DICKENS STUDIES ANNUAL
Essays on Victorian Fiction

DICKENS STUDIES ANNUAL
Essays on Victorian Fiction

EDITORS

Stanley Friedman
Edward Guiliano
Michael Timko

DICKENS STUDIES ANNUAL

Essays on Victorian Fiction

VOLUME
30

Edited by
Stanley Friedman, Edward Guiliano, and Michael Timko

AMS PRESS
NEW YORK

DICKENS STUDIES ANNUAL
ISSN 0084-9812

COPYRIGHT © 2001 by AMS Press Inc. *Dickens Studies Annual: Essays on Victorian Fiction* is published in cooperation with Queens College and the Graduate Center, CUNY.

International Standard Book Number
Series: 0-404-18520-7
Vol. 30:0-404-18930-X

Dickens Studies Annual: Essays on Victorian Fiction welcomes essay- and monograph-length contributions on Dickens and other Victorian novelists and on the history of aesthetics of Victorian fiction. All manuscripts should be double-spaced and should follow the documentation format described in the most recent *MLA Style Manual*. The author's name should appear only on a cover-page, not elsewhere in the essay. An editorial decision can usually be reached more quickly if two copies of the article are submitted, since outside readers are asked to evaluate each submission. (Return postage is not required; providing an e-mail address may expedite communication.) If a manuscript is accepted for publication, the author will be asked to provide a 100- to 200-word abstract and also a disk containing the final version of the essay. The preferred editions for citations from Dickens's works are the Clarendon and the Norton Critical when available, otherwise the Oxford Illustrated or the Penguin.

Please send submissions to The Editors, *Dickens Studies Annual,* Ph.D. Program in English, The Graduate Center, CUNY, 365 Fifth Avenue, New York, NY 10016-4309. Please send inquiries concerning subscriptions and/or the availability of earlier volumes to AMS Press, Inc., 56 East 13th Street, New York, NY 10003-4686.

Manufactured in the United States of America

All AMS books are printed on acid-free paper that meets the guidelines for performance and durability of the Committee on Production Guidelines for Book Longevity of the Council on Library Resources.

Contents

Illustrations

Errata

Harland Nelson's "Recent Dickens Studies: 1998," which appeared in volume 29 of *Dickens Studies Annual,* contained a large number of errors, none of them the fault of the author. AMS Press was just then switching from the older, traditional typesetting practices to printing directly from authors' computer disks. Somewhere on this slope between composition and computer, we slipped, and offer our apologies to Professor Nelson and to the readers of the annual.

Of the numerous typographical mishaps, we list below a sample of some of the more egregious:

Page 388, line 28: *For* perception *read* perceptive
Page 396, line 32: *For* an field *read* an antinomic field
Page 400, line 5: *For* in hospital *read* inhospitable
Page 403, line 16: *For* consequentially *read* consequentiality
Page 404, line 11: *For* apartment *read* argument
Page 415, line 17: *For* literally *read* literary
Page 426, line 36: *For* drawing *read* dawning
Page 430, line 26: *For* sensations *read* assertions
Page 437, line 3-4: *For* discussing *read* dismissing
Page 464, line 6: *For* Resonance *read* Romance

Preface

In the second scene of *2 Henry IV,* Falstaff exults, "I am not only witty in myself, but the cause that wit is in other men." For Dickens and many of his contemporaries, we believe that a like claim may be made, since their creative art retains the power to stimulate perceptive, lively discussions.

We express our gratitude to all who have submitted their essays to us, and we also sincerely thank those scholars who have generously served as outside readers. These reviewers, who help keep *DSA* receptive to an exceptionally wide range of students and approaches, have in many cases provided detailed responses that enabled contributors to revise and strengthen their work.

We thank Professor Michael Lund for his extensive survey of Dickens studies published in 1999.

For support, both practical and moral, we are indebted to the following administrators: President Frances Degen Horowitz, Provost William P. Kelly, Ph.D. Program in English Executive Officer Joan Richardson, and Linda Sherwin, Assistant Program Officer, Ph.D. Program in English, all of The Graduate Center, CUNY; and Interim President Russell Hotzler, Deans Raymond F. Erickson and Tamara S. Evans, and Department of English Chair Nancy R. Comley, all of Queens College, CUNY.

We extend thanks to Professor John O. Jordan, Director of The Dickens Project at the University of California, Santa Cruz, and to Jon Michael Varese, the web programmer for The Dickens Project, for placing on the Project's website the tables of contents for volumes 1-27 of *DSA*, as well as abstracts for subsequent volumes. (These materials are included in the Project's Dickens Electronic Archive.) The Dickens Project can be reached at http: //humwww.ucsc.edu/dickens/index.html.

Once more, we express our appreciation to Gabriel Hornstein, president of AMS Press, for his steady encouragement and assistance. We are also grateful to Jack Hopper, our editor at AMS Press, for his skill and congenial, resourceful cooperation. We thank, too, our editorial assistant for this volume, Andrea Knutson, for her valuable help.

—The Editors

The Editors are delighted to announce that in preparing future volumes they will be joined by Professor Anne Humpherys, of The Graduate Center, CUNY, and Lehman College, CUNY, a distinguished scholar who has made many valuable contributions to Victorian studies.

Notes on Contributors

PATRICK BRANTLINGER, professor of English at Indiana University, edited *Victorian Studies* for a decade (1980–90). Among his recent publications are *The Reading Lesson: The Threat of Mass Literacy in Nineteenth-Century British Fiction* and, forthcoming, *Who Killed Shakespeare? What's Happened to English since the Radical Sixties.*

ELENI COUNDOURIOTIS is associate professor of English and Comparative Literary and Cultural Studies at the University of Connecticut. She is author of *Claiming History: Colonialism, Ethnography, and the Novel.* Her research interests are divided between postcolonial studies and comparative approaches to nineteenth-century fiction.

SIMON COOKE is a senior lecturer at Coventry University and co-ordinator of the certificate and diploma programs in the History of Modern Art in the School of Continuing Studies, University of Birmingham, England. He teaches a range of courses to adult students, specializing in the interdisciplinary study of Victorian art and literature. He has published several essays on Wilkie Collins, and is currently working on a study of the role of painters in Sensational fiction.

AMANPAL GARCHA is a PhD candidate in the Department of English and Comparative Literature at Columbia University. He is writing a dissertation on the relationship between the sketch and the novel in nineteenth-century fiction.

JOHN GLAVIN teaches in the Department of English at Georgetown University.

MARK M. HENNELLY, JR. is the chair of the English Department of California State University, Sacramento, and has published widely on Victorian fiction, especially Dickens studies. His most recent work appears or is forthcoming in *Dickens Quarterly, The Thomas Hardy Year Book,* and *College Literature.* He is currently working on a carnivalesque reading of *Martin Chuzzlewit.*

xi

MICHAEL LUND, professor of English at Longwood College in Virginia, is the author of *Reading Thackeray* (1988) and *America's Continuing Story: An Introduction to Serial Fiction, 1850–1900* (1993). With Linda K. Hughes he is the co-author of *The Victorian Serial* (1991) and *Victorian Publishing and Mrs. Gaskell's Work* (1999).

MICHELLE MANCINI teaches in the Department of English at the University of California, Berkeley.

JAMES MARLOW is a graduate of Dartmouth College and the University of California at Davis. He teaches literature and semiotics at the University of Massachusetts at Dartmouth. He recently published *Charles Dickens: The Uses of Time*.

GOLDIE MORGENTALER is assistant professor of English at the University of Lethbridge. She is the author of *Dickens and Heredity: When Like Begets Like*. She has also published articles on Dickens in *SEL* and *Dickens Quarterly*.

REGINA B. OOST is associate professor of English and director of the Honors Program at Wesleyan College in Macon, Georgia. Recent publications include articles on Mary Shelley and James Hogg.

CAROLYN OULTON did her PhD on Dickens, Wilkie Collins, and the Broad Church response to evangelicalism in the mid-nineteenth century. In addition to her research interests, she is a poet. She currently works in London for the National Trust.

CLARE PETTITT is director of studies in English at Newnham College, Cambridge University.

ROBYN L. SCHIFFMAN is a doctoral candidate in the Department of Comparative Literature at the University of Chicago. Her research interests include the British reception of German Romanticism and psychoanalysis.

BARRY STILTNER is currently a lecturer in English at Purdue University. He recently completed a doctoral dissertation entitled " 'Ideological Fabrications': Charles Dickens and Michel Foucault" and is working on a book examining the theoretical connections between Dickens and Foucault.

JONATHAN TAYLOR is currently a lecturer at the English and Drama Department, Loughborough University. He is completing his doctoral thesis on "Masters and Mastery in Victorian Writing." He also has an essay on "The

Music Masters and the 'Jew' in Victorian Writing'' which will be published in a collection of essays entitled *The Idea of Music in Victorian Fiction.*

JUDITH WILT is professor of English at Boston College. She has written books and essays on nineteenth- and twentieth-century British fiction and teaches courses in Victorian literature, Women's Studies, Catholic Studies, and popular culture genres. She is currently writing an essay on the Hannibal Lector novels, and is completing a book-length study of the novels of Mary Arnold Ward.

Styles of Stillness and Motion: Market Culture and Narrative Form in *Sketches by Boz*

Amanpal Garcha

Dickens began his literary career by writing short tales before finding greater success with the primarily descriptive, plotless sketches that comprise much of Sketches by Boz. *His move from narrative tale to nonnarrative sketch corresponds to a change in focus: he shifts his attention from the suburbs to the city and from the relatively comfortable middle ranks of society to the struggling lower class. Owing to its participation in the restless, dynamic culture of the market, the middle class is easily narrated: it is intensely interested in time and always orients itself toward the future. The capitalist culture the middle class inhabits imagines the urban poor, on the other hand, as locked in a static, unchanging existence that can only be described, not plotted. The dynamism of the market is not absent from Dickens's descriptive sketches, though; rather, it is manifested in Dickens's restless, often violently energetic style, which serves as a counterpoint to the abject stasis of the lower-class characters he describes. This descriptive style becomes the most important factor in the success of his early novels, which are distinguished more by their stylistic force than by the coherence of their plots.*

In the preface to the first edition of the First Series of his first published volume of literary work, Dickens is already looking ahead:

In humble imitation of a prudent course, universally adopted by aeronauts, the Author of these volumes throws them up as his pilot balloon, trusting it may catch favourable current, and devoutly and earnestly hoping it may *go off well* . . . . Unlike the generality of pilot balloons which carry no car, in this one it is very possible for a man to embark, not only himself, but all his hopes of future fame, and all his chances of future success.   (7)

The next several years will indeed bring him fame and success, but here at the beginning of *Sketches by Boz,* Dickens does not just imagine himself moving in time to reach these goals. For Dickens, the moment of future literary glory is also a moment that must be met by travelling in space—in a "pilot balloon" that catches a "favourable current." That Dickens imagines himself making such a journey might otherwise be unremarkable, were it not for the fact that the vehicle he chooses for the trip is a volume of sketches. The sketch, after all, is primarily a *static* form, usually focusing on one place at one moment, and resisting spatial or temporal changes—differentiating it from the short story, which, like the novel and other narrative forms, is predicated on change. If *Sketches by Boz* is to carry Dickens into another place and time, in other words, it is a strange vessel in which to travel, since sketches themselves rarely go anywhere at all.

Dickens's sketches, although often busy in their depictions of day-to-day life, nevertheless lack a sense of meaningful progression; the actions they show are routine and repetitive, suggesting consistency and permanence rather than directed movement. Often, the sketches simply do away with action completely, "present[ing] little pictures of life and manners" rather than sustained diegesis (Preface First Series 7). Creating a "little picture" out of life also means stopping it, and this stasis is imposed by the sketches' dominant mode—description. Description produces a pause in narration, interrupting narrative's forward movement (Bal 94). So, for example, when Boz recounts the horrors of Seven Dials—the "streets of dirty, straggling houses . . . [h]ere and there, a little dark chandler's shop with a cracked bell hung up behind the door to announce the entrance of a customer . . . long rows of broken and patched windows"—he aptly calls the image he has created "the 'still life' of the subject" (94). The description, in recording all the aspects of the neighborhood in minute detail, gives us a picture of objects existing in a moment in time that is arrested indefinitely.[1]

Perhaps, though, the opposition between descriptive stasis and narrative progression is exactly what the *Sketches* works to overcome. As J. Hillis Miller points out, Dickens's arrangement of his sketches into three major categories, starting with "Scenes" and then moving on to "Characters" and finally to "Tales," [2] constitutes a move away from stasis and toward narrative, a move that in some ways reflects the evolution of Dickens's literary technique. According to Miller, Dickens constructs each individual sketch, as well as the volume of sketches as a whole, according to the logic of metonymy, so that the reader is first presented with "the scene, with its inanimate objects, then the people of whose lives these objects are the signs, and finally the continuous narrative of their lives which may be inferred from the traces of themselves they have left behind" (127). Such a movement, "from things to people to stories," is replicated both by Dickens's "realistic" literary mode (whereby the social and physical environment gives rise to characters and then narratives of those characters) and by the progression from Scenes to Characters to Tales in the collected *Sketches by Boz* (Miller 129). Realism's logic dictates that out of the still lifes of the sketches, narratives will arise; Dickens's Tales eventually "emerge as linear narrative out of the static poses of the earlier Scenes and Characters" (Miller 133).

The difference between the temporal and spatial stasis of the sketches and the narrative movement of the Tales, however, is much more profound than Miller believes: as we will soon see, this difference is rooted in and corresponds to a stark *social* division between a lower-class world that can only be represented in a static mode, and a middle-class world amenable to narrative. To clarify this point, though, we should first look at the most concrete problem with Miller's analysis, namely his assertion that Dickens moved progressively from static scene to diachronic story. Following the final arrangement of the pieces in the 1839 volume of *Sketches by Boz*, Miller insists that the Scenes and Characters precede, "anticipate," and give rise to the narrativity of the Tales (133). The initial publication history of the individual sketches, though, tells a much different story—one that is indeed the reverse of what Miller presents. Dickens's first published works were, in fact, his Tales: starting with "Mr. Minns and His Cousin,"[3] which appeared in *The Monthly Magazine* in December 1833, Dickens produced "Mrs. Joseph Porter," "Horatio Sparkins," "The Bloomsbury Christening," "Sentiment," and "The Boarding House"—all *before* he published the first of his Scenes ("Omnibuses" in *The Morning Chronicle*, September 26, 1834).[4] In terms of the trajectory of Dickens's work, then, we cannot say that the narrativity of the Tales naturally "emerges" from the static sketches. Rather, Dickens seems consciously to move away from narrativity as he progresses through his earliest writings.

This turn from narrativity brings up another problem with Miller's account of the *Sketches* and their relation to Dickens's overall literary project. Implicit in Miller's analysis is the idea that the progression from nonnarrative sketch to narrative Tale extends further—that is, that the Tales then evolve into his longer narrative works.[5] Yet commentators have traditionally viewed the Tales as the works least indicative of Dickens's later novelistic genius. Kathryn Chittick, in her review of contemporaneous criticism, points out that the sketches, with their "acuteness of observation," were "praised far more highly'' than the early, more facetious tales (48); and as Michael Slater remarks, while the *"Monthly Magazine* stories attracted a certain amount of approving notice,'' Dickens's "real originality emerged in the five 'Street Sketches' '' he published in the *Morning Chronicle* (xii). Dickens's own assessment of his early work comes to a similar conclusion. Writing the preface to the Cheap Edition of the *Sketches* in 1850, Dickens, now a highly successful novelist, denigrates the *Sketches* as a whole, but is especially critical of the Tales: "I am conscious of [the sketches] often being extremely crude and ill-considered, and bearing obvious marks of haste and inexperience; particularly in that section of the present volume which is comprised under the general head of Tales'' (11). What Dickens's evaluation reveals is not, as Miller would have it, that the sketches begot the narrative Tales, which in turn evolved into Dickens's novels, but rather that in comparison to the nonnarrative sketches, the Tales were most alien to Dickens's later literary masterpieces. Clearly, narrativity did not inevitably arise from the static sketches—instead, narrativity was precisely what Dickens had to reject, at least provisionally, in order to come into his own as a writer.

Instead of Miller's idea of a continuum between the narratively static Scenes and Characters and the narratively progressive Tales, then, we see a rupture. But this rupture is not just present in terms of form: the Tales also differ significantly from the Scenes and Characters in content, specifically in their geographical and class settings. Almost all of the early Tales take place in the suburbs, and even those that include urban settings, like "Mr. Minns and His Cousin,'' quickly move their focus from London to its outer communities. The centrality of the suburbs in the early Tales is nicely summed up in "Horatio Sparkins,'' in which we find out that the main characters, the Malderton family, "assiduously kept up an extensive acquaintance among the young eligible bachelors of Camberwell, and even of Wandsworth and Brixton; to say nothing of those who 'dropped in' from town'' (409–11). The geographic world of the Tales is represented by this remark—attention is concentrated on the suburbs (Camberwell, Wandsworth, and Brixton), and London is a marginal presence from which others "drop in.'' So, the settings of the early tales—Stamford Hill in "Mr. Minns and His Cousin,'' Clapham Rise in "Mrs. Joseph Porter,'' and Islington in "The Bloomsbury Christening''—are places away from the urban center of London (Chittick 46).

In contrast, the nonnarrative Scenes and Characters focus relentlessly on the city—Dickens dedicates himself almost exclusively to representing London's distinctive neighborhoods, shops, characters, institutions, and phenomena. Importantly, this change in geographical space from the suburban to the urban also entails a shift in socioeconomic class. With the exception of "The Drunkard's Death,'' the Tales center around characters who are at least middle-class, ranging from those like Mrs. Joseph Porter who live comfortably in suburban villas, down to the occupants of "The Boarding House," whose lives are not luxurious, but who are certainly not wanting for food or clothing. On the other hand, the personages of the Scenes and Characters are almost all of the lower orders, ranging from stable, but far from wealthy, characters like the carpenter Samuel Wilkins of "Miss Evans and the Eagle," whose "earnings were all-sufficient for his wants" (266) to the more marginal "Shabby-genteel People" to the assortment of sweeps and cads barely making a living, to the almost destitute customers of the "The Pawnbroker's Shop" and, finally, to the penniless and hopeless "Hospital Patient." As Chittick puts it, when Dickens stopped writing about "suburban entertainments" and started writing about the streets of London, he moved not only into a different geographical region, but also into a different (and lower) "literary and social caste" (47).[6]

In sum, Dickens's stories are not simply "narrativized" sketches; rather, there is a significant break in terms of both form and content between the Tales and the Scenes and Characters. His formal move from narrative Tale to nonnarrative sketch corresponds to a move in geography from the suburbs to the city, and a move in social milieu from the relatively comfortable middle ranks of society to the struggling lower class. But what explains this correspondence? Why did Dickens find the suburban middle class easily "narratable"[7] while the lower class resisted being put in a plot?

After our initial observations on the link between temporality and form, we might pose the problem another way: Why does the middle class, for Dickens, exist in a world of time and motion (and therefore narrative), while the lower class is excluded from this world? The historian Thomas Haskell, in his work on philanthropy and the rise of capitalism between 1750 and 1850, gives us one answer. Rather than dealing directly with the issue of the class divisions produced during this period, Haskell's work traces a more subtle change in "cognitive style" among those individuals taking part in the commercial and industrial revolution (547). This new way of thinking—which involved a new way of thinking about time and futurity—was predicated on the centrality of contractual obligations in Britain's emerging market culture. Contracts allow commerce, and therefore capitalism, to function—in order for a merchant to order goods from a distant producer, or for a laborer to put himself or herself consistently in the employ of a factory or firm, both parties involved in such a transaction must make promises and take them seriously. As Haskell puts it, "a growing reliance on mutual promises, or contractual relations, in lieu of relations based on status, custom, or traditional authority comes very close to the heart of what we mean by the 'rise of capitalism' " (553).

The centrality of promises to the market in turn produced—by rewarding—individuals who "live[d] partly in the future" (Haskell 560). A contract or promise forces one to think ahead; it makes each party "[commit] himself to bring to pass some designated future event" in order for the promise to be fulfilled (Haskell 553). In other words, a culture of promises is intensely interested in time; it is a culture in which individuals project themselves in the future and are therefore acutely sensitive to time's movement forward. In reference to our concerns here, we might say that such a culture is both narratable and receptive to narration, since narrative is the literary mode that depends on, and seeks to record, time's passing.

It is not surprising, then, that this world of promises and futurity is also the one that Dickens's narrative Tales present to us. For example, the plot of "Mr. Minns and His Cousin" is set in motion when Mr. Minns's relation calls and insists on Mr. Minns coming to dinner. Minns, "driven to despair, accept[s] the invitation and promise[s] to be at Poplar-walk on the ensuing Sunday, at a quarter before five to the minute" (366). The specificity of time here (Minns is expected at 4:45 "to the minute") is not incidental—Minns's promise ends up structuring the Tale by setting up a situation in which time matters, and much of the story is taken up by Minns's effort to abide by his cousin's request to "be punctual" (366). So, the story minutely records the passing of time, as when Minns has to deal with a cad who assures him that "the vehicle would start in three minutes," although a quarter of an hour elapses, and then "five minutes more," and five minutes more, with "no signs of moving," leaving Minns "desperate [because of] the lateness of the hour, and the impossibility of being in Poplar-walk at the appointed time" (367).

Such promises and appointments saturate the Tales; they are the primary narrative devices in Dickens's stories. The purpose of the appointment may be violent, as in "The Great Winglebury Duel" when Horace Hunter writes to Mr. Trott, "I shall be waiting there alone, at twenty minutes before six o'clock to-morrow morning. Should I be disappointed of seeing you there, I will do myself the pleasure of calling with a horsewhip" (468). Or the appointment may be amiable, as in "Horatio Sparkins," when Mr. Malderton says to Horatio, "It will give me the greatest pleasure, sir, to see you to dinner at Oak Lodge, Camberwell, on Sunday next at five o'clock, if you have no better engagement" (415). The appointment may have an ulterior motive, as in "Mr. Minns and His Cousin" when Mr. Budden makes his invitation to Minns in the hopes that "he might take a fancy to our Alexander, and leave him his property" (363). Or it may be made in the best of faith, as in "The Bloomsbury Christening" when Charles Kitterbell informs his uncle that his child will be "christened at twelve o'clock on Friday, at Saint George's church" and asks him, "Pray, don't be later than a quarter before twelve" (540). And this is not to mention the mysterious appointment that is the central focus of "The Black Veil" or the secret rendezvous or promises of marriage that play important roles in "The Boarding House," "Sentiment," and "Passage in the Life of Mr. Watkins Tottle."

Going back to Haskell's thesis, though, we should note that these promises are certainly not commercial contracts, and none of them are made in a business setting. Still, the coincidence between the relatively privileged class status of the characters of the Tales and their propensity to make promises is far from an accident. The world of the Tales, while not exactly the world of commerce, is nevertheless inhabited by those who have internalized the future-orientation required by market culture and who have been rewarded for it. So, not only does Mr. Minns make and keep promises with his cousin, but he also holds "a responsible situation under Government" that provides "a good and increasing salary" (already indicating his ability to fulfill contractual requirements), while having "some 10,000*l*. of his own" that is "invested in the funds" (361). These "funds," or investment securities, typify the way capitalism is dependent on forward-looking individuals—such securities, which mature after several years and reward those who wait that long, can exist only if there is a class of people who live "partly in the future." This class of people is, of course, not only the rich bourgeoisie, but also the members of the middle-class world of the Tales. Used to the idea of obligations, timeliness, and futurity, these individuals exist in a world in which they make promises and work to keep them, a time-intensive world that is easily narratable.

In some ways, such a world is one of relative freedom. Unlike the static, lower-class characters of the sketches, the people in the Tales are able to project themselves forward in time, a fact that allows them to work toward fulfilling their monetary and sexual desires. In other words, a culture of promises and futurity also allows for a certain amount of individual freedom and agency—a point Nietzsche makes in his *Genealogy of Morals*, in which he links promises with both an orientation toward the future and the development of a "will." For Nietzsche, the keeping of promises requires a subject who possesses

a desire for the continuance of something desired once, a real *memory of the will*: so that between the original "I will," "I shall do this" and the actual discharge of the will, its *act*, a world of strange new things, circumstances, even acts of will may be interposed without breaking this long chain of will. But how many things this presupposes! To ordain the future in advance in this way, man must first have learned to distinguish necessary events from chance ones, to think causally, to see and anticipate distant eventualities as if they belonged to the present, to decide with certainty what is the goal and what the means to it, and in general be able to calculate and compute. Man himself must first of all have become *calculable, regular, necessary*, even in his own image of himself, if he is able to stand security for *his own future*, which is what one who promises does! (Nietzsche 58)

Narratively speaking, this new, distinctively promise-oriented subjectivity and epistemology is identical to the epistemology that underlies narrativity. The centrality of "a desire for the continuance of something desired once;" the idea of a "long chain of will" that remains unbroken while assimilating "strange new things, circumstances," and other acts of will; the emphasis on goals and on cause and effect: these are the primary aspects not just of the new promise-keeping subject, but also of the nineteenth-century novel and its heroes and heroines.

Yet, if this kind of "will" implies a certain kind of freedom and agency, it also, as Nietzsche points out, requires an internalization of the rigid *constraints* imposed by a market-centered culture—namely, the demand that the subject be "*calculable, regular, necessary.*" These constraints are evident in many of the characters of the Tales, not least Mr. Minns, whose ability to hold down a regular job and maintain his investments goes along with a "love of order" that is "as powerful as his love of life" (363). But even less rigid and more seemingly free characters in the Tales are constrained by the very temporality that allows them to engage in purposive action. Percy Noakes, for instance, in "The Steamboat Excursion," appears as the epitome of middle-class privilege and freedom, neglecting any kind of serious work and devoting himself solely to a dilettantish life in which he "talk[s] politics to papas, flatter[s] the vanity of mamas, do[es] the amiable to their daughters, make[s] pleasure arrangements with their sons, and romp[s] with the younger branches" (438). His main occupation, in fact, is "planning some party of pleasure, which [is] his great *forte*" (440).

Dickens's humorous enumeration of such activities reinforces our vision of Percy as a lazy and dissolute floater, far away from the serious world of labor, effort, and production. Yet, Percy's apparently "free" realm of middle-class leisure is one that is also palpably time-intensive and is in many ways modeled around the most bureaucratic capitalist institutions. Percy's pleasurable steam excursion, which is the subject of the Tale, is arranged by a "committee of ten" who "manage the whole set out" by having a long meeting, in which motions are opposed and supported, and in which members pledge their share of the expenses. In other words, when Mrs. Taunton says of Percy, "What a manager you are!" the intended irony of the statement should not blind us to its validity (441–42). While the market has provided the middle-class with a certain amount of freedom and leisure, that is, it also has produced members of that class who, like Percy and his circle, end up structuring their free time in terms of the characteristic institutions of the market.

After all, the excursion itself is simply another appointment, which gives the piece its temporal and narrative dimension, but which also imposes certain demands upon the characters of the story—especially upon Percy himself.

When the day of the excursion arrives, "the anxiety of Mr. Percy Noakes [knows] no bounds," and the same time-sensitivity that allows for the excursion to take place becomes the stuff of nightmares: Noakes has "confused dreams of steamers starting off, and gigantic clocks with the hands pointing to a quarter past nine, and the ugly face of Mr. Alexander Briggs . . . grinning as if in derision of his fruitless attempts to move" (447). The dream suggests that what seems like the "freedom" of Percy's ability to move in time and space—his ability to plan for the future and to travel between locations—is equally a *compulsion* to do so: a compulsion that carries with it anxieties about being late and not being able to move, and inevitable social penalties for not fulfilling his obligations.

In fact, this nightmare is almost exactly the same as one that appears in "Early Coaches," a sketch that uncharacteristically focuses on the figure of the businessman. The sketch starts as the man "receive[s] an intimation from [his] place of business . . . that it will be necessary to leave town without delay"—an "intimation" that, like all requests from an employer, obviously has the force of an order (161). After the conscientious man takes great pains to book a seat on the coach, he is left to worry about getting to the stand on time. We find out the next morning that he has "done nothing all night but doze for five minutes at a time, and start up suddenly from a terrific dream of a large church-clock with the small hand running round, with astonishing rapidity, to every figure on the dial-plate" (162). The obvious similarity between Noakes's dream and that of the businessman points to the fact that at least in *Sketches by Boz*, the middle-class dilettante and the middle-class career-minded functionary are far from opposites—rather, as members of a class that has been created and rewarded by market culture, they both have internalized the anxieties about time, obligations, and promises such a culture produces.

But while the middle-class people of the Tales are certainly constrained, this is not to say that they are not privileged. The mobility in time and space that they enjoy is still preferable to the enforced stasis of the characters delineated in Dickens's sketches who, for one reason or another, fall outside the margins of market culture. The relationship between the stasis of the inhabitants of the sketches and their position in such a time-oriented culture can best be perceived in the moments when the two worlds—the "timely" world of the mobile middle class and the world of the static underclass—are juxtaposed. One such moment occurs in one of Dickens's most famous sketches, his "Visit to Newgate." Dickens, in introducing his sketch, discusses the way in which the men

> whose road to business every morning lies through Newgate-street or Old Bailey . . . pass and repass this gloomy depository of the guilt and misery of London, in one perpetual stream of life and bustle, utterly unmindful of the throng

of wretched creatures pent up within it . . . not even knowing, or if they do, not heeding the fact, that as they pass one particular angle of the massive wall with light laugh or a merry whistle, they stand within one yard of a fellow-creature, bound and helpless.   (234)

Although the businessmen are forced hurriedly to "pass and repass" the same spot each day on their way to work, suffering the constraints of such a routine is still more appealing than being "bound and helpless" like the prisoners. The opposition between the two groups, moreover, suggests how the population of *Sketches by Boz* is divided in terms of time—the mobility of the middle-class individuals is a function of their consciousness of time (they are walking hurriedly because they must get to work and not be late), while those who are imprisoned exist in a world where time does not signify, outside the "perpetual stream of life and bustle" that comprises existence in commercial London. In fact, the linkage between temporal stasis and criminality is the logical extension of the market culture's requirement of future orientation. While the good citizen looks ahead, the criminal does not or cannot do so—a point Herbert Spencer makes in his essay on "Prison Ethics" when he writes that criminals are those "who dwell only in the present . . . [and] who do not recognize the contingencies of the future" (216–17).[8]

While such static individuals are unfit for capitalism, they are perfect for the sketch form—with its emphasis on description, the sketch depends on a static object that can be apprehended patiently and in detail. The middle-class life of movement, mobility, and narrativity renders description problematic: the businessmen who hurriedly pass the prison disappear immediately into the stream of London's traffic, but those who are "bound" can be held up for intense scrutiny and description. But the businessmen's motion doesn't just make them difficult to perceive; it also seems to interfere with their own ability of perception. The fact that they are in a hurry and are walking by quickly makes them "utterly unmindful" of the jail, suggesting that description not only requires a static object, but a static observer as well. Rushed movement makes it impossible to see one's environment clearly, or even at all: as a cab driver in "The Tuggs' at Ramsgate" remarks, "surrounding objects [are] rendered invisible by hextreme welocity" (394).

The idea that the sketches' descriptions are produced only when both observer and observed are rendered motionless may explain the moments of seeming identification between the Dickensian narrator and the marginal, underclass individuals he sketches.[9] Yet, while it is true that total inattention and "hextreme welocity" may make description impossible, *some* amount of motion is in fact required for a person to describe a still object completely. Hermann Helmholtz, in his 1866 *Treatise on Physiological Optics*, the first modern scientific work on human perception, demonstrates this link between a subject's movement and his or her perception of the surrounding environment.

> Suppose, for instance, that a person is standing in a thick woods, where it is impossible for him to distinguish, except vaguely and roughly, in the mass of foliage and branches all around him what belongs to one tree and what to another, or how far apart the separate trees are, etc. But the moment he begins to move forward, everything disentangles itself, and immediately he gets an apperception of the material contents of the woods and their relations to each other. (295–96)

As Helmholtz points out, observers who remain motionless are unable to see their environment properly; in order to differentiate objects from one another and to see the different dimensions of those objects, the subject must move.

And, in fact, despite Boz's criticism of the hurried businessmen, he himself rarely stops in his tour of Newgate; like the subject Helmholtz imagines, the narrator's powers of observation and description are rooted in his ability to keep moving. So, even though he gives a prolonged account of the section of the jail devoted to female prisoners, this account is not produced by stopping for an extended amount of time to look at (or, for that matter, interact with) those women. "The period of our stay among them . . . was very brief" (240), Boz remarks after "passing hastily down the yard, and pausing only for an instant to notice the little incidents we have just recorded" (239).

Again, of course, Boz's mobility signifies his privileged position in respect to the prisoners; whereas he can move about, the prisoners are held fast. But this privilege is not just apparent with respect to those in Newgate—in fact, Boz's mobility is constantly emphasized by its contrast to the stasis of the figures in the sketches who are frozen in space and time. These figures, like the prisoners in Newgate, are outside the dominant capitalist economy—their inability to move forward, either spatially or temporally, is always linked to their lower-class, impoverished status. From the poor man in "Our Parish" who is reduced to penury and "can take no heed of the future" (17) to the "presiding genius of Scotland-yard" who "sits from day to day, brooding over the past" while "misery and want are depicted in his countenance" (89–90) to the "numerous groups" in "Seven Dials," who "are idling about in the gin-shops" and who "have no enjoyment beyond leaning against posts" in "listless perseverance" (93) to the inhabitants of Monmouth streets who are "deeply engaged in sedentary pursuits" (96) to the drunkards of every neighborhood who, like the one appearing in "The Pawnbroker's Shop," enjoy "a little relaxation from [their] sedentary pursuits" by drinking more and abusing their families (225), the motionlessness and inaction of the lower class—the "listless," "idling," and "sedentary" nature of their existence—keep them both economically disadvantaged and frozen in time and space.

Boz, on the other hand, is constantly on the move: he is "the speculative pedestrian" (223) who is "very fond of speculating as we walk through a street, on the character and pursuits of the people who inhabit it" (58).[10] So, his observation of "Shops and Their Tenants" is made as he "passe[s]" it periodically (82); after imagining the death of one of the imaginary figures summoned from the clothing in Monmouth Street, Boz takes "a step or two further on" in order to restore "the naturally cheerful tone of our thoughts" (101); he ends up in "Doctor's Commons" while "[w]alking . . . through St. Paul's Churchyard" (109); and the overall impression we get from the numerous neighborhoods, locations, and institutions described in *Sketches* is of a narrator who gets around.

Boz's constant movement, moreover, may also explain the near obsession he has with omnibuses and hackney-cabs, which not only appear in many of the sketches, but are also the focus of several of them ("Hackney-coach Stands," "Early Coaches," "Omnibuses," and "The Last Cab-driver, and the First Omnibus Cad"). David Payne has discussed the way in which Boz (and Dickens himself) identifies with the energetic cab drivers, who seem to embody the vital forces of modernity (55). Indeed, in Dickens's letters, he often writes excitedly about his life as a reporter and the constant travel it required. In a May 2, 1835, note to Thomas Beard, for instance, he describes his effort to meet his deadline and beat out the *Times* in reporting an election speech in Exeter: "On the first stage we had very poor horses. At the termination of the second, The Times and I changed horses together; they had the start two or three minutes: I bribed the postboys tremendously & we came in literally neck and neck—the most beautiful sight I ever saw" (58). The contest was made even more exhilarating for Dickens because he was writing his article while travelling, a skill Dickens mastered in his career as a journalist. He would often find himself, as he remarked later, "writing on the palm of my hand, by the light of a dark lantern, in a post chaise and four, galloping through a wild country, all through the dead of night" (qtd. in Ackroyd 155).

Such moments bring together all of the issues we have been dealing with so far: for one thing, Dickens's hurried travel is a consequence of his immersion in a literary culture that is ruled by the deadlines and competition of the market; and, for Dickens, writing and movement seem to be inextricably bound together—like Boz, Dickens produces text while on the move. But if the cabs and coaches in which he finished off his reportage embody the energy and excitement of the market and of literary production, those same cabs, as Payne remarks, are also "the tyrants of the London streets," often violently and callously victimizing others (Payne 53). While Dickens's writing about London transportation gives us some of the most hilarious and brilliant moments in the volume, and while "our very particular friends, hackney-coachmen, cabmen, and cads" (254) certainly provide "excitement" in a world that tends otherwise toward "universal lassitude" (172), we also are often reminded of the decidedly unfriendly aspects of coach travel. The spirited, competitive energy that makes it so lively also punishes the customers, making Boz wonder "how many months' incessant travelling in a post-chaise, it would take to kill a man" (159) especially since, on one route, "each coach had averaged two passengers killed and six wounded" (390–91).

Likewise, as his association between coaches and writing might suggest, the wonderful energy of Dickens's text also claims its own victims. We should not forget, after all, that Dickens's best writing—and, consequently, the fame and success it gained for him—was produced by representing in great detail the sufferings of the lower class. Of course, the writing is often "sympathetic," as many commentators have remarked, but Boz's sympathy only goes so far. Take, for instance, his portrait of a woman in "The Streets—Night":

> That wretched woman with the infant in her arms, round whose meagre form the remnant of her own scanty shawl is carefully wrapped, has been attempting to sing some popular ballad, in the hope of wringing a few pence from the compassionate passer-by. A brutal laugh at her weak voice is all she has gained . . . . How few of those who pass such a miserable creature as this, think of the anguish of heart, the sinking of soul and spirit, which the very effort of singing produces. Bitter mockery! Disease, neglect, and starvation, faintly articulating the words of the joyous ditty. (77)

Boz to some extent is clearly able to understand and sympathize with the woman, even going so far as comprehending the subtleties of "the sinking of soul and spirit, which the very effort of singing produces." But, if the "compassionate passer-by" is marked by his willingness to give "a few pence" to the woman, then Boz certainly does not qualify for such status. The woman has still only gained "a laugh at her weak voice" when Boz starts to depict other subjects, allowing her most probably to "turn away, only to die of cold and hunger" (78). In other words, Boz's sympathy toward the underclass is coincident with an acknowledgment of his privileged status in regards to it—whereas the woman must go off and die, Boz moves on to describe other people and places, a movement that both precludes any extended interaction with the poor woman and that is indicative of his absorption into a market culture that demands and rewards such motion.

We even might say that his virtuoso descriptions reveal an investment in such a figure's debasement—an investment that is analogous to the market's own stake in maintaining an exploited lower class. In a striking moment in the original published version of "The Prisoner's Van"—so striking, perhaps, that Dickens later had to strike it out of the final edition of the *Sketches*—we get a glimpse of this investment:

> Whenever we have an hour or two to spare, there is nothing we enjoy more
> than a little amateur vagrancy—walking up one street and down another, and
> staring into shop windows, and gazing about . . . . We revel in a crowd of any
> kind—a street "row" is our delight—even a woman in a fit is by no means to
> be despised, especially in a fourth-rate street . . . . Then a drunken man—what
> can be more charming than a regular drunken man?   (qtd. in Tillotson 44)

Here, and throughout the *Sketches*, Dickens seems to use the figure of Boz as
a way both to disguise and disavow many of his investments and motivations,
although this process ends up revealing much more than it hides. Boz's characterization of himself as an "amateur vagrant," for example, spins Dickens's very professional and purposive travelling as the activity of a careless
flâneur.[11] As Celeste Langan has argued, though, the artist's pose of "vagrancy" is always a giveaway: under a capitalist system that demands constant circulation, "the alienated condition of vagrancy is the *pathos*
of . . . negative liberty: the 'freedom to come and go' become[s] the obligation
to mobility" (19). And while Boz's delight in a "woman in a fit" or in the
charms of a "drunken man" is disavowed through the irony of the passage,
we can't help noticing that Dickens's fame arose partly by capitalizing on
just such a delight, on the fascination he was able to create through depicting
abused women (like the one in "The Hospital Patient") and abusive men
(like the drunkards in "Pawnshops" and "The Drunkard's Death").

On the bodies of these static, debased characters, Dickens writes his most
energetic prose. While in the hospital, for example, we see the

> ghastly appearance of the hapless creatures in the beds . . . . In one bed lay a
> child enveloped in bandages, with its body half consumed by fire; in another,
> a female, rendered hideous by some dreadful accident, was wildly beating her
> clenched fists on the coverlet, in agony of pain . . . . On every face was stamped
> the expression of anguish and suffering. The object of the visit . . . was a fine
> young woman of about two or three and twenty. Her long black hair had been
> hastily cut from about the wounds on her head, and streamed over the pillow
> in jagged and matted locks. Her face bore frightful marks of the ill-usage she
> had received.   (281)

John Kucich has discussed the way in which Dickens's parodic voice often
seems to run away with itself, creating a state of stylistic excess in which
nothing escapes from the text's lacerating irony. In this case, we can see a
kind of *descriptive* excess that over-indulges in the agonies of its objects.
Dickens's stylistic energy seems to exult in the pain the patients are suffering,
so that the "frightful marks" of violence and the anguish "stamped" on
every face almost become identical to the textual marks the description itself
produces—as if the descriptions were written *on* the women's faces, inflicting
their pain.

In other words, Dickens's style creates its share of casualties, and we have to look no further for them than the numerous dead bodies that have piled up by the end of *Sketches by Boz*. The sketches' move toward death may seem to contradict our earlier assertion of their essentially static character, but in fact the characters' deaths epitomize this stasis rather than negate it. Many characters, after all, seem almost dead already—the Broker's Man, in a typical remark, says of one impoverished woman, "if ever I saw death in a woman's face, I saw it in hers that night" (51); and the "cold, wretched looking creatures, in the last stage of emaciation and disease" who, because of their frequenting of "Gin Shops," have one foot in the gutter, clearly have the other one in the grave (219). The prisoners of Newgate, likewise, are living in a state in which they are "dying as surely—with the hand of death imprinted upon them as indelibly—as if . . . loathsome corruption had already begun" (235). Such characters, living in a state of morbid stillness, are perfect for the sketch form, as they take on death's key quality: its "fixing of every line and muscle" (66). The "indelible" imprint of death, in other words, practically turns body into text: it "fixes" it, making "every line" absolutely readable and unerasable.

The sketches, therefore, construct characters, only to summon them to their death—the text works to bring death on. It is as if Dickens's style, with its excess energy, reaches forward in time in order to fix the characters once and for all. Take, for example, the second couple presented to us in "London Recreations." Unlike the vulgar and greedy family that starts out the sketch, this couple is living "that quiet domestic life" that the text applauds, having "within themselves, the materials of comfort and content" which make their life almost idyllic (119). Yet, while this couple is clearly valorized, the text can't seem to leave them in this state of contentment; it constantly invokes death in order to move them toward a more profound stasis. The labels the husband puts near his garden flowers end up looking "like epitaphs to their memory" (118) and, as proof of the couple's love, we find out that "the only anxiety of each, is to die before the other" (119). While they are "sitting happily together in the little summer-house, enjoying the calm and peace of the twilight," the text goes out of its way to remind us of "the years that have silently rolled over their heads, deadening in their course the brightest hues of early hopes and feelings which have long since faded away" (119). The text's anxiousness to emphasize the couple's old age and fading prospects here gets the better of its ability to make sense: how, we might ask, can something deaden the hues of hopes and feelings, when those hopes and feelings have already ("long since") faded away? It's as if the energy of Dickens's style makes the text overstep itself; in its desire to kill off the couple, the sentence keeps on going a bit too long.

This excessive moment of Dickens's style, in which it "keeps on going" in a quest to put a stop to what it is describing, is representative of the style's own aggressive ambition. The style works toward its ideal condition: the permanent stasis of what it is describing; description's release from the constraints of narrativity and time, so that the text may have free reign to record every detail, make every satiric or sympathetic comment, and exhibit each facet of its own stylistic virtuosity. Yet we should not see this work as constituting a liberation from time's demands; rather, the ceaseless and often merciless activity of Dickens's style is more likely the ultimate sign of subordination to time's constraints. By reaching toward the death of its objects, Dickens's style reaches for the future, demonstrating its own desire to move forward and therefore its existence within the realm of temporality. Unlike the stasis it describes, the style of the sketches is oriented toward the future—as we see in "London Recreations," it works in time to achieve its goals.

Such timeliness makes sense: it appears as the result of the conditions of the text's production and as a mark of the competitive pressures under which Dickens labored. Unlike the static characters he portrays or even the *flâneur* persona he cultivates, Dickens worked hard on his sketches, constantly racing to produce text and meet his deadlines. Such feverish activity undoubtedly accounts for some of the energy of his prose—it is the energy unleashed by the demands of a newly capitalist literary field, characterized by contractual obligations and hurried production in the face of time limits. [12] Marked by the demands of temporality and the market, this energetic style, appropriately enough, becomes the vehicle that propels Dickens forward toward fulfilling his ambitions; it allows him to achieve the financial and artistic success he so ardently desires.

The sketch mode, therefore, with its foregrounding of style at the expense of narrative, is the perfect showcase for Dickens's talents and the appropriate form with which to launch his career. Yet Dickens's rejection of the narrativity of the Tales for the stasis of the sketches certainly requires additional comment. Why, after all, should his forward-looking style inhabit static description instead of diachronic plot? We can certainly think of works in which style has a complementary, rather than oppositional, relationship to narrative.[13] For Dickens, though, narrative seems to interrupt the energy of his style; as we saw earlier, he only comes into his own as a writer by abandoning the plots of the Tales for the nonnarrativity of the Scenes and Characters.

But Dickens had a peculiar conception of plot, a conception that was heavily influenced by the formal qualities of the short theatrical pieces Dickens often enjoyed at the time and one that, perhaps, necessitated his eventual rejection of narrative in the *Sketches*. The dominant narrative mode of the Tales, after all, does not resemble that of the literary short story, but rather the mode of the theatrical farce. The farcical nature of the Tales is made obvious by the preponderance of plots based on mistaken identity, threatened sexual transgression, and comedic coincidences. Indeed, Dickens transformed one of his Tales, "The Great Winglebury Duel," into a farce called *A Strange Gentleman* (subtitled "a comic burletta in two acts") and another author, John Buckstone, according to Dickens, appropriated "The Bloomsbury Christening" for a "Farce entitled 'The Christening' " (535).[14] The influence the theater had on Dickens's writing has been commented on extensively, with many critics drawing a link between the idea of theatricality and Dickens's style. J. Hillis Miller, for example, talks about the way that "theater permeates the *Sketches*" by being "one of Boz's major sources of metaphorical language" (136), and Robert Garis discusses Dickens's style "*as* theater," because it calls attention to its own "explicit artifice" and "verbal figurations," creating in the reader an "impulse to applaud" Dickens's stylistic expertise (8–9).[15] But while Dickens's writing in both its form and content makes reference to the stage, the actual demands of writing for the theater in some ways make prose style impossible. Everything written in a play must be able to be *acted*, especially when that play is a fast-moving comic farce—there is no room for the extended descriptions or authorial meditations that foreground style; in farce, narrative movement and performable action take precedence over the purely textual demands of style.

We might say, using Roland Barthes term, that Dickens's farce-like Tales therefore tend toward the "operable"—they can be "simply *executed*" in a way that "realistic" texts can never be. "Imagine the disorder," Barthes writes, that would be created if a novel's "descriptions [were] taken at face value, converted into operative programs" (80). Such a feat would be next to impossible, since "what we call 'real' (in the theory of the realistic text) is never more than a code of representation . . . it is never a code of execution: *the novelistic real is not operable*. To identify—as it would, after all, be 'realistic' enough to do—the real with the operable would be to subvert the novel at the limit of its genre" (80). For Barthes, the requirement of operability that exists in writing for performers (either on stage or, as Barthes discusses, on film) spells death to the purely *textual* world of realistic fiction.[16] By placing emphasis on what can be performed in the "real world," the demands of operability prevent the foregrounding of literary style, since style is an aspect of the text that only signifies on the level of the text itself.

Dickens's movement away from the theatrically-oriented Tales to the static sketches, then, is a move from performable action to his own type of "realistic text"—he releases himself from executable narrative and finds a form in which textual style dominates, a form that allows him to create a mode of "the novelistic real" that can evolve into his longer works of fiction. The energy of this mode soon produces *The Pickwick Papers*, a text that is a triumph of pure style—as Steven Marcus argues, Dickens creates it by "letting [his] language improvisationally, incontinently . . . run on," giving the reader an impression "of endless movement, of incessant motion" that resists the confines of plot (216, 226). But if *Pickwick* projects a sense of total stylistic "freedom," the *Sketches* show the origin of this sense—the dynamism of Dickens's style, like the brutal yet progressive capitalist energies that fuels it, erects itself on the bodies of a "static" class that feels the effects of such force without receiving any of the benefits of it. It is this exhilarating and violent style, though, that will finally transport Dickens to a place and a time where "all his hopes of future fame, and all his chances of future success" are realized. Despite and because of his production of a static form that depicts the future-less realm of lower-class London, in other words, Dickens moves ahead and finds a future for himself.

NOTES

1. It should be noted that the sketch form is not always narratively static—as the *Oxford English Dictionary* points out, a sketch can provide a "brief account . . . or narrative" of an incident, as well as simply giving a "description" of a place or a person. And, as many of Dickens's sketches show, even when description dominates, there is always an element of narrativity—description, as Gerard Genette argues, "is never found in a so to speak free state" that dispenses with narrative movement altogether (134). Nevertheless, descriptive stasis is clearly the dominant attribute of the sketches, as can be easily recognized when comparing the sketches to Dickens's plotted, narratively dynamic Tales.

    Others have recognized the stasis of Dickens's sketches: Virgil Grillo, in *Charles Dickens' Sketches by Boz: End in the Beginning*, differentiates between the two fictional modes within which Dickens initially worked by observing that "Dickens' sketches . . . describe . . . places, events, institutions, and occasions, without any plot or sustained focus on real or imagined characters," while "his *short stories* are papers written as fiction, presenting real or imagined characters in a plot" (14). Duane DeVries also remarks that Dickens's sketches are "predominantly descriptive essays" unlike his earlier farcical tales and discusses at length the formal distinction between the narrative and nonnarrative pieces in *Sketches by Boz* (70). J. Hillis Miller, as I discuss below, invokes a similar distinction between Dickens's sketches and stories.

2. In addition to these three large categories, Dickens also includes a smaller division of "Seven Sketches from Our Parish" at the beginning of the volume. The seven pieces in this section are essentially similar to the sketches included among the Scenes and Characters.

3. Originally entitled "A Dinner at Poplar Walk."

4. See DeVries 147–57 for the complete publication history of each of Dickens's sketches and of *Sketches by Boz* as a whole. I should also note that Miller does admit that "when Dickens collected the various texts from their random appearance over a period of three years in various periodicals, he rearranged the *Sketches*

in a way which does not correspond to the chronological order of their original publication'' (131). Miller's subsequent analysis of the ''progression'' of the *Sketches*, though, clearly fails to take this problematic fact into account. Moreover, by characterizing their initial appearance as ''random,'' he obscures the fact that the Tales were the one group of sketches that did not really appear haphazardly distributed among his writings—the majority of the Tales were written in the earliest phase of Dickens's periodical publication, from December 1833 to February 1835.

5. Miller asserts, for example, that the Tales ''contain all of Dickens' later work in embryo'' (124) and ''anticipate the grimmer side of Dickens' later fiction'' as well as its comic elements (133).

6. This concentration on the lower orders of London, in fact, became a distinguishing characteristic of Dickens's sketches in the eyes of contemporary reviewers, whether they liked the works or not. For example, the *Morning Post* of March 12, 1836 commended Boz because ''the varied aspects of society in the middle and lower classes are touched off with admirable truth and veracity,'' while the *Mirror* laments that the sketches ''savour too strongly of low London life'' (qtd. in Dexter 261–62).

7. For the concept of the ''narratable,'' see D. A. Miller's *Narrative and its Discontents: Problems of Closure in the Traditional Novel* (Princeton: Princeton UP, 1981).

8. Also quoted in Haskell 562. This opposition between the good, future-oriented citizen and the criminal, static character is apparent, for example, when Dickens talks about one of the men held in the ''Criminal Courts.'' Whereas the man's mother ''had borne misery without repining'' because she was ''looking steadily forward to the time when he who had so long witnessed her struggles for himself, might be able to make some exertions for their joint support,'' the man himself has had no such sense of the future. His ''idleness [has] led to crime:'' his ''idle'' nature has found its logical home in a prison (231).

9. For example, the ''shabby-genteel man'' in the slums of ''Seven Dials'' who never seems to leave his room except to get a ''half-pint of coffee every morning from the coffees shop,'' is ''naturally suppose[d]'' to be an author (95). Moreover, it's often not clear how Boz's endless, almost pointless travels around London differentiate him from those who ''have no enjoyment beyond leaning against posts'' (93)—although, as we will soon see, there is a crucial difference between Boz's mobile ''vagrancy'' and such static loafers.

10. ''Speculation'' is, of course, a word that neatly encapsulates Boz's connection to market culture. It suggests at once his ability to ''observe'' (from its etymological root *specula*, to watch or examine) and to ''take part in a business enterprise or transaction'' (*OED*), linking together Boz's habitual mode of observation and description with his professional aspirations to sell his work to the public for monetary gain.

11. See Jaffe 25–26 for a discussion of Boz as a *flâneur*.

12. In a letter to Catherine Hogarth in November of 1835, Dickens discusses his ''peculiar'' method of composition: ''I never can write with effect—especially in the serious way—until I have my steam up, or in other words, until I have

become so excited with my subject that I cannot leave off'' (25 November 1835). Dickens's image of his "steam"-powered writing is an appropriately industrial one, linking the vitality of his prose with the energies of industrialization and capitalism.

13. For example, Peter Brooks, in his discussion of *Le Rouge et le noir*, relates Stendahl's use of "hypothetical grammatical forms" to the novel's problematic narrative structure, both of which serve to foreground "the consonance and disjunctures . . . of event and might-have-been, of biological pattern and concerted deviance from it" (75, 88).

14. Dickens places this comment at the start of "The Bloomsbury Christening," where he stakes his claim to being the first creator of the plot: "The Author may be permitted to observe that this sketch was published some time before the Farce entitled 'The Christening' was first represented" (535). See DeVries 30–59 for a more thorough discussion of the influence of farce on Dickens's Tales. DeVries argues that Dickens turned to the farce because of his desire to "amuse readers" and because farcical tales offered greater "opportunities for satire" than other forms (56).

15. See Costigan for a definitive account of how "Dickens imitates the substance and structure of stage comedy . . . in the tales" of the *Sketches* (404).

16. Barthes talks of "the inevitable destruction of novels when they are transferred from writing to film, from a system of meaning to an order of the operable" (80–81).

WORKS CITED

Ackroyd, Peter. *Dickens.* New York: HarperCollins, 1990.

Bal, Mieke. *Narratology: Introduction to the Theory of Narrative.* Toronto: U of Toronto P, 1985.

Barthes, Roland. *S/Z.* Trans. Richard Howard. New York: Hill and Wang, 1974.

Brooks, Peter. *Reading for the Plot: Design and Intention in Narrative.* Cambridge: Harvard UP, 1984.

Chittick, Kathryn. *Dickens and the 1830s.* Cambridge: Cambridge UP, 1990.

Costigan, Edward. "Drama and Everyday Life in *Sketches by Boz.*" *Review of English Studies.* New Series 27 (1976): 403–21.

DeVries, Duane. *Dickens's Apprentice Years: The Making of a Novelist.* New York: Harvester, 1976.

Dexter, Walter. "The Reception of Dickens's First Book." *Charles Dickens: Critical Assessments.* Volume 1. Ed. Michael Hollington. Mountfield, East Sussex: Helm Information, 1995. 256–62.

Dickens, Charles. Preface to the First Edition of the First Series. February 1836. *Sketches by Boz*. Ed. Dennis Walder. London: Penguin, 1995. 7.

——. Preface to the First Cheap Edition. October 1850. *Sketches by Boz*. Ed. Dennis Walder. London: Penguin, 1995. 10.

——. Preface to the Original Edition. 1837. *The Pickwick Papers*. Ed. Robert Patten. London: Penguin, 1986. 41.

——. *Sketches by Boz*. Ed. Dennis Walder. London: Penguin, 1995.

——. "To Catherine Hogarth." 25 November 1835. *The Letters of Charles Dickens, Volume 1: 1820–1839*. Ed. M. House and G. Storey. Oxford: Clarendon P, 1965.

——. "To Thomas Beard." 2 May 1835. *The Letters of Charles Dickens, Volume 1: 1820–1839*. Ed. M. House and G. Storey. Oxford: Clarendon P, 1965.

Garis, Robert. *The Dickens Theatre: A Reassessment of the Novels*. Oxford: Clarendon Press, 1965.

Genette, Gerard. *Figures of Literary Discourse*. Trans. Alan Sheridan. New York: Columbia UP, 1982.

Grillo, Virgil. *Charles Dickens* Sketches by Boz*: End in the Beginning*. Boulder: Colorado Associated UP, 1974.

Haskell, Thomas L. "Capitalism and the Origins of the Humanitarian Sensibility." *American Historical Review* 90 (1985): 339–61, 547–66.

Helmholtz, Hermann. *Treatise on Physiological Optics*. 1866. Ed. J. P. C. Southall. New York: Optical Society of America, 1925.

Jaffe, Audrey. *Vanishing Points: Dickens, Narrative, and the Subject of Omniscience*. Berkeley: U California P, 1991.

Kucich, John. *Excess and Restraint in the Novels of Charles Dickens*. Athens: U Georgia Press, 1981.

Langan, Celeste. *Romantic Vagrancy: Wordsworth and the Simulation of Freedom*. Cambridge: Cambridge UP, 1995.

Marcus, Steven. "Language into Structure: *The Pickwick Papers*." *Representations: Essays on Literature and Society*. New York: Columbia UP, 1990.

Miller, J. Hillis. "The Fiction of Realism: *Sketches by Boz*, *Oliver Twist*, and Cruikshank's Illustrations." *Victorian Subjects*. Durham: Duke UP, 1991.

Nietzsche, Friedrich. *On the Genealogy of Morals and Ecce Homo*. Trans. Walter Kaufmann. New York: Vintage, 1969.

Payne, David. "A Field of Disenchantment: Poetics of Incarnation and Atonement in the Victorian Novel 1836–1861" Diss. Columbia U, 1998.

"Sketch." *Oxford English Dictionary*. 2nd ed. 1989.

Slater, Michael. Introduction. *Sketches by Boz and other early papers, 1833–39*. Columbus : Ohio State UP, 1994. xi-xxii.

"Speculation." *Oxford English Dictionary*. 2nd ed. 1989.

Spencer, Herbert. "Prison Ethics." *Essays Moral, Political and Aesthetic*. New York, 1888.

Tillotson, Kathleen. "*Sketches by Boz*: Collection and Revision." *Dickens at Work*. John Butt and Kathleen Tillotson. London: Methuen, 1957. 35–61.

Clock Work: *The Old Curiosity Shop* and *Barnaby Rudge*

Robert Tracy

Like The Old Curiosity Shop, Barnaby Rudge *originally appeared within the framing narrative of* Master Humphrey's Clock, *in which Master Humphrey reads aloud stories written by his listeners. Dickens soon found the* Clock *device inhibiting, and later published both novels without it. But elements from the* Clock *survive in* The Old Curiosity Shop *and* Barnaby Rudge. *Humphrey's quaint rambling old house reappears as the Curiosity Shop, the Maypole Inn, and the Warren. These antique settings invoke the atmosphere of Gothic fiction as Dickens knew it, with threatened maidens (Nell, Dolly Varden, Emma Haredale). As in Gothic fiction, they are threatened sexually and often financially, by sinister predators, in labyrinthine or half-ruined structures. The Catholic theme in* Barnaby Rudge *adds another traditional Gothic element. Gothic fiction frequently depends on the villain's manipulation of the victim, either by guile or by terror. Dickens's chief villains in* Barnaby Rudge, *Sir John Chester and Gashford, also manipulate, controlling Lord George and Hugh, and through Hugh the actions of Barnaby and the mob. Their control of characters and plot allows Dickens to query a novelist's manipulation of characters and plot.*

"The plot demands my utmost energy."
—Simon Tappertit, *Barnaby Rudge* 51

The Old Curiosity Shop and *Barnaby Rudge* reached their earliest readers as fictions set inside another fiction, Dickens's sustained but rather prosy account

---

23

of Master Humphrey, his quaint old house, his clock, and his little group of cronies who came to him each week to listen as he read aloud from a manuscript deposited by one of them in the clock-case. Though Dickens came to find the framing narrative about Humphrey and his friends an impediment in developing each novel, and ignored it for long periods, that narrative played an important role in shaping both *The Old Curiosity Shop* and *Barnaby Rudge*. At the same time, it gave Dickens a chance to play with issues of fiction and reality, to some extent blurring the traditional distinctions between them.

In July 1839, with *Nicholas Nickleby* close to completion, Dickens proposed to his new publishers, Chapman and Hall, a weekly periodical which he would edit. He would write most of the contents, which would include tales of old London, letters from imaginary correspondents, and satirical pieces, in the tradition of *The Spectator*, *The Rambler*, and *The Idler* (Johnson 1:261). The weekly's persona, or presiding presence, would be one Master Humphrey, an "old file" in a "queer house" who reads manuscripts kept in "the old, deep, dark, silent closet where the [clock] weights are" (Johnson 1: 295).

The reclusive Master Humphrey describes himself in the first number of *Master Humphrey's Clock* (4 April 1840). Under a drawing by George Cattermole, specially recruited for the *Clock* because of his skill at rendering old rooms and buildings, Humphrey warns the reader "not to expect to know where I live . . . never expect to know it." The drawing shows an old-fashioned room, beamed and wainscoted, in what is clearly an ancient building; the famous clock beside a capacious fireplace; and six stately chairs around a table. "I am not a churlish old man," Humphrey assures us;

> Friendless I can never be, for all mankind are of my kindred, and I am on ill terms with no one member of my great family. But for many years I have led a lonely, solitary life;—what wound I sought to heal, what sorrows to forget, originally, matters not now; it is sufficient that retirement has become a habit with me, and that I am unwilling to break the spell which for so long a time has shed its quiet influence upon my home and heart.
>
> I live in a venerable suburb of London, in an old house, which in bygone days was a famous resort for merry roysterers and peerless ladies, long since departed. It is a silent, shady place, with a paved court-yard so full of echoes, that sometimes I am tempted to believe that faint responses to the noises of old times linger there yet, and that these ghosts of sound haunt my footsteps as I pace it up and down. I am the more confirmed in this belief, because of late years, the echoes that attend my walks have been less loud and marked than they were wont to be; and it is pleasanter to imagine in them the rustling of silk brocade, and the light step of some lovely girl, than to recognize in their altered note the failing tread of an old man.   (*MHC* 27–28)

Humphrey, then, nurses a secret sorrow about some aspect of his past. He is romantic and imaginative, probably a reader of Walter Scott. Apart from *The Old Curiosity Shop*, the fictions he reads to his little club are historical fictions, set in Elizabethan or Stuart times, or the late eighteenth century.

When he first came to live in his mouldering old house, he tells us, he was disliked by his neighbors and rumored to be

> a spy, an infidel, a conjuror, a kidnapper of children, a refugee, a priest, a monster. Mothers caught up their infants and ran into their houses as I passed, men eyed me spitefully, and muttered threats and curses. I was the object of suspicion and distrust: ay, of downright hatred, too.

But in time he came to be accepted, and even popular: "now I never walk abroad, but pleasant recognitions and smiling faces wait on Master Humphrey" (*MHC* 28–29).

Humphrey offers us a partial explanation for his solitude and the initial hostility of his neighbors by his "confession . . . that I am a mis-shapen, deformed, old man" (*MHC* 31), a fact, he tells us, it no longer pains him to confess. But he still vividly remembers that day in his childhood when he realized he was not like other children, and came to understand his mother's sorrow and pity.

Master Humphrey lives in some comfort, with a housekeeper and the daily attendance of a barber. He is a great reader, and, like Dickens, a student of London life, especially nocturnal London life, wandering "by night and day, at all hours and seasons, in city streets and quiet country parts," where "I came to be familiar with certain faces, and to take it to heart as quite a heavy disappointment if they failed to present themselves each at its accustomed spot" (*MHC* 33).

This eagerness for the reappearance of familiar faces suggests a long suppressed gregarious instinct. Eventually Humphrey makes a friend, another solitary, a deaf man he finds eating Christmas dinner alone in a dreary tavern (*MHC* 61–62). Together they establish "Master Humphrey's Clock," a club which meets once a week at Humphrey's house, from 10 p.m. until 2 a.m., partly for conversation and fellowship but primarily to listen to Humphrey read aloud from the anonymous manuscripts deposited in the clock-case. The clock measures time but is also a kind of library of stories to be told at night, like those Scheherazade tells the sultan. Appropriately, both *The Old Curiosity Shop* and *Barnaby Rudge* are nocturnal books, with much of their action occurring at night. Dickens underlines this minor Gothic element by supposing the stories read at night in an ancient decaying building.

In the first number of *Master Humphrey's Clock*, Humphrey tells us that the club meets beside the clock, at a table with six chairs, a statement Cattermole's drawing substantiates. Initially there are only four members: Humphrey himself; the "deaf gentleman," whose name Humphrey never learns;

Jack Redburn, who comes to live with Humphrey; and Owen Miles, a retired businessman and widower, who becomes Redburn's particular friend. Like Humphrey, the deaf gentleman nurses a sorrow which remains as secret as his name. Redburn "has been all his life one of that easy wayward truant class whom the world is accustomed to designate as nobody's enemies but their own. Bred to a profession for which he never qualified himself, and reared in the expectation of a fortune he has never inherited, he has undergone every vicissitude of which such an existence is capable." He has lived with Humphrey "these eight years past" as

> my librarian, secretary, steward, and first minister: director of all my affairs and inspector-general of my household. He is something of a musician, something of an author, something of an actor, something of a painter, very much of a carpenter, and an extraordinary gardener: having had all his life a wonderful aptitude for learning everything that was of no use to him. He is remarkably fond of children and is the best and kindest nurse in sickness that ever drew the breath of life.   (*MHC* 64)

Redburn plays lugubrious tunes on the flute when depressed, and re-arranges the furniture in his room almost daily. He sometimes disappears for a few days. As for Owen Miles, he is "an excellent man of thoroughly sterling character: not of quick apprehension, and not without some amusing prejudices" (*MHC* 66). Miles has known Redburn for many years, and admires him extravagantly.

The first number of *Master Humphrey's Clock* sold very well, but sales fell off dramatically when readers discovered that the new work was not a sustained novel by Charles Dickens but a miscellany of grotesque tales written for one another by a group of eccentrics. Dickens's initial formula emerges as mysterious and sinister stories about old London, each to some extent characteristic of the club member who wrote it. In effect the club is a club of novelists, a kind of creative writing seminar in which new work is read aloud to the group, and perhaps criticized. The first two numbers of the *Clock* contain the deaf gentleman's story, the first and, as it turned out, the last of the "Giant Chronicles," stories about London's past told by Gog and Magog to each other at night in the Guildhall, this one overheard by a concealed listener—presumably *not* the deaf gentleman. In the story, Hugh Graham, an apprentice bowyer, loves his master's daughter, as is the custom of apprentices. She is seduced by a courtier, and vanishes for twenty years. When she returns in shame, Hugh kills her seducer and is then killed himself. Jack Redburn's story, supposedly a recalled dream (*MHC* 65), is a murderer's confession from the time of Charles II.

These tales, plus a comic letter from a reader offering to join the club and citing his intimate knowledge of society gossip as his qualification, comprise

Numbers 1–3 of *Master Humphrey's Clock*. With Number 4 (25 April 1840), Dickens began to take desperate but ingenious steps to save the weekly. "Personal Adventures of Master Humphrey," subtitled *The Old Curiosity Shop*, is chapter one of that novel, describing the narrator's encounter with Little Nell in the streets, late at night and far from home, his escorting her home, his meetings with her grandfather and Kit Nubbles, and his image of "the beautiful child in her gentle slumber" in "the old dark murky room," surrounded by "gaunt suits of mail with their ghostly silent air—the faces all awry, grinning from wood and stone—the dust and rust, and worm that lives in wood" (*OCS* 56). Master Humphrey's fascination with Nell makes it clear that there was more of her story to come, as it does, interspersed with other material, in Numbers 7, 8, 9, 10, and 11; from Number 12 (20 June 1840), containing chapters nine and ten of *The Old Curiosity Shop*, the story continues unmixed with other material until its conclusion in Number 45 (6 February 1841). In Number 45 Humphrey implausibly admits to his listeners that the story is indeed a personal adventure, and that he is, in fact, Nell's great-uncle, who searched for her so eagerly only to find her too late.

Dickens first thought of Little Nell and her story in March 1840, though she seems to have originally been intended to figure only in a "little tale" (*OCS* 13), probably no more than the first four chapters of the novel. By chapter four, Dickens had realized that he was embarked on a novel, and that it would rescue *Master Humphrey's Clock*, as indeed it did. At the end of chapter 4, Master Humphrey withdraws as narrator, leaving "those who have prominent and necessary parts in it to speak and act for themselves." Though Dickens's prepublication plans and comments about the *Clock* say nothing about including a sustained story over many numbers, in his 1848 preface to *The Old Curiosity Shop* he declares that he had all along intended "to include one continuous story, to be resumed, from time to time, with such indefinite intervals between each period of resumption as might best accord with the exigencies and capabilities of the proposed Miscellany." In that same preface he is quite frank about his own and his readers' uneasiness with "the desultory character" of the *Clock* as planned, and his need to "set about . . . cheerfully . . . disentangling myself from those impediments as fast as I could" (*OCS* 41).

Beginning *The Old Curiosity Shop* in *Clock* Number 4 was not Dickens's only device for saving his weekly. In Number 5 (2 May 1840) he brought back Mr. Pickwick, together with Sam Weller, his father Tony, and little Tony, Sam's son. Their presence raises interesting questions about Dickens's fictive world and its intersections with reality. Pickwick calls upon Master Humphrey because he has been reading *Master Humphrey's Clock* and wants to join the club, to occupy one of the two empty chairs at the table beside the clock. One fictional character has been reading about another, and wishes to know him personally. As for Humphrey, he recognizes Pickwick immediately because he has read *The Pickwick Papers*, and can ask the right questions about the Wellers and their current activities. The other club members are also readers of *Pickwick*, and know Phiz's illustrations. Though Owen Miles considers Pickwick's recorded adventures "unbecoming a gentleman of his years and gravity" and disapproves of his treatment of Mrs. Bardell, the others welcome him to the club warmly, and Humphrey assures Pickwick that the members are even " 'quite attached' " to Pickwick's gaiters (*MHC* 108–10).

Pickwick provides a story, and is eager that the group approve it. It is the melodramatic account of young Will Marks, who agrees to keep watch beside the gallows lest witches steal the body of a hanged man. The witches are in fact the victim's relatives, who persuade Marks to help them remove the body and carry it to a London church for burial. He does so, then spins a wild tale of witches to explain the absence of the body. Pickwick also proposes his friend Jack Bamber to take the final chair beside the clock, describing him as

> "living, and talking, and looking, like some strange spirit, whose delight is to haunt old buildings . . . . He lives . . . in one of those dull lonely old places with which his thoughts and stories are all connected; quite alone, and often shut up close, for several weeks together. . . . he broods upon the fancies he has so long indulged, and when he goes into the world . . . they are still present to his mind . . . he is a strange secluded visionary, in the world but not of it."
>
> (*MHC* 113–14)

Pickwick reminds the company of Bamber's brief appearance in *Pickwick Papers*, where he tells "The Tale of the Queer Client."

Pickwick's description does establish Bamber's eligibility to join Humphrey's circle. But it is more interesting as a little description of a storyteller, a novelist, whose fancies are continually alive to him, and who continues to tell himself his story even when far from his desk. It is close to Anthony Trollope's description of his own working methods in *An Autobiography* (42–43), and presumably to Dickens's own practice.

We hear no more of Bamber and his candidacy, but Dickens brings the Wellers back in Numbers 6, 9, and 11. There is some labored humor about Tony Weller's anxiety lest Humphrey's Housekeeper turn out to be " 'a widder' " (*MHC* 105). In Number 9 (30 May 1840), the Wellers join with Humphrey's housekeeper and barber to create their own club, "Mr. Weller's Watch." Dickens may have intended to vary the Gothic atmosphere of the tales read upstairs with humorous stories downstairs: Sam Weller does tell two brief anecdotes about barbers. If there was such a plan, it was quickly abandoned. We learn in Number 45 (6 February 1841) that the downstairs group had been listening to the reading aloud of *The Old Curiosity Shop* ''outside our door''; they are invited into the clock room to hear *Barnaby Rudge* and ''accommodated with chairs at a little distance'' (*MHC* 138), but they neither speak nor act.

When we recognize that ''Master Humphrey's Clock''—the club, not the periodical—was both the framing narrative and the catalyst for two of Dickens's fifteen novels, we need to consider how the imagined club shaped and to some extent controlled the development of those novels, even though Dickens and his readers quickly found the device clumsy and impeding. After all, Dickens brings the clock company back to hear Humphrey's claim to have acted in as well as written *The Old Curiosity Shop*, and again at the completion of *Barnaby Rudge*, when Master Humphrey dies after reading the final chapter to his friends, the clock stops, and the club is wound up.

Dickens had used the club formula already, in *The Pickwick Papers*, which were initially imagined as communications to the general membership of the Pickwick Club from a travelling committee consisting of Pickwick and three associates: a gang of four, like the Clock before Pickwick joined, or the three regulars who sit with John Willet at the Maypole in *Barnaby Rudge*. The Pickwickians were on a roving commission to report on their adventures and encounters, and, while Pickwick himself becomes the primary subject, the various interpolated tales he hears or reads resemble the device of manuscripts extracted from the clock-case and read aloud.

The framing fiction, then, is an account of a group of lonely men who write and consume fiction, a self-enclosed model of the novelist and his readers. Master Humphrey himself is the author of *The Old Curiosity Shop*, gifted by Dickens with all his own humorous, melodramatic, and sentimental powers. Despite his initial fumbling with point of view, and his eventual claim that the story is true and he played a part in it, Dickens has endowed him with a conspicuous talent for fiction. Does Dickens also imagine the story of Little Nell as a projection, so to speak, of Master Humphrey's personality? Has he imagined a novelist and then imagined what kind of a novel that novelist would write? In Chaucer's *Canterbury Tales*, some of the stories seem to tell us something about their tellers. The Prioress, who cannot marry and become a mother, tells a story about a murdered child; in the Wife of Bath's tale, a young man is rewarded for kissing an older woman; the Nuns' Priest, who works for the Prioress, tells a story about Chantecler, the rooster who is henpecked. Does Dickens fit the tale to the teller in a similar way?

Master Humphrey, like Jack Bamber and Anthony Trollope, is one of those who continually tell themselves stories. He imagines romantic relationships or enmities between various portraits of unknown subjects which hang in his house. ''With such materials as these, I work out many a little drama, whose chief merit is, that I can bring it to a happy end at will,'' he tells us (*MHC*

76). An ugly carved stone face, or a latticed window, will also set his imagination to work on a story. Silas Wegg develops a similar ongoing story about the inhabitants of the house where the Boffins later settle.

As he begins to describe that "Personal Adventure" that becomes *The Old Curiosity Shop*, Humphrey explains that he usually walks at night, primarily "because it affords me greater opportunity of speculating on the characters and occupations of those who fill the streets," that is, of making up stories about them. "The glare and hurry of broad noon are not adapted to idle pursuits like mine;" he tells us;

> a glimpse of passing faces caught by the light of a street lamp or a shop window is often better for my purpose than their full revelation in the daylight, and, if I must add the truth, night is kinder in this respect than day, which too often destroys an air-built castle at the moment of its completion, without the smallest ceremony or remorse. (*OCS* 43)

Dickens is describing his own nocturnal rambles and their importance for his art, especially in so many scenes where we see a character by lamplight, fire light, candlelight, and the lighting is revealing precisely because the character is imperfectly lit. The opening chapter of *Bleak House* is a study in this kind of chiaroscuro, when Dickens makes the courtroom's obscurity a metaphor for Chancery proceedings. There are occasions when we glimpse Fagin or Little Dorrit in such a way that, by not seeing them clearly, we understand them better. Little Nell is often seen in this way, from her first appearance in the street at night to her last days in the gloom of the ancient church; there is a shadow on her always, which hints at her early death, in effect predicts the outcome of the story.

"Mis-shapen, deformed," and lame as he is, acutely aware that he is unlike other men as he was unlike the beautiful children who were once his playmates, Humphrey has chosen to write his novel about his opposite, "a pretty little girl"—the words with which he introduces Nell (*OCS* 44). She is Humphrey's dream child as she was Dickens's dream child. But at the same time he introduces himself into her story, first as a passer-by intrigued by the mystery she represents, then as her feeble grandfather, and eventually as the energetic and impetuous "single gentleman" who enters the story in chapter 34 to search eagerly for Nell and her grandfather, his brother as it turns out. By inventing this active and shrewd version of himself, Humphrey creates an alter ego, the man he might have been if he had been born with health and vigor. But even here Humphrey does not cease to weave his story out of himself. Does he also re-imagine himself as the sinister and preternaturally agile Quilp, misshapen and malevolent, sexually aggressive, and particularly eager to get his hands on Nell? Is part of the novel's energy a strongly felt prurient interest in Nell, which Dickens shares and with which he endows Master Humphrey? Is *this* story the one that Humphrey is eager to imagine and to tell?

In addition, Humphrey seems to draw on his own curious old house for the atmosphere of the Curiosity Shop, and perhaps for the old monastic ruin where Nell and her grandfather find sanctuary and where she dies. Like other novelists, he puts a friend into the story: Jack Redburn's obsessions about his room, and his melancholy flute-playing, along with his impracticality and thwarted hopes of a legacy, re-appear in Dick Swiveller. As for Dickens, he is telling his favorite story, of a genteel child in danger in the streets of London, where child prostitution was all too common. Dickens even introduces his personal bête noire, Warren's Blacking. The poet Slum writes advertising doggerel for " 'the blacking-makers' " and offers Mrs. Jarley an acrostic on Warren which can easily be converted to Jarley (*OCS* 282); in *Barnaby Rudge* Mr. Haredale's house is called The Warren, and Dickens has the satisfaction of burning it to the ground.

Once Master Humphrey has revealed himself in *Clock* Number 45 (6 February 1841) as a participant in the adventures of Little Nell and her grandfather, in fact the single gentleman who tried to help them, he returns the manuscript of *The Old Curiosity Shop* to the clock-case and brings out the manuscript of *Barnaby Rudge*, just as "the deep and distant bell of St. Paul's" strikes midnight. " 'This,' " he tells his companions, " ' to be opened to such music, should be a tale where London's face by night is darkly seen, and where some deed of such a time as this is dimly shadowed out' " (*MHC* 134). Humphrey describes a recent visit to the clock-room at St. Paul's, where he imagines that the great clock "was London's heart, and that when it should cease to beat, the City would be no more." Now, he reminds his listeners,

> It is night. Calm and unmoved amidst the scenes that darkness favors, the great heart of London throbs in its Giant breast. Wealth and beggary, vice and virtue, guilt and innocence, repletion and the direst hunger, all treading on each other and crowding together, are gathered round it. Draw but a little circle above the clustering house-tops, and you shall have within its space, everything with its opposite extreme. . . . Where yonder feeble light is shining, a man is but this moment dead. The taper at a few yards' distance is seen by eyes that have this instant opened on the world. There are two houses separated by but an inch or two of wall. In one, there are quiet minds at rest; in the other a waking conscience that one might think would trouble the very air. In that close corner where the roofs shrink down . . . there are such dark crimes, such miseries and horrors, as could be hardly told in whispers. In the handsome street, there are folks asleep who have dwelt there all their lives, and have no more knowledge of these things than if they had never been.   (*MHC* 135–36)

The passage is a kind of summary for all of Dickens's novels, emphasizing especially those social and moral contrasts which shape them, and his readiness to show complacent middle-class readers how unjust, wicked, and fragile their society is.

As Humphrey prepares to begin reading *Barnaby Rudge* aloud, unaware of its authorship, the deaf gentleman proposes a new rule for these narratives. Since Humphrey's own activities were part of *The Old Curiosity Shop*,

> "... if such of us as have anything to relate of our own lives, could interweave it with our contributions to the Clock, it would be well to do so. This need be no restraint upon us, either as to time, or place, or incident, since any real passage of this kind may be surrounded by fictitious circumstances, and represented by fictitious characters."   (*MHC* 137)

Dickens is defining his own practice, drawing on his own childhood grievance to portray a series of neglected children suitably disguised: Oliver, Smike, Nell, Pip, Little Dorrit. But he is also preparing us for *Barnaby Rudge*, whose supposed author has written about his own past, disguising it as an historical novel set in a period more than sixty years earlier—the canonical distance, as established by Sir Walter Scott with *Waverley*. When the deaf gentleman's proposal is accepted, Humphrey points out that, although the manuscript before him was not written to conform to this new rule, nevertheless it may conform: perhaps " 'the writer of this tale—which is not impossible, for men are apt to do so when they write—has actually mingled with it something of his own endurance and experience' " (*MHC* 137). When no one demurs, Humphrey assumes this to be the case, and indeed detects a slight sign that *Barnaby Rudge* is in part a disguised autobiography by one of his friends. The novel begins in *Clock* Number 46 (13 February 1841) and proceeds with no further reference to Humphrey and his circle, usually at the rate of two chapters each week, ending in a double Number (87–88; 27 November 1841). In 88 we learn that Humphrey died alone beside the clock after he had finished reading *Barnaby Rudge*. Before he dies, Humphrey imagines a whole alternate life that he might have lived, with a wife, children, and grandchildren, and writes it all down. He leaves his house to Jack Redburn and the deaf gentleman, who are to live there together; eventually the house will be closed up but will remain as Humphrey left it, including the silent clock, the six chairs, and Humphrey's stick (*MHC* 145–47).

In those final pages, the deaf gentleman, who reports Humphrey's death and the disposal of his estate, also suggests that the story told by Magog, about the bowyer's daughter who ran off with a nobleman, but later repented and atoned, draws on his own similar loss of a daughter. More to the point, he identifies Jack Redburn as the probable author of *Barnaby Rudge*: "From certain allusions which Jack has dropped, to his having been deserted and cast off in early life, I am inclined to believe that some passages of his youth may possibly be shadowed out in the history of Mr. Chester and his son: but seeing that he avoids the subject, I have not pursued it" (*MHC* 146). Master Humphrey had introduced Redburn by describing him as impractical, easy-going, and at times melancholy. He explained that Redburn had been raised to expect a rich inheritance, but his younger brother had managed to exclude him from his wealthy relative's affection:

> too indolent to court, and too honest to flatter, the elder [Jack] gradually lost ground in the affections of a capricious old man, and the younger, who did not fail to improve his opportunity, now triumphs in the possession of enormous wealth. His triumph is to hoard it in solitary wretchedness, and probably to feel with the expenditure of every shilling a greater pang than the loss of his whole inheritance ever cost his brother.   (*MHC* 64)

Jack's two contributions to the *Clock*, "A Confession Found in a Prison in the Time of Charles the Second"(Number 3; 18 April 1840) and *Barnaby Rudge* tell a different story. The narrator of "A Confession" describes himself as "of a secret sullen distrustful nature." He is jealous of his brother, who is cheerful, generous, and popular; he hates his brother's wife, who seems to fear him. Left guardian of their child when they die, the narrator comes to hate the child and crave his fortune. After he murders the child and buries him in the garden, the crime is discovered; the narrator writes his confession on the eve of his execution.

Redburn's "Confession" is a revealing fiction, offering at once a hostile portrait of his usurping brother as secretive, sullen, and capable of murder, and expressing his own rage and capacity for murder. He understands the murderous impulse, as Dickens understood it in portraying Bill Sikes during and after the murder of Nancy. In composing *Barnaby Rudge*, Redburn has more elaborately explored that rage, chiefly in the character of Hugh, also dispossessed and so another self-portrait, darkened and melodramatic, but understandably resentful at the way society, and especially his father, have used and mistreated him. Sir John Chester, Hugh's father, is as artful and ingratiating as Redburn's younger brother, and as ruthless. In portraying Hugh, Redburn has imagined himself as a victim of family indifference. He does so again, less savagely, in portraying Edward Chester, Sir John's legitimate son; Sir John schemes to prevent his marriage, then curses and dispossesses him. Redburn may project another aspect of himself, his incapacity for practical activities, in Barnaby, another son repudiated by his father. John Willet makes the fourth in a quartet of fathers who mistreat their sons, and whose presence in *Barnaby Rudge* hint at its supposed author's resentments and obsessions—as they also hint at Dickens's own obsession with irresponsible parents and neglected children.

Master Humphrey, then is the author of *The Old Curiosity Shop*; Jack Redburn is the author of *Barnaby Rudge*. Though Dickens pretty much ignores these concepts for the duration of each novel, they are an important part of the shaping of both stories, and imply a certain interplay between author and audience. As reader of the stories, Humphrey anticipates that need to see his audience face to face, and to gauge their responses to his tales, which later motivated Dickens's public readings.

Though *Barnaby Rudge* is the second of the *Clock* novels, it may have played a part in Dickens's development of the *Clock* around a club that gathers to hear stories. We know that he planned a novel about the Gordon Riots as early as May 1836, to be called "Gabriel Vardon, the Locksmith of London," based on a real but nameless locksmith who refused to aid the mob by picking the lock of Newgate Prison during the riots. By July 1837, in negotiations with Richard Bentley, he was calling this unwritten novel "Barnaby Rudge." These negotiations dragged on into 1840, as Dickens became increasingly dissatisfied with Bentley. Meanwhile, he had begun *Barnaby Rudge*, writing a few pages in January 1839, and a little more in late September-early November of that year: 48 manuscript pages, comprising what are now chapters 1 through 3, which introduce John and Joe Willet, the Maypole Inn, Barnaby, Edward Chester, and the sinister man who follows and robs Chester on the London road.

These chapters introduce the four-man club that meets nightly at the Maypole. On the night when the novel begins, 19 March 1775, they listen as Solomon Daisy re-tells the story of that night twenty years before when Reuben Haredale and his steward Rudge were murdered. This Maypole club was perhaps transmuted by Dickens into the four-man club that listens to Master Humphrey's stories—only to become eventually a part of one of those stories. The Maypole club meets in a quaint old room not unlike Humphrey's room, and in describing them, Jack Redburn may have slyly caricatured at least one of his *Clock* associates: we hear of John Willet's "profound obstinacy and slowness of apprehension" (*BR* 45); Owen Miles, though "an excellent man of thoroughly sterling character," is "not of quick apprehension, and not without some amusing prejudices" (*MHC* 66). Miles, like John Willet, tends to be testy and peremptory. In his solemnity, sleepiness, love of eating, and slowness, Willet also resembles John Podgers in Mr. Pickwick's tale of witches, midnight burials, and masked noblemen (*Clock* 5–6; 2 and 9 May 1840). The deaf gentleman's story of Hugh Graham, "a bold young 'prentice who loved his master's daughter" (*MHC* 45), is a kind of fiction that Sim Tappertit would have found to his taste.

The company assembled beside Master Humphrey's clock favors stories about an earlier London which emphasize how dangerous and unsanitary the old city was. The story of Hugh Graham ends in a full-scale riot, citizens

against courtiers; when Will Marks conveys the body removed from the
gibbet to burial at St. Dunstan's, he passes

> low wooden arches . . . in every one of which ill-favored fellows lurked in
> knots of three or four . . . thrusting out their uncombed heads and scowling
> eyes . . . the rain . . . had converted [the streets] into a perfect quagmire, which
> the splashing water spouts . . . and the filth and offal cast from the different
> houses, swelled in no small degree . . . left to putrefy in the close and heavy
> air . . . . There were kites and ravens feeding in the streets . . . . There were
> distant fires whither crowds made their way clamouring eagerly for plun-
> der . . . yelling like devils let loose . . . single-handed men flying from bands of
> ruffians, who pursued them with naked weapons . . . drunken desperate robbers
> issuing from their dens and staggering through the open streets where no man
> dared molest them.   (*MHC* 97–98)

In *Barnaby Rudge*, Dickens describes the poorly lighted streets of London in
1775, and their convenience for robbers, in similar terms, implying that the
reader of 1840 would find them unrecognizable—a subtle irony from the man
who had recently described Jacob's Island:

> in the lighted thoroughfare, there was at every turn some obscure and dangerous
> spot where a thief might fly or shelter, and few would care to follow. . . . It is
> no wonder that . . . street robberies, often accompanied by cruel wounds, and
> not infrequently by loss of life, should have been of nightly occurrence in
> the very heart of London . . . night-cellars . . . yawned for the reception and
> entertainment of the most abandoned of both sexes.   (*BR* 177–78)

Dickens also contrasts then and now in more neutral ways. Clerkenwell was
cleaner and more rural then; St. George's Fields really were fields (*BR* 75,
446).

Dickens treats the past as another country, exotic and dangerously unpredictable. In doing so he draws upon the tradition of the Gothic novel as it
developed in England at the end of the eighteenth century, partly as a reaction
against eighteenth-century rationality. The irrational, the fantastic, the wild
and strange could be introduced, even the supernatural. Dickens very deliberately emphasizes Sir John Chester's identity as an eighteenth-century rational-
ist by calling attention to his favorite reading, Lord Chesterfield's
Letters . . . to his Son (1774), a book Chester has clearly acquired on publication. " 'In every page of this *enlightened* writer' " Chester, who shares part
of his name with Chesterfield, finds " 'some captivating hypocrisy which has
never occurred to me before, or some superlative piece of selfishness to which
I was utterly a stranger' " (*BR* 233; italics mine). Chesterfield's letters advise
his son how to get on in the world, how to ingratiate himself with those who
can advance his fortunes, by learning how to accommodate himself to his

company and assume at all times the mask they wish to see. Emotion is to be suppressed, and goals rationally identified and rationally pursued. The book has often been criticized for its cold-blooded advice about pursuing worldly success; Samuel Johnson described it as teaching " 'the morals of a whore, and the manners of a dancing master' " (Boswell 188). For Dickens, Chester, who had modeled himself on Chesterfield, represents rationality without compassion or charity, like the Poor Laws he criticizes in *Oliver Twist*. Chester advances his rational schemes by manipulating those less clever than himself, notably Hugh of the Maypole; in controlling others, he resembles Miss Havisham in her inculcation of Esther and in her allowing Pip to consider her his benefactor.

In *Barnaby Rudge* Dickens sets this manipulative rationality in the atmosphere of a Gothic novel, as earlier masters of that genre had done. As defined by Horace Walpole in *The Castle of Otranto* (1764), and subsequently developed by "Monk" Lewis, Charles Robert Maturin, and especially Mrs. Radcliffe, the Gothic novel usually featured a young woman, heiress to a great estate, who is threatened by the villain both sexually and financially. He entraps her, imprisons her in a gloomy and labyrinthine castle or monastery, and plans either to marry or murder her, perhaps even to frighten her to death, in order to gain control of her estate. Her sanity is also threatened, by real or contrived apparitions or other apparently supernatural manifestations intended to terrify her into surrender. The setting is usually Spain, Italy, or France, for the Gothic novel depended heavily on the English reader's prejudice against Catholicism and the Latin nations. Monks and nuns usually play sinister roles. They are wicked, it is implied, because of the repressive nature of Catholic teachings and institutions, and especially because of the unhealthiness of a cloistered life. Each writer naturally varied the basic formulae: Scott developed it into the medieval romance; writers like Emily and Charlotte Brontë retained mostly the sinister atmosphere, the dark, dangerous male protagonist, and the young woman who feels herself threatened.

Dickens had already employed Gothic elements in *Oliver Twist*, where Fagin's labyrinthine lairs are a slummier version of the Gothic castle or monastery. There too the young protagonist is threatened with the loss of fortune, reputation, and virtue. Fagin as Jew is presented as foreign, other, like the Catholics of the Gothic genre, and Oliver's chief tormentor is Gothically named: Monks.

By making the anti-Catholic Gordon Riots central to his novel, Dickens was able to draw on popular ideas about Catholics as presented in Gothic fiction. Though he deplores the mob's violence and suggests that its members were for the most part more interested in robbery and violence than in defending Protestant principles, he surrounds the novel's most prominent Catholic, Geoffrey Haredale, with an air of gloomy mystery, and finally sends him into a monastery abroad. Like Haredale, the novel's two villains, Sir John Chester and Mr. Gashford, have been educated by the Jesuits at St. Omer in France, from 1592 until the French Revolution a gathering place for English Catholics. There priests were trained to serve in England, and English Catholic laymen were educated; both activities were considered subversive by the English government. Priests who came to England from St. Omer were often executed in the sixteenth and seventeenth centuries, sometimes deported in the eighteenth. As Dickens implicitly reminds us, the only Catholic churches operating legally in England were chapels attached to the embassies of Catholic powers. The Bavarian and Sardinian chapels were destroyed in the Gordon Riots.

By making Sir John Chester and Mr. Gashford graduates of St. Omer, Dickens associates them with all the disagreeable traits that Englishmen traditionally associated with the Jesuits: duplicity, manipulation, subversion, slyness, furtiveness, an eagerness to control governments from behind the scenes, and a trick of ingratiating themselves with people of rank and power and coming to control them. Even in depicting his anti-Catholic villains, Dickens is able to draw on anti-Catholic clichés, and combine them with the sinister aura which the Gothic novel bestows on Catholics.

Gothic is both an architectural and a literary style, and in its literary manifestation often employs as setting a Gothic building, loosely defined as any structure that is old, quaint, and rambling. Dickens hints at the "Gothic" aspects of Master Humphrey's house, and various settings in *The Old Curiosity Shop* place the threatened heroine in a Gothic context: her bed in the shop among the fragments of armor and antique furniture; the Gothic arch from which Quilp suddenly emerges like a gargoyle fallen from one of its empty niches (*OCS* 276); the old church where she spends her last days among Crusader tombs and other fragments of armor, an appropriate setting for her seduction by death. All are duly illustrated by Cattermole rather than Phiz. *Barnaby Rudge* starts with an elaborate description of the Maypole Inn and Cattermole's drawing of the structure. Built probably in the time of Henry VIII, the inn is rich in abandoned rooms, numerous ells and additions, and paneled rooms with richly carved mantels. The nearby Warren, with its towers and turrets, wears a general air of isolation and gloom. Sim Tappertit's 'Prentice Knights meet in a dank subterranean vault, and eventually several characters end up in the dungeons of Newgate—vaults and dungeons are also favorite Gothic settings.

Sinister events occur in the Gothic settings of *Barnaby Rudge*. Reuben Haredale is murdered at the Warren, and later the mob destroys the house and also the Maypole. Solomon Daisy is alone in Chigwell church when he hears the alarm bell on the night of the Haredale murder; years later, again in the church, he has a glimpse of the supposedly dead Mr. Rudge. Dickens describes the Maypole initially as a place where the smoke that rose from its "huge zig-zag chimneys . . . could not choose but come in more than naturally fantastic shapes." The "vast stables" are

> gloomy, ruinous, and empty. . . . Its windows were old diamond-pane lattices, its floors were sunken and uneven, its ceilings blackened by the hand of time, and heavy with massive beams. Over the doorway was an ancient porch, quaintly carved . . . two grim-looking high-backed settles . . . like the twin dragons of some fairy tale, guarded the entrance to the mansion.
> In the chimneys of the disused rooms, swallows had built their nests for many a long year . . . . The bricks . . . had grown yellow and discoloured like an old man's skin; the sturdy timbers had decayed like teeth.   (BR 43–44)

But at the same time, Dickens insists that the inn was "a hale and hearty age, though, still." He stresses the snugness of its bar, the excellence of its food and drink, and the general sense of hospitality and good cheer which it exudes. In the same way, Humphrey's gloomy mansion is also a place of hospitality and fellowship, and at the Warren, despite its gloomy history, Emma Haredale has made herself a comfortable boudoir.

Despite its potential for cheer, we enter the Maypole on the night of 19 March 1775, the anniversary of that 1753 murder which has blighted Barnaby by darkening his mind and marking him with what seems a spot of blood—he was born on the night of the murder. That murder has cast a shadow over the life of Geoffrey Haredale, the victim's brother, suspected to be the murderer, and over the life of Mrs. Rudge, whose husband was also a victim—though we soon begin to suspect that the furtive stranger in chapter one may in fact be the supposedly murdered steward Rudge. It is curious, by the way, that the Maypole regulars do not recognize him in the inn's well-lighted bar, but one of them, Solomon Daisy, does so five years later at midnight near Chigwell church.

The undead Rudge and his furtive comings and goings are yet another Gothic element, a ghost story hovering at the edges of Dickens's novel. Like Gashford, Rudge represents a kind of motiveless malice and wickedness. We never learn why he killed Reuben Haredale, nor why he lurks miserably around London and Chigwell, where even the lowest avoid him, and he is without shelter, friends, or money. His crime seems one more irrational element.

In certain important ways, Barnaby Rudge himself embodies irrationality, as do Hugh and Lord George Gordon. All three characters are easily manipulated: Barnaby by Hugh, Hugh by Gashford and Sir John Chester, Lord George by Gashford. The presence of Barnaby throughout the story allows Dickens to give us a continuing portrait of a madman, harmless but, as Gabriel Varden recognizes, capable of being " 'put to bad uses' " (BR 261). By letting us into Barnaby's fantastic mind, Dickens allows us to understand Lord George's more dangerous fantasies about Catholic plots, and to understand how the mad lord himself is caught up in an irrational course of conduct that he cannot understand. We know that Dickens carefully researched Gordon and his riots, but as a novelist he understood that he could more readily convey Gordon's madness by creating a parallel figure who could be presented without obligation to the historical record. That record limits the novelist's ability to enter Gordon's fantasies, but Dickens can range freely through Barnaby's fantasies.

George Gissing long ago pointed out that , though Barnaby is occasionally spoken of in the novel as an idiot, he is not. He is a madman (Gissing 109), and a literary madman at that. Perhaps "flighty," Pumblechook's word for Miss Havisham, describes him best. When Dickens wants to give us a sense of the imaginative world where Barnaby dwells, it resembles the fantastic world evoked in "Tom o'Bedlam's Song":

> With a host of furious fancies,
> Whereof I am commander,
> With a burning spear
> And a host of air
> To the wilderness I wander.

Barnaby's fantastic dress represents his fantastic mind; "the steel hilt of an old sword without blade or scabbard; . . . Girt to his side" (*BR* 74) hints at that propensity for military action later provoked by the riots. " 'Look down there,' " he orders Sir John Chester, pointing at clothes drying on a line:

"do you mark how they whisper in each other's ears; then dance and leap, to make believe they are in sport? Do you see how they stop for a moment, when they think there is no one looking, and mutter among themselves again; and then how they roll and gambol, delighted with the mischief they've been plotting? Look at 'em now. See how they whirl and plunge. And now they stop again, and whisper, cautiously together—little thinking, mind, how often I have lain upon the grass and watched them . . . how much better to be silly, than as wise as you! You don't see shadowy people there, like those that live in sleep—not you. Nor eyes in the knotted panes of glass, nor swift ghosts when it blows hard, nor do you hear voices in the air, nor see men stalking in the sky—not you! I lead a merrier life than you, with all your cleverness. You're the dull men. We're the bright ones." (*BR* 133)

His movements are as erratic as his mind. Traveling with his mother, he yields

to every inconstant impulse . . . now leaving her far behind, now lingering far behind himself. . . . Now he would call to her from the topmost branch of some

high tree . . . now using his tall staff as a leaping-pole, come flying over ditch
or hedge or five-barred gate.   (*BR* 248–49)

By depicting Barnaby as erratic and fantastic in the first or 1775 half of the
book, Dickens is preparing us for the appearance of Lord George Gordon in
chapter 35 (*BR* 331–33), just after Dickens, easily transcending five intervening years, brings us back to the Maypole Inn on 19 March 1780, a dark and
stormy night. Crazy Barnaby and crazy Lord George are thereafter paralleled,
especially once they meet on Westminster Bridge, where Gordon urges Barnaby to join his following. When Mrs. Rudge pleads that her son is " 'not
in his right senses' " and should be left alone, Gordon blushes "deeply,"
half-realizing the affinity between Barnaby and himself. " 'It is a bad sign
of the depravity of these times . . . that those who cling to the truth and support
the right cause, are set down as mad,' " he tells her, then appeals to Gashford:

> "He has surely no appearance . . . of being deranged? And even if he had, we
> must not construe any trifling peculiarity into madness. Which of us,"—and
> here he turned red again—"would be safe, if that were made the law!"
>   (*BR* 443–44)

On Gordon's first appearance, Dickens notes his "restlessness of thought and
purpose . . . an indefinable uneasiness" (*BR* 336), constantly in need of the
reassurance Gashford is ready to supply. John Grueby offers an immediate
diagnosis: " 'Between Bloody Marys, and blue cockades . . . and no Pop-
erys . . . my lord's half off his head' " (*BR* 341). Grueby later makes the
parallel between Barnaby and Lord George explicit. When Lord George asks
him if Barnaby's manner strikes him as " 'at all wild or strange?' " Grueby
replies " 'Mad' . . . with emphatic brevity." When Gordon objects, Grueby
thrusts home: " 'My lord . . . look at his dress, look at his eyes, look at his
restless way, hear him cry 'No Popery!' Mad, my lord.' " Uncomfortable,
but unwilling to hear the truth, Gordon refuses to recognize madness in Barnaby or, by implication, in himself: " '*This* a madman!' " he exclaims; " 'I
am proud to be the leader of such men as you' " (*BR* 520–21).

The unity of *Barnaby Rudge* depends in part on parallel stories of fathers
mistreating sons: John Willet, Sir John Chester, and Mr. Rudge all act in this
way (Marcus 184–204). But it also depends on the parallels between Barnaby
and Lord George as madmen manipulated by cynical schemers. Dickens treats
Gordon with considerable sympathy, and his defense of Gordon is similar to
Gabriel Varden's defense of Barnaby, which procures Barnaby's pardon:
neither man is really responsible for his actions, but is manipulated by others.
Dickens makes this defense more clearly for the fictional Barnaby, but his
sympathy for Gordon as Gashford's pawn is evident. At times Gordon half
realizes that something is wrong, even expresses self-doubt, only to be assured

by Gashford that all is well. When Forster objected that Dickens had been too sympathetic to Gordon, Dickens insisted that

> he must have been at heart a kind man, and a lover of the despised and rejected, after his own fashion . . . was known to relieve the necessities of many people; . . . did great charities in Newgate. He always spoke on the people's side, and tried against his muddled brains to expose the profligacy of both parties. He never got anything by his madness, and never sought it.
>
> (*Letters* 2: 294–95)

Chester and Gashford control Lord George. They also control Hugh, and through Hugh, Barnaby; they even control Sim Tappertit and his 'Prentice Knights. Hugh encourages Barnaby's wild behavior during the riots, as Gashford encourages Lord George. The presence of Grip the raven underlines these chains of manipulation. Like a parrot, Grip repeats what he has been encouraged to say, phrases like " 'Never say die!' " and " 'Polly put the kettle on.' " When he joins the rioters with Barnaby, he quickly learns to cry " 'No Popery!' " His witless repetitions serve as an ironic commentary on Barnaby, Hugh, Lord George, and the rioters, all of whom repeat the slogans that others have imposed upon them by the clever ones who through them control the mob.

Like a raven, Dickens's writing-desk was well supplied with quills, essential instruments for the imaginative and manipulative activity that is the making of fictions. Apart from stressing a kind of psychological twinship between Barnaby and Lord George, Dickens incorporates into his plot the concocting and shaping of that plot: that is, while Dickens is manipulating his characters and their adventures as a novelist must do, he incorporates into his story manipulative plotters who are trying to control the story, are bringing people together or putting them apart just as the novelist himself is doing. He even attributes the novel to Jack Redburn, who has his own scores to pay off and his own psychological reasons for telling this story.

In *Oliver Twist* Fagin and Monks are trying to control the plot of Oliver's story, to make it the story of a criminal who will figure in the *Newgate Calendar*, while Nancy and Mr. Brownlow strive to write that story differently. Dickens's handling of his plotters in *Barnaby Rudge* is less sophisticated, but in making Chester and Gashford manipulate people and events, Dickens ambiguously hints at the similarity between making fictional plots and making conspiracies, and the questionable morality of such manipulations. The novelist is licensed to concoct and tell a tale, but in doing so develops some affinity with more sinister types of plotters, whose actions have consequences in the real world. This is particularly true of Chester and Gashford, whose plots are motivated by a love of power for its own sake, as well as by hatred, and who operate without scruples. In making the manipulations by his two principal villains a version of his own working methods,

Dickens recognizes the ambiguous nature of the creative imagination, the creative process.

WORKS CONSULTED

Andrews, Malcolm Y. "Introducing Master Humphrey." *Dickensian* 67 (1971): 70–86.

Boswell, James. *Life of Johnson.* Ed. R.W. Chapman. New edition corrected by J. D. Fleeman. London: Oxford UP, 1970.

Butt, John, and Kathleen Tillotson. *Dickens at Work.* London: Methuen, 1957.

Cohen, Jane R. *Charles Dickens and his Original Illustrators.* Columbus: Ohio State UP, 1980.

Davis, Earle. *The Flint and the Flame: the Artistry of Charles Dickens.* Columbia: U of Missouri P, 1963.

Dickens, Charles. *Barnaby Rudge.* Ed. Gordon Spence. London: Penguin Books, 1997. Designated in text as *BR.*

———. *The Letters of Charles Dickens.* Ed. Madeline House and Graham Storey. Volume 1, 1820–1839. Oxford: Clarendon, 1965.

———. *The Letters of Charles Dickens.* Ed. Madeline House and Graham Storey. Volume 2, 1840–1841. Oxford: Clarendon, 1969.

———. *Master Humphrey's Clock.* By "Boz." In 88 weekly parts (4 April 1840–27 November 1841). London: Chapman and Hall, 1840–41.

———. *Master Humphrey's Clock.* 3 volumes in one. London: Chapman and Hall, 1840–41.

———. *Master Humphrey's Clock and other stories.* Ed. Peter Mudford. London: Everyman, 1997. Designated in text as *MHC.*

———. *The Old Curiosity Shop.* Ed. Angus Eason. Harmondsworth: Penguin Books, 1972. Designated in text as *OCS.*

Forster, John. *The Life of Charles Dickens.* 2 volumes. 1872–74. London: Chapman and Hall, 1899.

Gissing, George. *Charles Dickens: a Critical Study.* London: Blackie, 1903.

Johnson, Edgar. *Charles Dickens: His Tragedy and Triumph.* 2 volumes. New York: Simon and Schuster, 1952.

Kincaid, James R. *Dickens and the Rhetoric of Laughter.* Oxford: Clarendon, 1971.

McGowan, John P. "Mystery and History in *Barnaby Rudge.*" *Dickens Studies Annual* 9 (1981): 33–52.

McMaster, Juliet. " 'Better to be Silly': from Vision to Reality in *Barnaby Rudge.*" *Dickens Studies Annual* 13 (1984): 1–17.

Marcus, Steven. *Dickens from Pickwick to Dombey.* New York: Clarion/Simon and Schuster, 1968.

Patten, Robert L. *Charles Dickens and his Publishers.* 1978. Santa Cruz: The Dickens Project, University of California, 1991.

Rice, Thomas Jackson. *Barnaby Rudge: an Annotated Bibliography.* New York: Garland, 1987.

Steig, Michael. *Dickens and Phiz.* Bloomington: Indiana UP, 1978.

Trollope, Anthony. *An Autobiography.* London: Oxford UP, 1950.

Executing Beauty:
Dickens and the Aesthetics of Death

Goldie Morgentaler

Dickens was notoriously reticent on the subject of aesthetics. There is, in the whole of his work, very little philosophizing about the nature of art or beauty. This reticence means that what Dickens understood by art must be inferred from his fiction and this inference leads directly to the startling observation that the few times when Dickens does raise issues of aesthetics in his fiction occur within the context of violent death. In fact, virtually the only characters in the Dickensian canon who are self-proclaimed as artists are those who make a profession of death—Mr. Venus in Our Mutual Friend *and Dennis the Hangman in* Barnaby Rudge. *This essay explores the paradoxical association of art, extinction, and execution in Dickens's fiction. It suggests that by yoking the three, Dickens was speaking indirectly of his own novelistic enterprise and that Dickens's fascination with such gruesome topics as dismemberment, dissection, and decapitation had implications for his literary style, so that a study of these matters may contribute to our understanding of his aesthetic beliefs.*

One of the anomalies of Dickens's career as novelist is that for an author so prolific and so obsessed with his own creative productions and activities, he was remarkably reticent on the subject of aesthetics. In the whole of Dickens's work, there is very little philosophizing about the nature of art or beauty, although there are numerous allusions in his correspondence to novel-writing as a craft. Dickens the novelist was quite capable of presenting an extended fictional portrait of another novelist, David Copperfield, without once broaching the subject of art, or suggesting that there was any significant difference between novel-writing and shorthand—or any other occupation that requires mastery through hard work and application. A partial, if not very satisfying rationale for this reticence can be found in a letter Dickens wrote to the journalist Richard Henry Horne: "A man makes a weak case when he tries to explain his writing. His writing should explain itself. . . ." (Lettis 2).[1]

Dickens followed his own advice and his silence on this subject means that what Dickens understood by art must be inferred from his fiction. And this inference leads directly to the rather startling observation that the few times when Dickens does raise issues of aesthetics in his fiction occur primarily within the context of death—violent, grotesque death, not the sentimentalized passing of a Little Nell or a Paul Dombey. In fact, virtually the only characters in the Dickensian canon who are self-proclaimed artists are those who make a profession of death—Mr. Venus in *Our Mutual Friend* and Dennis the Hangman in *Barnaby Rudge*.[2]

What I would like to do in this essay is explore this paradoxical association of art, extinction, and execution, and to suggest, that by yoking the three, Dickens was speaking indirectly of his own novelistic enterprise. The primary text I will be using to prove my argument is *Barnaby Rudge*, since in that novel about the Gordon Riots of the 1780s, the relationship between executed and executor is depicted as in some ways analogous to that between created and creator. I also intend to argue that Dickens's fascination with such gruesome topics as dismemberment, dissection, and decapitation had implications for his literary style, so that a study of what Harry Stone has aptly labeled "the night side"[3] of Dickens may contribute to our understanding of his aesthetic beliefs.

It is a commonplace of Dickens scholarship to point to his fascination with death. In fact, there are so many possible illustrations of just how obsessed Dickens was with this topic that I will limit myself here to just a few examples: In his early essay "A Visit to Newgate," published in *Sketches by Boz*, Dickens describes with fascinated horror how, in Newgate prison chapel, condemned men were once forced to sit next to their own coffins and murmur the responses to their own funeral services on the Sundays before their executions. In fact, this sadistic practice had been abolished by Dickens's time, and on his visit to Newgate in the 1830s, Dickens did not see any condemned men praying next to their own coffins, but the idea obviously had such a strong hold on his imagination that he could not resist adding the detail to his description of Newgate (67–83).

When he visited France, Dickens's favorite tourist spot was the Paris morgue, and in England he attended public executions, most famously that of the Mannings, a husband and wife who were executed together for the murder of their lodger. Dickens wrote two angry letters to the *Times* after the execution, in which he railed against the morbid curiosity and bad behavior of the spectators without pausing to consider that he had been one of them. Dickens routinely made pilgrimages to the places where violent crimes had been committed. On his second trip to America, he made a point of visiting the laboratory of the Harvard chemistry professor and murderer John Webster to see for himself where Webster had disposed of his victim's body.

Dickens's fiction reflects this peculiar attraction to the macabre—he likes to write about amputated legs and bottled babies, bodies eviscerated, bodies made up of artificial parts, bodies dug up after death. This seeming necrophilia may be understood as an attempt on Dickens's part to face his anxiety about death head-on, to exorcise the demon by staring it in the face. Dickens himself understood it this way, and connected his morbidity to childhood terrors of death. But I would like to suggest another reason for the prevalence of this motif in the Dickensian oeuvre, namely, that the anxiety being confronted has less to do with an actual fear of physical extinction than it does with an unease about the validity of art and its proper relationship to the processes of life.

Here, for instance, is a catalogue Dickens made of all the places he visited during a stay in Paris: "... Hospitals, Prisons, Dead-houses, Operas, Theatres, Concert Rooms, Burial-grounds, Palaces, and Wine shops" (Ackroyd 517). It is striking that the operas, theaters, and concert rooms are sandwiched between hospitals, prisons, and dead-houses on the one side and burial grounds on the other. The juxtaposition appears random, especially since it trails off to palaces and wine shops. Nevertheless, the world of art in this list remains rounded by the sleep of death, as if to emphasize its precariousness, its intermediate position between death and death. The operas, theaters, and concert rooms mentioned here appear as an unwarranted interruption to the catalogue of human pain, degeneracy, and decomposition epitomized by the hospitals, prisons, and dead houses. They are a bright inconsequential distraction to the real business of life—which is death.

This link between the aesthetic and the macabre can be found throughout Dickens's fiction. It occurs, for instance, in the following tribute paid to a newly deceased workhouse attendant in *Oliver Twist*: "A many, many beautiful corpses she laid out, as nice and neat as wax-work."[4] The idea of juxtaposing "beautiful" with "corpses" and transmuting both into the artistic artifact of a waxwork is typical of Dickens at his most ghoulish—and most sardonic.

The association of the macabre with the beautiful is especially notable when Dickens deals with the female victims of judicial execution, whom he often locates within the realm of the hypothetical and the metaphoric. For instance, in *Bleak House*, when Lady Dedlock realizes that she is in danger of exposure by the unscrupulous lawyer Tulkinghorn, she reaches for a gallows metaphor to describe her feelings. Says she: "I am to remain upon this gaudy platform, on which my miserable deception has been so long acted, and it is to fall beneath me when you give the signal?" (BH 659).

More ghastly still is the compliment paid to Lucie Manette, the heroine of *A Tale of Two Cities,* by one of the revolutionaries: " 'She has a fine head for it [the guillotine],' croaked Jacques Three. 'I have seen blue eyes and golden hair there, and they looked charming when Samson [the executioner] held them up.' " To which the narrator adds: "Ogre that he was, he spoke like an epicure" (388).

In this chilling juxtaposition of beauty and execution, Dickens merges the concept of unnatural death with that of aesthetics—the living woman's present beauty exists only to enhance the pictorial qualities of the tableau of her death. Beauty is here created at the expense—quite literally—of life. At the same time, the imagined execution constitutes a desecration of beauty, beauty here being made synonymous with female innocence. We are being asked to shudder at the thought of the angel defiled, and that shudder incorporates frissons of simultaneous horror and arousal. The scene balances on the border between aesthetics and pornography, where the quality of the emotion that is being evoked defines the base as purged of its lasciviousness through the reader's moral outrage at the desecration involved.

There is, of course, an irony in the fact that Jacques Three's statement is a compliment—it is a tribute to Lucie's beauty. But it deliberately turns inside-out the usual association of human beauty with human life, thereby transforming Jacques Three's leering admiration into the obverse of a far nobler sentiment—aesthetic appreciation—and suggesting how short is the distance from one emotion to the other. By calling Jacques Three an epicure—that is, someone with a discriminating taste in food—Dickens further confounds the horror of execution with the refinement of aesthetics.

Dickens is, of course, treading on well-traveled ground here, the death of a beautiful woman having been identified by Edgar Allen Poe as "unquestionably, the most poetical topic in the world" (756). Dickens, however, is more forthright than Poe when he hints at the sexual element that underlies a fascination with the morbid and refuses to disguise or justify the lascivious by labeling it as poetic. This kind of gleeful sexual predation, occasioned by the victimization of others—and especially women—can be found often in Dickens's fiction, especially in the earlier novels. The villainous dwarf Quilp's sadistic mistreatment of his wife in *The Old Curiosity Shop* is a good example of this, as is the fact that Mrs. Quilp loves her deformed husband no less for his abuse. In fact, she is certain that other women would find Quilp's behavior just as arousing as she does: "Quilp has such a way with him when he likes that the best-looking woman here couldn't refuse him if I was dead . . . and he chose to make love to her" (OCS 76).

A similar example of how Dickens depicts sexual arousal—this time male sexual arousal—as being directly linked to female victimization occurs in *Barnaby Rudge* when Emma Haredale and Dolly Varden are abducted by Hugh and Dennis the Hangman. Rape is in the air, as the narrator bursts into the following rhetorical raptures:

> What mortal eyes could have avoided wandering to [Dolly's] delicate bodice, the streaming hair, the neglected dress, the perfect abandonment and uncon-sciousness of the blooming little beauty? Who could look on and see [Dolly] lavish caresses and endearments [on Emma], and not desire to be in Emma Haredale's place; to be either her or Dolly; either the hugging or the hugged?
>
> (BR 541)

Note here the deliberate diminishment of the very idea of beauty by having it qualified by the adjective ''little'' in the phrase ''blooming little beauty.'' What is more, the paragraph's last line hints at the undifferentiated sameness of women, at their interchangeability, at the same time as it makes no bones about the self-referential nature of male arousal. There is no room for an ''other'' in the wish to be either the hugging or the hugged. There is merely the longing for self-gratification in both its active and its passive forms. But what is especially interesting in this passage is the picture it paints of the potential desecration of the beautiful—especially the beautiful woman—a desecration effected by sex in this case and by death in the earlier example I gave from *A Tale of Two Cities*. Dickens likes to inhabit the territory between admiration for the beautiful and arousal at its destruction, and he returns to it often.

In *Bleak House*, Krook, the repulsive owner of a foul rag and bone shop, suddenly beholds Ada Clare's golden hair: ''Hi!'' says Krook: ''Here's lovely hair! I have got three sacks of ladies' hair below, but none so beautiful and fine as this. What colour and what texture!'' (BH 100). Krook then proceeds to draw one of Ada's tresses through his ''yellow'' hand—yellow here stand-ing as the dirtier flip side of ''golden'' in much the same way as Jacques Three's leering admiration of Lucie in *A Tale of Two Cities* is the flip side of the ennobling appreciation of beauty.

Both of these scenes—Jacques Three's imaginary decapitation of Lucie and Krook's running his hand through Ada's hair—equate the pretty with the blond and locate the angelic associations thus evoked within the context of execution. And not just any kind of execution, but a decapitation—that is, an attack on the part of the body that most sins with its beauty—the head that contains the hair. Of course, Lucie's imagined beheading in *A Tale of Two Cities* occurs naturally within the context of the French Revolution during the reign of the guillotine. But in *Bleak House*, where he does not have such a realistic background at his disposal, Dickens manages to suggest the same kind of fate for the blond Ada by punctuating the scene with the entrance of Lady Jane, Krook's cat. The cat's name is an allusion to Lady Jane Grey, who was beheaded in the Tower in the sixteenth century. Krook is a dealer in body parts, in cat-skins and human hair. He regards Ada's hair as a desirable commodity because it is beautiful, but this is beauty that only acquires value when it is severed from the head that makes it grow.

However, women are not the only characters whom Dickens locates within the nexus of physical perfection, execution and death. In *Barnaby Rudge*, the recipient of such dubious flattery is Hugh, the disenfranchised, illegitimate son of the aristocrat John Chester by a gypsy woman. The narrator describes Hugh as follows: "Muscular and handsome. . . . A young man of a hale athletic figure, and a giant's strength, whose sunburnt face and swarthy throat, overgrown with jet-black hair, might have served a painter for a model" (BR 138).[5]

The suggestion that Hugh's physical proportions would make him ideal as a painter's model foreshadows a later remark by Dennis the Hangman about Hugh's suitability for hanging, which is also based on his physical beauty. Dennis remarks first that Hugh is "a fine-built chap." He then goes on, with what Dickens terms "a horrible kind of admiration, such as that with which a cannibal might regard his intimate friend, when hungry": "Did you ever . . . see such a throat as his? . . . There's a neck for stretching . . . !" (BR 360).

The intimation that Hugh's physical assets make him an ideal candidate for the noose reappears in different guises throughout *Barnaby Rudge*. These uses for Hugh's physical perfection—painting and hanging—are complemented by a third suggestion of a similar order when John Chester, Hugh's biological father, speculates that, once executed, Hugh's body "would make a very handsome preparation in Surgeon's Hall, and would benefit science extremely" (BR 671). In all these instances, Hugh's beauty is defined as having no value unless it can be anatomized by others. He is all object and all body—a beautiful animal just waiting to be dissected, hanged—or reproduced on canvas.

All these activities are mirror-images of one another. In fact, the connection between art, reproduction, and execution is an old one, often linked, for instance, in the literature on maternal impressions, where pregnant women who have witnessed executions are said to give birth to children with the marks of hanging or torture on their bodies, in much the same way as pregnant women who viewed paintings were thought to pass on the characteristics of the paintings to their offspring (Huet 71–72). Language itself provides a link between the two, since one can execute both a painting and a human being, and both may be hung.

Furthermore, execution in *Barnaby Rudge* is defined as a thing hereditable, handed down from mother to son—thereby further confounding the relationship between biological processes and unnatural death. All of the gypsies in this novel lose their lives by hanging, as if this type of death were both hereditable and racially determined. As the half-gypsy Hugh puts it, just before his own execution, his mother had "died the death in store for her son" (669). Hugh's proleptic construction of this thought, with its confusion of past and future, collapses the distinction between generations. The destiny of the mother is relived by the son—or, more accurately, re-died.

Dickens is not merely being fanciful when he juxtaposes the three images of Hugh as a perfect specimen for painter, hangman, and dissecting surgeon. Historically these activities were all linked. In 1752, an Act of Parliament gave judges discretion, when imposing sentence for murder, of substituting dissection for gibbeting (gibbeting was the practice of hanging the body in chains after execution). Since, by the 1750s the death penalty was being imposed for crimes against property, dissection after hanging was a way of singling out the punishment for murder. Dissection—as Ruth Richardson points out in her extraordinary book, *Death, Dissection and the Destitute*—was widely considered a fate worse than death, because it obliterated the body and, by law, denied the malefactor a grave. It is this total erasure of the body that Dickens finds so horrifying when he writes in his essay on the condemned of Newgate: "Imagine what have been the feelings of the men . . . of whom between the gallows and the knife no mortal remnant may now remain" (Dickens, "Visit," 76).

Like executions, dissections were public. Part of the punishment was the very publicity involved in the delivery from hangman to surgeons at the gallows, and later in the public exhibition of the opened body itself. As Ruth Richardson suggests, "Dissection was added to the array of punishments available to the bench . . . so that the punishment inflicted upon the body of the murderer should publicly transcend that already inflicted by the scaffold" (34).

The 1752 Act that permitted dissection benefitted both anatomists and artists, thus turning the judiciary into an unwitting instrument for the advancement of both medicine and art, since bodies hanged at Tyburn ended up either at the College of Surgeons or at the Royal Academy of Art, which was founded by authority of George III in 1768. The two institutions even shared the services of the same professor of anatomy, William Hunter. The following anecdote will illustrate just how close was the link between them: In 1775, the College of Surgeons acquired the bodies of eight men at once from Tyburn. Professor Hunter thought that the physical development of one of the men would benefit the artists, and the body was conveyed to the Royal

Academy of Art while still warm, before rigor mortis had set in. Hunter then arranged the body in an attitude in which it was allowed to stiffen. It was then flayed, so that the external muscles were exposed ready to make a mold. According to Richardson (37), the Royal Academy houses to this day a cast of the body of this man taken from the Tyburn gallows.

Dissection constitutes a man-made violation of the integrity of the human body, a reduction into parts and pieces of that which had once been whole and recognizably human. Dickens, as might be expected, was drawn by what he called "the attraction of repulsion" to the idea of dissection, and the practice is several times referred to in his novels. In *Pickwick Papers* it is the object of some stomach-turning jokes. "Nothing like dissection." says the aptly named medical student Bob Sawyer, "to give one an appetite" (PP, 494). But Dickens could also put the horror of dissection to more metaphorical use and integrate it into the larger intentions of his fiction, as he does quite poignantly in *Oliver Twist*, where the bodies of parish children who have died of neglect and starvation are opened and nothing is found inside.

Dickens's fascination with dissection, with the anatomizing and categorizing of the human body is reflected in his narrative style. He is the master of the synecdoche, of the part standing for the whole, and more often than not the part in question is a body part. One of the hallmarks of Dickens's descriptive method is his tendency to divide the human body into its components and then give those components a life of their own—Carker's teeth, for instance, in *Dombey and Son,* or Wegg's leg in *Our Mutual Friend.*

This is dismemberment translated into metaphor, and Dickens's increasing sophistication in using this technique can be traced in the trajectory of his career. At first, his fascination with dismemberment reveals itself simply in gruesome jokes of questionable taste: In *Pickwick Papers*, we read of the mother of five children: " ... Tall lady, eating sandwiches—forgot the arch—crash—knock—children look round—mother's head off—sandwich in her hand—no mouth to put it in—head of a family off" (PP 79). The pun at the end is a harbinger of things to come, when Dickens's delight in the macabre for its own sake begins to shade into an appreciation of its larger metaphoric possibilities—an appreciation which reaches its apex in *A Tale of Two Cities*, where dismemberment and beheading stand as grisly tropes for a society which has literally and figuratively been torn limb from limb, which has literally and figuratively lost its head.

Hugh is not the only character in *Barnaby Rudge* to be portrayed in terms that confound artistry with execution. Dennis the Hangman is presented in those terms as well, as if the relationship between executed and executor were analogous to that between created and creator. Dennis and Hugh both take part in the Gordon Riots of 1780, the historical incident around which the plot of *Barnaby Rudge* revolves. It is Dennis who recruits the stable-hand

Hugh as one of the rioters, thus playing "godfather"—as Dennis himself puts it—to Hugh's rebirth into violence. It is also Dennis who is responsible for supplying Hugh's new identity—on the very eve of both men's executions—as the unacknowledged and rejected son of the aristocrat Sir John Chester.[6] What is more, it is his privileged position as hangman hearing the last words of the condemned that permits Dennis to piece together the clues to Hugh's identity, thus making Hugh a child of the gallows in more ways than one and turning Dennis into an ironic model of his creator.

More significant, however, is the fact that in *Barnaby Rudge*, the hangman Dennis is presented as an aesthete of execution. Dennis's art consists of improving on "natural death," a talent for which he has, as he says himself, a "natural genius" (BR 372). Dennis habitually uses the language of aesthetics when speaking of his work. Says he: "I may call myself a artist—a fancy workman—'art improves natur'—that's my motto" (BR 372).

Not only is Dennis a man in love with his work, but he also manifests that most admirable quality of the committed seeker after truth, beauty and aesthetic transcendence—he is consumed by the search for perfection. Here is Dennis describing a successful hanging: " . . . When it's well done, it's so neat, so skilful, so captivating, if that don't seem too strong a word, that you'd hardly believe it could be brought to sich perfection" (BR 668).

He praises his own hand for the many jobs it has done with "a neatness and dex-terity [*sic*], never known before," and when he remembers the "helegant bits of work it has turned off," he might as easily be mistaken for a painter or a sculptor as for a hangman. In fact, one of his listeners does mistake him for an artist and assumes that the carved reproduction of Dennis's face on the knob of his walking stick—another example of the link between reproduction and death—is Dennis's own work, whereas it is actually the work of one of Dennis's victims, described by Dennis as "one of the finest stand-up men, you ever seen" (BR 372). (Dennis's use of the term "stand-up man" refers, of course, to someone about to be hanged. It is ironic, then, that in our own day a stand-up man has come to mean a comedian.)

Dennis's role as an aesthete of the gallows encompasses the dramatic as well as the plastic arts. Here is his description of what constitutes an aesthetic hanging, which might be easily confused with a prescription for a stage performance:

> I've heerd a eloquence on them boards—you know what boards I mean—and have heerd a degree of mouth given to them speeches, that they was as clear as a bell, and as good as a play. There's a pattern! And always, when a thing of this natur's to come off, what I stand for, is, a proper frame of mind. Let's have a proper frame of mind, and we can go through with it, creditable—pleasant—sociable. Whatever you do . . . never snivel. I'd sooner by half . . . see a man tear his clothes, a' purpose to spile 'em before they come to me, than find him snivelling. (BR 591)

Dickens even allows Dennis to attribute universality to the art of hanging. Dennis believes that hanging is a "Universal Medicine applicable to men, women and children, of every age and variety of criminal constitution" (BR 664). In other words, hanging is an activity the whole family can experience; it is an equal opportunity employer that does not discriminate between men, women or children "as a proof"—in Dennis's words—"of the amazing equalness and dignity of our law" (BR 542). Hanging is thus portrayed as a fate universally imminent, since to the eye of the hangman any passing stranger potentially represents an execution—in much the same way as human nature in general may be said to be grist for the novelist's mill. This is illustrated in the following passage in which Dennis describes his victim's clothes and how they came to be his. (One of the perks of the office of hangman was first dibs on the clothes of the executed):

> "I've often walked behind this coat, in the street, and wondered whether it would ever come to me: this pair of shoes have danced a hornpipe for another man, afore my eyes, full half-a-dozen times at least: and as to my hat . . . I've seen this hat go up Holborn on the box of a hackney-coach —ah, many and many a day." (BR 373)

In addition to suggesting the inevitable fate of all those with whom Dennis comes in contact, no matter how casually encountered, the passage also stands as another example of synecdoche. In this case, however, the various items of clothing do not so much stand for the human being who wears them; they obliterate him. The human is by definition expendable in this context, because he may be executed, whereas the clothing lives on after the man.

When Dennis claims that art improves nature he is alluding to an aesthetic philosophy which is not ordinarily associated with his profession. Dennis's "art," after all, consists of improving on "natural death." His job is to impose an artificial end on a natural process. Execution, therefore, belongs to the world of the man-made, to the world of craft and art, in much the same way as painting itself does—or novel-writing for that matter. It takes the natural as its raw material and converts it into a thing subject to human will.

Dickens returns to this unholy alliance between life, death, and artistry late in his career, when in *Our Mutual Friend,* he introduces Mr. Venus, the taxidermist—whose very name, *Venus,* alludes to the processes of procreation. Mr. Venus counterfeits life through manipulating the raw material of death and he too considers himself an artist—"a workman without equal" is his boast. His is the art of making the dead seem alive. Because Mr. Venus eats and drinks while he works, Dickens suggests a cannibalistic relationship between aesthetics and the processes of existence. The remodeling, reassembling, and reanimating of inert materials into a new reality is the domain of the artist, who dissects the living in order to create a semblance of life, and who furthermore lives off the results of his labor.

Dennis the Hangman and Mr. Venus are portraits of the artist as a dealer in death—they are businessmen living off the extinction of others. The same might be said of Dickens himself, who, as a novelist transformed his own obsessive fascination with death into material for his fiction. The frequent descriptions in Dickens's novels of those whose business is death—of the undertakers, resurrectionists, Thames body-fishers—suggest perverse analogues to the author's own occupation.

Or do they? Is there not an essential difference between Mr. Dickens the novelist and that of his death-dealing characters? The question is rhetorical, because the answer is obvious. Of course there is. Dickens despises Dennis the Hangman, who is, after all, the craven functionary of an unjust judiciary. Why then does he have Dennis proclaim himself an artist? Dennis's claim to being an artist calls into question all the life-affirming values traditionally associated with art, and locates the concept of aesthetics at the very door of death. Granted that the claim is ironic, at whom is the barb aimed—the hangman or the artist?

And why all the other gruesome juxtapositions? Why does Dickens consistently filter the biological process of extinction through the aesthetic one of reproduction and art, making the one relate equivalently to the other? It is true that he lived in an age that was much more comfortable than we are today with death and with using the dead as the raw material for artifacts—witness the Victorian habit of photographing dead children and the much older practice of making death masks of the famous and infamous. In *Great Expectations*, the lovable family-man Wemmick is a collector of the death masks of the hanged—and he is no less lovable for that.

But even if one takes into account Victorian attitudes towards death, the concordances in Dickens's fiction between aesthetics and violent death are nevertheless startling and seem to signify a profound questioning on Dickens's part of the relationship between life and art. I believe that they betray his profound unease with the idea that art should take as its raw material the lived life that ends inevitably in death, that it should attempt to transform the ephemeral into the immortal, in the process exploiting and dissecting that which is always in the process of dying, "dust with the breath of life in it," as Dickens called the living in *Edwin Drood*. Viewed in this light, the act of creating becomes an act of cannibalism, of reproducing life by drawing sustenance from inevitable death. From this perspective, novel-writing becomes an act of simultaneous execution and reproduction—in both senses of both those words.

NOTES

1. Richard Lettis, who wrote two books on Dickens's aesthetics, is forced to admit his frustration at the paucity of material available on Dickens's understanding of his own art form. Lettis begins *Dickens on Literature* with the remark that "a study of Dickens' comments on literature must begin with the reminder that he hardly ever wrote at length about his profession." See p. 1.
2. I am ignoring here Miss La Creevy of *Nicholas Nickleby*, who makes her living as a painter of miniatures and the feckless and unpleasant Henry Gowan of *Little Dorrit*. Both of these characters clearly engage in artistic pursuits, but in both casestheir artistic endeavor is defined by Dickens as marginal. Harold Skimpole in *Bleak House* is another example of a man whose artistic pretensions define him as an irresponsible dilettante.
3. This is the title of Stone's last book on Dickens: *The Night Side of Dickens: Cannibalism, Passion, Necessity* (Columbus: Ohio State UP, 1994), in which Stone deals at length with the morbid side of Dickens's nature. Other notable works that have covered this ground are Philip Collins, *Dickens and Crime* (Bloomington: Indiana UP, 1968) and John Carey's *The Violent Effigy: A Study of Dickens' Imagination* (London: Faber and Faber, 1973).
4. *Oliver Twist* (Harmondsworth: Penguin, 1985), 225. All future references to Dickens's novels are to the Penguin editions and appear in the text. 5. Sections of this and the following discussion of Dennis the Hangman have appeared in another context in my article "Dickens and Reproduction," *Dickens Quarterly* 14, 1 (March 1997): 24–32.
6. Dickens based his Dennis the Hangman on an actual historical figure, Edward Dennis, the public hangman from 1771 to 1786, who took part in the Gordon Riots of 1780 and was condemned to death. Dickens has his fictional hangman executed, probably because he liked the poetic justice inherent in the idea of the hangman hanged. But what really happened makes, in some ways, a better story: The historical Ned Dennis was reprieved and pardoned so that he could hang his fellow rioters. See note 2, p. 754 of the Penguin edition of *Barnaby Rudge* (Harmondsworth, 1984), edited by Gordon Spence.

WORKS CITED

Ackroyd, Peter. *Dickens*. New York: HarperCollins, 1990.

Dickens, Charles. "A Visit to Newgate." *Sketches by 'Boz': Illustrative of Everyday Life and Everyday People* London: Nicholson, n. d.

Huet, Marie-Hélène. *Monstrous Imagination*. Cambridge: Harvard UP, 1993.

Lettis, Richard. *Dickens on Literature: A Continuing Study of His Aesthetic*. New York: AMS Press, 1990.

Poe, Edgar Allen. "The Philosophy of Composition" (1846). Reprinted in *The Norton Anthology of American Literature* (Shorter Fifth Edition) (New York: W.W. Norton, 1999), 75.

Richardson, Ruth. *Death, Dissection and the Destitute*. London: Routledge, 1987.

Did Dickens Have a Philosophy of History? The Case of *Barnaby Rudge*

Patrick Brantlinger

Despite its flaws, Barnaby Rudge *is a remarkable achievement for Dickens at the very outset of his career. In it, Dickens not only attempts to write a historical novel on the model of Scott and the spate of Scott imitators in the 1830s, but he seems also to be struggling to articulate a philosophy of history. The oxymoron "grotesque populism" is perhaps as accurate a designation as any for this philosophy of history. Populism refers to the belief that all moral virtue and political legitimacy reside in the common people, not in their rulers. But populism turns grotesque when misrule has so deluded and deformed the common people that they themselves emerge, as in the foolish rituals and plotting of Simon Tappertit's 'Prentice Knights and the mob violence of the Gordon rioters, as a nightmarish caricature of what the common people might have been if wisely ruled. In short, in political terms, all of the nightmarish aspects of* Barnaby, *including its often slapstick violence, add up to the grotesque results of a balked or thwarted populism. And grotesque populism is registered, too, in Dickens's treatment of time in the novel. As in the narrative frame of* Master Humphrey's Clock, *Dickens in* Barnaby *is fascinated by grotesque distortions of time, which in turn point to the grotesque distortion of history represented by the Gordon Riots. Even though Dickens never attempted to give a philosophical explanation of grotesque populism, from* Barnaby Rudge *onward all of his novels express that near-philosophy of history with a visionary intensity that give them a depth and seriousness very different from the view of those critics who have seen him as a shallow, inconsistent thinker, a mere "sentimental radical."*

Coming to it from *Pickwick Papers*, readers of *Barnaby Rudge* must wonder where Dickens's humor went? Of course *Barnaby* contains many risible moments similar to those in more plentiful supply in *Pickwick*. Maybe the later novel is less amusing because Dickens did not create another Sam Weller? But it seems harder to laugh when Sim Tappertit gets his legs mangled than when Pickwick gets thrown into debtor's prison. There is obviously a lot of violence in *Barnaby*, including slapstick violence, that is absent from Dickens's first, funnier novel. Besides the violence, what is it about *Barnaby* that disrupts Dickens's humor, at least when compared to *Pickwick*? Because *Barnaby* is Dickens's first historical novel, the answer would seem to be history. Many historical novels falter because their authors can't integrate fact and fiction, or history in the textbook sense with imagination. This isn't exactly the case with *Barnaby*, however. In *Dickens at Work*, John Butt and Kathleen Tillotson noted that "What is most remarkable in his powerful narrative of the [Gordon] riots is the way he combines fidelity to fact with the doings of his fictitious characters. He adds, but never falsifies" (85). In this respect, *Barnaby* is on a par with Sir Walter Scott's best "historical romances."

What ordinarily defines the historical novel is the representation of actual events of national consequence like the Gordon Riots. However, that version of history does not enter *Barnaby* until midway through it. And the Gordon Riots do not make the novel tedious; they make it exciting. For the first half, the plot consists mainly of fathers quarreling with sons and with each other, complicating the romantic prospects of Emma Haredale and Dolly Varden. Not until chapter 34, when Lord George Gordon rides into the novel, does History with a capital H also ride into it. Then the plot thickens even as it accelerates. So it may be that what makes much of *Barnaby* comparatively tedious isn't history, but whatever is not history—that is, the private lives and doings of the characters before the Gordon Riots begin.

Yet from the outset, Dickens is setting the stage for history's violent entrance. The first half of the novel is slow-moving, perhaps, because Dickens is trying to figure out how best to represent the collision between the private and public spheres, between the lives of peaceable citizens like Gabriel Varden and history as the explosive disrupter of those lives. This is not to say that everyday life is peaceful while history is violent; the Haredale murder, after all, serves as the private, originary trauma foreshadowing the public violence of the Gordon Riots. Innocent Barnaby and his mother are caught between both forms of violence, the first seemingly buried in the past but continually haunting the present, and the other an unpredictable but very public outburst of rage and intolerance that sweeps everything before it, including those who seek to control it. Anyway, what seems to put the first half of *Barnaby* into slow motion is not history as such, but Dickens's attempt to think about the relationship between history and everyday life. In short, Dickens seems to be trying to articulate a philosophy of history—one that I will call "grotesque populism." By grotesque I mean all of those features of Dickens's novels that are monstrous, demonic, and nightmarish, including dreamlike violence in slapstick mode. Populism, on the other hand, involves the belief that the sole source of political legitimacy is the common people. Taken together, the two terms form an oxymoron or contradiction that informs everything that Dickens wrote.[1]

1.

But how can a contradiction, even a self-conscious one, add up to a philosophy of history? By "philosophy of history" I mean any thoughtful effort to understand the relationship of the collective or societal past to the present and future. There are many degrees and variations between the full-scale, systematic philosophies of history developed by, for instance, Hegel, Comte, and Marx, and merely random notions about the past picked up from reading this or that history. Dickens was not trained as a philosopher *or* a historian, so if in the 1830s he was developing a philosophy of history that can be called "grotesque populism," it was an amateur, unsophisticated one. Perhaps ideology would be a better term for it than philosophy of history, and yet from *Barnaby* forward Dickens's novels all express grotesque populism with a visionary intensity that makes the relatively straightforward humor of *Pickwick Papers* the anomaly among his works. Though Dickens never tried to explain grotesque populism in philosophical terms, he strove to articulate it in many ways throughout his career, especially in the novels. Here I agree with William Palmer, who in *Dickens and New Historicism* argues that, after *Pickwick*, "Every Dickens novel . . . attempts to formulate a self-reflexive philosophy of history" (169). I disagree, however, that an accurate name for this philosophy of history is what Palmer calls "realist evolutionary humanis[m]" (170), though this phrase certainly would fit George Eliot. Nevertheless, in relation to the grotesque, I will return to Palmer's important claim that Dickens's novels register history as "the irruptive violence of time" (168).[2]

Rather than insisting that Dickens foreshadows the New Historicism or even, prior to the 1859 publication of *Origin of Species*, Darwinian evolution, it is important to ask what philosophies of history were on offer in the 1830s, and whether *Barnaby* reflects any of these? Clearly, Dickens did not subscribe to any orthodox, religious theodicy—certainly not to any religious fundamentalism: *Barnaby* condemns precisely such fundamentalism and the intolerance it breeds. On the other hand, Benthamite utilitarianism and its ideological ally, political economy, offered a secular, reformist philosophy of history—one that, however, entailed a negation of history that Dickens could not accept. Bentham and his followers rejected the past in favor of the quasi-utopian category of utility. Society was to be stripped of its antiquated customs and superstitions, and treated as a blank slate by enlightened legislators focused solely upon "the greatest happiness of the greatest number." Like most of the great Romantic poets and intellectuals, Dickens believed both that the past had far too powerful a hold on the present for it to be easily swept aside and that utility was a mechanical, shallow measure of value. Further, again like the Romantics, he believed that Enlightenment rationalism, as expressed in Benthamism and political economy, overlooked the irrational but necessary and often wise, emotional aspects of human nature, including the imagination. He would go on to critique utilitarianism most fully in *Hard Times*, under the rubric of Gradgrindism.

Dickens may not have been well-versed in philosophy, but *Oliver Twist* shows that even in the 1830s he was capable of launching a powerful attack on some of the leading social and economic theories of his day, including the Malthusianism that shaped the New Poor Law of 1834. Moreover, that he even tried to write historical fiction as early as *Barnaby* suggests that he held some quite definite opinions about history. Whether we call these opinions a philosophy of history or merely an ideology will depend in part on just how self-conscious we judge him to have been, and also on whether he expresses his ideas in a consistent manner, more or less free from contradiction. But herein lies a problem: Grotesque populism involves the recognition that history itself is a contradictory, grotesque, often monstrous process. Dickens's novels illuminate this process without reducing it to, for instance, Macaulay's Whig-liberal version of human, or at least English, perfectibility through the triumph of science, industry, and free trade. That is one reason why Macaulay, reacting to *Hard Times*, called Dickens a "sullen socialist," which is perhaps not too different from calling him a "grotesque populist" (Macaulay qtd. by Orwell in Wall 298).

Ever since Walter Bagehot in 1858 declared that Dickens was a "sentimental radical . . . utterly deficient in the faculty of reasoning" (Bagehot in Wall 136, 124), the common assumption has been that, though a wonderfully imaginative writer, Dickens was anything but a systematic thinker.[3] So entrenched is this view that even to ask if Dickens had a philosophy of history sounds rather preposterous.[4] But, though Dickens was unaware of Hegel, Marx, and perhaps even John Stuart Mill, perhaps he was the novel-writing version of Thomas Carlyle? Another common assumption has been that, if Dickens did hold any systematic ideas about the past, he got them from Carlyle. On at least one key point, however—Hero-Worship—Dickens disagreed with Carlyle. Yet toward the end of his career, he declared that Carlyle was the thinker "who had most influenced him" (qtd. in Goldberg 2), and he directly acknowledged the influence of Carlyle's history of the French Revolution on his second historical novel, *A Tale of Two Cities*.[5]

But what about his first historical novel? Though it, too, was undoubtedly influenced by Carlyle, Dickens's historical sources for *Barnaby* were many and various. Moreover, if the main influence on *Tale of Two Cities* was Carlyle, a key influence on *Barnaby* was Scott. Yet while Dickens may have set out to rival Scott by writing a historical novel, *Barnaby* is quite different from any of Scott's novels in its conceptualization of the past and of the trajectory from past to present. In *Modern Romance and Transformations of the Novel*, Ian Duncan notes that, unlike Scott, "Dickens recognizes no spiritual authority in prior [historical] formations" (16). I would qualify this claim by adding that Dickens recognizes no *positive* spiritual authority in human history, a view that puts him at odds with both Scott and Carlyle. Dickens does not romanticize the past in a nostalgic or utopian vein; but he does demonize it, at least metaphorically, which is partly what I mean by "*grotesque* populism." For Dickens, the past offers no viable alternatives to the present, which struggles to exorcize history's demons and ghosts; those ghosts are powerful and perhaps inescapable, not to be shaken off by any shallow, pseudo-scientific doctrine like Bentham's "felicific calculus" of utility.

Besides Scott, Dickens was perhaps just as interested in the competition offered by the spate of historical novelists who, also imitative of the Waverley novels, entered the bestselling lists in the 1830s: William Harrison Ainsworth, Edward Bulwer-Lytton, and G. P. R. James. These would-be Scotts both sensationalized and trivialized the genre in ways Thackeray would mock in his series for *Punch*, "Novels by Eminent Hands," while in 1846 George Henry Lewes could declare that the readers of recent historical novels were "either very good-natured, or very ignorant; or both" (qtd. in Tillotson, *Novels* 41 n. 1). Especially shallow are James's many celebrations of chivalry and the Middle Ages. James and Dickens may have been on friendly terms (Ellis 230), but Dickens clearly detested nostalgia for what he called "the fine old English Tory times." That phrase comes from his 1841 political poem, "The Fine Old English Gentleman" (reprinted in Forster 1:278–79):

> I'll sing you a new ballad, and I'll warrant it first-rate,
> Of the days of that old gentleman who had that old estate;
> [. . . When] The good old laws were garnished well with gibbets,
>   whips, and chains,
> With fine old English penalties, and fine old English pains,
> With rebel heads and seas of blood once hot in rebel veins;
> For all these things were requisite to guard the rich old gains
>   Of the fine old English Tory times

While this poem is focused on the late eighteenth century and the Tory regime of William Pitt—in other words, on the same time period as *Barnaby*—Dickens elsewhere attacks romantic idealizations of the Middle Ages, as in "Old Lamps for New Ones," his diatribe against the Pre-Raphaelite Brotherhood, which he dubs "the Pre-Perspective Brotherhood." This *Household Words* essay specifically condemns John Everett Millais's painting, "Christ in the House of His Parents," but it is more generally a diatribe against all versions of "the great retrogressive principle" which celebrate past ages as better than the present. Thus, Dickens imagines a "Pre-Henry-the-Seventh Brotherhood," which would cancel "all the advances of nearly four hundred years" and return society "to one of the most disagreeable periods of English History," in which "We should be certain of [having] the Plague among many other advantages" (257–59). In any event, no more than *Tale of Two Cities* is *Barnaby* a celebration of "the bad old times" of the 1780s or any other era—think of the passages in which Dickens contrasts eighteenth-century London with the improved London of the 1830s. And *Barnaby* may also have been, in part, Dickens's attempt to rescue historical fiction from just such celebrations, as in James's romances.

Though it implies intellectual vacuity, Bagehot's label "sentimental radical" connects Dickens to a sizable number of intellectuals in Britain in the 1830s and 40s—the *Punch* radicals, Mark Lemon, Douglas Jerrold, Tom Hood, Henry Mayhew—who were at once critical of narrow versions of utilitarian theory and attuned to melodramatic versions of populism. It would be easy to dismiss such petit-bourgeois populism as unsystematic and therefore unphilosophical, and yet sentimental radicalism was more than just an incoherent bundle of fantasies about the past.[6] As with most political ideologies, populism has taken various forms in various historical contexts. Like stage melodrama, all of these forms share a belief in the common people as the sole source of virtue and of political legitimacy together with a more or less paranoid suspicion of existing governmental institutions, laws, and authorities as working against the interests of the people.[7] Populism can be understood as a variety of liberalism up to the point where it turns into a conspiracy theory about laws and institutions that are themselves liberal and at least semi-democratic. Dickens's distance from a liberal like Macaulay is evident in his 1855 remark that "I have no present political faith or hope—not a grain" (*Letters* 1:404–06). Macaulay believed in the gradual, progressive development of democracy in Britain from the time of the Glorious Revolution of 1688 forward. "Better an acre in Middlesex," he opined, "than a principality in Utopia." In contrast, Dickens the populist had little or no faith in most of the existing laws and institutions of government, except for the police, the post office, and the Bank of England. But neither did he think that any past form of government—feudalism, for example—had been any better.

In 1857, James Fitzjames Stephen came close to distinguishing between liberalism and populism when he wrote:

> Everybody has read chapter 10 of *Little Dorrit*; but we are not equally sure that everybody has asked himself what it really means. It means, if it means anything, that the result of the British constitution, of our boasted freedom, of parliamentary representation, and of all we possess, is to give us the worst government on the face of the earth. . . .

Stephen goes on to note that "The cover of [the monthly parts of *Little Dorrit*] is adorned by a picture [of] Britannia in a bath-chair, drawn by a set of effete idiots, an old woman, a worn-out cripple in a military uniform, and a supercilious young dandy. . . . The chair is pushed on by six men in foolscaps. . . ." (Stephen in Wall 108).

The illustration by "Phiz" and Stephen's commentary on it should be compared with the full passage, from his 1855 letter to W. C. Macready, in which Dickens expresses his lack of political faith:

> As to the suffrage, I have lost hope even in the ballot. We appear . . . to have proved the failure of representative institutions without an educated and advanced people to support them.

Dickens goes on to excoriate "flunkyism, toadyism, [and] letting the most contemptible lords come in for all manner of places, reading *The Court Circular* for the New Testament," and then concludes:

> . . . I do reluctantly believe that the English people are habitually consenting parties to the miserable imbecility into which we have fallen, *and never will help themselves out of it.* Who is to do it, if anybody is, God knows. But at present we are on the downhill road to being conquered, and the people WILL be content to bear it, sing "Rule Britannia," and WILL NOT be saved.
> (*Letters* 1:404–06)

Stephen's commentary, Phiz's illustration, and Dickens's letter together capture the essence of grotesque populism. While political legitimacy rests solely with the common people, to explain how all forms of government, both past and present, have exploited the people and trampled upon their true interests, the populist must also explain why the people misrecognize their interests. Populism turns grotesque when it focuses upon the ways the people themselves have been crippled or deformed by history—that is, by centuries of misrule. There is no more monstrous, grotesque distortion of the common people than the sort of mob violence depicted in *Barnaby*.

Stephen is right that, as Michael Steig puts it, Browne's illustration depicts "the blind and halt . . . leading a dozing Britannia with a retinue of fools and toadies'' (Steig 159). In equally grotesque fashion, Phiz's cover illustration for *Bleak House* offers a related caricature, with lawyers in the top panel playing a vicious game of blindman's buff. In both illustrations, not the common people, but those apparently closest to governmental power are depicted as blind or foolish. But of course, to allow Britannia to be led by a bunch of ''effete idiots,'' as Stephen puts it, the common people must themselves be duped, coerced, or both. In short, rather than some repository of political innocence, the common people are subjected to (and become the subjects of) grotesque distortion and, in all senses of this term, *mis*representation. As in the distorted, often monstrous imagery of dreams, the grotesque is for Dickens a powerful visual register for representing the forms of both verbal and political misrepresentation. And of course the grotesque was the main mode of political cartooning back to the eighteenth century and beyond.

Kafka, who acknowledged Dickens's influence on *The Trial* and his other stories, also knew how to use the grotesque to render his central themes of nightmarish mis- or even missing representations. Both Dickens and Kafka recognized on some level that populist trust in the people is ultimately mistrust, because throughout history the people have been deceived, crushed, and exploited. They have no resources of their own left on which to base political legitimacy. Dickens suspected, at least, that the democratic ideal of the sovereignty of the people may only be the ultimate nightmare, not history's cunning so much as its surrealism. The people have been so badly misruled throughout history, and are so badly misruled in the present, that their only possible responses are either acquiescence in their continued exploitation or, what for Dickens is sure to be worse, the mob violence of revolution. Either way, the result is a collective nightmare.

Up to a point, just as Dickens is close to Macaulay's liberalism, so is he close to Tom Paine's revolutionary radicalism. In his *Rights of Man*, Paine declares that throughout history there are three primary sorts of government (Paine 81). The first is government by fraud; the second is government by force; and the third, yet to come, will be government by reason. Paine identifies fraud with priestcraft and force with aristocracy, and adds that when these two combined in the union of Church and State, the bondage of the people was perfected. Just how the people can escape from that bondage and form the new, democratic government of reason is unclear, although for Paine revolution is the starting point. In his *Child's History of England*, Dickens makes priestcraft, or the deception of the people through religious fraud, a main theme. Thus, in Britain's ancient religion, druidism, ''Most of [the] ceremonies were kept secret by the priests . . . who pretended to be enchanters'' and deceived ''the ignorant people'' with what they knew were lies (*MHC* 132). And of course force is another main theme, including the Roman, Teutonic, and Norman invasions and the creation of aristocracy through conquest and violence, lording it over the common people.

But what *A Child's History of England* mostly expresses is rather different from Paine's radicalism, which pointed optimistically to a democratic future. In general, it is a version of the "crimes and follies" interpretation of history, one often articulated in the eighteenth century. Thus, Edward Gibbon declared that "history is little more than the register of the crimes, follies and misfortunes of mankind."[8] Now, the obvious, chief difficulty with this dismal view of history is that it cannot account for progress, or even change in any direction: there is just ongoing, hopeless repetition of "crimes and follies." Clearly, even though this idea was articulated by many Enlightenment intellectuals including Gibbon, it couldn't be squared with their belief in Enlightenment and, therefore, in progress. The antithesis of the Enlightenment doctrine of human perfectibility, moreover, was Joseph de Maistre's reactionary claim that the two essential officials for maintaining social order were the pope and the executioner (Maistre 131–42, 191–92). Both Dickens's fiction and his *Child's History* do a nightmarish tightrope dance between these views—optimistic faith in Enlightenment and progress, versus the pessimism of the "crimes and follies" thesis. It is in part this nightmarish tightrope dance that I am calling "grotesque populism"—not a systematic philosophy of history, perhaps, but also not the superficial, lightweight set of opinions that Bagehot dismissed as "sentimental radicalism."

2.

Still another critical commonplace about both *Barnaby* and *Tale of Two Cities* is that they are only superficially about the past—that they are really "tracts for their times" more than genuinely historical works of fiction (see Butt and Tillotson 76). The Gordon Riots equal Chartism, Simon Tappertit's Prentice Knights equals the trade unionism of the 1830s, and the Protestant Association of 1780 equals the Protestant Association of 1839.[9] Of course Dickens stresses these parallels or repetitions between past and present, along with the "lesson" or warning that, unless his fellow-citizens act to prevent it, something like the Gordon Riots could very well reoccur. Just so, Carlyle wrote his *History of the French Revolution* as a lay sermon to his contemporaries to go and do otherwise, and just so, *A Tale of Two Cities* insists that the threat of revolution, even in liberal, socially progressive London, has not vanished.

But parallels between past and present, suggesting the possibility, at least, of historical repetition, are only one sort of anachronism. From Quilp's counting-house clock whose "minute-hand had been twisted off for a toothpick" to Miss Havisham's stopped clocks in *Great Expectations*, Dickens is fascinated by misshapen versions of time.[10] Stoppages, displacements, or distortions of time come in many shapes and sizes in *Barnaby*, and they aren't mere accidents or inconsistencies. This is what Palmer means by "the irruptive violence of time," which for Dickens is both a cause and a primary form of the grotesque. The focus on Barnaby's confused mental processes is one way that Dickens emphasizes the grotesque, and Barnaby's confusions about memory and time are especially nightmarish. In the last chapter, Barnaby remembers "his condemnation and escape" as "a terrific dream" (737). But even that model of brave, industrious good cheer, Gabriel Varden, has strange dreams in which time is grotesquely distorted. On the road to London in chapter 3, Gabriel finds that his drowsiness causes him "to mingle up present circumstances with others which have no manner of connection with them; to confound all consideration of persons, things, times, and places; and to jumble his disjointed thoughts together in a kind of mental kaleidoscope, producing combinations as unexpected as they are transitory." In this state, Gabriel dreams about "picking a lock in the stomach of the Great Mogul," and as he is waking, he "mixe[s] up the turnpike man with his mother-in-law who had been dead twenty years" (70–71).

This phantom mother-in-law is also an instance of the most obvious way that Dickens insists upon anachronism, and that is through the demonic figure of the ghost, whether literal or metaphoric. Out of its due time, in a liminal or spectral condition belonging neither to this world nor the next, a ghost is simultaneously anachronistic and grotesque. And *Barnaby* is full of phantoms who are there to tell us, among other things, that history haunts the present. Wolfgang Kayser's claim that the grotesque arises from the "attempt to invoke and subdue demonic aspects of the world" seems especially germane to *Barnaby*, with its elaborate ghostly apparatus.[11]

It is precisely the insistence upon anachronism, which involves seeing in the present the threat, at least, of a repetition of the past, that is one key difference between Dickens and Scott. This is not to say that there are not plenty of anachronisms in the Waverley novels, but *Barnaby* elaborates them into a poetics of time that is intrinsically dreamlike, violent, and grotesque. *Master Humphrey's Clock*, the weekly serial in which *Barnaby* originally appeared, emphasizes this poetics of time. The stories that Humphrey and his cronies pluck from the clock and read or tell each other are themselves historical fictions, begging comparison with *Barnaby*, and they are also full of spectres and metaphoric hauntings of the present by the past. Further, they too treat time in ways that are dreamlike, violent, and grotesque, as in Humphrey's description of the clockworks inside the steeple of St. Paul's:

> . . . a complicated crowd of wheels and chains in iron and brass,—great, sturdy, rattling engines,—suggestive of breaking a finger put in here or there, and grinding the bone to powder,—and these were the Clock! Its very pulse, if I may use the word, was like no other clock. It did not mark the flight of every moment with a gentle second stroke, as though it would check old Time, and

have him stay his pace in pity, but measured it with one sledge-hammer beat,
as if its business were to crush the seconds as they came trooping on, and
remorsely to clear a path before the Day of Judgment.   (107)

The passage personifies both the clock and "old Time," and puts them at
odds with one another. Old Time sounds like a flexible, potentially kindly
fellow—he might "stay his pace in pity"—while the clock is a remorseless
executioner of the also personified seconds. As in the chapter on "Time, the
Great Manufacturer" in *Hard Times*, there is something quite murderous
about the way St. Paul's clock mechanically crushes the seconds "as they
[come] trooping on."

Various sorts of time—old and new, leisure and mechanical, slow and fast,
quotidian and apocalyptic—reappear in *Barnaby*. "Old Time" shows up
again both under that name (725) and others—for instance, as "that Great
Watcher with the hoary head, who never sleeps or rests" (687). Time's or-
derly passing, moreover, is often thrown into disorder, and not just in dreams.
For example, when Dennis the Hangman tries to delay his execution, a turn-
key says to him: "I say,—your watch goes different from what it used
to . . . . Once upon a time it was always too fast. It's got the other fault now"
(686). Both in *Master Humphrey's Clock* and in *Barnaby*, the failure to make
allowance for the past is just as monstrous as any ghostly visitation. Dickens
seems to see in past violence—the Haredale murder, the Gordon Riots—both
threats to the present and the flight of the present from the past as another
sort of violence, a form of repression that only encourages repetitions or
hauntings by the past in the present.

In contrast to Dickens's insistence upon anachronistic, often nightmarish
imbrications of past and present, Scott usually presents history as a relatively
straightforward, linear narrative of progress with a united Great Britain in
the enlightened present as the outcome. Paradoxically, the Tory Scott emerges
from the comparison as more liberal than Dickens, or anyway, as having a
firmer faith in progress. Dickens's anachronisms, including his ghosts, suggest
that time and history do not automatically follow a linear, straightforward
march from past to present, with a better future in the offing. Rather, everywhere in his novels, past and present are complexly, grotesquely entangled,
with the outcome, the future, hanging in the balance. On one hand, history
for Dickens is, as Benedetto Croce called it, "the story of liberty" (see
Croce). On the other, it is only very faintly or tentatively "the story of
liberty." And "liberty" means primarily the freedom of every individual to
go about his or her private business without interference either from other
individuals or from any of the numerous forms that tyrannical power has
taken through the ages. Above all, in *Barnaby* "liberty" means freedom to
believe what one wants, especially in regard to religion. What turns Dickens's

liberalism into grotesque populism, however, is mob violence on the one hand and tyrannical power on the other, including both government power and religious fantacism, versions of Paine's force and fraud. Intrinsically grotesque, mob violence is the result of both fraud and force (although government in *Barnaby* is as much characterized by its inaction as by its oppressions). Further, mob violence is the result of individual selfishness—not original sin, perhaps, but wickedness of a sort that, in every melodramatic plot, imperils virtue at every moment, and even in the denouement, in the moment when virtue triumphs (momentarily).

The triumphs of virtue are always momentary, both in stage melodrama and in Dickens's novels, because those triumphs are only private and individual. The translation of virtue to the public sphere and on into a utopian "reign of virtue" threatens always to become another reign of terror. And it is precisely this blockage that Dickens seems finally unable to explain in systematic, philosophical ways, though he dramatizes it obsessively: how or why the story of liberty is aborted at the moment when private virtue fails to become public virtue. This inexplicable and, except in grotesque ways, unrepresentable moment turns upon the "traumatic kernel" that Slavoj Žižek identifies with the originary lack in both human identity and history.[12] But it isn't originary in the sense either of infantile desire or of original sin. It is instead the contradiction between the proliferation of private desires, goals, and ambitions and the collective, public need to prevent those desires, goals, and ambitions from interfering with and thereby thwarting each other. Despite ghosts, Dickens was no believer in an "invisible hand," capitalist or other, harmonizing the private with the public.

In pointing out that, when writing about the past, Dickens is often anachronistic, Humphry House long ago also noted that "Among the false book-backs with which [Dickens] decorated his study at Gad's Hill was a set called: 'The Wisdom of our Ancestors—I. Ignorance. II. Superstition. III. The Block. IV. The Stake. V. The Rack. VI. Dirt. VII. Disease' " (House 35). How Dickens interpreted these fake books is unclear, but there are two main possibilities.[13] First, he often expresses the view that society has made much progress, as he does in his attack on Pre-Raphaelitism and other versions of "the great retrogressive principle." If all that "the wisdom of our ancestors" amounts to is ignorance, tyranny, dirt, and disease, there is nothing of value in it—nothing worth celebrating or trying to restore. Second, however, present-day society is of course the product of "our ancestors" and their "wisdom": there is no escaping the heritage or bondage of the past; albeit in new forms, ignorance, tyranny, dirt, and disease have not and perhaps never will be eradicated. As I have been arguing, between these two contradictory interpretations of the past, one optimistic and one pessimisitic, Dickens's populism turns grotesque. The contradiction itself he seems to have regarded as both unavoidable and supremely grotesque.

If the murder mystery and the father-and-son subplots in *Barnaby* underscore the old theme that the sins of the fathers—the ancestors—shall be visited upon the heads of the sons, the Gordon Riots, as Dickens portrays them, are the ultimate consequence of that theme. Instead of the narrative of historical progress that Dickens might have offered if he had been a Whig-liberal like, say, Macaulay, both in *Barnaby* and in *A Tale of Two Cities* he renders history as a nightmare from which we are always vainly trying to awake. In Dickens as in Marx, "The tradition of all the dead generations weighs like a nightmare on the brain of the living" (Marx 595). But whereas for Marx, the final revolution of the proletariat would dispel the nightmare, for Dickens, such a revolution, like the Gordon Riots or like the great French Revolution of 1789, would only be nightmare compounded. It is James Joyce's Stephen Dadaelus who says, "History is a nightmare from which I am trying to awake." Well before Joyce, Dickens understood this thought and made it central to what I have called his philosophy of history, his "grotesque populism."

NOTES

1. Major studies of the grotesque include Bakhtin, *Rabelais and His World*, and Kayser, *The Grotesque in Art and Literature*. See also Harpham, "The Grotesque: First Principles," and Hollington, *Dickens and the Grotesque*. For populism, see for instance Peter Wiles's definition: "Any creed or movement based on the following premise: virtue resides in the simple people, who are the overwhelming majority, and in their collective traditions" (qtd. in Canovan, *Populism*, p. 4).
2. Palmer gets this phrase from Michel Foucault. More generally, I disagree with Palmer's argument that "Dickens never, out of neglect, rapacious exploitation, or intentional suppression, allows history to become monstrous. Instead, he listens to its many voices . . . and forms a benevolent philosophy of history that functions as a fulcrum between past and present" (4). On the contrary, history for Dickens is generally "monstrous" and violent. While Dickens's intentions, moreover, are always "benevolent," that does not make grotesque populism a benevolent philosophy of history. Gothic, nightmarish, and surreal would be more like it.
3. Bagehot was expressing an emerging consensus. In 1844, R. H. Horne opined that Dickens was "an instinctive writer" who "does not tax his brain," while in 1872 George Henry Lewes declared that "Thought is strangely absent from his works" (Wall 73 and 201).
4. It seems presumptuous, moreover, if not exactly preposterous, even to expect Dickens to have a "philosophy of history," when "philosophies of history" are being relentlessly questioned and deconstructed in our own postmodern era. Philosophy tries to construct systems, total explanations of history; the "hermeneutics of suspicion" from Nietzsche through Adorno to Derrida and Lyotard

undermines or deconstructs those systems. According to Derrida, "What we must be wary of . . . is the *metaphysical* concept of history. This is the concept of history as the history of meaning . . . fulfilling itself. And doing so linearly . . . in a straight or circular line" (*Positions* 56). And Lyotard famously defines the postmodern as "incredulity toward metanarratives" (*The Postmodern Condition* xxiv).

5. Golberg thinks the influence of Carlyle on *Barnaby* is "uncertain" (101), though Dickens had probably read both *The French Revolution* and "Chartism" while he was writing it. Anyway, Carlylean "Hero-Worship" is hardly a theme either in the novels or in *A Child's History of England*. (In the latter, there are some national heroes—Alfred the Great, for instance—but even more villains, and Dickens does not preach worship of the great dead.) Of the various historians besides Carlyle whom Dickens read, Henry Thomas Buckle is the one who espoused a liberal philosophy of history that Dickens most explicitly agreed with. Buckle's liberalism contradicts Carlyle's authoritarianism in many ways, so part of the answer to the question, "Did Dickens have a philosophy of history?" must involve deciding whether Dickens was able to recognize and at least try to think through these contradictions, or instead simply shuttled back and forth between them as occasion demanded.

6. Bagehot says that "sentimental radicalism" was needed in the 1830s and 40s, when so much of the governmental machinery of Britain was harsh and "unfeeling," but he doesn't credit it with anything like philosophical consistency. He asserts both that Dickens persisted in "repining at" various social "evils long after they ceased to exist" and that, whenever he tried to think deeply, he wound up, like Stephen Blackpool, in a muddle. Dickens, says Bagehot, "is often troubled with the idea that he must reflect, and his reflections are perhaps the worst reading in the world" (Wall 124). So we get the still-current idea of the world's most popular novels as emotive, knee-jerk responses to experience written by an author who, apparently, couldn't think his way out of a paper bag. But even if they do make for tedious reading, these moments of reflection are, I believe, fascinating for what they tell us about Dickens, and especially about the young Dickens, at the start of his sky-rocket career.

7. For an analysis of Dickens's ideas about history in relation to melodrama, see "History and the Melodramatic Fix," ch. 3 of Christina Crosby, *The Ends of History*, 68–109.

8. Similarly, Voltaire opined that "history is [only] a picture of human crimes and misfortunes," and Oliver Goldsmith wrote that the history of Europe is "a tissue of crimes, follies, and misfortunes."

9. In my *Spirit of Reform*, I emphasize the parallels with Chartism and trade unionism, and did not say enough about religious intolerance and the anti-Catholicism rampant in the 1830s and early 40s in Britain.

10. See Franklin for these and other examples in Dickens. On different conceptions, theories, and shapes of time in history and historiography, see, among other works, Manuel, Munz, Whitrow, and Wilcox.

11. This apparatus, of course, starts up immediately in chapter 1, with Solomon Daisy's recollection of ringing the death knell on the night of the Haredale

murder, while terrifying himself with the legend that "on a certain night in the year . . . all the dead people came out of the ground and sat at the heads of their own graves till morning" (57).

12. A point Žižek, following Jacques Lacan, makes in all his works; see, for example, *The Sublime Object of Ideology.*

13. "Ancestors," perhaps, suggests versions of patriotism and racism that Dickens distinctly does not offer. Even in his *Child's History of England*, patriotism is downplayed and moments of racial uplift almost nonexistent. The following passage is a notable exception: under Alfred the Great, Dickens writes, "all the best points of the English-Saxon character were first encouraged, and in him first shown. It has been the greatest character among the nations of the earth. Wherever the descendants of the Saxon race have gone . . . they have" conquered. Everywhere "the Saxon blood remains unchanged. Wheresoever that race goes, there, law, and industry, and safety for life and property, and all the great results of steady perseverance, are certain to arise" (148–49). This was the standard rhetoric of both Tory and Whig historians.

WORKS CITED

Bakhtin, Mikhail. *Rabelais and His World.* Bloomington: Indiana UP, 1984.

Brantlinger, Patrick. *The Spirit of Reform: British Literature and Politics, 1832–1867.* Cambridge, MA: Harvard UP, 1977.

Butt, John, and Kathleen Tillotson. *Dickens at Work.* London: Methuen, 1957.

Canovan, Margaret. *Populism.* New York: Harcourt Brace Jovanovich, 1981.

Croce, Benedetto. *History as the Story of Liberty.* Tr. Sylvia Sprigge. New York: Norton, 1941.

Crosby, Christina. *The Ends of History: Victorians and "the Woman Question."* London: Routledge, 1991.

Derrida, Jacques. *Positions.* Chicago: U of Chicago P, 1981.

Dickens, Charles. *Barnaby Rudge.* London: Penguin, 1997.

———. "The Fine Old English Gentleman." Forster.

———. *Letters.* Ed. Mamie Dickens and Georgina Hogarth. 3 vols. London: Chapman and Hall, 1880.

———. *Master Humphrey's Clock and A Child's History of England.* Oxford: Oxford Illustrated Dickens, 1989. Abbreviated *MHC* in parentheses.

———. "Old Lamps for New Ones." *Household Words.* 15 June 1850: 254–59.

Duncan, Ian. *Modern Romance and Transformations of the Novel*. Cambridge: Cambridge UP, 1992.

Ellis, S. M. *The Solitary Horseman; or, the Life and Adventures of G. P. R. James*. Kensington: Cayme, 1927.

Forster, John. *The Life of Charles Dickens*. 2 vols. Boston: Osgood, 1875.

Franklin, Stephen L. "Dickens and Time: The Clock without Hands." *Dickens Studies Annual* 4 (1975): 1–35.

Goldberg, Michael. *Carlyle and Dickens*. Athens: U of Georgia P, 1972.

Harpham, Geoffrey. "The Grotesque: First Principles." *Journal of Aesthetics* 34 (1975–76): 461–68.

Hollington, Michael. *Dickens and the Grotesque*. London: Croom Helm, 1984.

House, Humphrey. *The Dickens World*. Oxford: Oxford UP, 1965.

Kayser, Wolfgang. *The Grotesque in Art and Literature*. New York: McGraw-Hill, 1966.

Lyotard, Jean-François. *The Postmodern Condition: A Report on Knowledge*. Minneapolis: U of Minnesota P, 1984.

Maistre, Joseph de. *The Works of Joseph de Maistre*. Ed. Jack Lively. New York: Schocken, 1971.

Manuel, Frank. *Shapes of Philosophical History*. Stanford: Stanford UP, 1965.

Marx, Karl. "The Eighteenth Brumaire of Louis Bonaparte." *The Marx-Engels Reader*. Robert C. Tucker, ed. New York: Norton, 1978: 594–617.

Munz, Peter. *The Shapes of Time: A New Look at the Philosophy of History*. Middletown, CT: Wesleyan UP, 1977.

Paine, Thomas. *Rights of Man*. Ed. Philip S. Foner. Secaucus, NJ: Citadel, 1974.

Palmer, William J. *Dickens and New Historicism*. New York: St. Martin's, 1997.

Steig, Michael. *Dickens and Phiz*. Bloomington: Indiana UP, 1978.

Tillotson, Kathleen. *Novels of the Eighteen-Forties*. Oxford: Oxford UP, 1954.

Wall, Stephen, ed. *Charles Dickens*. Harmondsworth: Penguin, 1970.

Whitrow, G. J. *Time in History: The Evolution of Our General Awareness of Time and Temporal Perspective*. Oxford: Oxford UP, 1988.

Wilcox, Donald J. *The Measure of Times Past: Pre-Newtonian Chronologies and the Rhetoric of Relative Time*. Chicago: Chicago UP, 1987.

Žižek, Slavoj. *The Sublime Object of Ideology*. London: Verso, 1989.

Masques of the English in *Barnaby Rudge*

Judith Wilt

Understanding the interaction of "Catholic" and "Protestant" in the novel means thinking not only about the events of 1780 dramatized there but also the Elizabethan/Jacobean witches' cauldron in which its primary images were formed, images which install an insistent dualism between (Roman) Catholic "duplicity" and (English) Protestant "authenticity" crucial to the formation of a new "national character." At the same time, as the novels of Scott show, the continuing return of the repressed Catholic plays out an English anxiety that the "Catholic" is in fact the authentic, and the "Protestant" a masquerade. A central figure for this anxiety in the English imagination is the conspiring Jesuit, who exists both as a political figure going ack to the Gunpowder Plot's myth of the "miner" beneath parliament, and as a hypermasculinist threat to the new erotic faith that enlisted the nineteenth-century novel to help create a new "national character" based in "the home." John Chester, plotting to explode the faith of the novel's erotic couples as well as of his Catholic schoolfellow, is this novel's conspiring Jesuit.

In December 1998, a film called *Elizabeth* made something of a splash, for Cate Blanchette's vivid portrayal of a title figure self-transformed from flesh to stone, and especially for its wickedly *Godfather*-like take on the making of the English nation in its golden age.

The film is a juicy trifle of Gothic melodrama and theatrical spectacle which attends in every moment to the artifice of "making." At one level,

Dickens Studies Annual, Volume 30, Copyright © 2001 by AMS Press, Inc. All rights reserved.

Lord Leicester's naive directive, "Remember who you are," projects a plot that believes in an authentic center of personal and national identity, could you just but find it again, a plot that climaxes when Elizabeth "remembers" she is not Anne Boleyn's daughter, the whore, but Henry VIII's daughter, the prince. But the father she identifies with is actually a Holbein painting, and the motor of the film's plot is actually Francis Walsingham's insinuating reflection on the death of (the single) God, marking the approach of modernity: "Perhaps there is nothing in this universe at all but ourselves, and our thoughts."

The spokesperson for the older plot of authenticity, uniform identity guaranteed by a single authentic God, is Mary Tudor, who peers at her desperately equivocating sister early in the film and hisses that Elizabeth may look like a subject on the surface but is probably a traitor "in your heart." The councilor William Cecil favors the standard path to identity for a female monarch—go to bed with a French or a Spanish prince and produce a male heir. But Elizabeth, pondering the new complications of divided nations and selves, reshapes the argument later in the film as she argues to parliament for an Act of Uniformity in worship based on a tense and jocular multiplicity rather than an authentic singularity: since some counselors favor a Spanish mate, some a French, and some will accept only an English, maybe she ought to marry one of each.

In this comic vision of a new trinity of husbands, Elizabeth affirms a new psycho-politics which holds the surface and depth ontology of the plot of authentic heart in suspension, available as rhetoric, but gone in fact: "I have no desire to make windows into men's souls," she says, "I simply ask, can any man in truth serve two masters?" The answer to this question in the film, of course, is—I certainly hope so. Elizabeth's masterly equivocation, expelling the site of "mastery" from the private heart, and reconstructing it in a public uniformity which leaves the prince legally blind to private soul, is not heresy, the queen concludes, but "common sense, which is a most English virtue."

In the film, "English virtue," or the virtue of "English," is imperiled by forces Spanish, French, Roman, whose uniformity is "the Catholic," whose phallic image is in candidate husbands, but whose true potency, virility, mobility, is in the striding black-cloaked figure of a priest who need not be named, so loudly do the echoes of English history supply the name—the Jesuit. If the last sincere person in England, peering into the body of the Protestant heir in search of her heart, is actually Bloody Mary, then her potent alter ego and double, the sly equivocator, the heartless dissembler, the plotting director of the show, is the conspiring Jesuit of the English Protestant imagination.

Called forth in the interlocking mirrors of Reformation and Counter-Reformation ideology, clothed in the theatrical extravagances of Renaissance self-fashioning, the conspiring Jesuit was caught red-handed, so we think we remember, in the Gunpowder Plot of 1605, which aimed at blowing up King James and parliament five years after the Essex rebellion missed dethroning Elizabeth.[1] But the Jesuit is much harder to kill than Bloody Mary, because the erotic/Gothic imagination of the virtue of Elizabeth, of English, needs him. By the time of the Gordon Riots, Bloody Mary is in her grave these 223 years, yet the Jesuit roves undiminished as her phallus, her unborn, never-conceived son. As the most faithful and truly English character, John Grueby, notes in *Barnaby Rudge*, Bloody Mary in her grave has done ten times the damage she did in her reign.

Patient scrutiny of *Barnaby Rudge* has failed, I admit, to turn up a Jesuit. And yet. There is a heartless dissembler, a smooth equivocator, a plotting director at the center of the show, who seems to be everywhere and nowhere, invulnerable and magical, the very avatar of psychic and national mobility, or instability, now a mere hollow dandaical shell, now a dense and serious figure of evil: one, moreover, who explicitly refers to the Gunpowder Plot as his analogue and inspiration. John Chester appears to be a staunch Protestant. All the more Jesuitical, is it not?

The Gunpowder Plot whose trail he lays, and mines, and explodes, is directed not at the Houses of Parliament but at The House—the novel's love story. Explode the idea of the heart and its invisible, risible faith, and that faith becomes, unmoored and airborne, available for a modern remaking. At the end of the film *Elizabeth*, the monarch remakes herself in the floating traits of the exploded Catholic feminine divine: holy woman, consoling mother— and one more. "I have become a virgin," Elizabeth notes in ironic elation. English virtue, or the virtue of "English," like Elizabeth's virginity requires of its nature to be recreated in numerous promiscuous exchanges, not least with its Gothic Other, "the Catholic."

My reading centers on the first part of *Barnaby Rudge*, on the history encapsulated in The Maypole and The Warren, and on the novel's love story, its investment in Dickensian "heart." The history I want to recall will be less the events of 1780 than the Elizabethan/Jacobean witches cauldron in which its primary images were formed, images which install an insistent dualism between (Roman) Catholic "duplicity" and (English) Protestant "authenticity" crucial to the formation of a new "national character." But at the same time, as the novels of Scott show, the continuing return of the repressed Catholic, in Stuart counter-revolutionary enterprises and Celtic resistances, in neo-medievalisms and pre-Raphaelitisms of all sorts, plays out an anxiety that "the Catholic" is in fact the authentic, and the Protestant a mere show, or shell. Scratch a Protestant and you find a hollow or a Catholic, as the grand psycho-political spectacle of John Henry Newman was reminding everyone.

Furthermore, in this early Victorian Age of Empire, the Elizabethan "virtue" of "English" fought back, as many have noted, by leapfrogging the old dualisms to form an intimately related new one, where the Colonial Other offered what the Continental Catholic before had offered, a way to remake the virginity of national identity in a Gothic-erotic exchange of international peril for internal power. *Barnaby Rudge* hovers at the meeting point of these exchanges: the younger (masculine) generation accesses its identity, and masculinity, in America and the West Indies, while the older generation, John Chester and Geoffrey Haredale, plays out the fatal masque of the Roman and the English, the Jesuit and the virgin.

I want in this essay, then, to revisit the Gunpowder Plot of 1605, which I will suggest is just as much in Dickens's mind here in the figure of John Chester as when in the first pages of his next novel he includes a surprisingly long and passionate satire on the Gunpowder plotters as the ancestors of that too too English line, the Chuzzlewits, with its most Jesuitical and Chesterian sprig Pecksniff.[2] But what about the much flaunted connection of Chester to Lord Chesterfield, whose letters to his son Chester reads approvingly a year after their publication? I'd call that a feint, a Jesuitical equivocation from Dickens. Aristocrat, flaneur, provocateur, John Chester defends the "holy bond" between father and son: "If there is anything real, he says, "this is real" (147). But deep in Dickens's consciousness the villain is defending here less the line of the patriarchal family than that long line of antidomestic brotherhoods for which the Jesuit stands, and for which increasingly "the Catholic" came to stand, in the myth of "the English,"—as over against that new "humanist" faith of the heart, holy domesticity, the state as the family, which characterized Victorian cultural and even political life, forwarded, as Robert Polhemus argues by the investment of the mainline Victorian novel not in religious or political but in "Erotic Faith."[3]

We can see the deep structure of Chester's evocation of the Conspiring Jesuit particularly if we look at two of Cattermole's illustrations for *Barnaby Rudge*.[4] We first meet John Chester, gentleman, in chapter 10, taking his ease in the best room of the Maypole, an ostentatiously lively, cheery, cozy public house which actually has a second, private identity (or rather first private identity) as a decaying mansion of the Catholic gentry. It is still the property of disenfranchised Catholic magnate Geoffrey Haredale, along with the decaying mansion a mile down the Road, the Warren, in which Haredale lives with his niece Emma, 23 years after (as we learn) the elder Rudge, his steward, robbed and killed Haredale's older brother and faked his own death to escape. The illustration emphasizes the Catholic, even the sacerdotal, ancestry of the Maypole: Chester sits warming his hands and feet before a fire that seems to be burning inside a cathedral facade—is he its priest or a triumphant usurper at third hand? He holds the room on lease from John Willet, the innkeeper, who holds it on lease from his landlord, Geoffrey Haredale. Mobilizing both identities, and two genders, Chester turns out in fact to be the true equivocal "sign" of the Maypole: it may serve some as a "sanctuary," but it is also, the narrator in more anxious mode laments, "a mercenary—a something to be bought and sold, a very courtezan, with equal and shallow smiles and warmth for all. God help the man whose heart ever changes with the world, as an old mansion when it becomes an inn" (128).

Chester has come for no casual purpose to the Maypole, however airy his manner: he has come to find and destroy a plot. And young Barnaby Rudge, a witless but imaginatively witting part of the plot, taxes him with it in a typically oblique way, dragging Chester to the window and pointing to a drying line full of animated shirts and tunics: "Look at em now. See how they whirl and plunge. And now they stop again, and whisper cautiously together . . . I say, what is it that they plot and hatch? Do you know?" (133).

Empty clothing, nothing in it, scoffs Chester, but the reader and Barnaby know better. A look at the second illustration can even help the reader put a name to the plot. In chapter 43 a Catholic gentleman walks through a London seething with political and religious animus. Crossing through Westminster he is accosted by two others, and drawn into dangerous conversation. Cattermole's snapshot of the scene puts the three together in a Gothic vault suggesting both a cathedral and a crypt: Dickens's text tells us that the three were "schoolfellows" together at St. Omer, which, it does not need to add, is the Jesuit school founded near Calais in 1593 for the sons of disenfranchised English recusants, some of whose pupils prepared the materials for, and whose Jesuit masters were, it was avidly asserted, the puppetmasters of, The Gunpowder Plot of 1605.

If there are three men in a cellar in Westminster in any moment for the next 250 years, one of them has to be a Jesuit. If all the men are gentlemen but one the most visibly gentlemanly of all, he is the Jesuit. If one of the three claims he was "a promising young Protestant at that time, sent to learn the French tongue" at St. Omer (403), well, the breathtaking laughability of this idea—on second thought the brilliant equivocation of this idea— makes him for sure the disguised Jesuit.

For just as in this novel the invisible figure of Elizabeth, seeking a new national-virginity, confronts that of Bloody Mary risen from her grave as the Jesuit, so does the visible book of the Protestant Manual, satirized but secretly seeking a new legitimacy, confront the invisible book of the Gunpowder Plot, the Jesuit, the "Catholic." It is a book that supplies the word Chester pretended to be looking for in chapter 12, when he protests Haredale's use of the word "lying" for their Gunpowder Plot against Edward and Emma: "O

Fig. 1. George Cattermole's *John Chester at the Maypole*

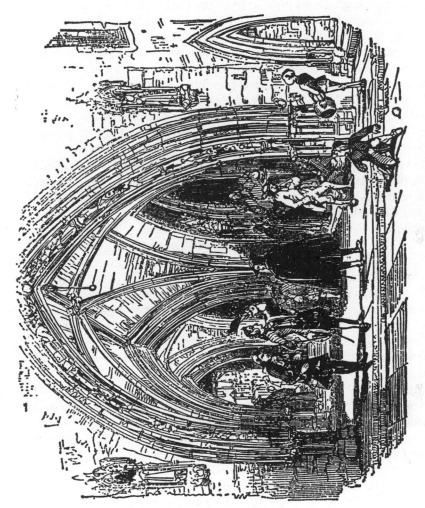

Fig. 2. George Cattermole's *Sir John Chester at Westminster*

dear no! Fie Fie! Not 'lying.' Only a little management, a little diplomacy, a little . . . '' (148). What *is* that word . . . ?

A Treatise of Equivocation by Henry Garnet, S.J. is the text that made the Jesuit into the adjective "jesuitical," part of a slide that made everything Catholic also Jesuitical on the tongue of the English. Still in manuscript in 1605, it wasn't a printed book until 1851, which makes it something of a Victorian document.[5] The *Treatise* is a poignant defense written out of a tradition of canon and civil law which is on its way to, but not yet arrived at, a doctrine of guarantees against self-incrimination. Written just after the 1595 trial and death of (Jesuit) Father and poet Robert Southwell, it is addressed to beleaguered Catholics both lay and clerical facing potential destruction of life and/or property and/or soul depending on how they answered questions like "are you a priest?" "Are you hiding a priest in this house?" "Do you believe the king [or queen] is damned for professing the Protestant faith?"

The *Treatise* is doubly poignant in that believing firmly as it does that Catholicism, the original faith, holds the high moral ground to Protestantism's belatedness and "bastardy," it must nevertheless base its argument on differences between legitimate and "fraudulent" dissimulation. Along the way it contains arguments not only for the justice of refusals to self-incriminate but also accounts of the way both the ancients and the saints and even the textual Christ himself can be found equivocating, metaphorizing, mystifying their identity and behavior.

These arguments were central to the issue of the mystery and mobility of "character" in art, and in the new modern nation-state which affirmed it would look only at a citizen's surface. They also opened the door to concepts of linguistically and artistically and morally legitimate equivocation that were matter for sly comedy in the Porter of Shakespeare's play *Macbeth* a few months later, as Gary Wills's comprehensive *Witches and Jesuits* (1995) has confirmed. Widely publicized in journals and sermons, moreover, these arguments were matter for condemnation and hanging in the state-sponsored drama called The Gunpowder Plot. Its climactic indictment was brought against the Jesuit superior in England, Fr. Garnet, by the great jurist and prosecutor Sir Edward Coke as the last act of what he called "that heavy and doleful tragedy." Citing the *Treatise* repeatedly, Coke called the Jesuit scholar a doctor of dissimulation, and argued, ingeniously, that as the author of this argument he had also to be regarded, despite the absence of proof that he forwarded or even knew about the plot, as "the author" of the Gunpowder Plot. (See Fraser, 254, 256).

For the next ten generations sermons on Jesuit equivocation proliferated, while partisans argued details of the Gunpowder Plot: Was it a full-scale international Catholic conspiracy? A fantasy invented by the Government to strengthen the still fragile Anglican ascendancy? A farce of history where a

few hotheaded zealots escaped the rational control of its marginalized community's elders and played out that community's repressed dream on a stage
controlled by Central Casting? Probably closer to the last. What is most
interesting to historians now is the place in the making of the nation held by
the government's strenuous restructuring of the undoubted "Powder Treason" of Francis Tresham, Robert Catesby, Guido Fawkes, and others into
the long-running and infinitely serviceable spectacle which we might now
call the Melodrama of the Conspiring Jesuits.

Two recent books remind us of the ways in which religious identity was
being, as we now say, "policed" in the service of national identity in nineteenth-century England, through ways of labeling good and bad conversions,
reversions, and perversions. Michael Ragussis's *Figures of Conversion*
(1995) is mainly concerned to trace the figure of the Jew as the scripturally
privileged Other in a stabilization of English national identity. "English"
was an identity fixed both as a culture of toleration leading to eventual conversion and assimilation, and as a racial body (Anglo-Saxon) capable somehow
of expansion without dilution, as the packed figure of Scott's Ivanhoe, dense
with absorptions of Franco-Norman, Palestinian, and Germanic life, demonstrates. Yet these virginity-enhancing transactions with The Other, Ragussis
shows, constantly projected a originary Third in palimpsest—Catholic under
Jew, Jew under Catholic, as political or imaginative circumstances warranted.
Burke's *Reflections on the Revolution in France* (1790), John Stockdale's
History of the Inquisitions (1810), and the whole elaborate edifice of the
Gothic novel from *The Castle of Otranto* (1764), supposed to be written by
an "artful priest" to defend his superstitions against the tide of modernity
to *Melmoth the Wanderer* (1820), which actually was written by an artful
Anglo-Irish priest—all these warn against the "secret race" allied with the
pope or descended from Judas who are coming to impose a malignant rever-
sion that will erase, or who are perversely faking the benign conversion that
produced the "English identity" readers now grasp as their own.

Stockdale's *History of the Inquisitions* is particularly interesting in this
respect. Marshalling history for an Anglican argument for keeping legal penalties on England's own Catholic minions of the Inquisition, the book interestingly forgets it is addressing a nation of recent post-Catholic conversos with
a decided nostalgia for "the Catholic" if not for the French or the Pope (see
Ragussis, 131–36). This nostalgia, along with other factors, would in the next
two decades produce the reinstatement of the Jesuit Order in England in 1829,
Catholic Emancipation in 1829, and the Oxford Movement of the 1830s,
whose climactic Tract 90 arguing that Anglicans already *were* doctrinally
Catholics came out in 1841 while *Barnaby Rudge* was running in weekly installments.

Dickens's eye is of course averted from these religious specifics in this
novel, and lifted instead toward the more abstract English identity contained

in the tolerance of difference promised by the modern nation-state. In postcolonial scholar Gauri Viswanathan's latest book, *Outside the Fold: Conversion, Modernity and Belief* (1998), *Barnaby Rudge* is a benchmark for
charting the literary imagination's contribution to (and in some ways contesta-
tion of) the state as guarantor-proselytizer for a ground of identity focussed
in the somewhat misleading concept of "the secular"—misleading because
the goal of the secular is assimilation and not the preservation of difference.
That is, as "the secular" state emancipates different religions within itself,
it arbitrates and disciplines them, houses them, puts them indoors.

As the national identity draws "secular" and "Anglican" ever nearer,
as over against the implied identity-threatening original Elizabethan-Mary
moment of "sectarian" difference, Viswanathan comments, novels about the
conversion of Hindus and Muslims to Christianity gained wide popular appeal, partly as displacements of the still active "sectarianisms" that accompanied the secularizing state's arbitration of Christian sects within England
(22–26). More importantly, these novels supplied a fantasy space in which
the reader could not only experience the exoticism of non-Christian beliefs
but also inhabit Christian belief itself with the dynamic and totalizing urgency
which was fading from "English identity." I need hardly add that in the
specimen novel for Viswanathan's analysis of this move to narratives of
empire and belief, Sidney Owenson's 1811 *The Missionary*, the villains of
the piece, defining truly urgent Christianity by their intrigues against it, are
a group of Spanish Jesuits (see Viswanathan, 27–31).

As history, then, the melodrama of conspiring Jesuits was useful in the
fragile business of holding the Converso identity of Anglican England steady
in an age of emancipation and empire. As literature, it went on to have a
spectacular run in nineteenth-century popular fiction. Books on the nineteenth-
century novel of religion by James Britten, Margaret M. Maison, and Robert
Lee Wolff have each the obligatory chapter on the Jesuit of popular fiction.[6]
He is pale and raven haired, he lies without qualm, he intrigues to divert both
money and virgins, especially male virgins, out of the normal systems of
inheritance and community and into the Order. For his real plot is the control
of men, the men of the future, the conversion—or perversion— of English
manhood to "the Catholic."[7] Like John Chester, the Jesuit believes only in
the reality of the power that multiplies between Father and Son, the overshad-
owing male intimacy that makes secondary, or artificial, or impossible, all
other forms of love.

It is, of course, a long, long cultural forgetting of maternity that proposes
as primary the intimacy between father and son, and it is a relatively new
cultural consciousness that wants to restructure this forgetting in the intimate
abstract identity-sharing between the Virgin-mother nation-state and the citizen. What can disrupt or purify these two kinds of love, both so unsatisfactory

in Dickens's analysis, the one so petrifying, the other so randomizing, ano-nymizing, for identity? In *Barnaby Rudge*, as elsewhere, Dickens recaptures English virginity, soul, sincerity beyond all irony, even Protestant sincerity, not through religious choice or conversion, but as Robert Polhemus argues (3), on the foundation of narrative itself, with nineteenth-century narrative's explicit investment in erotic faith.

It is as the enemy of erotic faith then, master of a counter-narrative, conspir-ing Jesuit, that John Chester is handed a secret scrap of paper by his valet in chapter 24 of *Barnaby Rudge*, and marvels "Where in the name of the Gun-powder Plot did you pick up this?" (244). "This" is a note from the self-styled revolutionary and conspirator Sim Tappertit warning of the involve-ment of his rival, his master, his master's daughter, the whole neighborhood, indeed the whole thrust of community narrative, in the plot of Erotic Faith against the Fathers.[8]

Sim is something of a conspiring Jesuit himself, or rather, in his own mind he is a kind of latter-day Knight Templar, a pre-Jesuit Catholic order with a similar conspiratorial history in the myth of the national identity, as readers of Scott's *Ivanhoe* (1819) will remember. He makes a ludicrous enough Brian de Bois Gilbert, does Sim, with his secret ruffles and midnight rituals, his hatred for the new constructed state that has filched what he thinks are the ancient privileges guaranteed by the constitution to his Templar order. Not to mention his avid kidnapper's eyes for a forbidden maiden. False claimant to the role of the disinherited knight, Sim in this secret note aims his borrowed sabre at the novel's true Ivanhoe, finds his true mentor in the name of the Gunpowder Plot in the disinheriting father, John Chester, and enlists under him in the effort to blow up the destined romance between the historically new and old, Norman and Saxon, Protestant and Catholic, Edward Chester and Edith Haredale.

Walter Scott has, of course, written this narrative twenty times already, with ingenious modifications Scottish, English, Orkneyan, Swiss, French, even Greek, over 800 years of history. Scott has even written this narrative into a post-Gunpowder Plot novel called *The Fortunes of Nigel* (1822). In this, his only thoroughly London-based novel, apprentices threaten to exercise the privilege of street warfare guaranteed by the old religious, now legal, liberties of "the Temple." An apprentice desires his master's daughter (a clocksmith, not a locksmith), and the young hero falls into the hands of an aristocratic mentor so villainous, says the heroine in chapter 19, that "since the Gunpowder Plot there never was a conspiracy so deeply laid, more basely and more deliberately pursued."

The Fortunes of Nigel seems to threaten an apprentice uprising in the streets all the way through, but so careful is Scott's narrative to recast public violence as erotic or commercial competition that even the promised duel between hero and villain at the end is replaced by a single shot in the dark from a thief, who is then captured and hung. So for a real London apprentice-Templars street fight, readers have to wait for *Barnaby Rudge*, which also delivers the promised duel between the contending parties of the culture in the making, a duel where, as it would seem, the engineer of the novel's Gunpowder Plot against erotic faith is hoist with his own petard.

The engineer and miner, John Chester, is the younger son of a younger son of the aristocracy: his name connects him with the ancient Saxon kingdom of Mercia. He married the daughter of an ambitious and wealthy barrister whose own father was a meat grocer (173) and he shudders delicately at the thought that his own son loves a woman whose father "was killed, like meat" (176). His foppery is comic, his class refinement hilarious, but Chester is also a damnably dangerous man.

His philosophy holds that all character and action is a glittering show wrapped around an existential hollow, like bubbles (145), all values a froth of infinitely changeable words whose substance or depth is a mirage. The words "frank," "love," and particularly "manly," rise constantly in his conversation, bubbles always elegantly popped by an accompanying "and so forth" or "that sort of thing." The unshakeable confidence with which he translates "what people call" their depths or hearts into what he says are their random surfaces, and with which he projects the dazzling charm of his own self-confessed surfaces, makes him a sort of mystic abyss into which all people lean, mesmerized and baffled, with a dread hardly distinguishable from desire.[9]

Prentices and masters, men who know better and women who feel more truly, all come nevertheless to this empty well with a pertinacity that enrages Dickens beyond the power of his analysis or satire quite to control. The force that attracts from the decorated hollow seems prodigious: it quells and binds Sim and Hugh and John Willet as well as the crowds of better informed men who flock around him in London. It made a scapegoat and drudge (291) of Geoffrey Haredale in the Jesuit school of St. Omer, and later, to hear Chester tell it, sapped Haredale's manhood to the point where he shrank away from the woman he loved, helpless to impede her enthralled passage toward Chester's bed.

Dickens's narrator applies firm moral reason and sharp sarcasm to this philosophy and philosopher, in vain: he fights the baleful intuition of modernity, to quote Elizabeth's Walsingham again, that perhaps the universe contains nothing but us and our thoughts, but he cannot vanquish it. "The thoughts of worldly men," the narrator intones, opening chapter 29, "are forever regulated by a moral law of gravitation which holds them down to earth . . . There are no signs in the sun or moon or stars for their reading. They know each planet by its Latin name [but] have quite forgotten such constellations as Charity, Universal Love, and Mercy, seeing only the images their minds already contain'' (280).

But this is a diagnosis which is its own undoing, because only those whose minds already contain the proper codes can read the planets and stars as constellations of love. Especially given that Chester has on the same page just mused, quite truly, on the moral gravity-defying Gunpowder Plot he has just set in motion: ''I have thrown the shell; it will explode, I think, in 8 and 40 hours, and should scatter these good folks amazingly'' (280).

Invisible action at a distance, subterranean sapping and mining, is Chester's forte. His interaction with his schoolfellow Geoffrey Haredale bears a striking resemblance to the relationship between the antagonists of *Our Mutual Friend*, Eugene Wrayburn and Bradley Headstone: the equivocally gendered being of impenetrable surfaces set against the frank and manly person, the opaque against the transparent, the man with no heart against the man, dreadfully in earnest, who wears his heart on his sleeve, Chester ''running'' Haredale until neither can escape the death that each craves more than the life promised by erotic faith. It is surely written that they too will end up wrestling each other into the river.

When Chester and Haredale were young men the plot of erotic faith was perverted by the awful attraction of the helpless woman to the hollow man: it is the maddening prospect of a repetition of this that drives the truthful and manly Haredale to league with his old enemy to prevent his new love, his niece Emma, from going the way of his old love. For make no mistake about it, for these two old men the young woman is the object both of the plot of erotic faith and of the Gunpowder Plot that should scatter it. Speechless she is in her first scene in chapter 14, merely a cloud of lovely dark hair flung onto Edward's breast, a waist to be gripped and drawn back onto Geoffrey's breast. But Emma Haredale is the symbol of faith in identity itself: while she lives in the Warren the building is for Geoffrey Haredale what it is for Edward Chester, ''the casket that holds the precious jewel of my existence'' (165), and his seizure of the jewel back from her Chester-lover is ontologically grounded.

Drained as she is of agency in the plot of erotic faith, Emma interestingly comes to life only in one scene of the novel, and that is when she walks out of the casket not to Edward but to John Chester, and falls to him, like Lucy to Bram Stoker's Dracula. It is an encounter brilliantly managed, one might say, both by Dickens and by Chester, to repeat for the reader the near rape of Dolly Vardin by Hugh the day before, which resulted in the theft of Emma's last letter to Edward, and to repeat for Haredale the scene years before in which Chester seduced his own mistress.

In this novel as in so many, the plot of erotic faith is a plot of letters and their interpretation: ''the relationship of sexuality, letters, and love,'' as Polhemus says, ''lies at the heart of any inquiry'' into the European novel

(19). Letters delivered by love-conspirators for years between Edward and Emma have stressed their love and faith: now as both Heavy Fathers descend, to decree Edward's disinheritance and to call upon Emma's Duty, Emma and Edward each write a letter. Each letter still contains, in the inimitable description of John Chester, "what people call tenderness and heart and all that sort of thing" (240). Tenderness and heart—and one more thing which the conspiring Jesuit, who has intercepted Emma's letter and secretly read Edward's, acutely pinpoints as erotic faith's new centerpiece—"disinterestedness."

Now, in the plot of erotic faith, the heartfelt expression of disinterestedness, each lover tenderly renouncing not the other but "possession" of the other, triggers the hermeneutic code which reads this renunciation as part of the constellation of love, the dimension of depth to the surface of desire. Renunciation becomes no hollow selflessness or mask of selfishness, but that Lacanean, or better, Levinasian, lack that hums with plenitude, intensifies interiority and its erotic and autoerotic strength, and draws to still more fervent faith.

It is this reading which John Chester sets out in chapter 29 to disrupt: his Gunpowder Plot is to burn Emma's letter and wire Edward's letter to explode in his face. In an elegantly conducted scene he rides out to the road between the Maypole and the Warren, and "entered the bounds of Miss Haredale's usual walk," waiting with exquisite fitness until "she crossed a little wooden bridge that lay between them," before he "threw himself in her way." In the encounter that follows he offers a sham act of disinterestedness as the credential of his Protestant sincerity—supplying her with Dolly's note explaining she had lost the letter actually stolen by Hugh and burned by Chester, thus excusing Edward's lack of reply to it. He then supplies her with a counter-hermeneutic for the letter he knows is on its way to Emma from Edward: the letter will "tell you that our poverty . . . forbids him to pursue his claim upon your hand, in which he talks . . . magnanimously of being in time more worthy of your regard, and so forth. A letter, to be plain, in which he not only jilts you, . . . but affects to make a merit and virtue of the act" (289).

We do not see the scene in which Edward, anxiously following up his letter, confronts an Emma who has like the letters been hermaneutically "tampered with . . . changed by vile means" (311). Instead we see Dolly reject Joe Willet in a similar but more culpable misreading. When next we see Mr. John Chester, the Gunpowder plotter, he has become Chester MP, as if he had served his political apprenticeship by blowing up the Parliament of erotic faith, Protestant sincerity, and taken back the Government for the Jesuits.

The narrative, however, is inevitably on the side of the plot of erotic faith, as we might have known from the closing sentence of its 1775 portion if we had remembered that Edward had proposed to Chester and presumably to Emma a five-year delay of their marriage as a disinterested example of his will to remake his own economic self and to retain his erotic self. In collaboration, the narrative absents itself for a strict five years, and returns to an Elizabethan scene of religious and political violence, 1780 completing 1605, another climax to the Gunpowder Plot, Bloody-Mary-out-of-her grave's threat to domestic natural order, national body at Westminster in danger, fifth column of recusants passing laws in the very halls looking to take power and subvert the Constitution.

In 1605 the national government deployed the spectre of Catholic invasion and usurpation with unparalleled speed and ingenuity, and exorcised it in a sublime display of foresight and force, entrapment and equivocation, capturing the conspirators, and more than the conspirators, and memorializing the narrow escape and divine justice in a great display of highly constitutional hanging, culminating in the splendid execution of Henry Garnet, S.J., author of *A Treatise of Equivocation*. In 1780, the narrative suggests, no one really believed in the grand drama of the international Catholic gun aimed by equivocating Jesuits at the unseeable Elizabethan heart. History's plot is groping instead toward modernity with its measures of tolerance and increments of liberties, while both government's stupor and rioter's rage seem products of private obsessions, ranging from Miggs and Simmun's sex-class frustration and Hugh's castration anxiety and young Barnaby's manic joy in the color of gold, to Dennis the hangman's fear of job downsizing.

Invisible for the long narrative spectacle of the riots in the last half of the novel, the plot of erotic faith circles just offstage in the haunted peregrinations of old Rudge and Geoffrey Haredale, who have each, 23 years apart, murdered loyalty and sleep and unknotted what ought to have remained joined, steward to his master, lover to his lover. Haggard, pale and thinned by his increasing fixation, haunted by his murdered brother as old Rudge is haunted, Haredale after five years needs only a slouched hat to *be* old Rudge, even after he arrests his quarry and alter ego in the smoking ruins of the desanctified Warren in chapter 56 and obsessively jails him in the midst of the London riots of chapter 61, leaving Emma and Dolly to be kidnapped—every honorable action of his forming inexorably, the narrator says, "another bead in the long rosary of his regrets" (557).

Returning simultaneously from soldiering in America and plantationing in the West Indies, Joe Willet and Edward Chester execute the demands of the plot of erotic faith fixed in Edward's statement, and in his memory, for five years. In the now standard parallel, the lower class Joe is the spokesman for both men: the genteel but remasculinized Edward provides, without a single word, the key actions. Dressed like one of the rioting throng he knocks Hugh off his horse in the rioters' attack on Haredale and rescues him, and knocks

Gashford down as he tries to kidnap Emma a second time, rescuing her.[10] The scenes clearing up misunderstandings between Joe and Dolly and establishing their readiness to marry stand for the undramatized actions in the genteel register reuniting Edward and Emma. Their breaches of erotic faith are presumably confessed and forgiven, before they depart again for the productive fields of Empire, leaving Joe and Dolly to rebuild the Maypole and furnish it with children too numerous to name.

Banking on good Protestant domesticity to save the national identity has its dangers, though. Mrs. Vardin coerced her household into contributing sixpences for the Protestant Association down the chimney of a bank designed as a little red house with a yellow roof. But in the end, Gabriel Vardin smashed it to pieces (387, 474).

Even the Maypole has always been a promiscuous and equivocal symbol, and retains what has always been its promiscuous and equivocal domesticity, as house and inn, embracing both the family and the stranger. The Maypole resembles the promiscuous pre-Reformation Christianity that gave houseroom to fairies and legends as well as to the Pure Doctrine. The original Pure Doctrine was enshrined in the Warren, the house of The Catholic, now seen as the house of that new Pure Doctrine, The Home. And that sanctuary is now embers. Shaken by the murder of master by steward, gutted by club and fire so that "every little nook which usages of home had made a sacred place" (505) was now profaned and open to "the coarse common gaze," the Warren, unlike the Maypole, will never be rebuilt. There remains only "the crumbled embers of a home [signifying] the casting down of that great altar where [even] the worst among us sometimes perform the worship of the heart" (725).

Contemplating this ruin "with an expression of . . . pleasure so keen that it . . . displayed itself utterly free from all restraint and reserve" (725) is the man drawn there for the last dramatic act of the novel, Sir John Chester, MP. Before the ruined altar of the worship of the heart, we are now encouraged to believe, all masks are off, all hearts visible. Here the hollow Chester reveals with evil glee that he fits the raven's curse, "I am a devil." The golden toothpicks and elegant paring knives with which he has ostentatiously decorated his surface become the sword which "restrained" and "reserved" in his scabbard in scene after scene, he finally draws, triumphantly pushing the frank and candid Haredale towards his destiny. Stricken, Haredale finally recognizes the part he is bound to play in the devil's masque, and in the national masque. The "childish spectre" he has been haunted by, perhaps since he and Chester were schoolboys together, is the killing of Chester. The killer he once sought will now be himself: the murderee with fiendish deliberation, in his final Luciferian act, has made him the phantom jailed and hanged man, the bad Catholic steward, the murderer. Geoffrey Haredale, murderer.

What does he remember in that moment: that on the March 19th of the novel's opening he forced an unwilling niece to go with him to a masquerade ball? that Edward Chester five years later gained access to defeat Hugh and to rescue himself by masquerading as one of the rioters? that to hold his dwindling English property under Catholic penal laws he has had to put some of it occasionally in a friend's name, or pay fines that were an open secret circumventing of the law? What, to paraphrase the narrator of *Bleak House* on Lady Dedlock at a similar moment, what was this death but the keystone of a gloomy arch removed, the arch of his identity as an Englishman? Does he remember, looking at the ruined altar of the worship of the heart, that the angel of his house had gone to John Chester, has gone to Edward Chester, partly because his worship has always been somewhat inward and solitary, when his "spirit should have mixed with all God's good creation" (705)? What was the hair-whitening blow of Emma's departure but the keystone of another arch removed, the erotic faith of the homebuilder, which falling in a thousand fragments, testifies to the artifice of all arches?

I leave it to the theologians to debate which Christian traditions claim more credibly the doctrine that the spirit should not hold apart, but should mix with all creation: in the nineteenth-century English novel this tradition belongs to the Anglican English. And, as the very keystone of its arch, incentive to its anxious rebuilding through love story after love story, domesticity after domesticity rebuilt, it requires a ruined altar at the core, leaving no property for the Catholic as original, as solitary. Hunted, he flies, to Europe, to cloisters in which, the narrative says equivocally, from the shelter of its inspirited, enamored worldliness, "a merciless penitence is exacted from those who sought . . . a refuge from the world" (731). There Geoffrey Haredale took vows, and within a few years died, the good Catholic alter ego to the bad Jesuit whom he killed. His undoubtedly Anglicized niece and her husband and their children build their new altar in the Indies and after many years and many children rebuild it in London. They may visit the Maypole but they leave the Warren alone, its ruined altar inviting still to reflection, and to endless rebuilding.

NOTES

1. I borrow the capitalized phrase from Antonia Fraser, whose book on the Gunpowder Plot draws particular attention to the way the political imagination of the time needed to transform the Powder Treason into "the Case of the Conspiring Jesuits" (206). Fraser's recent treatment is a thorough and vivid introduction to the Gunpowder Plot as fact and myth; a more focussed treatment of the Jesuits

in the case can be found in Philip Caraman's *Henry Garnet and the Gunpowder Plot* (1964)

2. The narrator of *Martin Chuzzlewit* typically has it both ways: his conjecture that a Gunpowder Plotter was "unquestionably" in the Chuzzlewit family background both satirizes their unwarranted sense of their innate nobility and uses Plot images—dark lantern, watching coals in a vault, destructive and "combustible" principles and engines—to lay the groundwork for character and event (14–16).

3. Polhemus's evocative treatment of this powerful idea links love as a mode of faith with the readerly faith built into narrative structure itself, pursuing the "reciprocity between love as subject, the novel as form, and faith as motive" in the English novel (3).

4. Dickens interestingly assigned two illustrators to this novel, Hablot K. Browne to specialize in character and George Cattermole in setting.

5. The title in full Elizabethan style is, "A Treatise of Equivocation: wherein is largely discussed the Question whether a Catholicke or any other person before a magistrate beying demaunded uppon his oath whether a Preiste were in such a place, may (notwithstanding his perfect knowledge to the contrary) without Periury and securely in conscience answere, No, with this secreat meaning reserved in his mynde, that he was no there so that any man is bounde to detect it." After its efficacious use in the Gunpowder Treason trials the manuscript lay in the Bodleian until resurrected for print by a Middle-Temple lawyer named David Jardine. In his preface Jardine reviews the history in a reasonably temperate spirit but feels it necessary to affirm strenuously that historical and philological reasons, not controversialist, have caused him to make the text accessible in print, notwithstanding "misapprehensions" that might be caused by its publication "at a time when events of a peculiar character have drawn much animadversion upon the principles of Roman Catholics" (xxix). These events included the restoration of Roman Catholic diocesan titles by Pope Pius IX and Archbishop Wiseman in 1850, which precipitated some mini no-popery demonstrations during the next several months.

6. James Britten's *Protestant Fiction* (1899) is an entertaining polemic with a chapter on Jesuits in fiction, noting that the term "Jesuit" seemed now to be bleeding out to encompass not only all priests but all Catholics as well: "I remember how, during my first walk with the late Lord Tennyson, he suddenly turned to me and said 'are you a Jesuit?' and when I said 'no,' rejoined 'well, you ARE a Roman Catholic,' as though the two were, to some extent at any rate, synonymous" (3). Writing in 1961 on Victorian religious novels Margaret M. Maison opens her chapter with the remark that the disguised or "crypto" Jesuit occupied the same place in popular fiction then as the Communist spy in the fiction of "today" (170). Several of the conspiring Jesuit novels cited in these studies, like Grace Kennedy's 1823 *Father Clement*, Frances Trollope's popular *Father Eustace* (1847), and Catherine Sinclair's enormously popular *Beatrice* (1852) were republished in the late 1970s as part of Robert Lee Wolff's project for Garland Press, along with his analysis of religious novels of the century, *Gains and Losses* (1977). Maison and Wolff also offer good treatments of more complex Jesuits in, for instance, Thackeray's *Henry Esmond* (1852), Charlotte Brontë's *Villette*

(1853), Joseph Shorthouse's *John Inglesant* (1880), and Mary Arnold Ward's *Helbeck of Bannisdale* (1898).

7. Herbert Sussman's *Victorian Masculinities* and James Eli Adams's *Dandies and Desert Saints* have reminded us of the importance of these part-demonized, part-glorified recapturings of the "Catholic" in the fashioning of new manhoods. Adams's section "The Fascination of Reserve" (83–106) suggests something of the erotic and even political resonance of the idea of brotherhoods "reserved" from domesticity, of masculinity understood as an "ascetic discipline" (230).

8. Stephen Marcus, whose *Dickens: From Pickwick to Dombey* did the best early critical groundwork on *Barnaby Rudge*, notes that Dickens reflected in his treatment of social change a curious reactionary impulse that ran through most English radical movements: "From the Peasants' Revolt and The Pilgrimage of Grace to the Luddite Riots and the Chartists, popular radical protest tended habitually to base its objections to a current law or condition on the ground that it was an infringement of some previously established one, and to demand that antecedent justice be restored" (181).

9. In this connection it is interesting to note the insistence of the Government during the Gunpowder treason trials that part of the Plot included the digging out of a "mine" beneath the Palace of Westminster, originally intended to convey the gunpowder from "cavity" to cavity beneath the buildings of Westminster. Though no trace was ever actually found of any such mine or tunnel, says Antonia Fraser, it "made an excellent focus for shock, horror" in pamphlets and sermons and official documents, as well as in songs and plays." "Vaults are his delight" is the comment on the devlish "miner" in Thomas Dekker's rhyming treatment of the Plot, whose title is the *Double PP. A Papist in Armes. Bearing Ten severall Sheilds Encountered by the Protestant. At ten several Weapons. A Jesuite Marching before them.* (110–11).

10. In nothing does Dickens resemble Scott more than the narrative evasion of Edward's violent actions: Alexander Welsh long ago pointed out that Scott's instinct was to elide as much as possible the ever-necessary violence by which the present civilized state of things had incrementally replaced the primitive state of things. We are told by Joe that the disguised Edward knocked Hugh off his horse (612). But the scene in retrospect obscures the issue, Hugh shouting "Whose hand was that, that struck me down?" (616) We see Gashford "felled like an ox in the butcher's shambles—struck down as though a block of marble had fallen from the roof and crushed him" (644) before we learn from Joe that the active agent of those passive verbs was Edward.

WORKS CITED

Adams, James Eli. *Dandies and Desert Saints: Styles of Victorian Masculinity.* Ithaca, N.Y.: Cornell UP, 1995.

Britten, James. *Protestant Fictions*. London: Catholic Truth Society, 1899.

Caraman, Philip. *Henry Garnet & the Gunpowder Plot*. New York: Farrar, Straus, 1964.

Dickens, Charles. *Barnaby Rudge: A Tale of the Riots of Eighty* (1841). Harmondsworth, Middlesex.: Penguin Classics, 1997.

————. *Bleak House* (1853). Rpt. Harmondsworth, Middlesex.: Penguin Classics, 1996.

————. *Martin Chuzzlewit* (1844). New York: New American Library, 1965.

————. *Our Mutual Friend* (1865). Harmondsworth, Middlesex.: Penguin Classics, 1976.

Fraser, Antonia. *Faith and Treason: The Story of the Gunpowder Plot*. New York: Doubleday, 1996.

Garnet, Henry, S. J. *A Treatise of Equivocation*. (1596). Published with introduction by David Jardine Esq. London: Longman, Brown, Green, and Longmans, 1851.

Marcus, Steven. *Dickens: from Pickwick to Dombey*. New York: Basic Books, 1965.

Owenson, Sydney (Lady Morgan). *The Missionary* (1811). Rpt. London: Charles Westerton, 1859 as *Luxima the Prophetess*.

Polhemus, Robert M. *Erotic Faith: Being in Love from Jane Austen to D. H. Lawrence*. Chicago: U of Chicago P, 1990.

Ragussis, Michael. *Figures of Conversion: The "Jewish Question" and English National Identity*. Durham, N.C.: Duke UP, 1995.

Scott, Walter. *The Fortunes of Nigel* (1822). Rpt. St. Albans, Hertfordshire: Panther Books, 1973.

————. *Ivanhoe* (1819). Rpt. New York: New American Library, 1962.

Viswanathan, Gauri. *Outside the Fold: Conversion, Modernity, and Belief*. Princeton, N. J.: Princeton UP, 1998.

Welsh, Alexander. *The Hero of the Waverley Novels*. New Haven: Yale UP, 1963.

Wills, Gary. *Witches and Jesuits: Shakespeare's "Macbeth."* New York: Oxford UP, 1995.

Wolff, Robert Lee. *Gains and Losses: Novels of Faith and Doubt in Victorian England*. New York: Garland, 1977.

Politics and *Barnaby Rudge:*
Surrogation, Restoration and Revival

John Glavin

Can Barnaby Rudge *be read as a political novel? Despite its historical subject, the answer would seem to be no. The novel does graphically portray the domestic and public tyrannies that drove the Gordon Riots. Here, as later in his career, Dickens is unrivaled as a social novelist, especially in his portrayal of the marginated and the powerless. But at the same time the novel confirms in a particularly clear way Dickens's deep and characteristic aversion to any structure or system which claims, for whatever cause, to impinge on or constrain the self. And it highlights his profound pessimism regarding any form of ameliorative, let alone revolutionary, development in British social life. In fact,* Rudge *reveals itself as so deeply anti-political that it can be read as an invaluable and illuminating proto-text in the development of European fascism, its rioters the sympathetically drawn precursors of all the ardent, rootless young men at the core of the full-fledged fascisms that followed.*

> "Even those critics who agree . . . on the stature of these novels, disagree markedly as to Dickens' own politics . . . there is a tendency to refashion Dickens . . . to make him seem safer than he was."
>
> Monroe Engel, *PMLA*

Barnaby Rudge raises in a particularly rich and pointed way the perennially vexed question of ''Dickens' own politics.'' This question I approach here

---

by deploying a discrimination, crucial to nineteenth-century architecture, between *restoration* and *revival*. For us restoration and revival seem virtually interchangeable. For architects contemporary with Dickens they marked not only different, but opposing projects. Here, for example, is the preeminent restorer of July Monarchy France, the France contemporary with the Dickens of *Rudge*, Eugène Viollet-le-Duc (born two years after Dickens). "To restore an edifice is not to maintain it, repair it or remake it, it is to re-establish it in a complete state that may never have existed at a given moment" (Murphy 2000, 18). To restore then is at once to memorialize *(re-establish in a complete state)* and to invent *(may never have existed)*, to look back in time on a new-made old work, a work made visible through being stripped of time. Such a notion of restoration can only come, as Kevin D. Murphy argues, from a sense "that the world has entered a new era, fundamentally disconnected from the rest of time, which is thereafter relegated to the status of 'history' " (18). Defined in this way, restoration represents a radically new idea. Indeed, Viollet-le-Duc insisted, "both the word and the thing are modern" (17): what the on-going nineteenth-century *now* does to an over-and-done- with *then*. We may delight (churches) or shudder (castles) to look back on the past we restore, but certainly we do not seek to re-enter or retrieve it, or even simply to continue with it. To re-enter, retrieve, continue, those are the goals of *revival*, as in, most conspicuously, the Gothic Revival, which subsumes the past into the practice of the present explicitly to erase, or at least to span, the gap that generates what Murphy means by history.

Writing history, in which direction does Dickens point *Rudge*? Does *Rudge restore* the Gordon Riots, marking them clearly as something Dickens's readers have moved on, or should have moved on, from? Or does *Rudge revive* the Riots, presenting them anew as a subject if not for emulation then at least for nostalgia? I skip completely the notion urged in earlier readings like those of Humphrey House or Steven Marcus, that Dickens is paralleling the Gordon Riots to Chartist agitation, warning his contemporaries against what the Riots might forebode. Gordon Spence nicely summarizes, and deflates, those arguments in his introduction to the 1973 Penguin edition of the novel (19–23, also the edition used in this essay). I am thinking instead of the darker implications of passages like this one, pointed out to me by Janice Carlisle, in which Lord George, in prison, is described by our author as "the unhappy author of all" (661). What should that shared authorship imply for our reading of Dickens's relation to Gordon, or of the Riot's relation to *Rudge*? If Gordon authors *all,* does that mean Gordon authors *Rudge*? And if Gordon authors *Rudge*, then, as Monroe Engel asked fifty years ago, how "safe" can "Dickens' own politics" be?

Politics Per Se

With *Rudge* Dickens begins to become the indispensable British *social* novelist. Here we find for the first time that broadly horizontal engagement with a society's problematic institutions that produces the most ambitious and (as we now think) the most typically Dickensian fiction, novels like *Bleak House, Little Dorrit, Our Mutual Friend*. But, if social, is *Rudge* also *political?* I do not mean by political here something like describing the element of hegemony inevitable to all relationships, and to all representations of those relationships. I mean something narrower, political as focusing on disputed public hegemony, the struggles to adjust the distribution of power within the state, and particularly within the institutions of the state, politics per se. In that sense I think I can claim that *Rudge* is not a political novel; indeed, that Dickens never wrote a political novel.

Throughout Dickens's fiction the state is always fundamentally bogus. Every regime we encounter, in England, in France, in the States, is invariably preposterous; its politics inevitably pretense. There is never any genuine possibility of reform—it is different in the ad hoc world of his journalism— no sense of a better government emerging through either internal or external pressure. *Rudge* dooms the Gordon Riots from the beginning because the rioters are inefficient and badly lead, but also (and for exactly the same reason that *A Tale* dismisses the French Revolution) because good government is always for Dickens an oxymoron. In novel after novel, trying to get good government only gets you more government, Circumlocution, which is inevitably worse government, because for Dickens the state, any state, is an imposition on the inherent liberty of the subject. Its political maneuvers vary only from imposture to light show to smoke screen. Of course, all the state's innate evils are horrifically magnified in *Barnaby Rudge*, where Dennis the Hangman is its ideal functionary and Sir John Chester its chief favorite. But Dennis and Chester merely ratchet the monstrous into the demonic.

We might try to counter that argument by following lines suggested by the British political philosopher Michael Oakeshott. Oakeshott admires a "traditional" politics that springs from "attending to the general arrangements of a collection of people who . . . compose a single community" (Oakeshott 1991, 56). Elective not electoral, traditional politics eschews programs. It builds instead a posteriori (certainly never a priori) descriptions of The Way We Live Now. Which certainly seems a notion congenial to a novelist, and especially to a novelist whose first, fame-garnering fiction detailed the extended Adventures of a Club, a "single community" bound together by civility, curiosity, and camaraderie. Theory-driven politics sets society on a journey. Oakeshott's displaces that journey with adventure, or better with plural and challenging adventures, always moving but getting nowhere in particular, which makes for a pretty good description of virtually every adult life in Dickens, where no one after childhood ever accomplishes a journey as planned.

But tempting as this alternative may be, it does not finally help us with Dickens because he cannot imagine that sustained, single community Oakeshott requires. Dickens rarely gets beyond the club or the quasi-domestic alternative family: Jarndyce and his wards; Sunday afternoons with the Manettes in Soho. And even these ad hoc groupings continually break down until finally, under the vicissitudes of experience, they evaporate. Thus Clennam and Little Dorrit, newly married, literally disappear into the London streets. And while we do get the Willets reconstituted at the end of *Rudge*, it's only at the price of a maimed husband and a demented old dad, just about the best he can imagine. Community, any kind of community, makes Dickens either suspicious or sad. He is rather an artist of the supreme and singular subject. He can't imagine any form of organized life which does not constitute per se an untoward imposition on the self. Something we see very clearly if we expand our inquiry into *Rudge* to include the alternative (hegemonic but not political per se) kinds of assembly it generates: theater, ceremony, and festival.

Theater

In *Rudge* nobody comes out intact after performing in anything resembling a theater. Throughout the novel theater and its synonyms are invariably dirty words for dirty events. It can be dirty-dopey. "Captain" Simon Tappertit climbing into a cellar in "gloomy majesty" is "theatrical" (109). Or dirty-deadly. The Warren is the appropriately "chosen theater for such a deed as it had known," the deed being the dual murder at the core of the mystery plot (254). Thus, when the Rudges and the Haredales reassemble in that "theater," they seem "all in keeping with the place, and actors in the legend"—a particularly pointed use of actor since this is a scene of almost continuous misrepresentation and misreading. But dopey or deadly, and more often deadly than dopey, theater invariably involves imposition and dissimulation.

Sir John Chester is thus always an explicit figure of theater, nowhere more damningly than after he ignores Varden's revelation that Hugh is his son. "Sir John's face changed; and the smile gave place to a haggard and anxious expression, like that of a weary actor jaded by the performance of a difficult part" (680). John Willet is forced by the rioters to watch the "destruction of his property, as if it were some queer play or entertainment, of an astonishing and stupefying nature'' (497). And the almost simultaneous burning of The Warren forms ''a scene never to be forgotten by those who saw it and were not actors in the work, as long as life endured'' (507).

Barnaby, captured by the soldiers as the riots wind down, is forced to become, literally, street-theater: ''he felt he was a sight; and looking up as they passed quickly along, could see people running to the windows a little too late, and throwing up the sashes to look after him'' (526). But where Barnaby associates public performance with shame, the unspeakable Dennis thrills to the performative possibilities of the scaffold-stage, before he senses what his own fate will be. ''I've heerd a eloquence on them boards—you know what boards I mean—and have heerd a degree of mouth given to them speeches, that they was as clear as a bell, and as a good as a play! That's a pattern!'' (591). London itself becomes a kind of command performance as it burns for ''the Lord Mayor, [who] with his hands in his pockets, looked on as a idle man might look at any other show, and seemed mightily satisfied to have got a good place'' (600). Indeed, the entire show-hungry town is so hardened by ''the frequent exhibition of this last dread punishment, of Death,'' that its denizens cannot think of the imminent death of incapable, inculpable Barnaby ''otherwise than as an actor in a show'' (682).

Of course, Dickens can imagine, even delight in, performance. We have only to look at Grip the Raven. Grip's ''surprising performances'' gratify him and reward the Rudges ''when he condescended to exhibit, which was not always, for genius is capricious'' (419). But when the drunken J.P. demands that Grip perform, the bird almost costs Barnaby and his mother their liberty. The ''genuine John Bull'' incarcerates them, then threatens flogging, and finally, on the boil at Grip's obstinate silence, demands the right to purchase him. The Rudges barely escape from this theater with their lives. And when, after Barnaby's pardon, Grip is presented at the window by Varden, to substitute for the hidden Rudge and thereby quell the demanding crowd, the bird does nothing. He merely suffers himself to be shown, only a slight improvement on his behavior earlier when, carried through the demanding ''multitude,'' he drew ''blood from every finger that came within his reach'' (712). For Dickens, then, authentic *performance*, Grip's par excellence, involves the freely chosen and freely given display by the self of the self.

Theater is that performance's grotesque parody: the self compelled to perform in a form not only other than its own, but distorting, and, if sustained, destructive of the self. Willet forced to participate in the ruin of the Maypole. Barnaby paraded down the street. Sir John playing Lord Chesterfield. Invariably, that same doubled imperative of dissimulation and imposition. (For a broad review of Dickens's anti-theatricality and performance anxieties, see my *After Dickens*.) All theater pivots on this process of simulation which

Joseph Roach has recently and memorably called *surrogation,* the broad spectrum of individual, domestic, and social strategies by which individuals or groups "make up for" unavailable originals, including performance in which the cavity of the scripted role becomes "filled" by the cast performer (Roach 1996, 2). However, both inside and outside the playhouse the fit, as Roach shows, "cannot be exact. The intended substitute either cannot fulfil expectations, creating a deficit, or actually exceeds them, creating a surplus" (2). We may not be able to tell the dancer from the dance, but the actor is never only the role, just as no substitute is ever entirely the original.

For Dickens, as famously for Rousseau, its dependence on surrogation makes theater a prime site of corruption. Rousseau argues against establishing theaters in places like republican Geneva and would-be royal Poland because a free-born people must lose its liberty when it emulates—that is, takes its form from—what it sees on a stage, the vicious values of corrupt courts and morally bankrupt dynasties. (One of the great intellectual games of the eighteenth century involved trying to figure out what Poland should be like, if there should ever again be a Poland. Rousseau thought Poland's best hope lay with folk-dancing. No plays, but a lot of polka [1972, 14–15]). Like Rousseau, *Rudge* routinely associates theater and its synonyms with imposture, loss of liberty, loss of life, dissimulation, and death. But not because a particular model of state has corrupted the playhouse. Rather because the playhouse, any playhouse, instances the corruption inevitable in any form of staging, the corruption of the Command Performance, where the individual is made to play the role the Other requires.

Paradoxically, in *Rudge* we see this hostility most powerfully directed not at anything explicitly called theatrical, but when we explore the most consequential show it refuses to stage, the "scene" of Barnaby's pardon. Though Barnaby's pardon is the final major moment in the novel, Dickens chooses not to describe it. We see Barnaby being lead out to execution. We assume he has died, and then, quite a while later, he magically reappears, rescued in the nick of time. Dickens can do nothing, except keep his, and our, distance from the degrading spectacle of Barnaby's performance in the state's self-serving interlude. In contrast, we find that Dickens can easily commandeer the spectacle of Hugh's hanging, using the state's means against itself, turning their criminal into his hero.

Hugh's execution is a public spectacle. It appals Dickens but he has no difficulty presenting it. Outside Newgate at high noon, that's where and how condemned men are hanged. And Hugh, as he insistently proclaims, is indeed guilty of the crimes for which he is being punished. He boldly, poignantly, performs himself throughout (695–97). Action and meaning perfectly coincide. Barnaby's execution, however, is a farrago of surrogacy. He is to be hung outside the standard site of execution in front of Lord Mansfield's town house, in the middle of Bloomsbury Square. But to set up a scaffold in Bloomsbury Square is to turn Bloomsbury Square into a set. And that is only the start of this sequence's extended process of standing-in. (As Roach shows, surrogation, always either deficit or surplus, must infinitely reproduce supplement.) Barnaby's "execution" attempts to restore a gutted ruin into a site of law, ostensibly to enforce the connection between a crime and its punishment. But Barnaby took no part in the attack on Mansfield's house. While that was going on, he and his father, just released from jail, were hiding out in Smithfield on their way to Finchley. This association between him and that arson is thus also added on. He is being made to stand in for the people who really did burn Mansfield's mansion, in a place that stands in for a place that has been destroyed, in an action that attempts a return for what is lost. All surrogation; all theater. Command Performance.

If written. But of course it is not written. In fact, Barnaby himself becomes un-written by passing through this gap in the narrative. "Passive and timid, scared, pale, and wondering, and gazing at the throng as if he were newly risen from the dead, and felt himself to be a ghost among the living, Barnaby" (711). Yet even as he rises from the dead he seems to vaporize. *Ghost* is the scene's key term. The reunion scene turns out be about the helpers, Varden, and Haredale. And we don't even get to see the reunion itself: "Barnaby, rushing up the stairs, fell upon his knees beside his mother's bed" (711). That's it. And after that non-scene, for the remainder of the novel, Barnaby seems virtually to vanish, leaving only a fugitive trace where before there had been a vivid character. He becomes someone who is, in the terrible word we have inherited from the recent history of the hemisphere, *disappeared*, a term I want to deploy with the full political resonance of what it means to us now: someone whom a regime has caused to vanish.

But Barnaby is "disappeared" not because of the riots, or the army, or even the prison, the usual causes for contemporary victims. The novel gives us memorable, forceful, affecting scenes that follow his involvement with each of those forms of state brutality. Clearly, what Barnaby cannot survive with any kind of vitality left intact is that unseen scene in front of Lord Mansfield's house, the scene, paradoxically, that ought to be all about his survival, the supreme moment not of the regime's barbarity but of its mercy. And it is not just that Barnaby as a character cannot survive that experience. Dickens cannot write it, because to write it effectively would be to endorse both the state that pardons and the theater in which the pardon is performed. Just imagine any way in which the scene could be narrated, and that conclusion becomes unavoidable. Of course, Barnaby must go free. The emotional and moral logic of the novel demands it. But Dickens cannot make his pen do the work common to both theater and politics: to submit the individual to the other's script, the playhouse audience, prepared to clap or hiss, or the great officers of state, with far more consequential forms of approbation or dismay. For Dickens, then, theater can never serve to organize a community alternative to the body politic. theater is invariably politics engrossed.

Ceremony

If theater makes Dickens profoundly anxious, ceremony, epitomized in the "dark and direful ceremonies" of the Apprentice Knights' initiation (116), merely piques his contempt.

Ceremony, here, does not mean quite the same thing as ritual. For many of Dickens's characters, especially the lower-class, the declassé, or the arriviste, the self is made and sustained by ritual, that is, by the performance of obsessive, codified repetition. In this novel we have only to think of Miggs. "At this spectacle Miggs cried 'Gracious!' again, and then 'Goodness gracious!' and then 'Goodness gracious me!' and then, candle in hand, went downstairs" (120). Ritual of this kind is about achieving coherence and sustaining continuity. Ceremonies, however, like that of the Apprentice Knights, are clearly about exactly the reverse: about discontinuity, about replacement, about making a difference, a change. Ceremonies claim to make something happen.

For Dickens that means all ceremony must be absurd. Official ceremonies are contaminated by the inherent corruption of the state. In his novels we never see a courtroom, a customs house, an inquest, without feeling their inherent silliness. This is true even in the final weddings of his favorite characters. The purely ceremonial aspects of the event, the clergyman, the verger, the pew-opener, the dusty church, are invariably ridiculed, to demarcate an authentic experience, marriage, something two loving individuals do, from an artificial experience, the wedding, the culture's imposition on those individuals.

And Dickens's satire becomes even sharper when he moves from ceremonies imposed on individuals to the ceremonies which groups like the Apprentice Knights impose on themselves. He treats them as a sort of group delusion. In theater individuals are constrained to play out the illusions of the other. In ceremonies individuals collude in believing that their shared, elective performances can effect a fundamental change in their lives and identities. Donning second-hand finery, bowing, orating, apprentices can become knights and effectively damn their unfeeling masters.

All such ceremony is silly because it depends on the fallacy—fallacy as Dickens insists—that individuals can share and circulate power in some middle, civic or quasi-civic sphere, intruded upon, or carved out between, the completely private and the entirely public. (Here we tread on the borders of, if not entirely within, Oakeshott territory.) Dickens has no belief in either the integrity or the potency of such a space. Ceremony is merely a compensatory fantasy, encouraged by the regime to mask the powerlessness imposed by the regime. Of course, then, the Apprentices meet in a no-thoroughfare, under a grating, along a cellar, kept by a blind man, selling broth made from scraps (108–18) . Where else, or better, Dickens asks, would you find ceremony going down?

Nowhere is Dickens more radically apolitical (not to mention, anti-democratic) than in this complete refusal to accept the possibility of community composed through positive, constructive associations, of non-domestic, elective, self-regulating and effective groups. To fall for their come-on, he maintains, is even worse than being forced onto a stage, worse than believing in the state. The stage leaves you a ghost, but with the dignity of a victim. Ceremonies just show you're a fool, or, more specifically: "a conceited, bragging, empty-headed, duck-legged idiot" (118).

Festival

One mode from our triad remains, which I'll call *festival*, since Dickens himself does not give it a name. Like theater and ceremony, festival fails Dickens, finally, but it comes closest to snagging his imagination, and that closeness, curiously, makes festival the most troubling and fascinating feature of the book.

We encounter festival most notably in chapter 48 as the rioters assemble on St. George's Fields before bringing their petition to Parliament. This exemplary scene seems to realize and relish everything missing from its counter-paradigm, the unpardon in Bloomsbury Square. It repays extended quotation.

> Here an immense multitude was collected, bearing flags of various kinds and sizes, but all of the same colour—blue, like the cockades—some sections marching to and fro in military array, and others drawn up in circles, squares, and lines. A large portion, both of the bodies which paraded the ground, and of those which remained stationary, were occupied in singing hymns or psalms. With whomsoever this originated, it was well done; for the sound of so many thousand voices in the air must have stirred the heart of any man within him, and could not fail to have a wonderful effect upon enthusiasts, however mistaken.
>
> Scouts had been posted in advance of the great body, to give notice of the leader's coming. Those falling back, the word was quickly passed through the whole host, and for a short interval there ensued a profound and deathlike silence, during which the mass was so still and quiet, that the fluttering of a banner caught the eye, and became a circumstance of note. Then they burst into a tremendous shout, into another, and another, and the air seemed rent and shaken, as if by the discharge of cannon.   (446–47)

Even if the narrator didn't explicitly tell us that it "was well done" and "could not fail to have a wonderful effect," we can hear admiration, thrilled awe, in the cadences of the prose, and in the rapt, respectful attention paid to this spectacle.

To appreciate that response contrast against the superb panache of this supremely efficient mass the condescending account of the Royal East London Volunteers, Gabriel Varden's troupe, just a few chapters earlier (chapter 42). Take note, too, of Royal and Volunteer, the conflation of theater (Royal) with ceremony (Volunteer).

> The Royal East London Volunteers made a brilliant sight that day: formed into lines, squares, circles, triangles, and what not, to the beating of drums, and the streaming of flags; and performed a vast number of complex evolutions, in all of which Serjeant Varden bore a conspicuous share. Having displayed their military prowess to the utmost in these warlike shows they marched in glittering order to the Chelsea Bun House, and regaled in the adjacent taverns until dark. Then at sound of drum they fell in again, and returned amidst the shouting of His Majesty's lieges to the place from whence they came.
>
>   The homeward march being somewhat tardy,—owing to the unsoldierlike behaviour of certain corporals, who, being gentlemen of sedentary pursuits in private life and excitable out of doors, broke several windows with their bayo-nets, and rendered it imperative on the commanding officer to deliver them over to a strong guard, with whom they fought at intervals as they came along . . . .
>   (392–93)

The Volunteers start out as a hodgepodge of ceremony and theater but quickly disintegrate, as does the prose, into carnival: the bibulous burghers' carefully policed day off. "We did have fun! Didn't we?" The time off is limited. The space controlled. Common purpose soon collapses, and the harm done is easily repaired. So much for carnival.

Festival is carnival's reverse, at least as Mona Ozouf defines it in her encyclopedic *Festivals of the French Revolution* (1988): "a people setting out . . . for the sheer pleasure of doing so, . . . go beyond the familiar bounds . . . [in a] spontaneous convergence of different wills" (16). That convergence results in "extravagant episodes" of "scandalous transgres-sion" which "spring from a violation of prohibitions" (31), but throughout remain ordered, "gratuitous," "ephemeral," even "musical" (17). The re-semblance to the scene on St. George's Fields is instantly striking.

Ozouf describes three other features crucial to the revolutionary festival.

1. *Rigid Segregation by Gender*, emphasized in *Rudge* by the forceful exclusion of Mrs. Rudge from her son. Festivity is all about virility.

2. *Eclipse of the Spectator*. A set-apart spectator is crucial to both theater and ceremonial. But on St. George's Fields no one's watching, or no one's only watching. Spectators and performers, all male, blend into a countless,

infinite one: "on and on, up this line, down that, round the exterior of this circle, and on every side of that hollow square; and still there were lines, and squares and circles out of number to review" (448–49).

3. A *Leader Who Emerges From Within the Mass*, feeling as Lord George claims "called" and "summoned" to review them in the excessive, exhausting heat (447). The leader may in fact be imposing on the crowd, but that is never their perception or his rhetoric.

On festive St. George's Fields, then, as in events like the Festival of the King's Death, or of 9 Thermidor, or 18 Fructidor, of the Taking of Toulon, even of the Retaking of Toulon (somewhat surprisingly the French Revolution turns out to have been unrelentingly festive; perhaps that's why it lasted so long), we encounter a "preoccupation with [a] situation of control, submissive behavior, extravagant effort, and the endurance of pain . . . two seemingly opposite states, egomania and servitude," that "take the form of a characteristic pageantry: the massing of groups of people; the turning of people into things"—all those squares, circles, and lines—"the multiplication or replication of things; and the grouping of people/things around an all-powerful, hypnotic, leader-figure or force." But that isn't Ozouf. That was Susan Sontag, in her famous essay on the films and photography of Leni Riefenstahl, characterizing fascist aesthetics (Sontag 1975–80, 91).

Fascist. The ugliest of all the f—— words. Now we begin to see what *unsafe* may really mean in this fiction, and to what being apolitical and antidemocratic might actually lead.

Those festive exercises on St. George's Fields conform precisely to the aesthetics of fascist maneuver we've seen filmed and photographed in the earlier parts of the past century. Group and mass ceremonies that transform men from spectators into participants, sacralizing and aestheticizing politics through liturgies of endless repetition and easy symbol (Mosse 1999, xii—xiii). But in *Rudge* this fascist quality goes beyond that relatively encapsulated moment on St. George's Fields. It's not merely this set of martial exercises that makes us anxious. Fascism uncannily seems to reach out to label the Gordon campaign itself. And Gordon, we remember, authors all.

Fascism

It's jejune to identify fascism simply with regimes that are "oppressive, authoritarian and elitist" (Griffin 1991, 2). Yet things become tricky when we try to go beyond that simplistic formula, because a key ideological outcome of the 1945 victory was to erase fascism not as a serious force but as a serious idea. Thus one of my colleagues, a political scientist, hearing what I am writing, remarks: "Oh yes, fascism, we think of it as socialism for the stupid."

Fascism is certainly not stupid, just as it is more complex and ubiquitous than its two monster-narratives: Hitler's and Mussolini's. We find it before World War II, in Spain, Romania, and Belgium. After the War, repeatedly in South America. Until recently in South Africa. Currently in what was Yugoslavia. And then, blushingly, the most successfully sustained fascist culture in history: the American South between Plessy v. Ferguson and Brown v. The Board. Broad differences among all these, yes, but also a strong family resemblance. Re-examined in this larger frame, then, I dare not say more sympathetically, but at least more respectfully, it's easy to see what Frederic Jameson means when he insists that fascism is modernism's twin (1979, 13). Or how Slavoj Žižik more recently could remark that Heidegger's "proto-Fascist decisionism is simply the basic condition of the *political*" (1999, 21).

Using Jameson, Sontag, Žižik and a wide range of other recent commentators (Eatwell 1995; Griffin 1991; Lamb 1997; Mosse 1999; Pinkus 1995; Spackman 1996) we can construct an encompassing model of fascism which includes:

- aggressive nationalism, seeking a middle or third way between the forces of the market and the mob, too populist to trust finance capitalism, too elitist to trust socialism, but which is also
- determined instead forcefully to reorder society in the light of a retrojected Utopia, the best of the past realized in the most up-to-date future, an "authentic popular longing . . . for a true community and social solidarity against fierce competition and exploitation" (Žižik 1999, 184). This new-old Utopia will be
- intolerant of ethnic and other internal differences, instead
- seeking legitimacy in that construction of a mythical past, which it
- enforces by continuously aggressive rituals of intimidation.

In short, the Gordon program. Or the Ku Klux Klan, a parallel too noticeable to ignore, or to bear.

Those June days in the London of 1780, then, seem to tell of a kind of Putsch. Much less successful than Rome 1922. But also much more effective than Munich 1923. In all three, a para-military band of disaffected, generally young men attempt "the violent establishment of an authoritarian nationalist regime" (Eatwell 1995, 92). Intolerant of internal differences, they are propelled by the ideal of a homogenous "natural community rising phoenix-like after a period of encroaching decadence," promising to "replace gerontocracy, mediocrity and national weakness with youth, heroism and national greatness" (Griffin 1991, 38, 47). But unlike revolutionaries of the more conventional right and left, they lack all concern for steady-state normalization, always embattled instead, and continuously aggressive, equating aggression with health.

But it is there, with aggression, that this linkage between *Rudge* and fascism ruptures. Warfare is to fascism what class-struggle is to Marxism: its fundamental dynamic. Dickens, however, is terrified by every form of violence, a terror made bare by his novels' obsessive return to passages of violence. *Rudge* handles this anxiety initially by trying hard and cleverly to distinguish two different strains "mingled" within "the [festive] concourse" (447): the destructive and the deluded. The first of these it energetically repudiates. That strain includes the dissimulation, the anti-Catholicism, and especially the mob's unchecked violence. But for the other strain, the dream of a renewed, anti-political social order, it frequently evokes a compelling sympathy. Describing the maneuvers on St. George's Fields before the march on Parliament, the novel ingeniously echoes the lines in *Paradise Lost* depicting the Fallen Angels as they reassemble for Satan's review before the building of Pandemonium (I: 541–622), even to the leaders' tears, in Satan's case "Tears, such as Angels weep" (620). Same details, same cadence, same tone. And the same doubleness. These are still Angels, at once thrilling and doomed, but not yet damned. Exactly like Gordon's troop: deeply mixed. Thus, in a typical gesture, we are told that the "throng" is "sprinkled doubtless here and there with honest zealots." If it comprises "the very scum and refuse of London," we must also recognize, as the sentence immediately goes on to claim, that their "growth was fostered by bad criminal laws, bad prison regulations, and the worst conceivable police" (447).

Listening more closely to what is being sung, the narrator can admit to finding "these fellows ... chanted any ribaldry or nonsense that occurred to them, feeling pretty certain that it would not be detected in the general chorus and not caring much if it were" (447). Gordon, however, it insists, "quite unconscious of their burden, passed on with his usual stiff and solemn deportment, very much edified and delighted by the pious conduct of his followers." He is being duped, but he is also being dissociated from all that is false and scabrous in the operation he ostensibly leads. Gordon can thereby emerge, in the novel's language, as really only a "poor gentleman," mislead and betrayed, an object of pity not scorn. It is Gashford, "cold" and "insidious," who is the real corrupting tempter. Thus, by chapter 53, after the failure to present the petition to Parliament, responsibility for the riots effectively shifts from Gordon to Gashford. At this point we have two groups, *rioters* (Gashford, Dennis, Hugh) and *fascisti* (Gordon, Barnaby, Sim), "men of capacity" v. "duller wits" (404). The former we loathe and fear. The latter we pity. Even stupid and vain Sim can sincerely justify himself as a would-be "healer of the wounds of his unhappy country," wounds we recognize as such (543).

Splits of this sort turn out historically to be a characteristic fascist move. Fascism routinely carries forward the thrust of the original putsch by a regular rhythm of the purge. Think SA and SS. Thus both Hitler and Mussolini repudiate with revulsion the French Revolution as their demonic inverse. And their apologists seek constantly to separate festivity from riot, the people from the mob, putsch from terror. Nevertheless, as the Gordon Riots conclude, this fascist-rioter distinction falters, overwhelmed by an entirely different alignment. Plot resolution springs, as it does in fascist myth, if not in fascist history, from the heroic efforts of *arditi*, the Italian fascist term for the bold young men who, coming together, risk all to overturn complacency and root out corruption, and whose equivalents are found in all fascist mythography and history. But the *arditi* in *Rudge* are not limited to, or identical with, the novel's *fascisti*. If that were the case, riotous Hugh would stay a villain, one with Sim and Gashford. Instead he emerges from the struggle as eloquent, justified, and tragic. And the Lost Boys, Joe and Ned, would probably remain far off among the Salwanners, rather than becoming indistinguishably part of the ardent band of brothers, one with fascist Barnaby and riotous Hugh (who is indeed Chester's half-brother).

By the riots' conclusion all the handsome young men together (looks exclude Sim from any sort of fascist virility) have distanced themselves from Dennis's mad vanity and Gashford's venality. Crucially, for this band of brothers, there is no sort of *duce* and no common ideology. (The palliated Lord George has of course gone missing.) What holds them together instead is their common aggressive virility, central to the imagery and narrative of fascist myth: not ideas or projects but "feverish sleeplessness, the forced march, the perilous leap, the slap and the blow with the fist" (Spackman 1996, 49). Predictably, it is the older men, comic Varden and dubious Haredale, who achieve results like Barnaby's last minute pardon. It's not the work of *arditi* to reason, only to do and, too often, die. (Which certainly suggests the seed for a follow-up study on Tennyson's fascism: perhaps "The Idylls of the Reich." As Jennifer Tolbert Roberts makes clear in *Athens on Trial* [1994], Dickens's contemporaries were much more prone to admire not Athens but Sparta.)

These deviations from the encompassing fascist paradigm tend to align Dickensian festivity with what Frederic Jameson calls protofascism: "a shifting strategy of class alliances whereby an initially strong populist and anticapitalist impulse is gradually readapted to the ideological habits of a petty bourgeoisie" (1979, 14). Actually, as Jameson refines that definition, in his study of Wyndham Lewis, it becomes clear that protofascism can apply only to twentieth-century experience. But the parallel remains suggestive because it calls attention to something characteristic of the protofascist that is crucial to Dickens: "a grinding contradiction between his aggressive critical, polemic and satiric impulses and his unwillingness to identify himself with any determinate class position or ideological commitment" (Jameson 1979, 17). Like the protofascist Dickens relies on the "fall-back" (17). Both feel profound repugnance for every organized form of contemporary life. Both yearn for a return to some idealized mode of origin. Both are, in Roger Griffin's term, "palingenetic," like an "archer who looks over his shoulder for guidance where to aim" (Griffin 1991, 36). But the fascist commits to action. Though he looks back, he acts forward. The protofascist, like Dickens, only looks, and draws, back.

Cities of the Dead convincingly argues that vital cultures, across the political spectrum, purchase continuity through those processes of surrogation described in our earlier discussion of theater. But there are also cultures, and psyches, which abhor surrogation, which refuse time, which repudiate the necessity of standing-in. A good term for both those psyches and those cultures is protofascist. Both turn their backs to time, and turn time back. Guided by a rearview mirror, these imaginations will not grow up, get on with it, adapt, look forward, accept change, remember by forgetting, see change as the cost of growth—all the attitudes that feed surrogation. We see then why, though Tennyson may be a fascist, the author of *In Memoriam* could never be called protofascist. Just as the author of *Peter Pan* could never be called anything but protofascist, dreaming like Dickens of the Never Land, where Permanently Lost Boys are Wanted, and where Wendy will ONLY keep house.

We find always proudly blazoned over every Dickens plot the imperative: Accept No Substitutes. Throughout his fiction, surrogation, constantly plotted, just as constantly fails. If you're lucky, the man who saves you is your biological grandfather, not just some kindly old man who can take your grandfather's place. If you're unlucky, you continually run into your cruel uncle who regularly attempts to arrange your sister's seduction. Or you are Recalled to Life only to find that it is, once again, your terror-driven life as the Bastille Prisoner. No one can take anyone's place in Dickens, and no place can replace the lost original. No one can change, and live. Thus, to use only the biggest examples, the Bleak House project does not work. John Jarndyce cannot recreate the ruined family around a different, kinder will, though he can replicate Bleak House South in Bleak House North. Mrs. Clennam as surrogate mother is Arthur's worst nightmare. Indeed, the kindest surrogate parent in the oeuvre, Magwitch, does no less harm than the most selfish, Miss Havisham. Of course, Sydney Carton can and does take Charles Darnay's place, on the scaffold. Which means that the price of successful surrogation is nothing less than death. It's all as it was, or not at all, originals or nothing.

It's this protofascist resistance to surrogation that frustrates any attempt to read *Rudge*—or any other Dickens fiction—as political. "Fascism," Žižik rightly claims, "combines organicist corporatism and the drive to ruthless modernization" (1999, 180). Dickens longs for the former, but loathes the latter, loathes it so throughly that he subverts any attempt by his characters to produce significant public change of any kind. Fascism trusts that the *arditi* well-led will bring about an ultimate, beneficial reshuffling of the public order. There Dickens balks. He can look back to the idealized image of a better past. But he cannot also look forward to that past's new and improved successor. Nor can he find, from any other vantage, a place that might generate a genuine public order. Thus, where fascism strives for the supremely efficient and the spanking new, protofascist *Rudge* fantasizes a return to the sentimental and the domestic.

The regime remains what is was at the start, the same bloodthirsty apparatus of imposition and repression. Hugh's final scene marks them as indelible. The bad fathers are gone, yes, but not the larger structures that enabled their domestic tyrannies. Instead, all the novel's sympathetic movements are retro. *Rudge* has only one goal for the future, to erase all difference and change. Thus the novel's final line insists that in 1840 Grip is still performing (738). As a result, it concludes as the most festive of Dickens's novels, on a par with *A Christmas Carol* (the major narrative in which Dickens comes closest to fully formed fascism). In town, the traitorous servants driven out, the locksmith's family is restored to connubial harmony. Ditto the rural Maypole, where, the perfidious father lobotomized, the young Willets are ever young, and ever reproductive of themselves—"more small Joes and small Dollys" (735)—never a Willy or a Sam. No future, no change, only the continuous reproduction of the now sanitized, forever undisturbed past. It's only the Catholic family, which has been "disappeared." Which perhaps says more about the novel's deepest links to the Gordon project than anything else I might point to.

Paradoxically, the very limitation which makes his politics nugatory renders Dickens also a towering social novelist, the hidden bonus, as it were, to his incapacity. Dickens can enter so graphically the experience of the marginal, the spurned, the impotent and impoverished, because that is where, throughout his life, despite his formidable success, Dickens dwells. He is forced to dwell there because he can imagine from that anguish no form of timely release. He is acutely fascinated by the state and its harsh apparatus: here Kings' Bench and the Fleet; later Quarantine, Chancery, Circumlocution, the Guillotine. And he is without equal in his commitment to, and skill at, showing how these apparatus interconnect, and undermine, widely diverse individual lives. But he constantly and irrationally interrupts those connections to displace them in favor of jejune fantasies of inviolable isolation. For Dickens the world, anonymous, dispersed, arcane, contains no possibilities for an authentic history which the subject might open for the self, or which the congregation of subjects might open for both community and individual. The ungrounded changing world is simply too risky for the always fragile

Dickensian subject, or for a collective project that depends on time. Insertion into or imposition of the self onto the world must always therefore cost the self whatever hope it might claim for an authentic history. The Riots destroy Hugh and nullify Gordon, just as later the French Revolution will consume the idealized figure of Carton. No Dickensian can ever become, in Monroe Engel's words, "safer than he was."

* * *

It is urgent that we notch precisely the implications of a novel like *Rudge*. Outside the United States, fascism—often tied to religious fundamentalism—continues to rise, in Europe, Africa, Asia, and in South America. Inside the United States protofascism has become virtually the hallmark of mainstream culture. In *Rudge*, writing history, Dickens neither *restores* nor *revives*. Those terms may help us approach the novel, but they cannot account for it. Dickens does not bring the past into the present. Nor does he mark the past as the present's other. He retires from the present into a past that never was. What's un-"safe," then, and deeply unsettling, are not Dickens's politics but the fact that he has none. He cannot restore. He cannot revive. He can only retreat. And what could be less "safe," for us all, than that?

I am happy to acknowledge the shaping debt this paper owes to the members of the Faculty Seminar on *Barnaby Rudge* at The Dickens Project, August 1999 (University of California at Santa Cruz).

WORKS CITED

Dickens, Charles. *Barnaby Rudge* [1841]. Edited with an Introduction by Gordon Spence. London: Penguin, 1973.

Eatwell, Roger. *Fascism A History*. London: Chatto & Windus, 1995.

Engel, Monroe. "The Politics of Dickens' Novels." *PMLA* 71 (1956): 945–74.

Glavin, John. *After Dickens: Reading, Adaptation & Performance*. Cambridge: Cambridge UP, 1999.

Griffin, Roger. *The Nature of Fascism*. New York: St. Martin's, 1991.

Jameson, Fredric. *Fables of Aggression: Wyndham Lewis, the Modernist as Fascist*. Berkeley: California UP, 1979.

Lamb, Richard. *Mussolini and the British*. London: John Murray, 1997

Mosse, George L. *The Fascist Revolution: Toward A General Theory of Fascism*. New York: Howard Fertig, 1999.

Murphy, Kevin D. *Memory and Modernity: Viollet-le-Duc at Vézelay*. University Park: Pennsylvania State UP, 2000.

Oakeshott, Michael. *Rationalism in Politics and Other Essays*. Indianapolis: Liberty Fund, 1991.

Ozouf, Mona. *Festivals of the French Revolution*. Translated by Alan Sheridan. Cambridge: Harvard UP, 1988.

Pinkus, Karen. *Bodily Regimes: Italian Advertising under Fascism*. Minneapolis: Minnesota UP, 1995.

Roach, Joseph. *Cities of the Dead: Circum-Atlantic Performance*. New York: Columbia UP, 1996.

Roberts, Jennifer Tolbert. *Athens On Trial: The Antidemocratic Tradition in Western Thought*. Princeton: Princeton UP, 1994.

Rousseau, Jean-Jacques. *The Government of Poland* [1772]. Translated with an Introduction by Willmoore Kendall. Indianapolis: Bobbs-Merrill, 1972.

Sontag, Susan. *Under the Sign of Saturn*. New York: Farrar Straus Giroux, 1980.

Spackman, Barbara. *Fascist Virilities: Rhetoric, Ideology, and Social Fantasy in Italy*. Minneapolis: Minnesota UP, 1996.

Žižik, Slavoj. *The Ticklish Subject: The Absent Centre of Political Ontology*. London: Verso. 1999.

Demons on the Rooftops, Gypsies in the Streets: The "Secret Intelligence" of *Dombey and Son*

Michelle Mancini

*An unusual perspective on Dickens's attitudes towards omniscience re-
sults from tracing through the "secret intelligence" that drives the plot
of* Dombey and Son. *On the surface, the novel links intelligence to new
technologies: the entrepreneurial speculations of the villainous Carker
and the rapidly expanding network of London's new railways. However,
another circuit for information gathering and purveying is created
through the wanderings of a very different character: the grotesque
beggar and rag-and-bone seller Good Mrs. Brown, whose characterization both hearkens back to fairy-tale conventions of the wicked witch
and anticipates an increasing interest in documenting the lives of London's street people. Her inexplicable speed and mobility, along with
her keen vision, make her a figure of narratorial omniscience, but one
whose greed and disfigurement trouble the Dickensian narrator's expressed hopes that greater knowledge may lead to increased Christian
charity. Dickens's concern with demonic observers and canny wanderers surfaces again in an 1854 article in* Household Words, *"A Tour
in Bohemia." Together with* Dombey and Son, *this essay hints at a
conjunction of artistic and sociological anxieties, as society's almost
invisible aliens come to seem both the model for Dickens's vision and
the one object capable of eluding it.*

In one of the most famous and most quoted passages from *Dombey and Son*, Dickens's narrator invokes what is often interpreted as the spirit of omniscient–or semi-omniscient—narration:

> Oh for a good spirit who would take the house-tops off, with a more potent and benignant hand than the lame demon in the tale, and show a Christian people what dark shapes issue from amidst their homes, to swell the retinue of the Destroying Angel as he moves forth among them! . . . Bright and blest the morning that should rise on such a night: for men, delayed no more by stumbling-blocks of their own making, which are but specks of dust upon the path between them and eternity, would then apply themselves, like creatures of one common origin, owning one duty to the Father of one family, and tending to one common end, to make the world a better place!   (620)

In the 1840s and early 1850s, Dickens returned again and again to the "lame demon in the tale," the title character and over-arching conceit of a now obscure eighteenth-century French novel and satire, Alain René Le Sage's *Le Diable Boiteux*. In this satire, a Spanish aristocrat liberates Asmodeus, the lame demon of the title, from the bottle where he has been imprisoned by a powerful magician. Asmodeus then entertains his liberator by lifting the roofs off various Madrid houses and using the revealed vices and follies as starting point for a series of satirical sketches. As a sort of prototype of the nineteenth-century flâneur, the figure has obvious attractions for Dickens, whose urban wanderings fuel his craft from *Sketches by Boz* on. But the devil's differences from the flâneur—vertical elevation and satirical detachment, rather than horizontal penetration and at least intermittent if ironic sympathy—make the figure an ambiguous role model for Dickens's own artistic practice.

Indeed, in its earlier appearance in *American Notes for General Circulation*, Le Sage's demon is a figure for Dickens's foe, the lurid American press:

> [F]ifty newspapers [are a kind of] amusement . . . dealing in round abuse and blackguard names; pulling off the roofs of private houses, as the Halting Devil did in Spain; pimping and pandering for all degrees of vicious taste, and gorging with coined lies the most voracious maw; imputing to every man in public life the coarsest and the vilest motives; scaring away from the stabbed and prostrate body-politic, every Samaritan of clear conscience and good deeds; and setting on, with yell and whistle and the clapping of foul hands, the vilest vermin and worst birds of prey.   (136)

Here the spirit is less satirist than pornographer, hawking falsehoods ("coined lies") as well as base facts. Questions of truth aside, this passage certainly makes clear the need for the "more benignant hand" called for in *Dombey and Son*. But the force of the language and imagery here in *American Notes* may well leave the reader wondering why Dickens craves a hand that is also "more potent."

Despite the frequency with which critics of all stripes and vintages quote the "oh for a good spirit" passage, relatively few have considered it in any detail. In an essay discussing structural and thematic similarities between Dickens's novel and *The House of the Seven Gables*, Jonathan Arac acknowledges early uses of the figure as embodying a "fantasy of detached, sadistic omniscience," abjured by both Hawthorne and Dickens. But in claiming that in *Bleak House* Dickens "does begin fully to realize the program of the good spirit," Arac minimizes the extent to which even after *Bleak House* the spirit's moral ambiguity continued to trouble Dickens (20–21). Audrey Jaffe helpfully enhances her discussion of the Asmodean spirit of omniscience by showing us Dickens proposing "a certain SHADOW, which may go into any place . . . loom[ing] as a fanciful thing over London" (15) as the unifying device for *Household Words*. But when she has the demon spend all his time "flying over rooftops" and embodying the "unmarked figure of the narrator," she imposes a view of omniscience very different from that suggested by Asmodeus's body (14–15). For what neither Arac nor Jaffe stop to consider are the implications of the stops built into Asmodeus as the "Halting Devil," a "lame demon," what various eighteenth-century English translations and continuations called "The Devil with Two Sticks."

To ask why the demon should be lame is to echo the words of the devil's original liberator, Don Cleofas. Confronted with a goat-legged demon, less than three feet tall, supported on crutches, a creature of yellow and black skin and small eyes like burning coals, Cleofas admits surprise at the generally unprepossessing appearance of this demon—who after all doubles as a mischievous cupid—but asks only one question: "*pourquois vous êtes boiteux?*" (31) Asmodeus's answer makes clear that *boiteux* is not just one physical trait among others but his identifying feature, albeit one resulting from historical accident rather than anything inherent or congenital. Contending with Pilladorc, the "demon of (self)interest," for the soul of a business man, Asmodeus is hurtled from mid-air onto the ground, just as Jupiter had thrown Vulcan—that other famous lamed divinity (31–32). And thus "my comrades named me *le diable boiteux*, a *sobriquet* that has lasted a long time" (32).

Nevertheless, Asmodeus makes haste to assure Cleofas that being *boiteux* is less a matter of being disabled than of being differently abled: "all crippled (*tout estropié*) as I am, I still set a good pace" (32). Ordering Cleofas to take the hem of his cloak, Asmodeus "split the air like an arrow violently released and perched on the spire of San Salvador" (34). Each time the pair changes locations, the movement occurs with the same invisible instantaneity. As Cleofas agrees politely, Asmodeus's speed proves the "falsity" of common report: far from a "*rude voiture*," "*le voiture du diable*" is instead "*très douce*" and so "*diligent*" that one doesn't have time to be bored on the way (34). The same ease applies to the demon's most characteristic action: he claims that his "diabolic power" enables him "to lift the roofs of houses," and indeed, "he simply extended his right arm and all the roofs were lifted" (34). But this "agility" and dexterity cannot precisely undo the force of the *boiteux*. Thus though it is true that Asmodeus "takes" (*emporta*) Cleofas from rooftop to rooftop, it is not precisely true that he is capable of spending time flying over the city; even more unequivocally, if "*le diable boiteux*" exemplifies a narrator, that narrator can hardly remain unmarked.

Although Asmodeus appears in *Dombey and Son* only within that single passage of wistful narratorial vision, his marks have far greater currency. Asmodeus's association with Vulcan and with a diabolical power of motion and revelation create clear links between him and the quasi-diabolical power of the railroads in *Dombey and Son*. Thus, as Murray Baumgarten has pointed out, it should come as no surprise that the very function Dickens imagines for the good spirit has already been performed by the trains, which offer a new access to and perspective on previously unknown neighborhoods (72), so that "through the *battered roofs* and *broken windows*, wretched rooms are seen . . . want and fever in many wretched shapes" (276). But the train cannot encompass all of Asmodeus's functions or characteristics: as a panderer prey-ing on lust, as a small and repulsive body, as a creature whose movements escape the eye and require no track, Asmodeus finds his match in one of the novel's minor characters, the primitive and sinister Good Mrs. Brown. She is like him a creature marked by "yellow skin" (73, 370); she has "lean" (75) and "shrivelled" (606, 690) arms, "withered hand[s]" (470), a "twisted figure" (700), and a "hobbling" (70), "limping" (473) pace, but these weak-nesses cannot undo the power of her grasp or her inexplicable mobility; most of all, she has an infernal power of vision: her eyes are variously described as "red-rim[med]" (70), "sharp" (693), "ferret eyes with their keen old wintry gaze" (702). It is her daughter Alice's eyes that most consistently "kindl[e]" (691), blaze, and burn, but though in this respect she surpasses her mother, she nevertheless clearly takes after her: though Alice's "glance was brighter than her mother's, and the fire that shone in it was fiercer," nevertheless, a few lines later, "the glance of each [was] shining in the gloom of the feebly-lighted room" (705). Following the lead provided by these physical resemblances should provide some new perspectives on the much contemplated problem of narrative omniscience. Rather than seeing only those parts of the Asmodeus precedent which confirm our preconceptions of Dickens's view of omniscience, I hope to show just how these various marks—the monstrous and infernal on the one hand; the incapacitated, abject, and needy on the other—inflect Dickens's fantasies and fears about observa-tion and narration.[1]

More specifically, I hope to show that the figure of Asmodeus in his particu-larity as demon, as lame, and as rooftop lifter, presides over what the novel presents as a tacit concurrence between Good Mrs. Brown and the railroad as systems of information and of motive force within the novel.[2] As spy, schemer, and plotter, Good Mrs. Brown is more than just the primitive and degraded double of the novel's far more public villain, the sinister Carker, whose financial and sexual machinations undo the house of Dombey and Son—in both its commercial and its domestic sense—from the inside out. Like any agent of surveillance, Good Mrs. Brown is able to ferret out secrets because she herself eludes observation, but the novel attributes her obscurity and near invisibility not to any sort of transcendent other-worldliness (a demon over the rooftops) but to an immanence within a world conceived in the most degraded and material terms. It is no accident that the character most closely connected with knowledge will also be most closely connected with the base facts of material existence; more importantly, it is no accident that Dickens cannot avoid an analogy that links the material with the incapable, the lame: to subject omniscience to figuration is to figure it as lame.

It is in the figure of Good Mrs. Brown that Dickens ties together the novel's two thematic registers: the old world of fairy tale and romance and the new world of trains, information, and capitalism. That these two registers are tied together, I argue, has implications for our understanding of two different strains of literary criticism: on the one hand, a Foucaldian genealogy of the novel as force of surveillance and discipline, and on the other, a Deleuzian celebration of the liberatory force of the nomadic as a new way of thinking and living with—and within—technology. As Miller supplements Flaubert's famous linkage of the author and God ("l'auteur, dans son oeuvre, doit être comme Dieu dans l'univers, présent partout et visible nulle part") with a reminder of the presence of that other "unseen over-seer," the police (24), so I too must push the envelope of surveillance to admit the demonic and the vagabond. But whereas Miller's all-encompassing view of surveillance easily drafts the outright criminal into its web, the very different diffuse illicitness of the demonic and vagabond makes them less easily assimilable to the concept of surveillance. Instead, they seem capable of unleashing a proto-Deleuzian form of resistance to systematic control: they thus elude the novel's system of knowledge even as they help to constitute it.

But just as Deleuze can help us to appreciate some of the mysterious force circulating around the figure of Good Mrs. Brown, attending to Good Mrs. Brown can also alert us to a rather disturbing genealogy of Deleuzian nomadology. Although critics have paid little attention to Good Mrs. Brown's role as a gypsy, a "wanderer about the country" (550),[3] Dickens's characterization of her as such does bring the novel into contact with a wide-ranging nineteenth-century fascination with gypsiness, a fascination that intermittently prefigures Deleuze's science of nomadology.

Finally, however, more than the claims of Miller or of Deleuze, it is the ambiguities and paradoxes of Asmodeus that most illuminate Dickens's treatment of Good Mrs. Brown. For just as I will argue that the railroad is ultimately more important to Dickens as a way of being within space than as a way of moving through it, so I will suggest that the real force of Good Mrs. Brown's nomadism is as a form of habitation rather than of travel. "Halting"—the ability to stop—is more important than the power to move; lameness can be glossed as a kind of staying power. Good Mrs. Brown stays behind to pick up what's left behind, and the novel's real secret intelligence is that knowledge—and its own omniscient narration—is largely a matter of picking up scraps. Herself something of a scrap from the more episodic and picaresque novels Dickens wrote in the thirties and forties, Good Mrs. Brown is seemingly ill-adapted for the more tightly plotted and psychologically introspective *Dombey and Son*. But recognizing the way *Dombey and Son* not only includes her but even makes her a kind of figure for authorial omniscience can precipitate the larger recognition that sopistication of narrative technique cannot eradicate a certain sordidness of basic narrative approach and material: like the blackmailing gypsy extortionist, the author too makes his living out of material that in other hands would have no value and endure only as trash.

Good Mrs. Brown's narrative role thus oscillates between eluding Dickens's practice and mirroring it, but in either of these two modes it troubles that practice: in the first case by disabling it, in the second by degrading it. The only solution the novel can offer is a far cry from the benevolent Christian vision called for in Dickens's explicit invocation of Asmodeus; it is that in the dark world of *Dombey and Son* degradation and elusiveness can always, paradoxically, find a place for themselves.

Proximity is only the most clearly demonstrated of the grounds for association between Good Mrs. Brown and the railroad. Of the four virtuoso passages of descriptions of the railroad (52–53, 184–85, 235–37, 651–53), three run smack against descriptions of Good Mrs. Brown and her various enterprises of information gathering and deployment; two, crucially, are not about the motion of trains at all but about the groundwork that must be laid before the train can begin to move and that remains even in the train's absence. While the usual theorists of technology and information tend to link these two concepts through a nexus of speed, this association with an old wandering woman on the one hand and with a landscape on the other suggests a more complex relation, lame but still powerful.[4]

At the conclusion of one of those four passages, the trains seem to be the entities in the know in *Dombey and Son*.

Night and day, the conquering engines rumbled at their distant work, or, advancing smoothly to their journey's end, and gliding like tame dragons into the allotted corners grooved out to the inch for their reception, stood bubbling and trembling there, making the walls quake, as if they were dilating with the *secret knowledge* of great powers yet unsuspected in them, and strong purposes not yet achieved.   (217–18, emphasis added)

Dickens's mythographic depiction of the trains in *Dombey and Son* exemplifies the excited ambivalence visible everywhere in contemporary discussions of the railroad phenomenon. On the one hand, confident predictions about the providential course of progress; on the other, turmoil about financial panics and horror at gruesome accidents, which drove home the trains' power to undo not only human dreams but human bodies. This excited ambivalence is familiar background to critical discussions of *Dombey and Son*, but can nevertheless appear in a new and startling light when considered in terms of a juxtaposition of Dickens and Deleuze. For the railroad, with its gridlike assault upon the pre-existing landscape, its neat geometry of two parallel tracks intersected at regular intervals by perpendicular ties, exemplifies with surprising ease the Deleuzian notion of striated space: the space that results from the state's process of territorialization, its translation of space into an archive of knowledge. And yet, in their liability to accidents, trains represent the way striation itself can get derailed, a demonstration of the claim Deleuze makes in a summation that is also a call to action: that the state apparatus cannot achieve its territorializing goals

without its flows forging further ahead . . . escaping . . . tending to enter into [other] connections that delineate a new land . . . following lines of flight that are themselves connectable. . . . The undecidable is the germ and locus par excellence of [the] revolutionary. . . . Some people [see revolution as impossible under] the high technology of the world system of enslavement, but even, and especially, this machinic enslavement abounds in undecidable propositions and movements that, far from belonging to a domain of knowledge reserved for sworn specialists, provides so many weapons for [minorities, nomads, etc.].
                                                                 (472–73)

The more complicated things get, Deleuze would seem to suggest, the more potential for breakdown and the more opportunities for the (ir)regular folks on the ground. Good Mrs. Brown is the novel's character on the ground, and though both she and the train seem to be within the control of the novel's own state apparatus, enslaved within its system of information retrieval, she will in fact exceed her function within that system. This excess suggests a flow, a slow seepage into the undecidable.

Undecidable in exactly what way? One advantage of bringing Deleuze into the discussion is that he allows a change in emphasis from that brought about by too exclusive a reliance on contemporary commentators, who would seem to suggest that the burning question about the railroad was only of good or bad, improvement or destruction. Deleuze, with his idea of the nomadic as the revolutionary that both precedes and succeeds the territorial state, makes the question one of new or old, difference or repetition: an emphasis more in keeping with the novel's slighting of the question of the value of technological change in favor of an engagement with the experience of the complex of change and continuity. The novel suggests the problem of the persistence of the old within the new in a number of ways, of which the most important are its depiction of the railroad as a landscape of unceasing (unchanging) change and of Good Mrs. Brown as a conventional gypsy wanderer of unceasing habitation. What is most important for the purposes of my argument is the way that these two paradoxes (railroad as landscape and gypsy as home-dweller) are inextricable both from each other and from the way the novel refers to both as systems of knowledge diffusion.

For Good Mrs. Brown is the other entity besides the railroad most clearly put in the know in the novel. In the course of a few pages of one scene alone, when her daughter Alice has suddenly returned from ten years' punishment in Australia, the words "I know" come from her "industrious mouth" (73) eight times, as simple statements ("I know all about him" [472]), as boast ("I know more than you think," "I know more than he thinks" [472]) and as pronouncement mysteriously expansive even in its tautology ("I know what I know" [470, 472]). What she never claims but what the novel repeatedly demonstrates is that she knows more than she or it says. Such knowledge puts her beyond the novel's account and so makes her a figure very much to be reckoned with in thinking about knowledge and omniscience in Dickens.

Nevertheless she has in fact thus far been served rather badly by the substantial and impressive criticism accumulating on *Dombey and Son*. Her relative neglect may be explained by the way the criticism tends to gravitate around one of two poles, neither one of which she quite seems to fit: the public, masculine, modern pole of the train, commerce, Dombey and Son; the private, feminine, "old-fashioned" pole of Florence, nature, feeling. Some of the most thoughtful examples of recent criticism tend to consider exactly how the novel works to maintain these separate spheres, meditating on how it deals with the paradoxical declaration that "Dombey and Son should be a Daughter after all" (191). These studies speculate on what changes must be effected in the social order by the exchange of Florence for the dead Paul. Feminist critics concerned with the exchangeability or non-exchangeability of Florence are happy to take into account the commodification of Edith and her resulting self-alienation and to glance both at Edith's mother's role in perpetuating this story and at Alice Marwood's degraded version of Edith's story: degraded because the market in which Alice sells herself is not the marriage market. But if these critics discuss Good Mrs. Brown at all, they limit themselves either to her role as Florence's abductor or as Alice's mother. As someone who both has a story of her own and who learns, deploys, and manipulates the stories of others, Good Mrs. Brown is largely ignored.[5]

Eventually the reader learns that the relationship between Alice and Edith is not merely one of formal parallels. It is not enough that Edith's would-be seducer Carker actually "ruined" Alice, nor that Alice and Edith, both beautiful, proud women, each lament their mothers' acquisitive pride in and cultivation of their beauty. Ultimately their relation exists not because of their mothers' similarity, but in their fathers' kinship. Good Mrs. Brown makes the revelation to Carker's sister Harriet, nurse to Alice on her deathbed:

> My daughter has been turned away from, and cast out, but she could boast relationship to proud folks too, if she chose. Ah! To proud folks! There's relationship without your clergy and wedding rings—they may make it, but they can't break it—and my daughter's well lated. Show me Mrs. Dombey, and I'll show you Alice's first cousin . . . . Though I am old and ugly now . . . I was once as young as any! Ah! as pretty as many! I was a fresh country wench in my time, darling, and looked it, too. Down in the country, Mrs. Dombey's father and his brother were the gayest gentlemen and the best-liked that come a-visiting from London . . . they were as like . . . as you could see two brothers.
> (784)

Until this revelation, Alice's grudge against Carker had seemed to have pride of place as motive force for many of the novel's events. Only at this late moment does the novel acknowledge Good Mrs. Brown's envious grudge against Ediths mother and Edith herself, the grudge of the seduced mother of the bastard against the properly married mother of the legitimate child.

Although this history may place Good Mrs. Brown at the primary moment of the novel's *fabula*, I would not want to claim that it places her at the novel's center. Indeed, some readers might say that by placing her at the center of coincidental connection—the artificial trappings of the novel's plot rather than the organic unity of its vision—this history in fact marginalizes her.[6] Nor would such readers see Good Mrs. Brown's survival as indication of any significant power of persistence; for them, Dickens does not let Good Mrs. Brown survive but rather forgets to have her die. Against this I will insist that, in fact, Good Mrs. Brown is made to embody the force of survival again and again and in various somewhat sinister ways.[7]

But no matter how much we marginalize Mrs. Brown's story of victimization and desire for revenge—her motivation—there remains the fact of her agency in providing the information that provides motivating force for the novel's most significant events. Interestingly, what she knows from the time before that narrated within the novel—that both Edith and Carker have shameful associations with Alice—informs her first few mysterious threats

of blackmail, but, kept secret until near the end, ultimately is far less significant than what she learns and reveals within the novel's own time frame.[8]
Thus her opportunistic observation precipitates both Florence's introduction
to Walter and Dombey's pursuit of Carker; her knowledge seems an agent
of the novel's justice, ensuring the happy marriage of the heroine and the
frightful death of the villain, although this last, of course, only with the
assistance of the train.

As a figure who crosses worlds and conveys information back and forth
among characters, who helps characters to know what they need to know
while at the same time enhancing the general atmosphere of mystery, Good
Mrs. Brown has her counterparts elsewhere in the Dickens canon and the
novel more generally—almost all of them minor characters who have heretofore largely escaped the critical gaze. In charting knowledge in Dickens's
novels, critics have tended to focus on the opposition between heroes and
heroines and villains: hero types who patiently move within a muddle until
the right—identity, partner, fate—comes clear in the end; villains who watch,
scheme, plot, but are somehow bested in the end. The difference between
innocence and guilt emerges clearly here, but such exclusive focus on these
extremes tends to obscure the strangest fact of all: the rarity of direct confrontation between innocent ignorance and evil knowingness. Curiously incurious,
the protagonist depends for ultimate clarification on a whole host of minor,
morally ambiguous and psychologically undeveloped characters, to whom is
delegated—or rather relegated—the capacity and responsibility to investigate.
The investigation itself takes place within a textually subterranean world of
eccentric and unmappable trajectories, coming at times asymptotically close
to the hero or heroine's but without touching it. To say that this is Dickens's
pattern does nothing to address why it should be—a question that I would
suggest involves lowering our sights and focusing on these characters.[9]

This is especially so in *Dombey and Son*, which places particular pressure
on these issues by explicitly thematizing them, both in Carker's entrepreneurial speculations[10] and in the depiction of the new rail lines as new conduits
of knowledge.[11] It is in this context that what is artificial and mechanical in
Good Mrs. Brown's plot function deserves to be rescued from the critical
obscurity it has suffered, a critical obscurity that is the lamentable consequence of the obscurity with which she operates. The source of her knowledge—and also of her livelihood—may be accounted for not by any grand
investigatory endeavors, but merely by the fact that she has "tramped about,"
"hung about," and "watched" (470). Nevertheless, for critics not to watch
and hang about with her is to miss the chance of seeing into the way Dickens
imagines a real world correlative for his own narrative practice.

Indeed, again and again, in both the way she gains her knowledge and
what she gains from it, Good Mrs. Brown wanders outside the terrain charted

and the events plotted by the novel.[12] As we will see, the information most crucial to the plot—and most remunerative to Good Mrs. Brown—is gained by her only because of her ability to trade on preexisting knowledge far outside the novel's purview. Moreover, what she does with that knowledge takes her even further beyond the novel's comprehension. Selling both silence (blackmail) and information for money is of a piece with all the other ways Good Mrs. Brown is constantly grasping after money, whether begging, pleading, or threatening. These may seem to make her needy and weak, but since the novel, like Mr. Dombey himself, can never really answer the innocent child's question, "Papa, What's money?" (93), the desire for money is as open-ended and undefined as everything else about Good Mrs. Brown.

Nevertheless, to the extent that it makes her a beggar, her relation to money constitutes one of a set of elements that brings the novel close to identifying Good Mrs. Brown's sociological status, an identification it also always backs away from. Although her knowledge lets her operate in the modern world of information and speed, it seems drawn from her apparently timeless existence as a kind of gypsy wanderer. As a gypsy-like crone, Good Mrs. Brown functions as a figure of conventional and familiar mystery. Both the narrator and her various interlocutors call her *hag* and *witch* time and again, and she performs both those offices typically assigned the gypsy crone: stealing children and telling fortunes. When Walter rescues young Florence following her misadventures with Good Mrs. Brown, the event provides the first chapter of Walter's fantastically romantic rags-to-riches, orphan-to-father narrative. Likewise, when Edith's mother Mrs. Skewton is told that Carker "spar[ed Edith] some annoyance from an importunate beggar," her willful romanticizing seems to allow her to intuit that more than just begging had been at issue, so that in her view there had taken place "one of the most enchanting coincidences . . . [with] such an obvious destiny in it" (372).

Although the narrator clearly distances himself from Mrs. Skewton's girlish enthusiasm, the staging of the encounter between Edith, Carker, and Good Mrs. Brown contains an undeniably strange set of coincidences. For at one and the same time it presents Good Mrs. Brown as a figure for the omniscient narrator and as almost unknowable sociological and biological type. The first thing that strikes the reader about the scene is the force with which it repeatedly violates characters' privacy: two characters, each of whom is confident of solitude or at least of not being observed, turn out not only to be in each other's presence but also within the observation and indeed the knowledge of a third character: "a withered and very ugly old woman" who "scrambled up from the ground—out of it, it almost appeared—and stood in the way" (370). The presence of both Carker and Edith may be surprising, but it is not inexplicable: the reader knows where they came from and where they're going. But in her inexplicable and indeed unnamed appearance, Good Mrs.

Brown takes on the most salient properties that Jaffe, following Shlomith Rimmon-Kenan, attributes to the Dickensian omniscient narrator: "a power and mobility that characters do not possess," a presence "in locations where characters are supposed to be unaccompanied" (9). True, here Good Mrs. Brown does not get behind any locked doors, but as the scene shifts from simple fortune telling to threatened blackmail ("What! You won't give me nothing to tell your fortune, pretty lady? How much will you give me *not* to tell it, then?" [370]), Good Mrs. Brown claims a knowledge that at least seems to know no limits.

The apparent limitlessness of her knowledge is reinforced by her own resistance to any easy description or naming by the Dickensian narrator himself. Not only does she appear out of nowhere—out of the ground—she seems to remain even when she must be gone: Carker's last glimpse is of her holding her ground; she points forward mysteriously and remains a haunting presence in Carker's mind. Moreover, her identity and activity both involve Dickens in a fevered rush of rhetoric: "A withered and very ugly old woman, dressed not so much like a gipsey as like any of that medley race of vagabonds who tramp about the country, begging, and stealing, and tinkering, and weaving rushes, by turns, or all together" (370). Dickens must be seen to be equivocating here: he doesn't exactly deny that Good Mrs. Brown is a gypsy, but does seem to insist that if she is one, she is so without any of the melodramatic and oriental conventions that in 1846 were already disparaged as unrealistic and unworthy of serious artistic practise. But if Dickens purports to offer us a real life vagrant and vagabond as opposed to a conventionally imagined gypsy, in fact, his multiplicity is also hard to accommodate within the real world: what would it mean, for instance, for a vagabond to be begging, stealing, tinkering, and weaving rushes *all together*? To the extent that it is a grotesque image, it is entirely in keeping with his other and even more mysterious description of Good Mrs. Brown from this scene:

> Munching like that sailor's wife of yore, who had chestnuts in her lap, and scowling like the witch who asked for some in vain, the old woman picked the shilling up, and going backwards, like a crab, or like a heap of crabs: for her alternately expanding and contracting hands might have represented two of that species, and her creeping face, some half a dozen more: crouched on the veinous root of an old tree, pulled out a short black pipe from within the crown of her bonnet, lighted it with a match, and smoked in silence, looking fixedly at her questioner.   (370–71)

When the omniscient narrator is driven to such a heap of analogies and similes, the reader cannot help but contemplate the limits of that omniscience.

The proliferation of these images cannot obliterate the contemporary reader's likely initial impression of Good Mrs. Brown: that of the mysterious, sometimes cajoling, other times threatening gypsy crone. A stock figure of melodrama and of cheap novels[13], the gypsy crone also made an appearance in more respectable reading. In *The Zincali*, George Borrow, author of the phenomenally successful *The Bible in Spain* and eventually nineteenth-century Britain's best-known writer about gypsies, presented the reading public with the unforgettable one-eyed sibyl Pepa; earlier, John Galt had made the eponymous hero of *Sir Andrew Wylie of That Ilk* dependent on a crafty but nameless old gypsy woman for many of his most celebrated accomplishments. Looming over both Pepa and Galt's crone was the gypsy nineteenth-century commentators wanted to believe was the grandmother of them all, the famous Meg Merrilies of Scott's *Guy Mannering*, who untangles the mystery of the lost heir's identity and then engineers his reinstatement.[14] All these crones are as canny as they are uncanny: Pepa is a creature of elaborate frauds as well as of eloquent curses, and Galt's old gypsy vies for consideration as the leading character in an interpolated plot that Gordon calls "one of the earliest examples in English of the murder-and-detection genre" (47). Earliest but largely ignored, raising what may seem a rather unexpected and unreasonable question: why have authors and critics alike been so reluctant to acknowledge the elderly gypsy female as a prototype of the alienated and morally dubious (hard-boiled?) detective? The question may seem at best tangential to my main line of inquiry, but in fact it offers new perspective on the question of narrative knowledge.

The answer is obvious but inadequate: in fictions and in journalistic accounts both, gypsies were—and are—much more liable to be seen as perpetrators of crime than as leaders in its detection. In fact, however, accounts of such crimes usually hint at the criminals' power to *detect* their victims' weakness, usually credulity. That Dickens as much as modern-day critics could fail to fathom the possibilities or problems of gypsy knowledge emerges from a brief article he published in *The Examiner* on April 29, 1848, soon after the release of the very last monthly number of *Dombey and Son*. As "an apt illustration of the shortcomings and inefficiency of what is called 'education' for the general people," Dickens offers an account recently "presented in the newspapers." The quoted account begins "Alice Lee, a pretty-looking young gipsy, with a child in her arms, was charged with fortune-telling" (98). But the subject of that sentence is not the object of Dickens's concern, which emerges only as the newspaper account switches from the passive position of being charged to the active one of accusing and testifying: "Susan Grant, a simple-looking young woman, about 24 years of age, stated that the prisoner came, on the 7th of February last, to her master's house in Ladbroke Square, and after a little conversation offered to read her fortune" (98). The narrative of repeated and escalating demands on Alice Lee's part—for a half-crown, for first one sovereign then for another, for all Susan

Grant's best clothes, all necessary for "properly ruling the planets"—emphasizes Susan Grant's passivity, victimization—"credulity" in the magistrate's terms. The court, however, gives her the active position, "complainant" and "witness," even though in fact Grant is testifying to her failure to witness—to see the imposition being perpetuated—and to complain—to object, to refuse (98).

Dickens's concern in telling the story is to point to the irony of the "elicited" fact that "the complainant had been educated at the Kensington National School": "As if any kind of instruction possessing the faintest claim to that designation [educated] in its lowest and most limited acceptance, could have left the complainant in the belief that a pretty-looking young gipsy with a child in her arms, could 'rule the planets' with a half-crown, a sovereign, two gowns, a shawl, and several new articles of body linen!" (98) In Dickens's admittedly ironic narrative, that belief already existed before the fateful day when, in his view, the young gypsy girl appeared exactly as she appeared in the court: it is a belief that survives because of the negligence of the National Schools rather than one that appears because of the active and canny cultivation by the gypsy girl—whose own education is utterly beside the point. In telling this bald narrative, Dickens himself fails to witness and to complain, fails to see all that the court and newspaper accounts leave untold. Far from trying to fathom how Alice insinuates herself into Susan's confidence, how she develops a penetrating insight into the precise points of her credulity, Dickens accepts the surface tale as the truth and so remains at the threshold: crucially "at her master's house in Ladbroke Square" and not within that house. For indeed, as countless other narratives of gypsy depredation make clear, the real threat offered by gypsy fortune tellers getting into the confidence of the servants was that they would thereby get into the master's house, that they would get not just the servant's best gown but various items not in fact the servant's to give away.

Why the discomfort with the full acknowledgment of the itinerant gypsy as an Asmodean figure and an authorial one? Two things I think: on the one hand, the threat posed by such real life figures to the sanctity of the author's home; on the other, the threat posed by the clichéd conventionality of such figures to the originality of the author's work. Gypsies are both not fictional enough and too fictional—or in Asmodean terms both too powerful and too lame.

The story of Alice Lee may seem to take us a long way from Good Mrs. Brown, who, despite her ability to keep up with the trains, never does seem to get inside any houses but her own.[15] Indeed the fact that she has a house at all takes her beyond the conventional image of gypsies and toward the novel's other identification of her, as a rag-and-bone seller. But in her house as much as in her wandering she will be an exception to the novel's general tendency to keep characters in place and within view. She will be an exception, paradoxically, because she will stay in that place too long. Moreover, she will show that too many other things also stay in place and so will supplement motion with stasis as part of the novel's secret system of knowledge collection and purveyance.

But though in this final section I want to focus on the rags and bones, the scraps of secret intelligence, I do not want to lose the sense of Good Mrs. Brown as gypsy, as nomad. For this ability to penetrate the homes of others is only half the story of gypsy wanderers; the other half is the ability to be at home even where conditions seem not to allow it.[16] Good Mrs. Brown's ability to find accommodation where and when none would seem to be possible is attested to both by the location of her home and its strange primitive permanence, permanence that would seem to fly in the face of the constant and chaotic change London was experiencing in the thirties and forties: as the *Dublin Evening Post* described it in 1840, London is "neither new nor old" but rather "a sort of Provisional City, a multitudinous congregation of houses that are constantly in a state of transition of being run up or run down." Within this simultaneous tearing down and rising up appears yet another of Good Mrs. Brown's ways of living and of the novel's playing with the idea of a lame demon above rooftops.

It is via Florence's abduction that the reader first encounters both Good Mrs. Brown and her home. The event represents the culmination of a series of steps away from the cold and ordered tyranny of the Dombey residence into a livelier and more chaotic London. Dickens's description of this chaos unfolds in three parts. First comes a lengthy catalogue of the many effects of a "great earthquake" in which the language replicates the excess and chaos of the scene:

> Houses were knocked down; streets broken through and stopped . . . enormous heaps of earth and clay thrown up . . . bridges led nowhere . . . temporary wooden houses [stood] in the most unlikely situations; carcases of ragged tenements and fragments of unfinished walls and arches . . . wildly mingled out of their places . . . unintelligible as any dream. Hot springs and fiery eruptions. . . . Boiling water hissed and heaved within dilapidated walls; whence, also, the glare and roar of flames came issuing forth; and mounds of ashes blocked up rights of way, [all] wholly changed.   (65)

Next comes the succinct real explanation: "In short, the yet unfinished and unopened Railroad was in progress; and, from the very core of all this dire disorder, trailed smoothly away, upon its mighty course of civilisation and improvement." The language is clear and to the point, although the point is less a statement of fact than a formulation of ideology, more or less ironically inflected by Dickens. But the description is not complete until Dickens also

catalogues the chaos that is index not of the railroad's progress but of resistance to it:

> But as yet, the neighborhood was shy to own the Railroad. One or two bold
> speculators had projected streets; and one had built a little, but had stopped
> among the mud and ashes to consider farther or it. . . . The general belief was
> very slow. There were frowzy fields, and cow-houses, and dunghills, and dust
> heaps, and ditches, and gardens, and summer-houses, and carpet-beating
> grounds, at the very door of the Railway. Little tumuli of oyster shells in the
> oyster season, and of lobster shells in the lobster season, and of broken crockery
> and faded cabbage leaves in all seasons, encroached upon its high places. Posts,
> and rails, and old cautions to trespasses, and backs of mean houses, and patches
> of wretched vegetation stared it out of countenance. Nothing was the better for
> it, or thought of being so. If the miserable waste ground lying near it could
> have laughed, it would have laughed it to scorn, like many of the miserable
> neighbors.   (65–66)

Change writ large in the "earthquake rent" landscape of the first passage
seems to be (re)written as lack of change, writ small, in the shyness of the
neighborhood to own the landscape. Note the number of repeated words and
phrases and images between the two. Part of this similarity is evoked by a
mere fact of linguistic coincidence: that *waste* is both a state of emptiness
prior to cultivation and a state of desolation subsequent to it. For obvious
reasons, the first meaning has temporal priority in England and a vast advantage in frequency of use; but in the wake of vast industrialization, the posterior
sense of waste begins to gain ground on its anterior rival.

Dickens never specifically activates this double sense of waste anywhere
within the impressionistic confusion of temporalities, but he does exploit the
potential of another phrase: "the carcases of tenements," which reappears in
the description of the same neighborhood five years later, when the railway
has been completed. At first, Dickens seems to have tidied everything up:
"Bridges that [had before] led to nothing [now] led to villas, gardens,
churches, healthy public walks. The carcasses of houses, and beginning of
new thoroughfares, had started off upon the lines at steam's own speed, and
shot away into the country in a monster train" (217–18) Given emphasis by
its position at the end of another long and convoluted description, *carcasses*,
with their connotation of death, seem a blight on a landscape of resplendent
glory. Knowing that *carcass* could refer to both the ruins of buildings, as
half-complete destruction, and the framework or scaffolding of a building,
half-complete construction, does little to undo that far more fundamental
sense of mortality, decay, decomposition. Especially when we recall that the
novel has only returned to what was once Staggs's Gardens because the dying
Paul wants to see the nurse of his infancy, we are unlikely to be able to
ignore the troubling implications of these repeated carcases. Houses without

roofs come to be seen as natural parts of life and death. Our grasp on life and on privacy seem equally tenuous.

That same complex of waste images inflects Mrs. Brown's hovel, both as Florence encounters it and as the reader does twice afterwards. In her first appearance as in every subsequent one, Good Mrs. Brown appears as a canny opportunist, able to make a profit from ruin, accident, and misfortune. Soon after the departure from Staggs's Gardens, a mad bull's rush separates Florence from the rest of the Dombey party and brings her into the clutches of Good Mrs. Brown, who apparently offers her protection but is in reality out to take her for all she can get. The old woman works by combining what she has heard Florence say ("Susan! Susan! oh, where are they?" [70]) with an ability to exploit the typical child's sense of guilt ("Where are they? Why did you run away from them?" [70]), willingness to believe adults ("Susan an't far off and the others are close to her" [73]), and desire to be reassured ("Is anybody hurt?" "Not a bit of it." [73]). Florence thus "willingly" accompanies her escort through "some very uncomfortable places, such as brick fields and tile-yards . . . down a dirty lane, where the mud lay in deep black ruts" (73) For the first and only time, the reader sees from the outside "a shabby little house, as closely shut up as a house that was full of cracks and crevices could be" (73). Again we are presented with a paradoxical combination: not a demon both lame and agile, but a house that induces both claustrophobia and a sense of exposure. Florence is pushed into a "back room, where there was a great heap of rags of different colours lying on the floor; a heap of bones, a heap of sifted dust or cinders; but there was no furniture at all, and the walls and ceilings were quite black" (73). Now apparently revealed as a rag-and-bone gatherer, one of the lowest of London's street occupations, Good Mrs. Brown obviously pursues various criminal sidelines: she proceeds to divest her victim of her clothes and—far more importantly—her name. When Florence is set on her confused and bewildered way and then rescued by Walter, the first-time reader may assume that Good Mrs. Brown has served her narrative function and may disappear.

Of course she does not: we encounter her several times again, gathering more information in various places. But finally, we see her at home again: a home that despite all the changes in the nearby Staggs's Gardens remains essentially unchanged.[17] Indeed, the only changes—the fire, the few sticks of furniture—are accounted for by the fact that we have gained access to the house's other room, and the house's unchanging primitiveness is made by the narrative to have a gnomic truth: when we meet Alice, returned after ten years' transportation, we learn that Good Mrs. Brown is "as much a mother as her dwelling is a home" (464). The line to that home is direct and straightforward, with no circuitous wanderings or searching; a few short paragraphs and a new chapter finds us "in an ugly and dark room [with] . . . a meagre

fire [and] . . . stray drops of rain fall[ing] hissing on the smouldering embers''
(465). When Alice arrives, she is so changed her mother doesn't recognize
her, but the place itself is exactly as it was, so the narrator reminds us, when
Florence saw it years before: ''a heap of rags, a heap of bones, a wretched
bed, two or three mutilated chairs or stools, the black walls and blacker
ceiling . . . the damp hearth of the chimney—for there was no stove'' (465).[18]
Not even Alice's continued presence will make much difference: the dwelling
is still ''poor and miserable [though] not so utterly wretched as in the days
when only Good Mrs Brown inhabited it. Some few attempts at cleanliness
and order were manifest, though made in a reckless, gipsy way, that might
have connected them, at a glance, with the younger woman'' (690). With this
second use of the word *gipsy*, Dickens again shows his sense of connection
between gypsiness and a way of being at home, and not, as we might expect,
with a way of travelling.

Despite her apparent position on the economic margins, in maintaining her
hold on this place of habitation, Good Mrs. Brown is somehow not one of
the dispossessed. A lapse on Dickens's part? A failure to offer a realistic
documentation of the vicissitudes of urban poverty? Perhaps, but if so, an
error that may be justified by its truth: the curiously resilient persistence of
the ragged and the ruined. The sordid exchange which provides bare subsis-
tence to the dealer in rags and bones cannot be denied its place in the economic and material order, even as the imagistic leakage between heaps of
rags and bones and carcasses of ragged tenements suggests that this sordid
exchange also cannot be kept in that place, but instead infiltrates the entire
system.

And so in Good Mrs. Brown's dwelling we come face to face with the
fundamental—and fundamentally unstable—structure of capitalism himself.
Playing off of Marx's famous statement that ''all that is solid melts into air,''
Marshall Berman replaces *melts into air* with a far less ethereal process:

> All that is solid—from the clothes on our backs to the looms and mills that
> weave them, to the men and women who work the machines, to the houses and
> neighborhoods the workers live in . . . to the towns and cities . . . that embrace
> them all—all these are made to be *broken* tomorrow, *smashed* or *shredded* or
> *pulverized* or dissolved, so that they can be recycled or replaced next week,
> and the whole process can go on again and again.   (99)

Dissolved may remain a possibility, but one that decreases in probability next
to the accumulated materiality of *smashed*, *shredded*, and *pulverized*. In this
accumulation of waste process, the rag-and-bone shop begins to seem the
lowest common denominator of the entire capitalist equation, its degraded
epitome, the dark cellar of its resplendent edifice.

Thirty years after the publication of *Dombey and Son*, George Borrow's
last published work explicitly discusses gypsy exploitation of capitalism's

dissolute tendencies. Borrow describes the potteries around Notting Hill in language highly reminiscent of Dickens's description of Staggs's Gardens:

> It is a neighborhood of transition; of brickfields, open spaces, poor streets . . . sites of intended tenements, or sites of tenements which have been pulled down; it is in fact a mere chaos, where there is no order and no regularity; where there is nothing durable, or intended to be durable; though there can be little doubt that within a few years . . . the misery, squalidness, and meanness will have disappeared, and the whole district, up to the railroad arches which bound it on the west and north, will be covered with palaces . . . or delightful villas . . . . At present, however, it is quite the kind of place to please the Gypsies and wandering people, who find many places within its bounds where they can squat and settle . . . without much risk of being interfered with. Here their tents, cars, and caravans may be seen amidst ruins, half-raised walls, and on patches of unenclosed ground; here their children may . . . be seen playing about, flinging up dust and dirt . . . and here, at night, the different families . . . may be seen seated around their fires and their kettles . . . and every now and then indulging in shouts of merriment, as much as to say,—
> What care we, though we be so small?
> The tent shall stand when the palace shall fall; which is quite true. The Gypsy tent must make way for the palace, but after a millennium or two, the Gypsy tent is pitched on the ruins of the palace.   (231)

The gypsies thus take Marx, at least Berman's Marx, one step further. Where Berman characterizes "even the most beautiful and impressive bourgeois buildings and public works" as "disposable" and so likens them metaphorically "in their social functions to tents and encampments" (99), Borrow both actualizes and reverses the metaphor, in order to claim that under capitalism, tents are the only enduring monument.

Seeing the rag-and-bone shop as capitalism's degraded epitome is, I think, an important and inevitable consequence of the line of inquiry I am pursuing here, but it must not be allowed to overshadow my more specific concern with Mrs. Brown's habitation as the degraded epitome of the novel's own gathering up and purveying of information. In her home, in the chapter entitled "Secret Intelligence" (note the echo of the trains' "secret knowledge"), Good Mrs. Brown most conspicuously trades in information, giving nothing away, selling a product (knowledge) but not the means of production (the ability to learn secrets). Carefully hiding Dombey behind a door, she sets out to obtain from Carker's spy Biler the secret of his and Edith Dombey's destination. Her impatience makes Biler wish he was the "electric fluency" (701)—an apparent reference to the telegraph, whose nearly simultaneous invention was crucial to the practical usefulness of the steam-powered locomotive. Her success punishes Dombey for his skepticism, which may well mirror the reader's: on first entering Good Mrs. Brown's home, he asks, "how does it happen that I can find voluntary intelligence in a hovel like this?" (692)

The answer is that Good Mrs. Brown in fact knows more than the novel itself does or wants to—a situation that results as much from her ability to persist within the hovel as her ability to move beyond it. First she is able to twist Biler's arm with her knowledge of his various past connivances and wrongdoing among the "pigeon-fancying tramps and bird-catchers" (610)—knowledge obtained outside the purview of what Dickens offers the reader in *Dombey and Son*. Second she knows that Biler, obtuse as he is, may well have knowledge that he would not seem to have. His protestations do him no good against her stubborn persistence: "how should I know, Misses Brown," he asks, and again, "How can I pronounce the name of foreign places?" but she "retorted quickly, 'you have seen it written, and you can spell it.'" Rob is "penetrated with some admiration of Mrs. Brown's cunning" (703) and agrees to tell her how it all came about:

> When a certain person left the lady with me, he put a piece of paper with a direction written on it in the lady's hand, saying it was in case she should forget. She wasn't afraid of forgetting, for she tore it up as soon as his back was turned, and when I put up the carriage steps, I shook out one of the pieces—she sprinkled the rest out of the window, I suppose for there was none afterwards, though I looked for 'em. There was only one word on it, and that was this, if you must and will know. (703–4)

Rob then proceeds to write the letters of the word, in chalk upon a table, extra large, as Dombey "looked eagerly towards the creeping track of his hand" (704). The creeping track echoes the train's own lines, but even more importantly the retrieved torn-up piece of paper echoes all the rags and bones and ashes and scraps and carcasses in and around Good Mrs. Brown's abode. Thus Biler's plight—that he can't escape his past, that it is always still there—turns out to be everyone's, and when he begs Good Mrs. Brown to "let the birds be" and regrets that "they're always flying back in your face when you least expect it," what he says of "them little creeturs" may be what we would all say of the scraps of our lives (610).

If the "Secret Intelligence" of *Dombey and Son* is a track (trace) of writing on a discarded scrap of paper, I too have had my own secret intelligence: that once more in the early fifties Dickens returned to the image of Asmodeus only, essentially, to scrap it. Inspired by the recent publication in Paris of Henri Murger's *Scènes de la Vie de Boheme*, Dickens writes an article in *Household Words* entitled "Tour in Bohemia," which turns from the lives of the Parisian artists considered by Murger to that of London speculators—a world more akin to Thackeray's *Vanity Fair* than to Puccini's *La Boheme*.[19]

Like Murger's before him, Dickens's invocation of gypsiness is immediately made subject to limitations (during the specification of which Dickens incidentally displays his familiarity with George Borrow's earliest published works, on Spanish gypsies):

> The Bohemians I tell of are the gipsies of civilisation. Their skins may be fair, their eyes blue, their skill in telling fortunes . . . and in speaking the Rommaney language may be limited; they may prefer the shelter of a tiled roof to that of a blanket tent . . . but they are essentially as nomadic, as predatory, as incorrigibly reluctant to any reputable task, and as diligent in any knavish operation; as dissipated, careless, improvident, and municipally worthless, as any Caloro or Rommaney chal that the Polyglottian Mr. Borrow has ever told us of.[20]

But though Dickens seems to promise us an introduction to the ways and means of this form of social existence, he ends his exposé with an admission that it would in fact take more than a tour guide's power to expose the entire truth:

> If I could drive some hundreds of the well-dressed units of what is called society into the pens of Smithfield market, and then have some Asmodeus at my bidding to untile, not the roofs of the houses, but the heads of the assembly, and read their working brains, what a well-informed man I should be to be sure! . . . Perhaps the most startling and instructive revelation of all would be to know where all the well-dressed inhabitants of Bohemia live. They swagger about Regent Street, they sit next us at dinner, they are at our evening parties, at the club, the theatre, but where do they live? Perhaps in Belgravia, perhaps in back streets off Leicester Square, or Clare market.   (500)

The rather macabre desire to untop heads and peer into brains shows Dickens undoing the force of a metaphor whose form he nevertheless clings to: usually to see into houses is to see into lives and hence into thoughts, but in this context the only way to see into thoughts is to see into brains.

In LeSage's original, Asmodeus complies with Cleofas's request to look into men's heads and see their dreams, but must suddenly leave off when the magician from whom Cleofas had liberated him discovers his escape and calls him back. This reassertion of the magician's power—anticipated in the novel's first chapters—provides LeSage with both a convenient and allegorically significant stopping point to what might otherwise have been an endless narrative: it is hard to avoid the sense that in penetrating men's dreams the demon has gone too far. But in the case of Bohemians, Dickens is nevertheless impelled to ignore this negative example, for only by looking into their brains can he know what roofs he can lift to see them at home—if they have any home at all. For a curiosity about "where the inhabitants of Bohemia live" is unlikely to be satisfied by any simple knowledge of where they stay, instead seeking to find where they may set aside pretense and be themselves—not where they hang their hats but where they let down their predatory and deceptive guard. Bohemians, who live by their wits, in some strange sense live only within their own heads; interiority moves from the inside of houses to the inside of heads.

But while Dickens is ostensibly concerned with obtaining knowledge of Bohemians, the passage itself, in the context of the reference to Asmodeus and all of Dickens's previous usages of the reference, cannot escape the realization that wherever Bohemians may be found, they are always in the know—knowing rather than to-be-known, subjects rather than the objects of knowledge. For if Bohemians' secrets are safe from the rooftop-lifting demon and his journalistic and novelistic others, it is because they have anticipated the demon as interlopers below those roofs, as deceptive, self-interested, and utterly unsuspected observers.

There are two things Dickens admits he is not telling us in the article in *Household Words*. At the very end of the two concluding paragraphs of the article, he leaves us hanging. First, immediately after the Asmodean passage quoted above, the exposition of the problem of where Bohemians live, he admits with a strange combination of candor and equivocation: "Perhaps *I* know, but while I tell of the chief features of Bohemia, scorn to uncover the nakedness of the land" (500, emphasis in original). That admission of the possibility of personal knowledge is startling, although what he goes on to say of this Upper Bohemia—that it has no rival for "mystery and subtlety of ways and means, and fertility of invention"—makes it perhaps reconcilable with the journalist, though hardly with the conductor of the properly domestic *Household Words*. Even more disturbing is the very end of the article: "It may be in days to come that if I have power and you inclination, I will treat of that Bohemia which lies at the very bottom of the social ladder—down among the straw and the mud, and which alone can be the parallel to the Bohemia I have attempted cursorily to describe." The contrast between the gilt of Upper Bohemia and the squalor of lower is exactly the contrast that Good Mrs. Brown and Alice make when they see Carker

> "so easy, and so trim, a'horseback, while we are in the mud"—
> "And of it," said her daughter impatiently. "We are mud, underneath his horse's feet. What should we be?"   (609)

Whether because of a deficit of authorial power or of readerly inclination, Dickens's explicit journalistic treatment of the world beneath the horses' feet never came to be. But that lack cannot undo the uneasy alliance suggested in the article between the "Upper Bohemia" of "the next railway mania, the next assurance mania, the next mining mania, the next gold-finding mania, the next emigration mania'' (500); the author; the Bohemia of straw and mud; and the proliferation of Asmodean interlopers.

In tracing *Dombey and Son*'s version of this alliance, I have attempted to show how Asmodeus's lameness calls attention to the various ways narrative knowledge is disfigured throughout the novel. Its associations with the cycle of waste, with dissolution and reassemblage, with gypsy wanderings and gypsy housekeeping—all these contribute to this process of disfigurement. Unlike the demon Asmodeus, the kind of knower represented by Good Mrs. Brown may not be able to unroof houses, but then she has no need to, instead she just hangs around and watches while the houses decay. That the "creeping track" of the writer's hand as well as the sharp gaze of his eye may be neither benignant nor potent but grasping, opportunistic, low—and yet enduring withal—may well be the secret intelligence *Dombey and Son* neither quite delivers nor quite finds deliverance from.

NOTES

1. In her discussion of references to Asmodeus in nineteenth-century Paris, Sharon Marcus suggests links to the "malignant" figure of the *portière*. Although the portière differs from Good Mrs. Brown in her identification with one particular place, the apartment house which she serves as porter, she is, like Good Mrs. Brown, a "bounded character who nevertheless has a boundless point of view" (53).
2. I borrow the phrase "tacit concurrence" from Miller, who in discussing *Oliver Twist* draws the reader's attention to the "tacit concurrence the text assumes between the law and its supplement" (8). In the linkage *Dombey and Son*, provides between the modern railroad and the primitive Mrs. Brown, I see a "tacit concurrence" between technology and its supplement.
3. The word *gypsy* is used twice in reference to Good Mrs. Brown, though neither is precisely an identification (370, 690).
4. On speed, see various works by Paul Virilio.
5. On business, finance, and the trains, see Marcus and Baumgarten. On the problem of the daughter, see Auerbach, Clark, Loesberg, Epstein, and Moglen. Waters suggests a swerve away from Auerbach's conclusion by arguing that rather than challenging the doctrine of separate spheres, the novel in fact criticizes Dombey's own failure to conform to that doctrine, adhering instead to an outmoded notion of the family and the family business as both matters of dynasty and lineage. Jaffe mentions Good Mrs. Brown along with Carker very briefly as a thematized figure of bad surveillance (88). Marsh comes closest to recognizing the importance of Good Mrs. Brown, but although she astutely recognizes that Good Mrs. Brown is drawn not only from the fairy tale world of bad witches but also from the procuress's world of Fanny Hill, she does not discuss her connections with the technology of observation and narration.

6. The fact that Good Mrs. Brown's story seems tacked on as a kind of afterthought to explain her various movements actually helps make possible the Deleuzian reading I will give. Were Good Mrs. Brown's psychological motivation more convincing, she like other characters would be constrained within various Oedipal' stories and would be unable to be a figure of "depsychologized desire."

7. Waters is typical in ignoring Good Mrs. Brown's survival when she builds her conclusion on the way that the "removal of Alice and Edith from the narrative paves the way for Florence to restore harmony" (52). In fact, Good Mrs. Brown is the "dark wom[a]n" the novel not only fails to assimilate but also fails to expel.

8. The distinction Welsh draws between knowledge and information may be of use here: information is "latent knowledge" (46); it "can be exchanged, collected from as many different quarters as possible" (43) finally, "if knowledge is power ... information is power to operate at a distance" (9). I am suggesting that Good Mrs. Brown's information is more important than her knowledge, though in fact, like Welsh, and like nineteenth-century writers, I continue to favor the word knowledge. Moreover, against the sharp distinction Welsh would draw between the detective (and the novelist) on the one hand and the blackmailer on the other, I am far more interested in the slippage between the two, found most notably in the way Good Mrs. Brown sells both silence and information.

9. As my earlier use of the term *fabula* suggests, the vocabulary of narratology and of narrative theory does offer some help in pinpointing Good Mrs. Brown, especially in a way that would enable more precise comparison with similar characters within other novels. For example, it is helpful to think of such characters as activating Barthes's hermeneutic code, which, as Brooks glosses it, "concerns ... the questions and answers that structure a story, their suspense, partial unveiling, temporary blockage, eventual resolution, with the resulting creation of a 'dilatory space'—the space of suspense." (Note the echo of Dickens's locomotives "dilating with secret knowledge.") But more than reading *Dombey and Son* through narratology, I am interested in reading narratology through *Dombey and Son*, specifically the way *Dombey and Son*'s mechanized forces can inform the reliance on language of mechanics and motive force in Brooks and others. See, for instance, Brooks, pp. 7, 14, 15, 20, 33.

10. In Waters's terms, Carker is an "entrepreneur" (41) who engages in "voracious business activity" by exercising his "native wits and power of surveillance" (45). The remarkable similarity in descriptive language, both the narrator's and various characters', as applied to both Carker and Good Mrs. Brown ("sharp," "acute," "knowing") has been little commented upon.

11. Recall that the years of *Dombey and Son* (1846–1848) overlapped with those of the "Railway Mania" and thus with a period of unprecedented attention to the funding, operation, profits and effects of the trains. The novel itself depicts the building of London's own second railway, the London-Birmingham, in the mid 1830s, a period of unequaled railway construction.

12. At least one of Good Mrs. Brown's wanderings in fact replicates a route set down by the railroad: Mr. Dombey and Major Bagstock travel from London to Leamington Spa by train (at least as far as Birmingham, where they pick up a coach); Good Mrs. Brown, on the other hand, simply and instantaneously is in

London at one point and at Leamington Spa at another. Compare the way that at two other points her actions apparently combine with those of the railroad: in getting Florence to Walter, and in ensuring Carker's death (he is terrified by Dombey's appearance, which Good Mrs. Brown's information has made possible, but in fact killed by the sudden appearance of the train).

13. See for instance the trio of gypsy novels published in the 1830s by Jones, the "Queen" of the penny-dreadful; as well as works by Bury and Ainsworth. For a quick survey, see Reed.

14. The list need not stop there, however: Meg herself bears more than a passing resemblance to the crone that appears in an early chapter of Lewis's *The Monk.* As I argue elsewhere, what makes Meg new is a thoroughgoing craftiness that allows her both to learn and to determine the fate of an old Scottish family and to craft her own identity as a "gypsy" rather than "any of that medley race of vagabonds."

15. In her first appearance, however, Good Mrs. Brown threatens Florence with just such an invasion: "If you don't [vex me], I tell you I won't hurt you. But if you do, I'll kill you. I could have you killed at any time—even if you was in your own bed at home" (73–74).

16. In *Little Dorrit*, Dickens describes a class he terms "gipsies of civilization" characterized by their insistence on making boudoirs out of broom closets and generally maximizing accommodations (359). His rather acerbic treatment of this class is contrasted by earlier uses of *gypsy* in this way. When David Copperfield visits the newly married Traddles in his chambers in Gray's Inn, he gleefully reveals that his apparently business-like chambers are actually home not just to himself and the new Mrs. Traddles, but to a slew of her sisters as well: "Sophy's an extraordinary manager! You'll be surprised how those girls are stowed away . . . We are prepared to rough it . . . and . . . improvise . . . there's a little room in the roof—a very nice room, when you're up there . . . and that's our room at present. It's a capital little gipsy sort of place. There's quite a view from it" (897–98). Along with David's early account of how the gypsy kettle whistled in the course of Dora's birthday picnic, this description ties gypsiness not only incidentally to young men's affairs of the heart but inherently to an incongruous, vaguely transgressive, and utterly unexpected plenitude. Kettles, the emblem of domesticity, shouldn't whistle outside; women shouldn't be in Gray's Inn chambers, nor in such a legalistic labyrinth should there be such unexpected accommodating spaces.

17. In fact, just how nearby remains unclear. When the mad bull appeared, Florence and the others had walked for "a good hour" (70) from Staggs's Gardens. Florence then "screamed and ran. She ran till she was exhausted . . . and then found . . . she was quite alone" (70). At that point she is accosted by Good Mrs. Brown (again present when a character seems to be alone); Florence then follows the old woman "not very far, but . . . by some very uncomfortable places." I doubt whether in fact Florence's run and their walk together in fact equalled the earlier "good hour's walk." Regardless of precisely where in London Good Mrs. Brown lives, textually when she leads Florence back through "brickyards and

tile yards,'' she is leading her back into the kind of space the novel identifies with Staggs's Gardens, with the railroad, with change.

18. Good Mrs. Brown's "hovel" reverses the claim made by Bachelard that walls are optional: "all really inhabited space bears the essence of the notion of home . . . . The imagination functions in this direction whenever the human being has found the slightest shelter: we shall see the imagination build "walls" of impalpable shadows, comfort itself with the illusion of protection. . . . " In Good Mrs. Brown's home, however, the physically present walls tend in the imagination to disappear into mere impalpable shadows—the walls of a cavern (cf. traditional gypsy dens) or of an engine room. Similarly, instead of serving as an anchor of comfort and security, the hearth becomes a kind of witch's altar.

19. The article from *Household Words* is most frequently cited today as offering a kind of gloss on the passage from *Little Dorrit* describing what turns out to be one of the places Bohemians of Society live, Mrs. Gowan's digs at Hampton Court. Note to Penguin edition. Armstrong discusses the passage in *Little Dorrit*, but only as a failure of home rather than as a manipulation of it (37, 109).

20. It is hard to exaggerate how little space Dickens gives to characters supposed to be seen as real gypsies, especially considering his interest in the dispossessed, the outcast, the vagrant. Gypsies are a vague but sinister presence during Nell's time in the world of the Derby in *The Old Curiosity Shop*; Hugh in *Barnaby Rudge* was born of a gypsy mother conveniently hanged long before the novel's action begins; in *Great Expectations*, Estella is ultimately revealed to have also had a gypsy mother—but one who has had the gypsiness greatly curbed by years of domestic service under Jaggers. But Dickens explicitly in the case of Hugh makes any interest in gypsies qua gypsies one with the sinister and hypocritical interest of John Chester—revealed at the novel's end to be Hugh's father. Similarly, a gypsiness apparently utterly evacuated of all its usual associations runs through the entire course of David Copperfield's involvement with the vacuous Dora in the form of her spoiled lapdog, "who was called Jip, short for Gipsy" (454).

Armstrong discusses Dickens's aversion to romanticized houselessness: "It does seem . . . that in Dickens's own view four walls and a ceiling are necessary if not sufficient physical conditions for a home. In spite of his enjoyment of long walks, he was no camper, and his characters get no pleasure from sleeping in the open air" (25).

WORKS CITED

Ainsworth, W.H. *Rookwood*. London: Bentley, 1834.

Arac, Jonathan. "The House and the Railroad: *Dombey and Son* and *The House of the Seven Gables*." *The New England Quarterly* (1978): 3–22.

Armstrong, Frances. *Dickens and the Concept of Home*. Ann Arbor: UMI Research Press, 1990.

Auerbach, Nina. "Dickens and Dombey: A Daughter After All." *Dickens Studies Annual* 5 (1976): 95–114.

Bachelard, Gaston. *The Poetics of Space*. 1958. Trans. Maria Jolas. Boston: Beacon, 1969.

Baumgarten, Murray. "Railway/Reading/Time: *Dombey and Son* and the Industrial World." *Dickens Studies Annual* 19 (1990): 65–89

Berman, Marshall. *All That Is Solid Melts Into Air: The Experience of Modernity*. New York: Penguin, 1988.

Borrrow, George. *Romano Lavo-lil*. London: John Murray, 1874.

———. *The Zincali*. London: John Murray, 1840.

Brooks, Peter. *Reading for the Plot*. Cambridge: Harvard UP, 1984.

Bury, Charlotte. *The Gipsy's Daughter*.

Clark, Robert. "Riddling the Family Firm: The Sexual Economy in *Dombey and Son*." *ELH* 51 (Spring 1984): 69–84.

Deleuze, Gilles and Guattari, Felix. *A Thousand Plateaus*. Trans. Brian Massumi. Minneapolis: U of Minnesota P, 1993.

Dickens, Charles. *American Notes for General Circulation*. 1842. New York: Penguin, 1972.

———. *Barnaby Rudge*. 1841. New York: Penguin, 1973.

———. *David Copperfield*. 1849–50. New York: Penguin, 1966.

———. *Dombey and Son*. 1846–48. Ed. Alan Horsman. Oxford: Oxford UP, 1974.

———. *Great Expectations*. 1860–61. New York: Penguin, 1965.

———. "Ignorance and Its Victims." *The Dent Uniform Edition of Dickens' Journalism*, Vol. 2. Ed. Michael Slater. Columbus: Ohio State University Press, 1996: 95–98

———. *Little Dorrit*. 1855–1857. New York: Penguin, 1967.

———. *The Old Curiosity Shop*. 1840. New York: Penguin, 1972.

———. "A Tour in Bohemia." *Household Words*. July 8, 1854.

Galt, John. *Sir Andrew Wylie of That Ilk*. 182?. Edinburgh: Blackwoods, 1877.

Gordon, Ian A. *John Galt: The Life of a Writer*. Edinburgh: Oliver and Boyd, 1972.

Jaffe, Audrey. *Vanishing Points: Dickens, Narrative, and the Subject of Omniscience.* Berkeley: U of California P, 1991.

Jones, Hannah Maria. *The Gipsey Chief.* London: 1840.

————. *The Gipsey Girl.* London: Tallis, 1836.

————. *The Gipsy Mother.* London: Virtue, 1833.

Lewis, Matthew. *The Monk.* 1796. Oxford: Oxford UP, 1973.

Loesberg, Jonathan. "Deconstruction, Historicism, and Overdetermination: Dislocations of the Marriage Plots in *Robert Elsmere* and *Dombey and Son.*" *Victorian Studies*, Spring (1990): 441–64.

Marcus, Sharon. *Apartment Stories: City and Home in Nineteenth-Century Paris and London.* Berkeley: U of California P, 1999.

Marcus, Steven. *Dickens from Pickwick to Dombey.* New York: Basic Books, 1965.

Marsh, Joss. "Good Mrs. Brown's Connections: Sexuality and Story-Telling in *Dealings with the Firm of Dombey and Son.*" *ELH* 58 (1991): 405–26.

Miller, D. A. *The Novel and the Police.* Berkeley: U of California P, 1988.

Moglen, Helene. "Theoriizing Fiction/Fictionalizing Theory: The Case of *Dombey and Son.*" *Victorian Studies* (1992):159–84.

Nord, Deborah Epstein. *Walking the Victorian Streets.* Ithaca: Cornell UP, 1995.

Reed, John. *Victorian Conventions.* Athens: U of Ohio P, 1970.

Samuel, Raphael. "Comers and Goers." *The Victorian City.* Ed. H. J. Dyos and Michael Wolff. London: Routledge and Kegan Paul, 1973. 123–60.

Schivelbusch, Wolfgang. *The Railway Journey.* Berkeley: U of California P, 1986.

Scott, Walter. *Guy Mannering.* 1814. London: E. P. Dent, 1921.

Tucker, Walter C. Ed. *The Marx-Engels Reader.* New York: W.W. Norton, 1978.

Virilio, Paul. *The Art of the Motor.* Trans. Julie Rose. Minneapolis: U of Minnesota P, 1995.

Waters, Catherine. *Dickens and the Politics of Family.* Cambridge: Cambridge UP, 1997.

Welsh, Alexander. *George Eliot and Blackmail.* Cambridge: Harvard UP, 1985.

"More Like Than Life":
Painting, Photography, and Dickens's
Bleak House

Regina B. Oost

In a recent article, Ronald R. Thomas writes that in Bleak House *"photographic images are contrasted . . . with a set of painted portraits which do not tell the truth." If we consider the novel in the context of contemporary writings on photography, however, this claim becomes problematic. The ubiquity of portraits among the novel's middle-class characters raises questions about representation that resonate not just through the 1830s (the era of the novel's setting), but also through Dickens's own era of the 1850s, a time in which the photograph had largely replaced the painted portrait as a means of memorializing the middle classes. Advertisements for John E. Mayall's photographic studio appearing in serialized issues of* Bleak House, *Dickens's letter to Angela Burdett Coutts describing his first sitting for Mayall in December of 1852, and articles published in* Household Words *in the early 1850s all attest to the popular fascination with photography, but also suggest the writers' ambivalence toward the new technology, ambivalence born of the rigidity, artificiality, and potential distortion of early photographic images. These same qualities are attributed to painted portraits in* Bleak House. *In subtly equating photography (the new technology of the middle classes) with painting (traditionally the means of preserving the images of the elite), the novel cautions readers against naive celebration of the documentary accuracy of any type of representation while also suggesting the susceptibility of the rising middle classes to the foibles of the erstwhile ruling classes.*

In "Double Exposures: Arresting Images in *Bleak House* and *The House of Seven Gables*," Ronald R. Thomas writes that "photographic images [in *Bleak House*] are contrasted . . . with a set of painted portraits which do *not* tell the truth" (103). Thomas makes this statement near the end of a discussion of Bucket's ability to fix in his mind the images which enable him to unravel the mystery of Lady Dedlock's illicit liaison and Tulkinghorn's murder. Thomas asserts that Bucket's ability is akin to that of the new photographic camera, which could capture the likenesses of criminals, thus aiding in crime detection.[1] While this reading of Bucket as proto-photographer is intriguing, the statement that the novel's painted portraits "do not tell the truth" merits further scrutiny. I concur with Thomas that *Bleak House* is concerned with the workings of new technology in a period of social change, but I am less convinced that the novel juxtaposes photography and painting so as to promote the truth-claims of the newer technology over those of the older. Paintings figure prominently in the novel, and several critics (including Thomas) have discussed the emblematic treatment of the Dedlock portraits, particularly that of Lady Dedlock at Chesney Wold.[2] Less frequently noted are the portraits of such characters as Guppy and the Snagsbys, and seldom are the thematic purposes of these works considered at length.[3] The ubiquity of portraits among the novel's middle-class characters invites such consideration, however, for the narrative treatment of these paintings raises questions about representation that resonate not just through society of the 1830s as depicted in the novel,[4] but also through Dickens's own society of the 1850s, an era in which the photograph had largely replaced the painted portrait as a means of memorializing the middle class. Was one form of representation more accurate, a more truthful and objective measure of reality, than the other? Based on the argument outlined above, Thomas's answer to this question would be yes. However, I believe that many of Dickens's contemporaries would have been harder pressed to answer in the affirmative, and that *Bleak House* bears the traces of considerable ambivalence about what any portrait—painted or photographed—can convey.

To analyze the novel's commentary on portraiture, it is helpful to distinguish the era in which the novel was written from that in which it is set. Living in an age of photography, Dickens and his contemporaries would have thought somewhat differently about portraiture than did the novel's characters. Of course, being fictional, the characters are limited to the perceptions that Dickens invented for them, and as subsequent discussion will demonstrate, Dickens did a fairly good job in attributing to characters insights about paintings that would indeed have been available during the 1830s. However, hindsight granted Dickens the ability to emphasize precisely those elements in representational art that would be nurtured by the later invention of photography, so that in writing about paintings of two decades earlier,

Dickens also explores issues that were relevant to readers of his own era. Walter Benjamin, in "The Work of Art in the Age of Mechanical Reproduction," describes the kind of relationship I am suggesting here between painting and photography: "The history of every art form shows critical epochs in which a certain form aspires to effects which could be fully obtained only with a changed technical standard, that is to say, in a new art form" (237). In *Bleak House*, Dickens depicts painted portraits as "aspir[ing] to the effects" of photography, the "changed technical standard" of the 1850s. An examination of the novel's portraits can thus begin by considering precisely which "effects" photography had achieved by Dickens's day, then turning to the novel to discern how such effects are attributed to the many painted portraits.[5]

With the development of photography in 1839 and the widespread establishment of portrait studies beginning in 1841,[6] a new era dawned in which people erstwhile unable to afford painted portraits of themselves had the means to pass their images to posterity. As Beaumont Newhall reflects, "All kinds of people sat before the camera; thanks to the relative cheapness of production, financial distinctions mattered little. Celebrated men and women as well as less renowned citizens who otherwise would be forgotten, have left their features on the silvered plate" (30). Thomas also emphasizes the democratizing potential of photography, stating that "Through the magic of the camera lens, the portrait, long an emblem of wealth and status among the privileged classes, became an affordable symbol of middle-class respectability and ascendancy" ("Double Exposure" 87). "Ascendancy" is an apt term, for the photograph was one of many commodities middle-class consumers acquired in the 1840s and 1850s to emulate the lifestyle formerly reserved for the gentry and aristocracy. In examining monthly issues of *Bleak House* published between March 1852 and September 1853, one encounters a brochure for Mayall's Daguerreotype Portrait Galleries (included with issue number 15, May 1853) among other advertisements for goods marketed to middle-class consumers aspiring to the tastes of the upper classes. Such advertisements include, in the first issue (March 1852), one from Watherston & Brogden, Manufacturing Goldsmiths, stating that in order to establish "a closer connexion than has hitherto existed between the real worker in the precious metals and the Public," the firm will begin manufacturing moderately-priced gold chains of reliable quality. The same issue (and several subsequent others) presents an advertisement for Mott's New Silver Electro Plate—a product "possessing in a pre-eminent degree the qualities of Sterling Silver"—assuring the reader that "a table may be elegantly furnished with this beautiful manufacture at a fifth of the cost of Silver, from which it cannot be distinguished." The fifth issue (July 1852) contains an advertisement for "Forster's Pocket Peerage" that promises to make accessible "to the million" information that has "hitherto circulated exclusively among the wealthier classes."

As Dickens's readers turned the pages of the serialized novel, they encountered myriad enticements to raise their standard of living through acquisition, and in this context the brochure for Mayall's studio is situated. Mayall's advertisement joins the others in emphasizing the attainability of luxury goods: it assures the reader that the "arrangement of charges" for the "highest class pictures" "place[s] them within the reach of all."

John E. Mayall's studio was well known to the author of *Bleak House*, for in December of 1852 (six months before the advertisement appears, and during the period in which *Bleak House* was written), Dickens sat for Mayall. The surviving daguerreotypes are the first known photographic images of Dickens,[7] and his letter of December 23, 1852, to Angela Burdett Coutts indicates his satisfaction with the sitting:

> I am happy to say that the little piece of business between the Sun and myself, came off with the greatest success . . . . The Artist who operated, is quite a Genius in that way, and has acquired a large stock of a very singular knowledge of all the little eccentricities of the light and the instrument. The consequence of which, is, that his results are very different from those of other men. I am disposed to think the portrait, by far the best specimen of anything in that way, I have ever seen. Some of the peculiarities inseparable from the process—as a slight rigidity and desperate grimness—are in it, but very greatly modified. I sat five times. (*Letters* 834)

Dickens's approbation of Mayall's skill is evident. Also discernible, however, is some ambivalence toward photography in general underlying the writer's comments about "peculiarities inseparable from the process." The "rigidity and desperate grimness" of which Dickens writes often characterized early photographic images; another writer quoted in Mayall's advertisement refers to much the same qualities in calling the products of operators other than Mayall "severe and morose." The rigidity and severity of early portraits were due to technological requirements of the new art, specifically the lengthy exposure time needed to produce a clear image and the bright lighting needed to sensitize the plate. After 1851 the introduction of the collodion process and new types of lenses reduced exposure time from several minutes to less than one minute, but during exposure the sitter was required to remain motionless, as even the slightest movement could blur the image.[8]

Further comment on the "desperate grimness" produced by the sitter's necessary immobility comes from Henry Morley and W. H. Wills, two writers for Dickens's *Household Words*. In an article entitled "Photography" that appeared on March 19, 1853, the writers record their impressions upon visiting Mayall's studio: "Beautiful women smiled out of metal as polished and as hard as a knight's armour on the eve of battle. Young chevaliers regarded us with faces tied and fastened down so that, as it seemed, they could by no struggle get their features loose out of the very twist and smirk they chanced to wear when they were captured and fixed'' (55). While the writers chivalrously refrain from disparaging the images of the women, their description of the distorted faces of the men evokes the sitters' discomfort and the viewers' dissatisfaction with the resultant images. In juxtaposing the apparently bad likeness of the men with acceptable (or at least unremarkable) ones of the women, the writers neither extol photography's achievements nor bemoan its failings, but instead appear to be yet weighing its merits. The article goes on to describe the history and science of photography in a tone that vacillates between wonder and apprehension. For example, when the writers ask the photographer whether the people pictured ''whose tongues were silent'' and ''whose limbs were fixed'' ''have all breathed and moved . . . about that very room,'' the photographer answers that ''they have all been executed here. If you mount further up you also may be taken'' (55). The double-entendre of this passages is amusing, but it also hints at the writers' ambivalence with both the products and the process of photography.

Also contributing to ambivalence about early photography's merits was the ease with which images could be made, which led to a proliferation of hack photographers. As Newhall notes, the proprietors of early portrait studios ''came from a wide variety of trades and professions: in two weeks almost anyone could gain sufficient technical proficiency to set up business'' (30). By 1850 numerous ''picture factories'' specialized in dividing the labor of photography so that a plate was prepared by one person and exposed by another, while yet more people developed, then gilded, then tinted the photograph. All of this was done cheaply and quickly, often to the dissatisfaction of the sitter (Newhall 39). To preserve their reputations and livelihoods, skilled photographers sought to distance their works from those of the hacks: in his advertisement in *Bleak House*, John E. Mayall asserts that his portraits are greatly superior to ''the many wretched abortions claiming the same nomenclature, and to be seen in almost every street.'' As a means of distinguishing his works from (to quote another portion of the same advertisement) the ''numberless daubs that meet the eye almost in every quarter,'' Mayall refers to them as ''art,'' an evaluation Dickens seems inclined to share when he refers to the photographer as an ''Artist'' whose ''results are very different from those of other men.''

Mayall and Dickens were not alone in considering a good photograph to be art: discussions of the relationship of photography to painting were commonplace. Some asserted that photography should be subordinated to painting, but that painters could benefit from the new technology by replacing live models with photographs. Morley and Wills, for instance, suggest that painters could substitute photographs for travel sketches (61). Others discerned a closer relationship between photography and painting, as did Sir

William Newton who, in an address to the newly-formed Photographic Society of London in 1853, denied that photography was an independent art (Newhall 73). Several prominent portraitists such as David Hill and Robert Adams were trained as painters (Jeffrey 28), and early photographers often relied upon what Ian Jeffrey calls "pictorial code" in the composition and arrangement of their portraits (23).

Early portrait photographers could manipulate many aspects of a sitter's appearance to produce a desired artistic effect. Mayall's advertisement, for instance, suggests dress for sitters that "adds to the beauty of the picture" and "enhances the general effect," specifically "shawls, scarfs, mantles and . . . flowing drapery" for women and "hair in ringlets" for children. In their visit to Mayall's studio, Morley and Wills comment on the attire of a sitter: "Now the lady's dress was not at all ill chosen for a picture sitting or a masquerade" (55). Another prominent London portraitist, Antoine François Claudet, was commended by the *Journal of Commerce* of March 25, 1842, for using "beautiful backgrounds, producing the most picturesque effect" (qtd. in Newhall 35). Color could be introduced by delicately hand-tinting daguerreotypes (Newhall 269), and Mayall specialized in what he called the "crayon daguerreotype," which framed the subject to result in "a picture upon which the head is engraved with unusual distinctness, and the bust is gradually shaded down into the general colour of the plate, so that the effect is that of a crayon portrait" (Morley and Wills 60). Finally, as Ian Jeffrey remarks, "European [as opposed to American] portraits often showed supporting details, which defined their subjects in social terms," signaling the class and status of the sitter (56).

The practice of arranging photographs so as to exhibit sitters to best artistic and social advantage was at odds with the belief that the camera provided an objective, accurate representation of the person being photographed, and claims for the documentary accuracy of photographic portraits were sometimes undercut even as they were advanced. Such is the case with Mayall's advertisement, which quotes a review from the *Manchester Examiner and Times* extolling the photographer's work for its documentary accuracy: "with regard to portraits we see our friends as they are, without a vestige of the tinselled flattery of bygone art, as true as the polished mirror would depict them." However, other parts of the same advertisement (as we have seen) advise sitters on costume, and comment on the "admirable tinting and execution of the drapery," elements of artistic arrangement that might indeed enhance or even change the appearance of the sitter. In claiming that the camera did not flatter, the writers of the *Manchester Examiner and Times* apparently place more confidence in its documentary ability than do the two writers who visited Mayall's studio. Morley and Wills report that in the hands of the women whose business it was to tint daguerreotypes, pictures were "undergoing flattery." One of the women told the writers, "When we don't paint coats bright enough, people complain. They tell us that we make them look as if they wore old clothes" (59).

Perhaps it is the knowledge that portraits do indeed flatter that leads Morley and Wills to conclude that, while a skilled operator can minimize the falsification of the camera's representation, "in the present state of photographic art, no miniature can be utterly free from distortion" (59), and that "it is not only—or indeed chiefly—by the reproduction of our own features that we bring photography into the service of our race" (61). The writers go on to speculate about other potential uses of photography: investigating natural phenomena, charting the moon's phases and observing its surface, creating facsimiles of historical documents (61). A year after Morley and Wills's suggestions were published, the April 29, 1854, issue of *Household Words* again took up the issue of photography's potential applications: writer William Blanchard Jerrold speculates that photography might chart the progress of building projects, aid scientific inquiry, lighten the load of the commercial traveler who could carry photographs rather than samples of wares, and provide witness before a coroner's jury in cases of railway accidents or other disasters (245). It is not far from Jerrold's last suggestion to the conclusion that photographs might aid law enforcement officers to track criminals, an application of photographic technology that Ronald Thomas considers at length.[9] However, even Jerrold, whose article largely celebrates photography's potential, appears somewhat ambivalent when he mentions that photographs could fraudulently duplicate bank notes, and concludes by characterizing photography as "strange, scientific, mournful, all at once!" (245). Not quite sure how best to apply the new technology, the writers in *Household Words* seem simultaneously excited by and wary of photography's documentary potential. With regard to portraiture, the contest between claims of documentary realism and art came to a head in 1855, when German photographer Franz Hanfstaengl showed a print made from a retouched negative at the Exposition Universelle in Paris (Newhall 69–70). From this point on, photographers routinely and openly retouched negatives rather than relying solely on more subtle arrangements of lighting, clothing, background, and props to enhance a sitter's appearance.

Given the popularity of portrait photography during the 1850s, as well as the proliferation of discussion about its uses and shortcomings—a discussion in which Dickens's *Household Words* often engaged—it is not altogether surprising that questions about the truth-claims of painted portraits resonate through *Bleak House*. Characters contemplate the likenesses of other characters and try from them to unravel family secrets, as Guppy does when he recognizes Esther's resemblance to two pictures of Lady Dedlock, one at Chesney Wold, the other hanging on the wall of his friend Weevle's chamber.

Or characters look up at the figure of Allegory on the ceiling of Tulkinghorn's chamber and wish it could give evidence as to who killed the lawyer. Or (less ominously) they try to discern the virtues of Mrs. Bayham Badger's two deceased husbands from the portraits hung proudly in her drawing room. In each of these cases the viewer is required to interpret the image, to ask what portion of reality it represents, which is to some extent what Dickens and his contemporaries did when they looked at a photograph: is the sitter truly as "rigid" and "grim" as the image suggests, or are contortions of face and body the result of "peculiarities inseparable from the process"? Do the photographer's trappings of dress and background and tint romanticize the sitter, or do props such as the "supporting details" Jeffrey mentions reveal a truth about the sitter—such as his or her social position—that might not otherwise be evident in the photograph? While parallels can clearly be drawn between the situation of Dickens's readers and those of his characters, and while this essay will later explore such parallels, at this point it is important to recall that *Bleak House* is set in the decade before photography's invention: although the novel presents for characters' and readers' contemplation several painted portraits, there are no photographs in the houses of the novel's characters. Consequently, if we wish to consider comments the novel may be making on technology of Dickens's day, we must rely upon inferences rather than explicit statements. Recalling Benjamin's description of the evolution of art, we can ask whether, in *Bleak House*, we do indeed see painted portraits that "aspire to the effects" of the "changed technical standard" introduced by the camera.

As indicated earlier, chief among these effects is memorialization of middle-class sitters, whose social ascendancy led to patronage of the new photographic portrait studios. With respect to historical accuracy, however, we must recognize that even before photography's invention in 1839, middle-class patrons were purchasing painted portraits of themselves in increasing numbers. As art historian William Gaunt points out, the economic prosperity of the Victorian era "produced a great age of picture-buying" (8) among those whose incomes derived from manufacturing, banking, and small business (Gaunt 25; Pelles 45). The tastes of these new patrons were apparently not as refined as many painters would have liked: Alan Bird writes that British artists were "faced with aggressive philistinism from the brash, self-opinionated and uncultivated Bounderbys of the Victorian Age" (199). Motivated by traditional associations between portrait ownership and class standing, such "Bounderbys" were interested in purchasing portraits of themselves rather than other types of subjects, and as growing numbers of artists competed for commissions (Pelles 23), portraiture became "the only sure way for an English artist to make a living" (Bowness 286). The artist skilled at portraiture was aided by new technology in the dissemination of his or her work: inexpensive reproductions of paintings by new methods of chromo-lithography and photoengraving made the paintings available to most middle-class purchasers (Ericksen 33). Not everybody was happy about the popularity of portraits, however: Thackeray, for instance, complained of the absence of pictures other than portraits in middle-class homes (Pelles 46), voicing a sentiment not uncommon among artists and art connoisseurs that the rising middle class was too unsophisticated to understand and appreciate more chal-lenging subjects. Nevertheless, Thackeray's yoking the middle class with por-trait ownership indicates the extent to which the two were joined in the popular imagination, and suggests the existence of a ready-made market for photography once the technology became available.

Walter Benjamin, again reflecting upon the development of art, writes that "social changes often promote a change in receptivity which will benefit the new art form" (250). It is precisely the moment of this "change in receptiv-ity" that *Bleak House* captures. In looking back the 1830s, Dickens (always an astute observer of his culture, and well-versed in contemporary painting[10]) depicts a society at a time of change, suggesting in patterns of portrait owner-ship a shift in power and prestige to the middle class that in his own era would benefit the new art form of photography.

There is no question that in *Bleak House*, the people we would traditionally expect to own portraits—the aristocracy and gentry—do so. In fact, the omni-scient narrator refers repeatedly to the pictures of the Dedlock ancestors hung on the walls of Chesney Wold. From the first allusion to these portraits, however, the reader realizes that they express not power, but decline. The novel's second chapter, describing a rainy November afternoon at the unin-habited Chesney Wold, states, "the pictures of the Dedlocks past and gone have seemed to vanish into the damp walls in mere lowness of spirits, as the housekeeper has passed along the old rooms, shutting up the shutters" (9). If, as Allan Pritchard has pointed out, Dickens made free use of Gothic conventions when he wrote *Bleak House*, here these conventions are inverted. Traditionally, portraits step out of their frames in Gothic novels to intervene in an action: in Walpole's *The Castle of Otranto*, for instance, a painting of Manfred's grandfather sighs and steps from its frame to lure Manfred away from Isabella, enabling her to escape his advances. In *Bleak House*, however, the Dedlock portraits have no such potency. Rather than moving away from the wall, they vanish lifelessly into it. Later in the novel, when danger to the family appears immanent, the portraits again are evoked as powerless: "As Sir Leicester basks in his library, and dozes over his newspaper, is there no influence in the house to startle him; not to say, to make the very trees at Chesney Wold fling up their knotted arms, the very portraits frown, the very armour stir? No" (410). As Skimpole observes, the Dedlock portraits are "perfectly free from animation" (532); they hang stupidly on walls of a house often shut up, and as J. R. Harvey has noted, they are frequently treated as a "comic chorus" (157) by the narrator and characters such as Skimpole.

The one Dedlock portrait still potent in this novel, having escaped ineffectual confinement at Chesney Wold, is the engraving of Lady Dedlock that Weevle owns as part of his collection of Galaxy Gallery of British Beauty. Thomas has pointed out that what keeps this particular image alive is new technology (such as the aforementioned chromolithography and photoengraving) that allowed for mass production of painted portraits.[11] Circulating in a consumer market, Lady Dedlock's Galaxy portrait no longer serves the function it did when families such as the Dedlocks were at the height of their social power: it no longer signals exclusivity. Instead, it indicates a technological and economic shift that makes such artwork, and presumably the prestige heretofore associated with such artwork, available to people other than the Dedlocks. This particular "speaking likeness" of Lady Dedlock (as Guppy refers to it) speaks the demise of the Dedlock dynasty, but neither Guppy, nor Tulkinghorn, nor Bucket, ultimately causes this demise. The family and the power base the family represents are already in decline when the story opens, as the novel's first description of the Dedlock portraits' vanishing into the walls makes clear.

Not all of the novel's portraits are as moribund as those of the Dedlock family. On the contrary, the novel presents several artworks that exude vitality, such as the portrait of Guppy hanging in his mother's sitting room that seems to Esther "more like than life: it insisted upon him with such obstinacy, and was so determined not to let him off" (541). This, too, is a speaking likeness, but it speaks aggressively, energetically, unlike the listless portraits on the walls of Chesney Wold. The suggestion that the portrait is "more like than life" echoes claims often made for photography in Dickens's day, such as those of French photographer Gaspard-Felix Tournachon (known as Nadar), who wrote of photography's ability to acquire "the moral grasp of the subject—that instant understanding which puts [the photographer] in touch with the model, helps [the photographer] to sum him up" (qtd. in Jeffrey 41). Like Nadar's later photographic portraits, the oil portrait of Guppy "sums him up" by revealing a quality the intensity of which becomes even more apparent in the artwork than in life: Guppy's determination not to be "let off," that is, to stamp his image upon society.

Guppy's is not the only middle-class portrait depicted at some length: the reader is also told of Guster's care in dusting portraits of Mr. and Mrs. Snagsby that are "displayed in oil—and plenty of it too" in their upstairs drawing room. These oil portraits may lack artistic merit, but they seem to have been painted with gusto, and in the servant's eyes, "are . . . as achievements of Raphael or Titian" (129). Significantly, the name of the artist who in Guster's view rivals the masters is left unspoken in this novel, as are those of the artists who painted Guppy's portrait, and even Lady Dedlock's. In showing visitors the house at Chesney Wold, Rosa reports that Lady Dedlock's portrait is "the best work of the master," but does not name him. Nor does the omniscient narrator, who merely records that the portrait was "painted by the fashionable artist of the day" (87). The anonymity of all the portrait painters in this novel[12] has the effect of calling attention to the sitter rather than to the imaginative or technical abilities of the artist: artistic skill is valued insofar as it produces a recognizable portrait, and the artist becomes an instrument by which to record a likeness. In this way painted portraits in *Bleak House* are much like photographs in Dickens's era, the majority of which bear no signature on the plate by which we might identify the photographer who took them (Newhall 32) . Although it is fair to assume that the portrait of Lady Dedlock was painted by a more delicate hand than the one that lavished plenty of oil on the Snagsby portraits, its value as an aesthetic object is subordinated to its social function, and the social function of Lady Dedlock's portrait is essentially the same as that of the Snagsby portraits: all attest to the prestige of their sitters. Once a marker of social difference, the portrait now marks an erasure of distinctions as a new class energetically claims the right to represent itself.

Supplementing the narrative's descriptions of portraits are illustrations that also link portrait ownership with the social aspirations of the middle class. Of the 40 plates that Hablot Knight Browne designed in collaboration with Dickens,[13] 22 picture characters' places of residence; of these 22 interiors, 18 have paintings hung on the walls. There are a total of 48 paintings depicted: 35 (or 75%) of these appear to be portraits, and portraits are hung in the homes of the novel's middle-class and professional characters—Vholes, Snagsby, Turveydrop, Bayham Badger—as well as of the aristocracy (the Dedlocks) and the gentry (Jarndyce) . The preponderance of portraits not only thematically supports a plot hinging upon revelations about identity, but also visually connects the homes of the middle class and those of the aristocracy and gentry. These connections are further strengthened by the presence of other decorative objects in the illustrations. While it is widely known that Browne deployed Hogarth's method of including in the backgrounds of illustrations paintings that comment on the action being depicted,[14] some of the decorative objects included in *Bleak House*'s illustrations seem at first oddly detached from the subject of the illustration. For instance, the plate "Mr. Chadband 'Improving' a Tough Subject" illustrates the Snagsby parlor. The preacher stands in the middle of the picture with one hand upraised, the other palm forward in front of him, while at his feet cowers the wretched Jo, and around him sit Mr. and Mrs. Snagsby, Mrs. Chadband, two apprentices, and Guster. The room depicted in this plate contains several pieces of art, including behind Mr. Chadband two small portraits that do not appear to be the ones of Mr.

and Mrs. Snagsby that Guster so admired, and a large picture of an evangelist: the figure in this canvas stands with one hand upraised, facing the same direction as Mr. Chadband, who is positioned directly below the picture. However, while Mr. Chadband's left hand is empty, the evangelist bears a cross. Obviously Mr. Chadband does not come to his task as fully prepared as did the evangelist, and here the plate provides the Hogarthian commentary on the inefficacy of Mr. Chadband's methods. But three other pieces of decorative art displayed along the parlor's side wall provide a greater challenge to interpretation. These pieces include a mounted fish hung over the fireplace, a porcelain shepherd and shepherdess standing upon the mantle, and a screen to the left of the fireplace. While these pieces may initially seem included merely to fill up empty space, they actually function thematically when one realizes that all three objects have been pictured or alluded to earlier in the novel: a plate entitled ''Coavinses'' depicts a room in Bleak House where a porcelain shepherd and shepherdess grace the mantelpiece; the mounted fish is mentioned in Esther's description of Bleak House (66); and Lady Dedlock is seen shading her face with a fire screen (albeit a hand-held one) when she encounters Nemo's handwriting among the papers Tulkinghorn has brought (14), as well as when Guppy first visits her (402). The decorative art displayed in the Snagsby parlor thus links the stationer's home with those of figures traditionally more elevated in social status and supports the suggestion of class ascendancy conveyed by the parlor's four portraits (the two pictured in the illustration, and the two of Mr. and Mrs. Snagsby described by the narrative).

In both illustrations and narrative, portrait ownership in *Bleak House* attests to a shift in social power from the erstwhile great old families to a new, rising middle class, and the ubiquity of the painted portrait in the parlors of the novel's middle-class characters evokes the popularity of the photographic portrait of Dickens's day. In the novel as in the homes of Dickens's contemporaries, portraits make the middle class a permanent feature of society. But what of the ambivalence with which many of Dickens's contemporaries regarded the photographic portrait? Does this ambivalence make its way into *Bleak House*? As the remainder of this essay will demonstrate, the answer to this question is yes. While Guppy and Snagsby seem perfectly content with the artistic merits of and social claims advanced by the portraits gracing their walls, in the end *Bleak House* leaves its reader unsure about the extent to which a painted image can be trusted. The grounds the novel presents for distrust are akin to those often cited in contemporary discussions of photography.

Some of the novel's portraits are clearly satirized for their stylized and flattering depiction of sitters. These portraits subordinate sitters' personalities to fashions of the age and myths of family glory:

There were such portentous shepherdesses among the Ladies Dedlock dead and gone . . . that peaceful crooks became weapons of assault in their hands. They tended their flocks severely in buckram and powder, and put their sticking-plaster patches on to terrify commoners, as the chiefs of some other tribes put on their war-paint. There was a Sir Somebody Dedlock, with a battle, a spring-mine, volumes of smoke, flashes of lightning, a town on fire, and a stormed fort, all in full action between his horse's two hind legs: showing . . . how little a Dedlock made of such trifles.   (532)

It is precisely the extravagant trappings of such paintings that, in the 1850s, photography was said to shun when it depicted sitters without the "tinselled flattery of bygone art" (to quote again from Mayall's brochure). However, in his description of the Dedlock portraits, Dickens calls attention to the very aspects of composition and arrangement that contemporary photographers were also known to manipulate, often to emphasize the social situation of sitters, and sometimes with the effect of misleading a viewer. A description of one of Mayall's portraits, for example, reveals the same kind of stylized presentation of its subject that a visitor to Chesney Wold might have discovered: Morley and Wills describe a photograph of "a belted soldier with a red coat, a large cocked hat, and a heavy sword," a stereotypical man of war. However, the writers are surprised to discover that the sitter is actually "a man of peace, a lamb in wolf's clothing; an army doctor, by whose side, if army regulations suffered it, there should have hung a scalpel, not a sword" (55). If stylized costume and background make some of the painted portraits in *Bleak House* dubious, then photography is no less subject to censure on the same grounds.[15]

It is sometimes difficult to say, however, when pictorial trappings convey the truth (as in instances where a photographer's props accurately communicated a sitter's class position or profession) and when they mislead (as in the above description of the physician-cum-soldier). The indeterminate status of the Galaxy portrait of Lady Dedlock hanging on Weevle's wall illustrates this difficulty. The portrait is described at some length: "she is represented on a terrace, with a pedestal upon the terrace, and a vase upon the pedestal, and her shawl upon the vase, and a prodigious piece of fur upon the shawl, and her arm on the prodigious piece of fur, and a bracelet on her arm" (448). This is another of the family's stylized paintings, particularly as it calls attentions to the accouterments of wealth that surround and define its subject. The tone with which the picture is described recalls the narrator's irreverent treatment of the other family portraits, and the narrator's verbal piling-up of objects on and around Lady Dedlock puts a reader in mind of the two pictures of the "Fancy Ball School" that Sir Leicester takes joy in contemplating, pictures "which would be best catalogued like the miscellaneous articles in a sale" (401). To readers who have encountered myriad descriptions of the staring ancestors on the walls of Chesney Wold, and who have one installment earlier seen Lady Dedlock—a "wild figure on [her] knees"—suffering when she discovers Esther's parentage (410), the portrait misrepresents Lady Dedlock by casting her as yet another superficial, decorated Dedlock. Yet Guppy praises this painting as "a speaking likeness," claiming for it a documentary accuracy much like that later attributed to photographs. Guppy does not comment upon, or even seem to notice, that this picture is stylized, that it represents a social position as much as (if not more than) an individual. Rather, his confidence in the accuracy of the likeness enables him to draw from it information that leads him to the same conclusions reached by Tulkinghorn and Bucket, characters who have considerably more prestige in the novel than Guppy. The "speaking likeness" does indeed provide crucial evidence in the revelation of Lady Dedlock's history. Is this painting, then, to be venerated or disparaged? Does it reveal or conceal truth? In the end, no simple answers to these questions are possible.

Lest we suspect that the fancy portraits of the Dedlocks are the only ones giving rise to such questions, we can once again turn our attention to Guppy's. To recall Esther's description, the portrait of Guppy is "more like than life: it insisted upon him with such obstinacy, and was so determined not to let him off" (541). Perhaps unwittingly, Esther points out what is ridiculous in the painting and its sitter: not the rising social status that enables Guppy to have the portrait made, but the vehemence and "obstinacy" with which he and the portrait assert his claims. In being "more like than life," the portrait not only reveals these attributes in its subject, but also exaggerates them and fixes them in time. The portrait allows Esther to learn in a moment what an acquaintance of Guppy's who hasn't seen the picture might require a much longer period to discern. But in exaggerating Guppy's ambitions and refusing ever "to let him off," the portrait begins to look remarkably like one that might hang on the walls of Chesney Wold: like Guppy's portrait, those of the staring Dedlock ancestors insist upon themselves with equal determination never to give way. When Guppy aspires to the social prestige and power of the Dedlocks, he also becomes susceptible to their weaknesses.

Perhaps it is coincidental that rigidity was one attribute of photographic portraits that Dickens found objectionable, but the paintings in *Bleak House* are frequently depicted as, and satirized for, sharing this same fault. Whether resulting from the stylized arrangement of the image or from the character of the sitter, the paintings' rigidity implicates them in the novel's indictment of paralyzed and paralyzing institutions such as the "deadened" world of fashion (8) and the "leaden-headed" Court of Chancery (2).[16] Portraits (whether painted, or made in a photographic studio such as Mayall's that pledged "every picture guaranteed permanent, and to stand the test of time") promise sitters a permanent place in history; to remain vital, however, a society cannot obstinately cling to fixed images. The portraits in *Bleak House* do indeed indicate a shift in the social position of the middle class, but they also caution a reader that the middle class could eventually become like the moribund Dedlocks if complacency wins the day.

Two years after completing *Bleak House*, Dickens wrote a letter to his friend and biographer John Forster reviewing (not favorably) an exhibition of British painting in Paris. In the letter Dickens observes that the paintings were "strangely expressive to me of the state of England itself" (qtd. in Ormond 17). This assertion echoes one made in the March 1853 issue of *Household Words*, but in the earlier instance, the art form "expressive of the state of England" is photography, "a liberal art born of our own days, and peculiarly marked with the character of our own time" (Morley and Wills 57). These two statements grant painting and photography equal status as reflections of an age, a similarity Dickens uses to full advantage in *Bleak House*. Obviously the novel deals with the theme of the trustworthiness of appearances, a theme of great significance in an era in which the camera was touted as "nature's pencil" and images the camera recorded were starting to be used as evidence in scientific and legal inquiries. While *Bleak House*'s historical setting requires that the theme is treated with reference to paintings, clearly the questions the novel raises about the reliability of representation did not lose their relevance with the invention of photography. In this light, it is difficult to concur with Thomas that in the novel, paintings that do not tell the truth are contrasted with photographs that do. Rather than contrasting the two art forms, the novel compares them. Sometimes its painted portraits do indeed obscure the truth; sometimes they reveal it. In all cases, the person standing in front of the painting must carefully weigh its claims, much as Dickens's contemporaries did when assessing the merits of the new photographic portraits, some of which obscured the truth, some of which revealed it. It is not always easy or possible to separate truth from untruth in art, as *Bleak House*'s readers learn when contemplating the paradoxically stylized yet perfect likeness of Lady Dedlock, and Dickens's readers discovered when seeing artfully arranged and tinted, yet often rigid, daguerreotypes of themselves and their neighbors. *Bleak House* invited contemporary readers to contemplate its painted portraits in much the same terms as they did their photographs, indeed encouraged such contemplation by establishing implicit parallels between the two art forms. And if Dickens and his contemporaries celebrated the wonders of the new technology at the same time as they found it "strange, scientific and mournful, all at once" (to recall Jerrold's conclusion), it is no great surprise that for *Bleak House*'s readers, paintings characterized as "more like than life" evoke similar ambivalence.

NOTES

1. Thomas makes essentially the same argument about Bucket in an earlier article, "Making Darkness Visible: Capturing the Criminal and Observing the Law in Victorian Photography and Detective Fiction," where he considers *Bleak House* in relation to Doyle's Sherlock Holmes stories.

2. In addition to Thomas, other critics discussing the Dedlock portraits at length include Donald H. Ericksen, Anny Sadrin, Jane R. Cohen, and J. R. Harvey.

3. J. R. Harvey is one of the few critics to comment upon portraits of the novel's middle-class characters. He writes, "The prosperity and self-esteem of the Snagsbies and Guppies is reflected in their own portraits"(156). Unfortunately, he does not further explore the implications of this observation.

4. Most critics have cited the novel's description of superannuated Chancery practices and the coming of the railroad in chapter 55 to establish the story's setting.

5. The limited scope of this article precludes me from considering novels other than *Bleak House*. However, this essay's discussion of art might well be extended to include other novels. For instance, the miniatures produced by Miss La Creevy of *Nicholas Nickleby* typify the works by obscure professional artists that flooded the market in the years proceeding photography's inception and fed the middle class's desire for portraits; the Veneerings' paintings in *Our Mutual Friend* proclaim the rising social status of their owners; and Bounderby's portrait in *Hard Times* boisterously lays claim to a prominent social position, much as Guppy's does in *Bleak House* .

6. See Newhall for a discussion of the proliferation of portrait studios in England and on the Continent.

7. There seems to be debate among scholars about dates of early daguerreotypes of Dickens. I am basing my claim on information related to me by Andrew Xavier of the Dickens House Museum, London, whom I would also like to thank for facilitating my research in the serial installments of *Bleak House*.

7. For more on technological developments in photography, see works by Jeffrey and Newhall.

9. In his analysis of *Bleak House*, Thomas writes that not long after the invention of photography, photographs were adopted as aides to social control and surveillance, which proved a source of contemporary anxiety. Thomas notes that Bucket, who represents the "panopticism" of the new technology, mitigates this anxiety by serving as a "beneficial rather than threatening" agent in the novel's plot ("Double Exposure" 101).

10. For discussions of Dickens's involvement with artists and the art world, see articles by Leonee Ormond, Donald H. Ericksen, and Richard Lettis, among others .

11. Thomas goes even further to speculate in "Making Darkness Visible" that Lady Dedlock's portrait "may have been reproduced by some primitive photographic process" (140), and in "Double Exposure" that "this copy may well have been reproduced . . . we may even speculate, on a collodionised glass plate" (95). These speculations do not seem altogether tenable, given the novel's setting before photography's invention.

12. For additional comments on the anonymity of *Bleak House*'s portrait painters, see Anny Sadrin's "Presence et fonction de l'art et de l'artiste dans *Bleak House*."
13. Jane Cohen discusses at length Dickens's role in designing the plates, indicating that he specified what he wanted in the illustrations, approved the preliminary sketches (often returning them to Browne with marginal suggestions), in general took pains to ensure that the illustrations achieved the desired effect (64).
14. See J. R. Harvey's *Victorian Novelists and Their Illustrators* for an extended discussion of Hogarth's influence on Browne's illustrations.
15. Leonee Ormond comments that Dickens "felt that there was a deep hypocrisy in representing people on canvas as quite unlike their true selves" (13). I suggest that Dickens disliked "hypocrisy in representing people" on the photographic plate as much as on canvas.
16. Writing of *Little Dorrit*, Martin Meisel arrives at a conclusion similar to mine: "The frozen image, in stone, paint, or flesh, is associated in the novel with both the intrinsic quality and the extrinsic effects of the deadly set who are allowed to preside over the social and political life of the community" (316).

WORKS CITED

Benjamin, Walter. "The Work of Art in the Age of Mechanical Reproduction." *Illuminations*. Ed. Hannah Arendt. New York: Schocken, 1969. 217–51.

Bird, Alan. "The Romantics." *The Genius of British Painting*. Ed. David Piper. New York: William Morrow, 1975. 198–248.

Bowness, Alan. "The Victorians." *The Genius of British Painting*. Ed. David Piper. New York: William Morrow, 1975. 249–90.

Cohen, Jane R. *Charles Dickens and His Original Illustrators*. Columbus: Ohio State UP, 1980.

Dickens, Charles. *Bleak House*. 1853. Introd. Osbert Sitwell. Oxford: Oxford UP, 1987.

———. "To Angela Burdett Coutts." 23 Dec. 1852. *The Letters of Charles Dickens*. Ed. Graham Storey, Kathleen Tillotson and Nina Burgis. Vol. 6. Oxford: Clarendon, 1988. 833–34.

Ericksen, Donald H. "*Bleak House* and Victorian Art and Illustration: Charles Dickens's Visual Narrative Style." *The Journal of Narrative Technique* 3 (Winter 1983): 31–46.

Gaunt, William. *The Restless Century: Painting in Britain 1800–1900*. Oxford: Phaidon, 1978.

Harvey, J. R. *Victorian Novelists and Their Illustrators*. New York: New York UP, 1971.

Jeffrey, Ian. *Photography: A Concise History*. New York: Oxford UP, 1981.

Jerrold, William Blanchard. "Busy With the Photograph." *Household Words* 29 April 1854: 242–45.

Lettis, Richard. "Dickens and Art." *Dickens Studies Annual* 14 (1985): 93–146.

Meisel, Martin. *Realizations: Narrative, Pictorial, and Theatrical Arts in Nineteenth-Century England*. Princeton, N. J.: Princeton UP, 1983.

Morley, Henry, and W. H. Wills. "Photography." *Household Words* 19 March 1853: 54–61.

Newhall, Beaumont. *The History of Photography from 1839 to the Present*. New York: Museum of Modern Art, 1982.

Ormond, Leonee. "Dickens and Painting: Contemporary Art." *The Dickensian* 80 (Spring 1984): 3–25.

Pelles, Geraldine. *Art, Artists, and Society: Origins of a Modern Dilemma*. Englewood Cliffs, N. J.: Prentice-Hall, 1963.

Pritchard, Allan. "The Urban Gothic of *Bleak House*." *Nineteenth-Century Literature* 45 (June 1990): 432–52.

Sadrin, Anny. "Presence et Fonction de l'Art et de l'Artiste dans *Bleak House*." *Home, Sweet Home or Bleak House? Art et Litterature a l'Epoque Victorienne*. Ed. Marie-Claire Hamard. Paris: Les Belles Lettres, 1981. 131–50.

Thomas, Ronald R. "Double Exposure: Arresting Images in *Bleak House* and *The House of Seven Gables*." *Novel: A Forum on Fiction* 31 (Fall 1997): 87–113.

———. "Making Darkness Visible: Capturing the Criminal and Observing the Law in Victorian Photography and Detective Fiction." *Victorian Literature and the Victorian Visual Imagination*. Ed. Carol T. Christ and John O. Jordan. Berkeley: U of California P, 1995. 134–68.

Wax-Work, Clock-Work, and Puppet-Shews: *Bleak House* and the Uncanny

Robyn L. Schiffman

While Esther has been discussed as a character who both experiences uncanny feelings herself and generates uncanniness in others, critical commentary has yet to pay attention to Esther's doll as an uncanny figure or to examine the uncanny relationship Esther has with her doll. Through close reading of those passages in which Dolly appears in Bleak House, *this essay reconsiders the Freudian uncanny and its presence in this novel by looking at the uncanniness of things, specifically Esther's doll. Additionally, analysis of the two key moments in the novel when Dolly reappears (during Esther's search for love and for her mother) illustrates how the uncanny is solidly rooted in the unconscious mind of the child and is brought about by the sexual life of the adult.*

> Mr. Tulkinghorn is . . . so oddly out of place, and yet so perfectly at home.
>
> —*Bleak House*[1]

Discussing *Bleak House* scholarship, Philip Collins observed in 1978 that "The character much the most has been written about . . . is Esther Summerson" (97). A survey of Esther's appearance in critical studies of the subsequent twenty years reveals that Dickens's narrator still commands her share of attention, though arguably not with as much regularity or playfulness.[2] One interpretive method that has been particularly profitable in analyzing Esther is psychoanalysis. The relationship between *Bleak House* and psychoanalysis goes back at least to 1883, when the twenty-seven-year-old

---

Freud (who is almost, we might point out, as old as *Bleak House*) wrote to his future wife, Martha Bernays, about Dickens's heroines and Esther in particular.[3] Over one hundred years later, the Anglo-American scholarship of the mid-1970s produced a number of psychoanalytic studies of *Bleak House*, and the end of that decade would yield more in-depth investigations, as critics used Freud's 1919 paper "The 'Uncanny' " as the framework from which to analyze Esther.[4] In this essay, I return to Freud's 1919 treatise and the criticism on *Bleak House* it has inspired as a way of theorizing about uncanny things, more specifically dolls. While Esther has been discussed as a character who both experiences uncanny feelings and creates the uncanny herself, critical commentary has yet to pay attention to Esther's doll as an uncanny figure or to examine the uncanny relationship Esther has with her doll.[5] The charting of Dolly's presence in the novel invites the critic to reconsider Esther's own humanness and returns the discussion of the uncanny back toward things.

Scholarly attention to the Dickensian uncanny has focused on "that class of the frightening which leads back to what is known of old and long familiar" as it relates to people (Freud, "The 'Uncanny' " 121). In his influential study, Robert Newsom reads closely those passages in which Esther's face is the cause of another character's *déjà vu* (50–64). Both Jo and Mr. Guppy, think they have met or at least seen Esther before and are visibly confused and upset. For Jo, bewilderment gives way to near hysteria as he wonders, in a memorable scene, "Is there *three* of 'em then," confusing Lady Dedlock, Mademoiselle Hortense, and Esther (488). Following in Newsom's steps, Maria Tatar sees Lady Dedlock as a character who activates uncanny feelings in Esther (180–81). At first, it is Lady Dedlock's face that causes Esther to be "fluttered and troubled" (304) when they meet early in the novel in church. Esther reports that Lady Dedlock's face was "like a broken glass" which had the power to evoke "scraps of old remembrances" (304). Later, it is Lady Dedlock's voice that forces Esther to recall "immumerable pictures of myself" (309).

The experience of the self seeing a disguised version of itself, whereby the self does not, at first, recognize the self (especially when seeing the reflection in a mirror), is a further uncanny experience.[6] This uncanny experience, as we will examine shortly, captures the two sides of uncanny: the strange familiarity of the other and the strange otherness of the familiar. A pivotal example of this duality comes in Esther's famous mirror scene, occurring about halfway into *Bleak House*. Having recovered from a disfiguring illness, Esther finally gathers her courage, for the first time since her convalescence, to look in the mirror. The act of glimpsing her altered complexion results in the following:

> My hair had not been cut off, though it had been in danger more than once. It
> was long and thick. I let it down, and shook it out, and went up to the glass

upon the dressing-table. There was a little muslin curtain drawn across it. I drew it back: and stood for a moment looking through a veil of my own hair, that I could see nothing else. Then, I put my hair aside, and looked at the reflection in the mirror, encouraged by seeing how placidly it looked at me. I was very much changed -O very, very much. At first, my face was so strange to me, that I think I should have put my hands before it and started back, but for the encouragement I have mentioned. Very soon it became familiar, and then I knew the extent of the alteration in it better than I had done at first. It was not like what I had expected.   (599)

In this passage, Esther describes the process of recognizing her face as it stares, unfamiliarly, back at her. Esther's attempt at seeing her reflection is burdened, at first, by two obstacles: the muslin curtain on the mirror and the cascade of her own hair. Nonetheless, Esther knows she is looking at herself; yet, she is so changed by her illness that she does not recognize herself. She records that her reflection is at first very strange to her, so much so that she even refers to her reflection, and her face, as "it." Gradually, the strange becomes familiar and Esther comes to recognize herself, returning to the first-person pronoun "I."

Sixty-six years later and countries away, Freud writes the following in a footnote in his "The 'Uncanny' ":

I was sitting alone in my *wagon-lit* compartment when a more than unusually violent jolt of the train swung back the door of the adjoining washing-cabinet, and an elderly gentleman in a dressing-gown and a traveling cap came in. I assumed that in leaving the washing-cabinet, which lay between the two compartments, he had taken the wrong direction and come into my compartment by mistake. Jumping up with the intention of putting him right, I at once realized to my dismay that the intruder was nothing but my reflection in the looking glass on the open door. I can still recollect that I thoroughly disliked his appearance.
(248)

Though different in tone, circumstance, and genre, Esther's and Freud's words above describe their reactions upon not having recognized their own mirror image. Uncanny feelings emerge, says Freud, when one experiences "that class of the frightening which leads back to what is known of old and long familiar" (220). After the reflection reveals what is "old and long familiar," that is, their own faces, the shock and fear are registered. Esther needs "encouragement" as she almost turns away from her strange face. Freud is rather upset by this experience: he is aggressive in his choice of words and in his desired course of action. Freud's German is even more emphatic: he uses the word "verdutzt," perhaps more commonly translated as "taken aback" or "astonished," rather than Strachey's "dismayed."[7]

Given the almost eerie pertinence of Freud's essay to Esther's reactions toward herself and the other characters in the novel, it is surprising that most psychoanalytic commentary on *Bleak House* has not gone further to explore what Freud considered one of the primary sources of uncanny feelings. "There is something," Siegbert Prawer contends, "uncanny in *things*" (19; emphasis by Prawer). In the remainder of this essay I will closely examine Esther's doll as an uncanny figure both in Esther's description of her and her reappearance at two critical moments in the text. As we shall see, the presence of this figure initiates a discussion about Esther's own doll-self in relation to the uncanny themes of the often unclear boundary between human and non-human.

Freud's "The 'Uncanny' " refutes and elaborates upon a 1906 paper by Ernst Jentsch. Jentsch concludes and Freud then reports that there is something uncanny about wax figures, automata, and dolls.[8] In our postmodern age replete with cyborgs appearing in literature and film, and with the ever more permeable boundary between man and machine, interest in automata may seem perfectly sensible and perhaps somewhat boring. But during the nineteenth and early twentieth centuries, automata still fascinated, perplexed, and frightened people. One has only to read E. T. A. Hoffmann's 1814 story "Die Automate" [Automata] (a story that Freud, curiously, does not even mention in his Hoffmann-centered essay), in order to understand a fictional account of an earlier culture's automaton fear and attraction.[9] By the time Charles Dickens was born in 1812, Madam Tussaud had already been exhibiting her collection of wax figures for ten years. She would continue to tour all of the United Kingdom in fairs and circuses until 1835, at which point London's Baker Street became her permanent home (Gurrey, 3).

Psychoanalysts and psychologists, notably Freud and Jentsch, inherited this fascination with wax figures, automata, and dolls and set out to explain the power these figures held over their viewers. Freud and Jentsch use the example of the German Romantic author Hoffmann (1776–1822), "a writer who has succeeded in producing uncanny effects better than anyone else" (227), to illustrate their respective theories about the appearance of the uncanny in literature. Hoffmann's 1816 novella *Der Sandmann* [The Sandman] contains the character Olympia, the automaton with whom the student Nathanael falls in love. Jentsch believes that dolls, because of their likeness to real life, create intellectual uncertainty, the inability to ascertain whether or not a figure is human. In Hoffmann's story, Nathanael's central problem, leading to his eventual suicide, is his inability to realize that Olympia is a wooden doll [Holzpüppchen]. This uncertainty, expressed by Jentsch as a feeling of "discomfort" or "ungemüthlichkeit," is more commonly expressed as uncanny, "unheimlich." Interested in the effect on viewers and readers, Jentsch writes that identification with the wax figure is based on fear, fear that the figure will come to life. Freud, on the other hand, understands the uncanniness of dolls not as fear but as desire and connects the uncanny with something, not surprisingly, that occurred in childhood. Using the example of children and their relationships with their dolls, Freud writes that children do not actually fear their dolls coming to life; in fact the opposite is true—they often wish it. Contrary to Jentsch's conclusion, Freud writes that "The source of uncanny feelings . . . is not an infantile fear . . . but rather an infantile wish" (233). Freud then resolves to "content ourselves with selecting those themes of uncanniness which are most prominent, and with seeing whether they too can fairly be traced back to infantile sources" (234).

Using Freud's and Jentsch's formulation of the uncanny as our starting point, we can trace the representation of Esther's doll, an uncanny figure in *Bleak House*. Most people familiar with *Bleak House* know that something remarkable happens in the third chapter: a first-person narrator, Esther Summerson, introduces herself to the reader. Esther's first words, "I have a great deal of difficulty in beginning my portion of these pages, for I know I am not clever. I always knew that" (62), have received much attention, and are widely recognized as characteristic of her self-effacing style. What has been less well analyzed is the sentence that follows. Here, three full sentences after Esther's first entrance into her portion of the narrative of *Bleak House*, Dolly makes her appearance. She disappears in this third chapter just as swiftly; she is eventually buried by Esther. In other words, Dolly lives and dies in the space of eight pages. While this may seem an insignificant amount of space in a novel that is almost a thousand pages long, Dolly remains important not only to the narrative of the novel as a figure of repetition, but also critical to Esther's simultaneous development as a young woman and author. As we shall see, Dolly reappears in the text not to haunt Esther or the novel, but to demonstrate how the uncanny is solidly rooted in the unconscious mind of the child and is brought about by the sexual life of the adult.

How does Esther introduce Dolly? First to see evidence of Dolly as an uncanny figure, we need only continue with Esther's introductory statements:

> I have a great deal of difficulty in beginning my portion of these pages, for I know I am not clever. I always knew that. I can remember, when I was a very little girl indeed, I used to say to my doll, when we were alone together, "Now Dolly, I am not clever, you know very well, and you must be patient with me, like a dear!" And she used to sit propped up in a great arm-chair, with her beautiful complexion and rosy lips, staring at me . . . while I busily stitched away, and told her every one of my secrets. (62)

What is significant about this passage is the immediate importance Dolly is given by Dickens. Dolly, described at length in subsequent paragraphs, is Esther's "only friend" and the only figure with whom she "felt at ease" (63), because, while she lived with her godmother, Esther never confided in anyone other than the doll. Introduced only two sentences after Esther, the doll is given almost equivalent narrative time and space in the first few paragraphs of this chapter. That there is something uncanny about Dolly is immediately established by Dickens, both by the ontological linkage developed and sustained between the two and Dolly's emergence in the text as human. Esther wishes Dolly to come to life and, through her narration, Esther does bring Dolly to life; Esther describes Dolly's "beautiful complexion" and "rosy lips" (62). Esther fancies that Dolly, "propped up in a great armchair," has been both "faithful" and "expecting" (62) her arrival home from school. Esther would then "sit down on the floor, leaning on the elbow of her great chair, and tell her all I had noticed since we parted" (62).

"Children do not distinguish at all sharply," Freud writes, "between living and inanimate objects . . . they are especially fond of treating their dolls like live people" (233). If the uncanny allows for the blurring of the boundaries between person and thing, between human and machine, we see how Esther and her doll, respectively, double as doll and human, versions of each. Indeed what is striking about these descriptions is the uncertainty the reader has in identifying precisely who the doll is: Esther or Dolly? Esther herself enables this point as she describes Dolly to the reader. Using what Jentsch calls the "finer details" [feineren Einzelheiten], Esther describes Dolly's humanized form and particular human body parts, all of which contribute in causing uncanny feelings: "The fact that such wax-figures do often represent anatomical details," Jentsch writes, "may indeed contribute to the intensification of the intended emotional effect."[10] Confusion about the real and the fake underlies the rest of the chapter as we learn Dolly's name before we learn Esther's, perhaps leading the reader to question which figure is more important. Additionally, Esther compares her upbringing to "the princesses in the fairy stories" (63). The language used here by Esther invokes a genre of literature in which fantastic elements, it could be said, are the norm. The princess remark, found in the third paragraph of the third chapter, plays on the reader's expectations of both novels and of fairy tales. Highlighting another level of the fictional process in the construction of narrative, Esther's comment supports the already established atmosphere of uncertainty regarding what is real and what is make-believe. Will Esther write her own a fairy tale as well?

Part of Esther's struggle as a young child is to become human. Her godmother treats her as a nonperson and, significantly, on the day allotted to celebrate life, issues her most damaging words: "It would have been far better, little Esther, that you had had no birthday; that you had never been born" (64). These words haunt Esther as she describes her own childhood as a lifeless, inarticulate being. Doll-like and unable to speak, Esther is mute: "I seldom dared to open my lips" (62). A few pages later she records, "I was not able to speak, though I tried" and "I was still less able to speak, than before" (69). It is only when Dolly is buried and gone that Esther becomes human and regains her speaking voice. Only when her own doll self is buried can Esther become the narrator who, with the hindsight of "seven happy years" (915), records her portion of *Bleak House*. Esther, unsure whether she is real, cannot emerge as fully human until she actively mourns a part of herself.

Esther's confusion regarding her own "thingness" is perhaps deeper. Since she has no knowledge who her real parents are, she has no concrete sense of her origins. After becoming accustomed to life at Greenleaf, Esther reports that "I seemed . . . almost to have dreamed rather than really lived my old life at my grandmother's" (72). She must construct her own fairy story and concludes that her life with her grandmother, and her life with Dolly, was more dreamlike than real.[11]

Additionally, Esther and Dolly are linked linguistically through the novel. Esther often inserts the adjective "old" before the word doll when she speaks of Dolly. "My dear old doll!" (62), she exclaims as she begins a memory of Dolly for the reader early in the third chapter. Again, when she buries Dolly eight pages later, Esther mourns for her "dear old doll" (72). While the use of the word "old" serves as a term of endearment (there is really nothing to suggest the doll is aged in any way), this adjective is the same one that will be used as Esther's own nickname when she becomes a ward of Mr. Jarndyce. In chapter 8, Esther, who has in the meantime become a young woman, records the following: "This was the beginning of my being called Old Woman, and Little Old Woman, and Cobweb, and Mrs. Shipton, and Mother Hubbard, and Dame Durden, and so many names of the sort, that my own name soon became quite lost among them" (148). Esther's nicknames desexualize her but they also connect Esther linguistically with the doll through the shared epithet. Moreover, as William Axton has pointed out, these nicknames locate Esther in contemporary and earlier fairy tale narratives.[12]

As swiftly as Dolly is introduced into the narrative, she is ushered out of it. The close of chapter 3, Dolly's burial by Esther, provides further evidence of Dolly as an uncanny figure.[13] Upon the death of Miss Barbary, Esther is to be taken to Greenleaf and placed under the care of the two Miss Donnys. Before she goes on this journey, she offhandedly mentions that she puts Dolly to rest: "A day or two before," Esther writes, "I had wrapped the dear old doll in her own shawl, and quietly laid her—I am half ashamed to tell it—in the garden-earth, under the tree that shaded my old window. I had no companion left" (70). Though in control in the present moment of narration, Esther is clearly affected by the reminiscence of this powerful emotional event. Esther becomes unsure of even the date; "a day *or* two before" (my emphasis), she writes. But Esther is sure of the exact location of Dolly's grave: "under the tree that shaded my old window." The seeming discrepancy between the uncertainty of the day and the certainty of the grave's location reveals how significant, in the space of one sentence, this moment is for Esther.

While this is not the last time we hear of dear old Dolly, it does mark a significant moment for Esther; as we have seen, the orphaned child has not only buried her ties with the past but she has also buried a part of herself. Burying Dolly is the burial of the child Esther; it is the burial of her childhood memories. Esther's transformation after this event is remarkable: she regains her voice and starts speaking with others. Esther may no longer be a doll herself but she has not given up her relationship with Dolly; Dolly is buried in the ground and she is also buried in Esther's unconscious mind.

Yet it is this uncanny figure who has the last word in Esther's life and loves. Esther will evaluate her future relationships in life through her one, powerful attachment to Dolly. Upon learning from her godmother that it would have been best not to have even been born, Esther records her profound despair and sorrow. She vows "to repair the fault I had been born with" (65): "Imperfect as my understanding of sorrow was, I knew I had brought no joy, at any time, to anybody's heart, and that I was to no one upon earth what Dolly was to me" (65). As we shall see, when this desire comes to fruition, Esther becomes frightened—and Dolly reappears.

At the closing of chapter 9, Mr. Guppy proposes to Esther. Rejecting his proposal immediately, she is disoriented and upset by his person and she orders him to leave, threatening to ring for a servant. She closes the chapter in a moment of reflection, very much characteristic of the way she ends each chapter she narrates. She writes:

> I sat there for another hour or more, finishing my books and payments, and getting through plenty of business. Then, I arranged my desk, and put everything away, and was so composed and cheerful that I thought I had quite dismissed this unexpected incident. But, when I went upstairs to my own room, I surprised myself by beginning to laugh about it, and then surprised myself still more by beginning to cry about it. In short, I was in a flutter for a little while; and felt as if an old chord had been more coarsely touched than it ever had been since the days of the dear old doll, long buried in the garden.   (178)

Why, we might ask, has this "unexpected incident" caused Esther to remember her doll, something, by her own admission, that is long buried in the ground? Speaking generally of uncanny moments in Dickens, Maria Tatar writes that the "remembrance of things past—of the distinct impressions registered on the child's mind as it grows to adolescence and maturity—holds the key to uncanny moments of recognition in Dickens' novels" (178–79). Esther's moment of recognition recalls her time as a child, as an innocent, pre-sexual being. After grounding herself in the controlled present moment of housekeeping, Esther allows herself an emotive response ranging from the comic to the tragic. "An uncanny experience occurs," Freud writes, " . . . when infantile complexes which have been repressed are once more revived by some impression" (249). The unhappiness Guppy's proposal unleashed recalls Esther's painful childhood memories, taking Esther and the reader are back to chapter 3 of the novel where Esther and Dolly both enter into the narrative of *Bleak House*. Guppy is the "impression" that had "revived" Esther's repressed childhood feelings. All Esther wanted as a child was to be loved and accepted. She was able to find this love and acceptance in a doll, a figure she then shamefully admits to burying. Repression, as well as its inevitable return, is the key to the Freudian uncanny and, herewith, Esther's reaction to Guppy's proposal.

When Guppy confesses his love to Esther—"Thy image" he cries, "has . . . been fixed in my breast" (177)—is Esther realizing that her wish to be something to someone has come true? Guppy's proposal represents the first time in her life that Esther is confronted as a sexual being, that is, as an object of man's desire. Esther is rather harsh in her rejection of Guppy (at one point he calls her "cruel miss" [177]) and orders him to leave, hoping that they both will forget that the encounter ever took place. Her anger is partially governed by fear; perhaps she is afraid that she can only attract men like Guppy and father/guardian figures such as Mr. Jarndyce, rather than dashing young surgeons such as Woodcourt. Esther, then, is trying to write her fairy tale, happy ending by rejecting the inappropriate suitor, Mr. Guppy.

For more than one hundred pages, both Esther and the reader forget about Dolly. But Dolly is recalled for the last time in chapter 18, this time in connection with an incident between Esther and Lady Dedlock. Not yet aware that Lady Dedlock is her real mother, Esther is repeatedly and profoundly affected when she sees the lady's face and hears her voice: "And, very strangely, there was something quickened within me, associated with the lonely days at my godmother's; yes, away even to the days when I had stood on tiptoe to dress myself at my little glass, after dressing my doll. And this, although I had never seen this lady's face before in all my life—I was quite sure of it—absolutely certain" (304). In this passage, Esther takes great pains to assure the reader that she had never seen Lady Dedlock before, yet she is drawn to her countenance, as if she should know it, but cannot explain why. Again, Dolly serves as a constant in Esther's past, part of Esther's daily dressing routine. Esther writes that she dresses Dolly first, then looks into the mirror only to dress her own doll self. Dolly, reappearing once more at a significant moment in Esther's life, serves as the anchor during an emotional crisis. Inching closer toward knowledge of her mother, Esther recalls the time in her life when she was a mother to a seemingly helpless thing while being motherless herself. We recall Esther's realization that as a child she "was to no one upon earth what Dolly was to me" (65). Dolly, then, links Esther to her mother. Both Guppy's proposal and the encounter with Lady Dedlock allow Dolly, who has been buried, to come back to life during Esther's sexual and then maternal interactions. Since the novel ends with both these issues of the sexual and the maternal resolved (Esther marries, has two daughters of her own, and finds her mother), Dolly's participation in the resolution of this fairy-tale ending deserves attention.

It is not surprising then, with the aid of psychoanalysis and the recognition of the dynamics of the uncanny, that it is only after Esther's search for love and her mother that Dolly finally exits her life and narrative. Dolly's textual presence, it is true, is confined only to the examples mentioned and analyzed in this paper. But, as I have tried to show, this is in no way a reflection of her importance to the themes underlying *Bleak House* and the development of its protagonist as she remembers and writes herself into adulthood. Therefore, the Dickensian uncanny must go beyond a theory of people in order to grapple fully with its earliest theoreticians who placed the importance of things at the heart of their inquiries.

NOTES

A previous version of this essay was presented at the *Third Annual Dickens Symposium* at Wilkes-University in October of 1998. I would like to thank the anonymous readers at *Dickens Studies Annual*, Dianne Hunter, Ron Thomas and, most especially, Kathryn Haines and Deniz Sengel, for very helpful comments and suggestions.

1. P. 217. All citations are from the Penguin edition edited by Norman Page (London: Penguin Books Limited, 1971). Page numbers are given in parentheses in the text.

2. Examples of more recent work done in the '90s include Richard T. Gaughan, " 'Their Places are a Blank': The Two Narrators in *Bleak House*," *Dickens Studies Annual* 21 (1992): 79–96 and LuAnn McCracken Fletcher "A Recipe for Perversion: The Feminine Narrative Challenge in *Bleak House*," *Dickens Studies Annual* 25 (1996): 67–89. Analyses from the '60s and '70s had particular fun with regard to titles: see William Axton, "The Trouble with Esther," *Modern Language Quarterly* 26 (1965): 545–57; Alex Zwerdling, "Esther Summerson Rehabilitated," *PMLA* 88 (1973): 429–39; Valery Kennedy "*Bleak House*: More Trouble with Esther?" *Journal of Women's Studies in Literature* 1 (1979): 330–47; and Crawford Kilian "In Defense of Esther Summerson," *Dalhousie Review* 54 (1974): 318–28.

3. Freud did not like *Bleak House* and much preferred *David Copperfield*, his favorite Dickens work. Ernest Jones reproduces a portion of this October 5, 1883 letter in which Freud refers to Dickens's heroines as "flawless," "colorless," and "selfless" (174).

4. See Albert Hutter's "The High Tower of His Mind: Psychoanalysis and the Reader of *Bleak House*," *Criticism* 19 (Fall 1977): 296–316; Lawrence Frank's

" 'Through a Glass Darkly': Esther Summerson and *Bleak House*," *Dickens Studies Annual* 4 (1975): 91–112; and Gordon D. Hirsch, "The Mysteries in *Bleak House*: A Psychoanalytic Study," *Dickens Studies Annual* 4 (1975): 132–52. The following critics specifically write on the Freudian uncanny: Robert Newsom, *Dickens on the Romantic Side of Familiar Things*: Bleak House *and the Novel Tradition* (New York: Columbia UP), 1977; and Maria M. Tatar, "The Houses of Fiction: Toward a Definition of the Uncanny," *Comparative Literature* 33.2 (Spring 1981): 167–82.

5. For example, Lois Rostow Kuznets's 1994 study of dolls and automata in literary history, *When Toys Come Alive: Narratives of Animation, Metamorphosis, and Development*, does not mention *Bleak House* at all.

6. See Otto Rank's classic text on this point, *The Double: A Psychoanalytic Study*, first published, prior to Freud's "Uncanny," as "Der Doppelgänger" in 1914.

7. The entire sentence reads: "Ich nahm an, daß er sich beim Verlassen des zwichen zwei Abteilen befindlichen Kabinetts in der Richtung geirrt hatte und fälschlich in mein Abteil gekommen war, sprang auf, um ihn aufzuklären, erkannte aber bald verdutzt, daß der Eindringling mein eigenes, vom Spiegel in der Verbindungstür entworfenes Bild war." See Freud's "Das Unheimliche" in the *Gesammelte Werke* (262–3).

8. My placing these three entities alongside one another, and using them as the title of this paper, follows the pattern of Wordsworth in the Seventh Book of his "Prelude." Describing a trip to the St. Bartholomew Fair of 1802, Wordsworth writes:

> All moveables of wonder from all parts . . .
> The Wax-work, Clock-work, all the marvelous craft
> Of modern Merlins, Wild-Beasts, Puppet-shews,
> All out-o'th'way, far-fetched, perverted things,
> All freaks of Nature, all Promethean thoughts
> Of man; his dullness, madness, and their feats,
> All jumbled up together, to compose
> A Parliament of Monsters. (706; 712–18)

9. In addition to Hoffmann's 1814 story mentioned, 1836 (just seventeen years before *Bleak House*) was an important year for the American reception of the automata-craze: "Perhaps no exhibition of the kind," writes Edgar Allen Poe, "has ever elicited so general attention as the Chess-Player of Maelzel" (78).

10. These quotations from Jentsch's article appear in Naomi Schor, "Duane Hanson: Truth in Sculpture," *New York Literary Forum* 8/9 (1981): 235–48. The one cited here occurs on page 243. Schor's essay uses the Freudian uncanny as a way of interpreting modern sculpture.

11. The fact that Esther has both a doll and knowledge of fairy stories contrasts her with other characters, Judy Smallweed in particular. We are told that "Judy never owned a doll, never heard of Cinderella, never played at any game" (354).

12. See William Axton (1966) on Esther's nicknames.

13. Even though Esther buries Dolly, the doll certainly fares better than, for example, another fictional doll several years later whose owner drives nails into her head. George Eliot's Maggie Tulliver is a memorable character for several reasons but surely no reader forgets the narrator's description in book one of *The Mill on the Floss* (1860) when Maggie's aggression and violence are taken out on her doll (79).

WORKS CITED

Axton, William. "Esther's Nicknames: A Study in Relevance." *The Dickensian* 62.3 (Sept. 1966): 158–63.

———. "The Trouble with Esther." *Modern Language Quarterly* 26 (1965): 545–57.

Collins, Philip. "Charles Dickens." *Victorian Fiction: A Second Guide to Research.* Ed. George Ford. New York: Modern Language Association, 1978. 34–113.

Dickens, Charles. *Bleak House.* Ed. Norman Page. London: Penguin, 1971.

———. *The Old Curiosity Shop.* Ed. Angus Wilson. London: Penguin, 1972.

Eliot, George. *The Mill on the Floss.* Ed. A. S. Byatt. London: Penguin, 1979.

Frank, Lawrence. " 'Through a Glass Darkly': Esther Summerson and *Bleak House.*" *Dickens Studies Annual* 4 (1975): 91–112.

Freud, Sigmund. "The 'Uncanny'." *The Standard Edition of the Complete Psychological Works of Sigmund Freud, Vol. 17.* Ed. and Trans. James Strachey. London: Hogarth Press, 1955. 212–52.

———. "Das Unheimliche." *Gesammelte Werke, Zwölfter Band, Werke aus den Jahren 1917–1920.* Ed. Anna Freud et al. Frankfurt am Main: S. Fischer, 1947–56. 229–68.

Gaughan, Richard T. " 'Their Places are a Blank': The Two Narrators in *Bleak House.*" *Dickens Studies Annual* 21 (1992): 79–96.

Gurrey, Gene. *America in Wax.* New York: Crown, 1977.

Hirsch, Gordon D. "The Mysteries in *Bleak House*: A Psychoanalytic Study." *Dickens Studies Annual* 4 (1975): 132–52.

Hoffmann, E. T. A. "Automata." *The Best Tales of Hoffmann.* Ed. E. F. Bleiler. Trans. Major Alexander Ewing. New York: Dover, 1967. 71–103.

———. *The Sandman. Selected Writings of E. T. A. Hoffmann.* Ed. and Trans. Leonard J. Kent and Elizabeth C. Knight. Chicago and London: U of Chicago P, 1969. 93–125.

Hutter, Albert. "The High Tower of His Mind: Psychoanalysis and the Reader of *Bleak House*." *Criticism* 19 (Fall 1977): 296–316.

Jentsch, Ernst. "Zur Psychologie des Unheimlichen." *Psychiatrisch-Neurologische Wochenschrift* 22 (1906): 198–227.

Jones, Ernest. *The Life and Work of Sigmund Freud: Vol. 1, 1856–1900.* New York: Basic Books, 1957.

Kennedy, Valery. "*Bleak House*: More Trouble with Esther?" *Journal of Women's Studies in Literature* 1 (1979): 330–47.

Kilian, Crawford. "In Defense of Esther Summerson." *Dalhousie Review* 54 (1974): 318–28.

Kuznets, Lois Rostow. *When Toys Come Alive: Narratives of Animation, Metamorphosis, and Development.* New Haven and London: Yale UP, 1994.

McCracken Fletcher, LuAnn. "A Recipe for Perversion: The Feminine Narrative Challenge in *Bleak House*." *Dickens Studies Annual* 25 (1996): 67–89.

Newsom, Robert. *Dickens on the Romantic Side of Familiar Things:* Bleak House *and the Novel Tradition.* New York: Columbia UP, 1977.

Poe, Edgar Allen. "Maelzel's Chess-Player." *The Works of Edgar Allen Poe in Ten Volumes.* Ed. Edwin Markham. New York: Funk & Wagnalls, 1904. 78–114.

Prawer, Siegbert S. *The 'Uncanny' in Literature: An Apology for its Investigation.* London: Watford. 1965.

Rank, Otto. *The Double: A Psychoanalytic Study.* Trans. Harry Tucker, Jr. Chapel Hill: The U of North Carolina P, 1971.

Schor, Naomi. "Duane Hanson: Truth in Sculpture." *New York Literary Forum* 8/9 (1981): 235–48.

Tatar, Maria M. "The Houses of Fiction: Toward a Definition of the Uncanny." *Comparative Literature* 33.2 (Spring 1981): 167–82.

Wordsworth, William. *The Prelude or Growth of a Poet's Mind.* Ed. Ernest de Selincourt. Oxford: Clarendon, 1959.

Zwerdling, Alex. "Esther Summerson Rehabilitated." *PMLA* 88 (1973): 429–39.

Towards A Dickens Poetic: Iconic and Indexical Elements in *Bleak House*

James E. Marlow

Readers have long felt that relying on the traditional means of criticizing narratives and realism were inadequate to appreciate the novels of Charles Dickens. By using the semiotic terms of Charles Peirce, Ferdinand Saussure, and Roman Jakobson, it may be possible to isolate some of his techniques and so to understand better the quality of Dickens's writing. This approach enables us to discover the effects both of Dickens's word-play and his elaborate structuring of sentences. In Bleak House *there is ample evidence of both. Words and names seem to be imposed on the text by the character of the object or person. In addition, he sculpts the sentences so that their arrangements reinforce, as icons, the symbolic meanings. This crafting of the sentences not only foregrounds the material, the language, of the novels, but it also seems to add a magic, a necessary, an essential character to what is supposed to be a conventional and arbitrary sign system. Dickens often deploys sentences to provide an iconic or indexical supplement to the conventional meanings of the words. If poetry is an art which is more opaque than prose, featuring the material of language—that is, signifiers—as part of its expression, and often requiring the reader to revisit the text a moment or two before deciding how best to decode the words, then Dickens's novels may be better appreciated for their poetic qualities.*

Dickens Studies Annual, Volume 30, Copyright © 2001 by AMS Press, Inc. All rights reserved.

During his whole career Charles Dickens experimented with the limits of the conventional sign system which is the English language. He seemed determined to broach the distinctions Charles Peirce later made between the kinds of representamens: the symbolic, the iconic, and the indexical.[1] As a comic writer, he constantly played with puns, malapropisms, and forms of catachresis which could raise a smile even as they manifested the uncertainties of a system often thought to be solidly objective. *Pickwick Papers* is filled with such humor. There is the delight in the expressiveness of slang phrases, such as "sawbones" for "doctor," a dysphemism which renders medical practice of the nineteenth century virtually iconic.

Pickwick Papers's most notorious send-up of language as a conventional system is generated by the discovery by Pickwick of a stone engraved with the following signs.

+

B I L S T
U M
P S H I
S. M.
A R K

Assuming the inscription to be an ancient one, Pickwick constructs twenty-seven different readings of it. However, all are wrong, for it was only Bill Stumps taking liberties with the rule, meant to insure legibility, that letters cannot be placed arbitrarily but must cohere consecutively as words. No doubt Bill Stumps was motivated partly by the width of the stone and perhaps by his own delight in balance. It seems, therefore, that aesthetic taste overrides the rule of consecutiveness; this is a principle of sculpture, not language. Moreover, as a sort of signature, another rule overrides the conventions of legibility. A signature seems to collapse Peirce's tripartition of the sign into representamen—object—interpretant. For, as a representamen, a signature's words become an inscribed shape, and so may operate not so much as a symbol as an index: a trace of the hand's movement as motivated by one's character. Thus, it is only a question of which rule to apply, which code to use, to understand any inscription. Such ambiguity raises a laugh because it makes a mockery of the cherished assumption that language is a definitive and rational system.

As Dickens gained confidence in his reception by his public, he experimented in many other ways with the language, going past simple words or names to whole sentences whose very shapes require decoding by means other than the conventional means. He was constantly experimenting with how far from its conventional field he could take language. His efforts resemble those of the expressionists who attempted to make two dimensional paintings move into the fourth dimension. Examples can be drawn from any of the novels but I intend to concentrate on *Bleak House*, so let me give an example from earlier and from later in Dickens's career.

In *Martin Chuzzlewit*, for example, he creates a sentence whose very rhythm provides redundant information about the feelings of Tom Pinch at being released from Pecksniff's employ. On a coach bound for London, "Tom could not resist the captivating sense of rapid motion" and fell in with the song of the road which is the implied metaphor of the coach trip:

> Yoho, past hedges, gates and trees; past cottages, barns and people going home from from work. Yoho, past donkey-chaises, drawn aside into the ditch, and empty carts with rampant horses, whipped up at a bound upon the little watercourse, and held by struggling carters close to the five-barred gate, until the coach had passed the narrow turning in the road. Yoho, by churches dropped down by themselves in quiet nooks, with rustic burial-grounds about them, where the graves are green, and daisies sleep—for it is evening—on the bosoms of the dead. Yoho, past streams, in which the cattle cool their feet, and where the rushes grow; past paddock-fences, farms, and rick-yards; past last year's stacks, cut, slice by slice away, and showing in the waning light, like ruined gables, old and brown. Yoho, down the pebbly dip, and through the merry water-splash, and up at a canter to the level road again. Yoho! Yoho! (ch.36)

The "Yoho" replaces subjects and verbs with an audible sound, and the skimming coach seems to be re-represented by means not of words but of a bugle sound. This onomatopoeia is best understood as an iconic sign.

The sculpting of sentences to create reiterations of their messages in other sign modes occurs all through Dickens's work. Many years ago Randolph Quirk pointed out that the "twisted syntax and images of Flintwinch in *Little Dorrit* are again typical manifestations of his twisted mind and are congruent with his twisted physique. On the other hand, virtue shines through the pure and obviously sanctioned lexis and syntax of Oliver Twist or of Lizzie Hexam in *Our Mutual Friend* . . . reminding us again that Dickens is not striving after a simple or slavish linguistic realism but after a linguistic congruence with fundamental intention" (Quirk 22). Dickens believed, to a very large extent, in physiognomy, the notion that character is revealed in the shapes of heads and faces and often, as with Flintwinch and Wegg and Uriah Heap, of bodies. Given that, it is not surprising that he attempted to create a physiognomic style, sculpting sentences to correspond to their meaning. His characters often do the same. *The Mystery of Edwin Drood* presents this example: " 'My informiation,' retorted the Billickin, throwing in an extra syllable for the sake of emphasis at once polite and powerful" (ch. 22). The amusement here is sharpened by the reader's intuition of the indexical nature of the usage. All through Dickens, therefore, the language tests the reader, often requiring a semiosis other than the standard one used for discursive language. To study this poetic style, this physiognomic register, in Dickens, let me turn to *Bleak House*, the towering novel published near the middle of his career.

I

To Roman Jakobson the poetic function is that quality in a message which draws the attention of the addressee—the reader—to the language, to the material of the signifier itself. "The set (*Einstellung*) towards the MESSAGE as such, focus on the message for its own sake, is the POETIC function of language" (Jakobson 1972, 93). As Sartre once wrote, poetry is opaque whereas prose intends to be transparent. To be opaque, writing as to evade the two primary causes of transparency: the orthodox operation of the referential function, and the linear or metonymic momentum of the narrative line. As Michael Riffaterre put it, "Each point of the text that holds up the superreader is tentatively considered a component of the poetic structure . . . " (Riffaterre 204). Dickens's writing slows readers with its humor, its many figures of speech, its polyphonic narrative structure and other techniques, making it evident that the text is a dance with language and not a rush to a conclusion. This focus on language itself, on the signifier as much as the signified, marks Dickens's style throughout his career. It is what made him "The Inimitable."

Dickens is able to use language to—as his friend Wilkie Collins said— "make 'em laugh, make 'em cry, make 'em wait." What differentiates Dickens's novels from those of Collins is precisely the opacity of his language, those qualities which Barthes called the "writerly." Dickens's work effects frequent changes in tone, uses word-play that may be pure play or may bear figurative or ironic import; it forces the reader to read between the lines, to render the unconventionalities along the paradigmatic or syntagmatic axes as significant—in a word, to commit a far higher degree of attention to the linguistic surface of the text than is asked for by most novelists. In this he seems to work in a manner more often ascribed to poets than to prose writers.

In poetry, argues Riffaterre, there occur signs which "*threaten the literary representation of reality, or mimesis,*" (Riffaterre 1978, 2). For Riffaterre, the "literary representation of reality" depends on the functioning of what Peirce called symbols, signs that require conventional codes to be understood. When smooth transitions between sign and code are derailed, these semantic blips Riffaterre calls *ungrammaticalities*. On those uncanny occasions, the reader must halt to negotiate new, non-standard significations.

In *Bleak House* there is frequent need to negotiate meanings. Some of the causes are evident in Knud Sorenson's list of techniques that Dickens uses in the novel, including free indirect style, that often seem to be "overstepping the normal limits of the grammatico-stylistic code" (Sorenson 238) and so mark themselves, in Riffaterre's term, as ungrammaticalities. For example, contrary to common practice in English literature, *Bleak House*'s third-person narrator, so wisely called the "anonymous narrator" by Hough (52), uses present tense for his narrative. At the time of the publication the unconventional choice of tense presented problems. Sylvère Monod documented these, pointing out that the present tense, "being unusual, occasionally disconcerted the compositors, and half a dozen preterits were substituted . . . here and there" (7). These changes Dickens had to reverse in the proofs. From the first, then, *Bleak House* put even professional readers on their mettle.

The different tenses used by the two narrators also lead to some valuable insights; for example, the anonymous narrator changes to the preterit in the passages of free indirect style. Sorenson writes,

> As far as I can see this is a deliberate attempt to convey normal points of view through the normal tense, the preterit, while the key theme of the law's delay as one manifestation of a corrupt society is foregrounded by the use of the present, partly perhaps to symbolize the eternal dragging of the lawsuit, but more importantly to conjure up a sinister atmosphere.   (Sorenson 240)

I am not convinced that a sinister atmosphere needs to be rendered in present tense in order to be compelling. But, because the traditional past tense is used only in those situations—after the telling absence of any tense and verbs at the beginning of the novel—the narrational artifice of present tense becomes strongly marked. As Sorenson suggests, present tense implies that events do not transpire. In Chancery Court, obviously, nothing of substance does happen. Where nothing happens, the past, the present, and the future have no separable entity, and therefore time cannot be perceived. This connoted message, so central to the thematic structure of the novel, is confirmed in Richard's touching admission, "There is no now for us suitors" (ch. 37).

Besides contrasting tenses for the two narrators, Dickens dares to write the first three paragraphs with no tense indications at all. "One of the remarkable features of Dickens *verbal syntax* is that he sometimes chooses to do without finite verbs. The best known example is probably the opening of *Bleak House*" (Sorenson 240). The novel opens with "London. Michaelmas term lately over, and the Lord Chancellor sitting in Lincoln's Inn Hall. Implacable November weather." In case the reader overlooks what is missing in the first long paragraph, Dickens performs the same sleight-of-hand with verbs for the second and third paragraphs. By excising verbs, Dickens is foregrounding the linguistic material of his novel by defying our normal expectations of well-formed sentences: "An extremely effective means of making linguistic forms visible is deformation" (Holenstein 85).

In terms of Dickens's poetic style, what shouts from these early passages is this: how can you expect a verb, a word referencing an action, where there is no action, only mud and stasis? A verb, after all, makes a proposition, impels us to the act of conjoining subject and predicate in some specified relation. The lack of verbs mires us in materiality, as if the objects in the fictive world prevent the language from performing those functions which give mankind some distance from, and so some sense of control over, mere matter. That is, the language seems formed by its referenced objects, inert though they be. Thus, magically, the language seems to have become a motivated or indexical sign of the referent.

The absence of verbs is powerfully metaphoric. As Jacques Derrida has pointed out: "The poetic force of metaphor is often the trace of its rejected alternative" (Derrida 90). When all alternatives are rejected, the absence of a verb is all the more forceful. Whereas metaphoric possibilities expand the offerings along the paradigmatic axis far beyond the usual range of synonymity and antonymity, to select "none of the above" in the slot where the verb should be draws even more attention to the very fact of selection because the lack of any verb offends our deeply engrained linguistic competence.

When dialogue finally begins, several pages later, we hear first the clearly indexical name, "Mr. Tangle," (a name that might have been generated by Chancery Court) and his response: "Mlud." Dickens has found a rich, ambiguous pun in this contraction of "my lord"; for, either "lud" or just the "l" can stand for "lord." If we use "lud" for "lord" we hear in it the echo of "mud," which the text has emphasized previously. But if we use "l," the Lord Chancellor's immersion as "l" into "mud" jokingly enacts the theme that Dickens is weaving about Chancery Court. Thus, the condition of the court is evident in the very material of the language. A potent magic confronts the reader when an author is able to sculpt language so that it enacts what it means. In such cases, Saussure's claim of an indivisible connection between signifier and signified is doubled.

As Krystyna Pomorska also points out, this unorthodox verbal behavior has special implications because of its position:

> The opening of a novel lends itself to a further principle of analysis after the model of poetry, pertaining to the very special, marked character of the beginning. As Jakobson has shown, the first line of a poem functions as a kind of tuning fork: it signals the rhythmical pattern, the cadence, even the sound pattern, the *paronomasia*, of the entire poem. As it turns out, prose behaves in a similar way, even though it operates with a different set of constituents. The first chapter of a novel, usually even the first scene, introduces all of the protagonists as well as all of the general themes.   (172–73)

At the beginning of *Bleak House* the major protagonist, Chancery Court, and the major theme, systemic catalepsy, are indeed introduced. The critical literature has commented extensively on the suggestion of the fog being emitted by the court, the metonymical connection of law and mud, and the allusions to an archaic world. Pomorska's point is only the more valid if we accept the idea that in *Bleak House* the language is the protagonist, as it is in poetry.

II

Besides employing poetic means such as metaphors, in *Bleak House* Dickens also carries out the difficult balancing act of maintaining credible symbolic representation while opening sudden shafts into the other modes of signification—indexes and icons.

Among the commentators there seems to be an uncertainty about the exact nature of an index. Peirce wrote that an index

> is a real thing or fact which is a sign of its object by virtue of being connected with it as a matter of fact and by also forcibly intruding upon the mind, quite regardless of its being interpreted as a sign. It may simply serve to identify its object as assure us of its existence and presence.   (359)

Peirce goes on to argue that a photograph is an index (as well as an iconic sign) "owing to its optical connexion with the object." That is, the material light reflected by the object has affected the film and hence its relation is a matter of fact, not convention. With indexes, Peirce is evidently focusing on material causes and effects.

One example of such an index in *Bleak House* is Snagsby's cough—a sign that his conscience as much as his lungs is having trouble taking in the situation with Jo, or with Guster, the abused servant. Another example of an index is Detective Bucket's large index finger, which he finally uses to indict Hortense for the murder of Tulkinghorn (ch. 55). Yet, rather than simplifying the characters, these gestural tags deepen them. For, the cough reminds the reader that Snagsby, for all the chilling effects of Mrs. Snagsby, Tulkinghorn, and commerce have exercised on his conscience, still retains one. Although a sign of his profession and of the essence of his character, Bucket's finger is mentioned so often that the reader begins to think him another "Allegory," as feckless as the painting of the pointing Roman. Therefore, when he "merely shakes his finger at" Hortense to arrest her, it comes as a surprise. It is an index not because it is used to point at Hortense but because it is connected to the character of Bucket.

Normally, names would not be considered indexes. For Peirce an index is a "real thing . . . forcibly intruding itself upon the mind." At least since names have ceased to reveal places of origin or occupations or fathers' names, they are conventional, mere symbols. However, Kaja Silverman and others consider that proper names can function as indexes. Although proper names are assigned social constructions and do not as such intrude upon the mind through the senses, they function unlike other nouns for they have the power to single out their objects and each can be assigned theoretically to but one object. Furthermore, in fiction names are in the not-so-arbitrary hands of the author, and Dickens, for one, discovers names that seem to spring from the essence of the character. Thus seemingly connected to their object "as a matter of fact," such names manage to cast doubt on the idea that names, like other words, are arbitrary, merely terms evoked by the principle of linguistic difference and agreed upon. Nor are the names such as Krook and Snagsby allegorical; they did not represent accepted ideas. All the names Dickens uses are real English names: he has simply disclosed a magic quality in them.

The signifier "Summerson," for example, is also apparently generated by the essence of the character, as she proves utterly different from the mud and fog and despair in the novel. These have no more influence on her character than they do on the sun (and *influence* is one of the major themes in the novel). Because of their dual role, as both proper name and potential index, Dickens's names often cause readers to pause to attune ourselves to the poetic function of language. To so play with words offends the orthodox notion that language—including names—is purely arbitrary, one of Saussure's and modern linguistics' founding principles. To consider language as other than arbitrary is to return us to a pre-analytic mentality, in which words have a magical connection to their referent. The argument that goes back at least to Plato's "Cratylus" was considered settled once and for all by Saussure. However, Jakobson does not wholly yield the question. He argues that the "iconic and indexical constituents of verbal symbols have too often remained underestimated and even disregarded" (Jakobson 1971, 357).

Although a real item from the paradigm of English surnames, the name "Boythorn" is a compound sign whose parts reveal his character: he is a boy still; he is a thorn (especially to Sir Leicester Dedlock). What's more, in his youth his heart was pricked by the character whom we know as Miss Barb/ery—the synonymity suggesting that they were meant for each other. Such names convey more than normal language is supposed to offer. Hence "Boythorn" appears as a kind of silhouette of the referent's history and character. Unlike the names "Smith" or "Carter," "Boythorn" still retains a living connection between signifier and signified. It is not an arbitrary and conventional reference but is an upwelling of essence. In this sense, such names can be seen as metaphors or indexes. Hence, in the criticism of Dickens's poetic mode the term "index" needs to be broadened to include the sign as a motivated expression of essence.

As indexes, Dickens's fictional names are linguistic atavisms perhaps. Ernst Cassirer has written,

> For it is characteristic of the earliest conscious reflection on the world as a whole that there was as yet no distinction between language and being, word and meaning, but that they still formed an indivisible unity.   (Cassirer I, 117)

The poetic mode in Dickens often manages to create the appearance that the two kind of index, of mind and reality, of essence and of existence, are of equal significance.

To pick up on the proper name's connection to essence, the reader must keep open the windows to childish word-play and archaic reflection, to magic, to the poetic mode.

> Now this close connection between word and object is an illusory one, even in the referential use of language . . . but it is a powerful illusion. And it is an illusion which the poetic use of language attempts to point up.   (Waugh 153)

Dickens's work is filled with names that are essentially indexes. They are not material signs, like symptoms, but they nevertheless seem to enjoy a non-arbitrary connection with "a matter of [fictive] fact." It is a technique Dickens constantly uses.

Perhaps the most ostentatious subversion of the socially accepted idea that names have a merely referential function occurs with the names Dickens provides for politicians *in Bleak House.* By calling the politicians William Buffy, Cuffy, Duffy, Coodle, Doodle, and the Lord of Foodle, Dickens lampoons the British political system. By means of this paronomasia, in which the differences between the signifiers are as slight as they can be and still mark separate verbal signs, Dickens is stipulating that the differences between the signifieds—the politicians and their parties—is equally negligible. Comically reversing the effect of names like Boythorn and Summerson, these proper names fail to single out individuals while nonetheless serving as indexes of the interchangeable essences of their characters.

In the real world of politics, of course, the names vary naturally, from Gladstone to Disraeli, for example; but to that extent, Dickens implies, those actual signifiers lie, and the "Buffy Cuffy Duffy" string is closer to the truth of their practice. The very absence of a reasonable range of selections on the paradigmatic axis for proper names of politicians is itself the message, signifying the insular, undistinguished, and indistinguishable members of the political elite of Great Britain. Because of the traces or echoes that accompany "Boodle," there is an insistence on the materiality of language. Whether the essence into which such symbolic indexes tap is particular or not, it gives the reader poetic pause. Such indexical signs, illusory as they may be from one point of view, control powerful poetic effects.

III

Onomatopoeia is the technique by which language is made iconic; as an imitation of a sound, it is the word's material that carries significance.

> [O]nomatopoeia [is] the phenomenon in which the sound of the word imitates that to which it refers by convention. Thus the noun "rumble" or "hiss" refer, as conventional symbols, to the relevant events. And since the use of every word not only expresses certain experiences of the speaker but also evokes a certain response in the listener, the symbolic and iconic elements are also joined by indication, indexical symptomatic, and signaling elements. And such a situation is perfectly normal. There are no "pure" signs.   (Pelc 13)

Pelc here provides a timely warning: there are no "pure" signs even in oral examples of onomatopoeia. "Cockadoodle-do" is as much English symbol as iconic sign. What's more, silent reading mutes onomatopoeia to a considerable extent. Writing, however, has other resources to generate iconic representamens, not so much through single words as through longer collocations of words, sentences, and paragraphs.

Dickens exploits the standard idea of iconic signs quite often: a mirroring of the physical object by the sign material. One example occurs when Krook "chalked the letter J upon the wall—in a very curious manner, beginning with the end of the letter and shaping it backwards" (ch. 5). Since Krook cannot read and therefore lacks the code by which the letter, when matched with the code, counts as a phoneme, he is not using the J symbolically. To him the J does not represent a sound. Hence, he is merely imitating what he has seen, and so creates an icon.

Another example of iconicity in *Bleak House* is a profound stroke by Dickens because it reveals the severe limits of understanding in Jo. Asking Mr. Woodcourt to write to Esther to beg her forgiveness of having infected her with smallpox, he says, "If the writin could be made to say it wery large, she might" forgive (ch. 47). To Jo, who like Krook is illiterate, letters are homeless signifiers, and he can only link their size (as compared to letters written ordinarily) to the degree of his regret (as compared with his usual feelings). If language is merely symbol and not index or icon, this notion is pure foolishness. However, Jakobson points out the curious growth in English of an adjective's size from its declarative to its comparative to its superlative forms, as in "high: higher: highest" (Jakobson 1971, 352).

In addition, Dickens's poetic style makes use of another form of icon. Richard Carstone had been engaged in writing a letter to Esther to try to explain his situation. When she shows up in his room, he has no need to send the letter or she to read it, for its contents are manifest: " 'Oh, my dear,' he returned with a hopeless gesture. 'You may read it in the whole room. It is all over here' '' (ch. 45). To express his mental condition in language is no longer necessary because the condition of the room is an unmistakeable icon for it. Such iconic signs are frequent in literature and in life, but Dickens has here markedly eliminated the symbolic message in favor of the iconic one.

Joseph Randall clearly explains the difference between symbolic and iconic comprehension.

> Roughly, whenever recourse to a code or rule of interpretation is *required* in order to understand what a sign means, one is insofar dealing with something symbolic (in Peirce's sense of 'symbolic'), whereas insofar as something is iconic, it represents (exhibits, displays, shows) in *itself* some relevant properties of the object—indeed, perceiving the object itself, partially or wholly—in the sign rather than *moving from* the sign according to some rule which "arbitrarily" correlates sign and object.   (Randall 65)

Krook's "J," Jo's "wery large writin," and the chaos of Richard's room have in common the fact that these signs unequivocally function without recourse to a code and therefore are not symbols but icons.

Yet, Dicken's most daring signs work first as symbols (requiring codes) and then make the leap to the level of icons, thus saturating the signs with meaning. That is, in a phrase, or syntagm, the way the words are ordered mirrors the way the parts of the object relate to each other.[2] This feature functions as an iconic sign in Peirce's sense of a *diagram*. "According to Peirce's theory of signs, upon which Jakobson builds in this connection, a diagram is a sign whose own constitution reflects the relational structure of the thing represented" (Holenstein 157). Hence, to trace his use of iconic language and so to describe Dickens's poetic style adequately, we must turn from single words such as names to "supersigns," or syntactical constructions.

These longer passages discover a similarity between the two halves of the sign, the signifier and the signified, between the perceptible and the intelligible. What appears to take place is that an author's reference has a shape imposed upon it by the referent. Such iconicity moves us toward a magical sense of language, for it argues that there is, after all, a necessary connection between signifier and signified. If the signifier is formed by the signified, an essence could be claimed and the symbol, a.k.a. the icon, would therefore verge upon being an index as we have understood it.

To illustrate the poetic ground which Dickens is tilling I turn to the criticism of Christopher Ricks. He argued that the "poet is always insisting, as if by magic, that his control of words is a control of experience" (Ricks 1963, 19). What I take him to mean is that the materiality of the poet's language, including its organization on the page, or on the breath of the speaker, is itself an icon, a diagram for the phenomenon which it is simultaneously signifying by conventional symbolic means. Milton's "grand style," Ricks writes, is marked by "this ability to harness the thrust of his syntax" in which "even the smallest passages have a dynamic force of the astonishing kind which one finds also everywhere in Dickens" (Ricks 1963, 31). I hope to affirm his insight by noting a number of such extraordinary passages.

Ricks proceeds to illustrate Milton's grand style:

> Aire, Water, Earth
> By Fowl, Fish, Beast was flow, was swum was walkt
> Frequent.   (P.L. VII. 502–04)

In these lines Milton desired, writes Ricks, "to suggest both the teeming activity of the earth, and the fundamental order and harmony of it. So he presents a throng of monosyllables while at the same time grouping them into a pattern of triplets" (Ricks 1963, 33). Thus, in one short passage Milton creates a net of signifiers that emulates and therefore supplements the complex signification provided by the conventional operations of language.

William Wordsworth, Ricks argues as well, learned from Milton and is, if anything, even more artfully insistent on the iconicity between the signifier and the signified (to substitute these terms for Ricks's). Ricks points out that Wordsworth exploits the graphic possibilities of line endings by fitting the sense to the graphic site. Thus the lines form a kind of mise-en-scene which mirrors the significance of the passage.

> Dreamlike the blending of the whole
> Harmonious landscape; all along the shore
> The boundary lost, the line invisible
> That parts the image from reality;
> (Wordsworth, Home at Grasmere, l. 574–77)

This technique of shaping the linguistic matter is directly relevant to Dickens's poetic, as I hope to show.

Discussing a famous passage from *The Prelude*, Ricks writes,

> And although the ambiguity would still exist if the lines were simply deployed as prose with no change of word-order, the ambiguity would be less tangible, since there would not be the possibility (created by the line-ending and its temporal pause) that the unit of sense is coterminous with line-unit . . . .
> (Ricks 1972, 515)

So, the meaning of those poetic lines—which is that of uncertainty—is enhanced, made "tangible," by a "flicker of hesitation" created in the moment during which the eyes travel to the beginning of the next line. And this would not happen in prose, where the subsequent sentence usually lies cheek by jowl with the antecedent sentence and the words are not physiognomically arranged, but are laid down only according to the rules of syntax and semantics only.

Ricks goes on to argue, "The change from verse to prose·would be the abolition of the implicitly metaphoric [or iconic] enactment [by the signifier of the signified]" (Ricks 1972, 519). Doubtless that is generally true, but Ricks's own vaunted Dickens serves to prove that prose has its own techniques for such enactments.

> Mr. Skimpole laughed at the pleasant absurdity, and lightly touched the piano by which he was seated.
> "And he told me," he said, playing little chords where I shall put full stops, "That the Coavinses profession. Being unpopular. The rising Coavinses. Were at a considerable disadvantage." (ch. 15)

Dickens cannot avail himself of the spacious white margins of poetry, or of the migratory moments from line-end to line-beginning, but he uses cadence and he uses a kind of counterpoint of codes: although the "full stop" can not be a full stop from the point of view of semantics, the reader must nevertheless decode it first by the rules of punctuation as a full stop, and then come around to reevaluate it. This return invests the message with much the same "momentary doubt" as the passages in Wordsworth cited by Ricks. If it is a "flicker of hesitation" that marks a poetic effect, then these full stops are, arguably, as poetic as the material of poetry. How better could the "language [be] deployed . . . so as to make the most of each word's eventfulness" (Ricks 1972, 506)?

The dynamic enactment of meaning, this "deployment" of language, is superbly illustrated in the initial lines of James Dickey's poem "Fence Wire":

> Too tight, it is running over
> Too much of this ground to be still
> Or to do anything but Tremble
> And disappear left and right
> As far as the eye can see
>
> Over hills, through woods,
> Down roads, to arrive at last
> Again where it connects
> Coming back from the other side
> Of animals, defining their earthly estate
>
> As the grass becomes snow
> While they are standing and dreaming
> Of grass and snow.

The mind's eye almost wearies following those fence lines over the spacious territory of two and a half stanzas. I think most readers would concede that his example of a signifier enacting what it is simultaneously expressing by symbolic means verges upon the magical.

Yet Dickens's poetic style can match the effect in prose. When Charley goes on her mission to fetch John Jarndyce's letter (a proposal of marriage) for Esther, the reader is also anxious to know its contents and so enjoys the suspense, the retardation of the plot, as "Charley went up the stairs and down the stairs and along the passages—the zigzag way about the old-fashioned house seemed very long in my listening ears that night—and so came back, along the passages, and down the stairs, and up the stairs, and brought the letter" (ch. 44). Those same passages (Dickens's pun?) create a different effect when introduced earlier and at much greater length: while an iconicity is sustained, the passages were then filled with intermittent surprises—like Dickens's style of discourse itself.

> Out of this room, you went down two steps, into a charming little sitting-room, looking down upon a flower-garden, which room was henceforth to belong to Ada and me. Out of this you went up three steps into Ada's bedroom, which had fine broad windows, commanding a beautiful view (we saw a great expanse of darkness lying underneath the stars), to which there was a hollow window-seat, in which, with a spring-lock, three dear Adas might have been lost at once. Out of this room, you passed into a little gallery, with which the other best rooms (only two) communicated, and so, by a little staircase of shallow steps, with a number of corner stairs in it, considering its length, down into the hall. But if, instead of going out at Ada's door, you came back into my room, and went out at the door by which you had entered it, and turned up a few crooked steps that branched off in an unexpected manner from the stairs, you lost yourself in passages, with angles in them, and three-cornered tables, and a Native-Hindoo chair, which was also a sofa, a box, and a bedstead, and looked in every form, something between a bamboo skeleton and a great bird-cage, and had been brought from India nobody knew by whom or when.   (ch. 6)

What a game this tour of the legible world is, as representamens of objects (including a chair which defies categorization) and spaces and directions turn up "in an unexpected manner" in the course of the three sentences, the last of which meanders for nearly 100 words. Yet all three are always in control, faithfully performing their syntactical as well as their sculptural duties. To what extent do these cozy, cluttered Victorian syntactical interiors contribute to our sense of the Victorian interior of Bleak House and, indeed, of *Bleak House*? Some of the hallucinatory qualities that G. H. Lewes diagnosed in Dickens may perhaps be traced to such sentences.

Perhaps it is not so astonishing that the signifier of a prose sentence can be deployed to make an icon for a still interior scene. It is more surprising to find that the shape of a sentence can also reflect the opposite: a dynamic, crowded exterior scene.

> Jostling against clerks going to post the day's letters, and against counsel and attorneys going home to dinner, and against plaintiffs and defendants, and suitors of all sorts, and against the general crowd, in whose way the forensic wisdom of the ages has interposed a million of obstacles to the transaction of the commonest business of life—diving through law and equity, and through that kindred mystery, the street mud, which is made of nobody knows what, and collects about us nobody knows whence or how; we only knowing in general that when there is too much of it, we find it necessary to shovel it away—the lawyer and the law-stationer come to a Rag and Bottle shop, and general emporium of much disregarded merchandise, lying and being in the shadow of Lincoln's Inn, and kept, as is announced in paint, to all whom it may concern, by one Krook. (ch. 10)

With the long-delayed introduction of the subjects (who seem more the recipients of the action), the very syntax seems mightily jostled. The sentence has all the hubbub and throng, all the hectic pace and general disorder of the scene it renders by conventional means. Dickens also interjects his solution for the mess in the streets (and in the courts)—a shovel. By the end of the sentence, with its large parenthetical statement in the center, we sense the anagogic point: this crooked way England has gone down will never be made straight without hard work and digging. The throw-away sarcasm here, of "forensic wisdom" erecting "a million of obstacles," with its echo of "a million of money"—which clues the reader in to what most of the obstacles to clarity and justice amount to—is one of Dickens's frequent transmogrifications of pat or proverbial phrases. Even the "lying and being in the shadow" provides a poetic figure called a zeugma, which foregrounds the individual words and makes us reprocess their meanings.

Another kind of sculpted sentence occurs when Dickens multiplies items along the syntagmatic axis yet manages to achieve a sense not of the possibility of endless addition but of closure:

> [George the Trooper] comes to a gateway in the brick wall, looks in, and sees a great perplexity of iron lying about, in every stage and in a vast variety of shapes; in bars, in wedges, in sheets; in tanks, in boilers, in axles, in wheels, in cogs, in cranks, in rails; twisted and wrenched into eccentric and perverse forms, as separate parts of machinery; mountains of it broken up, and rusty in its age; distant furnaces of it glowing and bubbling in its youth; bright fireworks of it showering about, under the blows of the steam hammer; red-hot iron, cold-black iron; and iron taste, and iron smell, and a Babel of iron sounds. (ch. 63)

The reader comes to realize that the idea that George's ironmaster brother might produce some product of some other metal, or might produce some iron product not listed here, or even that there might be some form of iron product not made by him is refuted by the exhaustive list of signifiers exhibited, mostly in triplets. The range of color too—black, white, red—completes a kind of spectrum. Not only are many shapes designated, what brings the list full circle, besides the sensual exhaustiveness, is that every typical (anthropomorphic) stage of iron's development is shown: bubbling youth, firey maturity, and rusty old age. The reader realizes that there is nothing left to add. George sees, and by the end of the sentence tastes, smells, hears, and even through the heat feels the iron; the sensual exhaustiveness also signals closure. What seemed like an unlimited enterprise has been neatly brought round by the tolling off of each of the five senses and so closed down but without diminishing the sense of repletion.

By completing a sensual inventory, Dickens's poetics here is able to iconicize a particular but extensive category such as products made of iron. A similar effect occurs when Dickens's style extends its reach, its inclusivity, and its single-breathed stamina to encompass all of England.

> Not only is it a still night on dusty high roads and on hill-summits, whence a wide expanse of country may be seen in repose, quieter and quieter as it spreads away into the fringe of trees against the sky, with the grey ghost of a bloom upon them; not only is it a still night in the gardens and in the woods, and on the river where the water meadows are fresh and green, and the stream sparkles on among pleasant islands, murmuring weirs, and whispering rushes; not only does the stillness attend it as it flows where houses cluster thick, where many bridges are reflected in it, where wharves and shipping make it black and awful, where it winds from these disfigurements through marshes whose grim beacons stand like skeletons washing ashore, where it expands through the bolder region of rising grounds, rich in corn-field, wind-mill, and steeple, and where it mingles with the ever-heaving sea; not only is it a still night on the deep, and on the shore where the watcher stands to see the ship with her spread wings cross the path of light that appears to be presented only to him; but even on this stranger's wilderness of London, there is some rest.   (ch. 48)

The accumulation of scenes are obviously meant to stand as a synedoche for all of England. But it is not only the net drawn by the signifieds that lends satisfaction to this magnificent sentence; the repetitions of signifiers provide the sense that all the signifieds—hill, woods, town, marsh, and sea—are connected because they are under the control of the syntax as much as the signified repose.

We begin with "high-roads" and conclude with the "deep"; we move from a "fringe of trees"—domesticated nature—to the shocking reversal of "the wilderness of London"; we move from "roads" and "expanses" and "spreads" and numerous other terms of motion through the "ever-heaving sea" to conclude with the final word, "rest." By naming opposites such as "high-roads" and "deeps," Dickens is creating a simple binary code based on perceptual experience. The opposed terms provide, again, a sense of exhaustiveness, for all else falls in between on the paradigmatic axis.

It is Dickens's poetic skill in holding all these signifiers together in one burgeoning, graceful sentence which ends in a definite closure that helps to convince us that peace has indeed settled upon everything. After each "not only," the clauses stretch on beyond the limits of the normal cumulative sentence, and with each new clause the syntax alters, adding distinguishing details in a different way each time. The "not only' patterns flow on like the river[3] itself until they come to an end with a "watcher" becoming self-conscious as he watches; thus the sentence brings about the long-awaited structural closure in the brilliant movement from God's point of view, suddenly, to that of one human individual. To funnel down from the illimitable "wide expanse," open to everyone's vision, down to the specific, self-conscious vision of one watcher watching what "is presented only to him," is to imply that every view of things possible has been incorporated into the stream of this sentence. The paradigmatic eddying from "still" to "repose" to "quieter and quieter," back to "still," to "stillness," and back to "still," finally concludes with "rest." The nature of language precludes totality; one can write on anything forever. Yet this sentence concedes no absences. Like a sculpture it imposes a sense of the totality. The concept of peace is provided the magic of poetry.

IV

I do not presume to have noted all the features of Dickens's poetics even in *Bleak House*. His other novels provide many more examples of his poetic style. What I have attempted to argue is that there is throughout Dickens's work ample evidence to support taking a poetic attitude towards it. We need to attend to the magical effect of many word choices, and to appreciate how often Dickens's sentences enact or are seemingly derived from their content. Hauntings of essence fill the pages, as the nature of the signs used are blurred. According to Jakobson, messages always have composite functions, and, according to Peirce, composite signs such as we have argued appear in Dickens's poetics are preferable:

> It is frequently desireable that a representamen should exercise one of those three functions to the exclusion of the other two, or two of them to the exclusion of the third; but the most perfect signs are those in which the iconic, indicative, and symbolic characters are blended as equally as possible.   (Peirce 361)

That is, they should if possible communicate not through a single system but through two or three simultaneously. If they do, they cannot but draw attention to the materiality of the language, to the poetic function.

The question will naturally be asked, would the examples of Dickens's icons and indexes be universally recognized if the symbolic code were not first understood? In the last example, would the iconic quality of the syntax be recognized without generating from the symbolic level an interpretant of expansive quietude? Perhaps not. Perhaps iconic signs too require some code to be read. Jerzy Pelc writes, "the iconic sign belongs, together with the symbol, to the class of objects that denote by convention and not by natural connection" (Pelc 10). But my object was only to call attention to Dickens's poetic style, to show instances of a wonderful match between an iconical or indexical sentence and its symbolic interpretant.[4] Our intention was to suggest that a signifier may be more vitally linked to its signified than Saussure's description condones; at least it appears so in poetry, like that of Dickens, which seems to create a living link between reference and referent that exceed our understanding, muddling the distinctions between icon, index, and symbol and liberating the reader's mind from the iron dictates of conventional decoding of language.

NOTES

1. Peirce's tripartition of the sign and Saussure's bipartition, into signifier and signified, are, I fear, used rather unrigorously in this paper, depending on the context and perhaps even the aesthetic sense of the author.
2. It is understood that "object" is illusory in fiction; it is virtual, and perhaps is indistinguishable from "interpretant." Perhaps Saussure's terms work better here: the signifier motivated by the signified.
3. As my colleague Bill Nelles pointed out to me, the passage of the river is awash with sibilants, heightening the demands for poetic attention.
4. In what I have called an iconic sentence the form of the sentence appears to serve as its own interpretant. By doing so, isn't the fearsome danger of an endless chain of interpretants short-circuited?

WORKS CITED

Barthes, Roland. "The Semiotics of the Object." In *The Semiotic Challenge*, tr. Richard Howard. New York: Hill and Wang, 1988.

Cassirer, Ernst. *The Philosophy of Symbolic Forms*. Three Volumes. New Haven: Yale UP, 1966.

Derrida, Jacques. *Writing and Difference*, tr. Barbara Johnson. Chicago: U of Chicago P, 1978.

Holenstein, Elmer. *Roman Jakobson's Approach to Language*. Bloomington: Indiana UP, 1976.

Hough, Graham. "Language and Reality in *Bleak House*." In *Realism in European Literature*. Cambridge: Cambridge UP, 1986.

Jakobson, Roman. *Selected Writings*. Vol. 2. The Hague: Mouton, 1971.

————. "Linguistics and Poetics." In *The Structuralists*, ed. R. & F. DeGeorge. Garden City, NY: Anchor, 1972, 85–122.

————. *Roman Jakobson: Verbal Art, Verbal Sign, Verbal Time*, eds. Krystyna Pomorska and Stephan Rudy. Minneapolis: U of Minnesota P, 1985.

Lewes, G. H. "Dickens in Relation to Criticism." *Fortnightly Review* 17 (1872), 141–54.

Monod, Sylvère. " 'When the Battle's Lost and Won . . . ' Dickens v. the Compositors of *Bleak House*." *The Dickensian* 69 (1973): 3–12.

Peirce, Charles Sanders. *The Collected Papers*. Vol IV. Eds. Charles Hartshorne and Paul Weiss. Cambridge MA: Harvard UP, 1960.

Pelc, Jerzy. "Iconicity: Iconic Signs or Iconic Uses of Signs." In *Iconicity: Essays on Nature of Culture*. Eds. Paul Boissac, Michael Herzfeld, and Roland Posner. Tubingen: Stauffenburg, 1985.

Pomorska, Krystyna. "Poetics of Prose." In *Roman Jakobson: Verbal Art, Verbal Sign, Verbal Time*. Minneapolis: Minnesota UP, 1985, 169–77.

Posner, Roland. "Iconicity in Syntax." In *Iconicity: Essays on the Nature of Culture*. Tubingen: Stauffenburg Verlag, 1985.

Quirk, Randolph. "Some Observations on the Language of Dickens." *Review of English Literature*, II iii (1961): 19–28.

Randall, Joseph. "On Peirce's Conception of the Iconic Sign." In *Iconicity: Essays on the Nature of Culture*. Tubingen: Stauffenburg Verlag, 1985.

Ricks, Christopher. *Milton's Grand Style*. Oxford: Oxford UP, 1963.

————. "Wordsworth: 'A Pure Organic Pleasure from Line.' " In *Wordsworth*. Ed. Graham McMaster. Harmondsworth: Penguin, 1972, 505–34.

Riffaterre, Michael. "Describing Poetic Structures: Two Approaches to Baudelaire's 'les Chats.' " In *Structuralism*. Ed. Jacques Ehrmann. Garden City, NY: Anchor, 1970.

————. *The Semiotics of Poetry*. Bloomington: Indiana UP, 1978.

————. "On the Diegetic Functions of the Descriptive." *Style* 20:3 (1986): 281–94.

Silverman, Kaja. *The Subject is Semiotics*. New York: Oxford UP, 1983.

Sorenson, Knud. "Charles Dickens: Linguistic Innovator." In *English Studies* 65 (1984): 237–47.

Waugh, Linda. "The Poetic Function and the Nature of Language." In *Roman Jakobson: Verbal Art, Verbal Sign, Verbal Time*. Minneapolis: U of Minnesota P, 1985.

Hard Times: The Disciplinary City

Barry Stiltner

As Dickens's "industrial novel," Hard Times confronts the complexities of the Victorian class structure. However, the novel also elaborates a critique of institutional mechanisms, in particular the disciplinary operations of Utilitarianism and coordinate industrial structures. As D.A. Miller, Jeremy Tambling, and Cynthia Northcutt Malone (among others) have well established, Dickens prefigures, if not precedes, Michel Foucault in recognizing the disciplinary machinery that insinuated itself into Western culture in the eighteenth and nineteenth centuries. Hard Times is one of the more extensive considerations of that recognition in the Dickens world; the novel dramatically diagnoses apparatuses of Foucauldian "discipline" in Victorian culture and problematizes the nature of the "self" in that paradigm.

One of the signal sites in Dickens's prefiguration of Michel Foucault's cultural theories (specifically *Discipline and Punish* and *The Order of Things*) is *Hard Times* (1854). Though *Hard Times* is Dickens's "industrial novel," his only book-length consideration of the British proletariat, it is also his most programmatic elaboration of mid-Victorian institutional circuits and disciplinary mechanisms. For *Hard Times* not only depicts the "antagonism of oppressing and oppressed classes" (Marx and Engels 77), but also uniquely delineates a cultural model where Gradgrind's Utilitarianism and Bounderby's factories form a disciplinary symbiont that regulates the lives of Coketown's populace. The novel's social terrain is defined by D. A. Miller's articulation of Foucault and the Dickens world: "Embodied in the prison, the workhouse, the factory, the school, discipline became . . . a *topic* of Dickensian representation . . . "

(59). In Coketown, Bounderby's textile mills and Gradgrind's school go beyond defining roles for people within the Victorian social contract; they are agents of a "disciplinary society" (Foucault, *Discipline and Punish* 183) that is focused on the refashioning of the "self" into a "docile," (136–37) institutional appendage. While a classed, economic oppression is central to the condition of Coketown's workers, the city's educational, industrial, and governmental institutions generate an encompassing disciplinary scheme of conformity, of "normalization" (183). Thus, in many ways, *Hard Times* confronts the cultural scripting of individuals, how "subjectivities" are formed and contested; it questions how, if possible, a person can maintain any authenticity in a mid-Victorian society invested with disciplinary institutions such as factories, workhouses, and Utilitarian schools.

However, *Hard Times*'s ideological structure is polarized. At crucial points, in particular those scenes foregrounding the "antagonism of classes" (cf. Slackbridge addressing the Coketown workers), "no actual revolutionary struggle against the Bounderby-Gradgrind regime is adumbrated" (Jackson 88). As the narrative accrues an oppositional voice, much of that opposition's value is undermined by the novel ultimately accepting the status quo of the Coketown social structure.

Despite possessing such an inconsistent thematic, *Hard Times* singularly transcends the traditional economic environs of the "Condition of England" novel to focus on institutional networks, to create a "disciplinary city" in Coketown:

> It contained several large streets all very like one another, inhabited by people equally like one another, who all went in and out at the same time . . . to do the same work, and to whom every day was the same as yesterday and tomorrow . . . .   (17; bk. 1, ch. 5)

Coketown's workers exist in a tireless present, traveling identical streets with people of identical routines. They are "a race who would have found more favor with some people, if Providence had seen fit to make them only hands, or like the lower creatures of the seashore, only hands and stomachs . . ." (49; bk. 1, ch. 10). This imagery of the workers as "non-human" or a collective of machines suffuses the novel. Louisa Gradgrind's received Utilitarian vision of them is an exemplary instance: "She knew of their existence by the hundreds and by thousands," not as "individuals" but more as machines that generate a respective amount of "work . . . in a given space of time" (120; bk. 2, ch. 6). The "Hands" of Coketown are, in effect, animated segments who are "manipulated, shaped" and "trained" (Foucault, *Discipline and Punish* 136) for service in the city's factory network.

They have lost much of their social currency as "people" as they are enmeshed in what Foucault calls the "historical moment of the disciplines" (138):

The human body was entering a machinery of power that explores it, breaks it down . . . . A "political anatomy", which was also a "mechanics of power", was being born; it defined how one may have a hold over others' bodies . . . . Thus discipline produces subjected and practised bodies, "docile" bodies. . . . In short, it disassociates power from the body. (138)

From a Foucauldian perspective, Coketown's industrial operatives are a new iteration of "humanity," " 'docile bodies' " produced by a disciplinary "machinery of power" that seeks to reduce individuals to malleable automatons. Throughout *Hard Times* Dickens underscores the power that produces "subjected and practised bodies" as a theoretical motif. Coketown's mill workers are characterized as "quiet servants with . . . composed faces and . . . regulated actions" (53; bk. 1, ch. 11). Their lives are a routine of "direful uniformity" (69; bk. 1, ch. 14) in which any aspirations beyond a "bare existence" are "utterly driven out of their souls" (125; bk. 2, ch. 6); they evince a marked "disassociation" from any personal power. In this original social "anatomy," Coketown's functionaries reflect not only the "estrangement" of people from their labor (Marx 119), but a disciplinary pandemic in which Victorian institutions were perfecting the normalization (Foucault, *Discipline and Punish* 182–83) symbolized by the Hands' "regulated actions."

If, as Friedrich Engels maintains, "the proletariat was called into existence by the introduction of machinery" (61–62), then what also distinguishes *Hard Times* from its Victorian counterparts is its focus on such an interpellative process (Althusser 174–75), specifically the oppressive interpellation of Utilitarian and capitalist discourses that script "uniformity" in workers such as Stephen Blackpool and "call in to existence" (174–75) a social equation between "looms . . . wheels, and Hands" (53; bk. 1, ch. 11). The linkage of these discourses is further underscored by the Utilitarian disciplinary product, Bitzer, an "excellent young economist" who feels "to buy . . . for as little as he could possibly give and sell . . . for as much as he possibly could get" is the philosophical datum of "man's duty" (88; bk. 2, ch. 1). This ideology of Utilitarian/laissez-faire self-interest drives the institutional spectre that haunts the lives of Coketown's underclass.

However, Dickens's portrait of the Coketown workers has long been a source of critical dissension on two fronts: that he lacked sufficient experience among the industrial class to write of them expertly and that *Hard Times* correspondingly displays this unfamiliarity. George Gissing (1903) argued that "the working class is not Dickens's field, even in London" (202), and that Stephen Blackpool, *Hard Times*'s central proletarian, "represents nothing at all; he is a mere model of meekness . . . " (201). Louis Cazamian (*The Social Novel in England: 1830–1850,* 1903) felt that "the details of the factory workers' lives come as brief interludes" and that the ethos of Coketown is "drawn in broad strokes" (168). In concert with Gissing, Humphry House

(*The Dickens World*, 1941) thought that the "most common general explanation of the book's failure is that Dickens was writing of people and things
quite outside the range of his own experience" (203–04).

These assessments are connected to what is traditionally seen as the origin
of *Hard Times*: Dickens's January, 1854 weekend excursion to the industrial
north of England ("On Strike" 453) to survey the effects of the Industrial
Revolution, specifically, the strike of twenty-thousand textile workers (Perkin
298) in Preston. In fact, Dickens was offended by "claims that he had gotten
the idea for *Hard Times* from the Preston strike" and he felt that he had a
more than sufficient theoretical and experiential base upon which to develop
characters of the industrial class (Kaplan 308).

It is true that the characterizations of workers such as Stephen Blackpool
and Rachael are not the material of a stridently transcriptive factory novel.
But perhaps the absence in *Hard Times* of such vivid Dickensian moments
as Oliver Twist gladly eating a dog's leftover food scraps is not a marker of
Dickens's failure in "realist" portraiture, but a sign of his actual focus: to
go beyond a documentary of the *belle époque* of industrial oppression. By
1854, when Dickens began writing *Hard Times*, novels such as Benjamin
Disraeli's *Sybil, or the Two Nations* (1845) and Elizabeth Gaskell's *Mary
Barton* (1848) had already conducted readers through the hovels of the Victorian proletariat. In contrast, Dickens's apparent project was to construct a city
based on disciplinary, Utilitarian ordering principles and follow the effects of
those principles through both personal and institutional lenses.

Hard Times has also been critically challenged in regard to Dickens's
understanding of systematic political principles (House 205; Holloway
159–61; Monod 451)—some maintaining that he was a "muddled thinker
with only a casual grasp" (Coles 153) of philosophical systems such as
Utilitarianism. However, *Hard Times* evidences a "clear understanding of
the theoretical tenets of the philosophy whose consequences the novel enacts"
(153). To Dickens, those "tenets" did not revolve around Utilitarianism's
ostensible "enlightened and emancipated thinking" that led to what many
saw as "comprehensive social welfare and reform" (Holloway 159). Instead,
Dickens saw workhouses and assembly-line schools as the actual impact of
Utilitarian "reforms"; thus *Hard Times* portrays Utilitarianism as an over-
arching disciplinary mechanism allied with industrial institutions such as
Coketown's factories.

Reciprocally, the workers of Coketown are not just defined as proletarians
economically exploited in an "ugly citadel" "where Nature was as strongly
bricked out as killing airs and gases were bricked in" (48; bk. 1, ch. 10), but
like Sissy Jupe in Gradgrind's school, they are "in all things regulated and
governed" (5; bk. 1, ch. 2) in that most prevalent of Victorian disciplinary
institutions, the factory. The oppressive factories and workhouses that define

the British Victorian social fabric are, in the Foucauldian world, extensions or a disciplinary apparatus that originated in "a whole set of regulations . . . and calculated methods relating to the army, the school and the hospital, for controlling or correcting the operations of the body" (*Discipline and Punish* 136).

This control of the "body" is evident in Bounderby's factory where Stephen Blackpool, as the symbol of all the Coketown Hands, labors: " Stephen bent over his loom, quiet, watchful, and steady . . . in the forest of looms . . . . So many hundred Hands in this Mill; so many hundred horse Steam Power" (53; bk. 1, ch. 11). Stephen is more than an overworked economic operative. His "quiet" and "watchful" routine is that of a controlled body—a body valued by the mill owners as only so much "Steam Power." Stephen's plight exemplifies Foucault's analysis that Victorian factories employed an "art of distributing bodies, of extracting time from them . . . of composing forces to obtain an efficient machine" (*Discipline and Punish* 164). As such an "efficient machine," Stephen's "self" is lost among the ironically juxtaposed "forest of looms."

In *The Rise of Industrial Society in England: 1815–1885* (1964), S.G. Checkland observes that though the "residual" agrarian mode of production (Williams, *Marxism* 122–24) was obviously exploitative for the worker, there was a limit to its oppression. Nature itself, the seasons, punctuated any working cycle (Checkland 244). However, the "emergent" (Williams, *Marxism* 122–24) industrial workplace, was interior, outside Nature; workers were now "intertwined with powered machines in a single process" (Checkland 244). In concert with this appraisal, Dickens's factory scenes construct a mechanical Anti-Nature where the shadows of the mills' engines on the factories' walls are "the substitute Coketown had to show for the shadows of rustling woods; while, for the summer hum of insects, it could offer, all the year round . . . the whirr of shafts and wheels" (85; bk. 2, ch. 1). In such an environment, the Hands of Coketown become correlative with the "shafts and wheels" to which they are bound. Dickens, like Ruskin, saw that in order to make people "work with the accuracy of tools," it was necessary to "unhumanize" them (Ruskin 2: 161). *Hard Times* echoes how "disciplinary power became an 'integrated' system, linked . . . to the economy" (Foucault, *Discipline and Punish* 176) with its representation of the disciplinary architecture of industrial sites.

As Foucault acknowledges, this culture of "discipline" was not unique to the institutional explosion of the Victorian era: "Many disciplinary methods had long been in existence—in monasteries, armies, workshops. But in the course of the seventeenth and eighteenth centuries the disciplines became general formulas of domination (*Discipline and Punish* 137). Dickens's Coketown displays just such an infusion of "disciplinary methods" with its Utilitarian schools and coordinate factories. One of the primary "formulas of domination" encountered in *Hard Times* appears in the first paragraph of the novel with Gradgrind's famous discourse on Utilitarian education: "Teach these boys and girls nothing but facts. Facts alone are wanted in life. Plant nothing else, and root out everything else. You can only form the minds of reasoning animals upon Facts; nothing else will be any service to them" (1; bk. 1, ch. 1). In transforming children into "reasoning animals," disciplinary productions, walking abacuses such as Gradgrind would write "the great book of Man-the-Machine" (Foucault, *Discipline and Punish* 136) via Utilitarian dicta where "any parcel of human nature" was "a case of simple arithmetic" (2; bk. 1, ch. 2). Such reduction of people to arithmetic, mechanized figures is a controlling image-pattern in *Hard Times*.

This iconography of the "machine" is immediately extended in the resumé of Gradgrind's classroom agent, M'Choakumchild. He "and some one hundred and forty other schoolmasters, had been lately turned at the same time, in the same factory, on the same principles, as so many pianoforte legs" (6; bk. 1, ch. 2). M'Choakumchild is a factory product, like a Coketown Hand, and his agenda is to make "the educational space function like a learning machine" (Foucault, *Discipline and Punish* 147), a machine that will erase Imagination and create disciplinary operatives who will "Never wonder"—never question their roles in the Coketown's institutional apparatus—for Gradgrind's disciplinary imperative centers on making the lives of these operatives a manageable formulation, "a mere question of figures" (2; bk. 1, ch. 2).

One of Dickens's early titles for what would become *Hard Times* was *A Mere Question of Figures* (Lindsay 310). A leitmotif in Dickens's representation of the disciplinary city revolves around figurality. At the opening of the novel, the imperious schoolmaster, Gradgrind, is imaged as a geometric figure, with a "square coat, square legs" and "square shoulders" (1; bk. 1, ch. 1). He is an animated Euclidean construction, a "wintry piece of fact" (48; bk. 1, ch. 9). The primacy of "fact" and the erasure of the imagination, "Fancy," are central to Gradgrind's Utilitarian norming process: "Herein lay the spring of the mechanical art and mystery of educating the reason without stooping to the cultivation of the sentiments and affections. Never wonder. By means of addition, multiplication, and division, settle everything somehow, and never wonder" (37; bk. 1, ch. 8). Gradgrind's school, the location for what Dickens labels "Murdering the Innocents" (2; bk. 1, ch. 2), is an appropriate setting for erasing students' "sentiments and affections" and replacing them with a "mechanical," arithmetic psychological register. Gradgrind's theater is a "bare, monotonous vault of a schoolroom" (1; bk. 1, ch. 1) where the "art" of producing docile bodies is developed and refined. It is not only the immediate students of Gradgrind, but also the populace of Coketown who are subject to the indoctrination of abstracting existence to a tabular scheme: "Facts," the gods of the Utilitarian pantheon, govern Coke-town: "Fact, fact, fact, everywhere . . . in the town . . . everything was fact between the lying-in hospital and the cemetery . . . " (17; bk. 1, ch. 5). The Utilitarian ideology even takes on an ontological imperative: "what you couldn't state in figures . . . was not, and never should be . . . " (17).

As Nicholas Coles stresses in the seminal "The Politics of *Hard Times*: Dickens the Novelist versus Dickens the Reformer" (1986), "All forms of statistical science are presented in effect as ideological instruments of class domination . . . " in *Hard Times* (160–61). Dickens was very prophetic of Foucault in recognizing the varied forces that normed people at the apex of the Industrial Revolution. These forces, Dickens recognized, were not just subsets of class warfare. They also included an institutional scheme of statisti-cal, co-opting discourse, what *Hard Times* terms "tabular statements" (18; bk. 1, ch. 5). These discourses reduce the workers of Coketown to figures in prescriptive statements of social control. When the workers do not attend church, the local religious authorities react by "indignantly petitioning for acts of Parliament that should make these people religious by main force" (18). The narrative lists a catalog of these statistical efforts:

> Then came the Teetotal Society, who complained that these same people *would* get drunk, and showed in tabular statements that they did get drunk . . . . Then came the chemist and the druggist, with other tabular statements, showing that when they didn't get drunk, they took opium. Then, came the experienced chaplain of the jail, with more tabular statements, outdoing all the previous tabular statements, and showing that the same people *would* resort to low haunts . . . .   (18)

These "statements, " along with Gradgrind's "Facts," constitute a cultural trope of figurality that informs the world of *Hard Times*. This discursive program of regulation and enforced docility confronts how Victorian society had turned "people" into manageable, scripted "populations":

> One of the great innovations in the techniques of power in the eighteenth century was the emergence of "population" as an economic and political prob-lem: population as wealth, population as manpower or labor capacity . . . . Gov-ernments perceived that they were not dealing simply with subjects, or even with a "people," but with a "population". . . .
>
> (Foucault, *History of Sexuality* 25)

According to Foucault, at a very elemental level the functioning of emergent social control in the eighteenth and nineteenth centuries relied on cataloguing people as a set of population "variables": "birth and death rates . . . state of health . . . patterns of diet and habitation" (25). The Hands of *Hard Times* are similarly categorized as "Something to be worked so much and paid so much, and there ended .... Something that increased at such a rate of percentage, and yielded such another percentage of crime, and such another percentage of pauperism ... " (120–21; bk. 2, ch. 6). Despite negative critical evaluations of Dickens as a social theorist, he was actually incisive and original in his diagnosis of institutional mechanisms and their "techniques of power" in Victorian England.

When Sissy Jupe enters Gradgrind's institutional world, the balance of his control in the school is disrupted. Sissy is a refugee of the Sleary circus, a residual "pre-capitalist" (Jackson 84) group that exists on the perimeter of the Coketown disciplinary network. In contrast to the production that defines Coketown, the Sleary circus group is a singular stratum of Victorian society that does not produce anything material, rather its "production" is entertainment and the engagement of Gradgrind's nemesis, "Fancy."

After Sissy's father disappears, she is brought into the Gradgrind household as a student and domestic servant to Mrs. Gradgrind. In Gradgrind's mind, Sissy's orphanage is a "miserable but natural end" to her "late career" (36; bk. 1, ch. 7) in the circus's roaming environment of anti-Reason, or "Imagination." Gradgrind's purpose is to bring her into the land and language of Coketown's institutional network: " ... one of the primary objects of discipline is to fix; it is an anti-nomadic technique ... " (Foucault, *Discipline and Punish* 218). In his norming exercises with Sissy, Gradgrind attempts to erase the "language" of her origins in the Sleary circus group and replace it with the discourse of regulation: " 'I shall have the satisfaction of causing you to be strictly educated; and you will be living proof to all ... of the advantages of the training you will receive. You will be reclaimed and formed' " (37; bk. 1 , ch. 7). Gradgrind's proposed "training" is not an invitation to Education, but a quintessential disciplinary program. Sissy is to be "reclaimed" in his institutional apparatus and "formed" in a "disciplinary coercion" that "establishes in the body the constricting link between an increased aptitude and an increased domination" (Foucault, *Discipline and Punish* 138). Gradgrind's school is, in effect, a disciplinary rookery.

The ambition of Gradgrind's effort at "reclamation" is total. He tells Sissy that " 'From this time you begin your history' " (36; bk. 1, ch. 7). Her life will cease to have a "past" and even her status as a person is effaced in the school with the assignment of a figural identity, " 'Girl number twenty' " (2; bk. 1, ch. 2). Sissy's resistance to this draconian taxonomy is successful due to her refusal to forget her history in the circus and replace it with the codes of governmental "tabular statements" that classify people as if they were so many statistical figures to be processed and manipulated (18; bk. 1, ch. 5). Sissy is representative of what Raymond Williams sees as the base of Dickens's conception of social reform: "For Dickens is not setting Reform against Exploitation .... It is not the model factory against the Satanic ....

It is rather, individual persons against the System . . . . It is the Circus against Coketown'' (*Culture and Society* 94–95). Williams underscores how one may see Sissy Jupe as a symbol of successful revolt against Gradgrind and Coketown; she succeeds at the "individual," local level. As opposed to the "systemization" of Bitzer, Sissy represents how the "unorganized life is the ground . . . of genuine feeling" (95). She frustrates the "System" of Gradgrind who recognizes that she retains an emotional capacity "that could hardly be set forth in tabular form" (71; bk. 1, ch. 14). Sissy's retention of her unreclaimed self is her revolt.

Jack Lindsay argues that "it is the opposition of the fantasy-life of the circus to the grinding round of toil which gives *Hard Times* its hint of a true revolutionary quality" (311). However, in a global cultural context, both Sissy and the Sleary Circus are islands of resistance. Though they evade the docility of a Stephen Blackpool, or the insidious self-fixation of a Bitzer, they are as agent-less as Stephen in effecting any enduring change in the Coketown power structure. Sissy and Sleary, are, in the end, catalysts in Gradgrind's Scrooge-like transformation in his rejection of "Reason," but the Utilitarian dynamic in Coketown is little altered.

The "star pupil," or homunculus of Gradgrind's Utilitarian training is Bitzer, one of Dickens's most originally drawn characters. The docile Stephen Blackpool is only a liminal figure in relation to this extremity of disciplinary production. Dickens, once again, is proleptic of Foucault in his creation of Bitzer. Bitzer is what Foucault would classify as a disciplinary product (*Discipline and Punish* 138), not an "individual" in the traditional humanist sense, but rather the robotic creation of a specific discipline, in this case, Utilitarianism.

Bitzer is the paragon of Gradgrind's Utilitarian formulae and their attendant system of surveillance. As Jeremy Tambling maintains in "Prison-Bound: Dickens and Foucault" (1986): "Something of the Panoptical Method is at work in *Hard Times* . . . the idea being thought suitable for schools and factories. In Gradgrind's school, the pupils are so raked that each can be seen at a glance" (13). In conjunction with Tambling, Cynthia Malone argues that "From the M'Choakumchild school in the opening chapter, to the fire-gazing conclusion, *Hard Times* represents . . . a hierarchical system of multiple gazes that enforce docility and obedience" (15). Both Tambling and Northcutt Malone are applying Foucault's discourse on the "Panoptic" impulse in disciplinary technologies (*Discipline and Punish* 195). This model originates in Jeremy Bentham's panoptic prison model where a central tower observes prison cells "like so many small theatres, in which each actor is alone, perfectly individualized and constantly visible" (200). The constant surveillance generates a condition where the inmate assumes scrutiny, whether existent or not; it "assures the automatic functioning of power" (201).

In an "automatic" progression, Bitzer gains the "respectable office of general spy and informer" (88 ; bk. 2, ch. 1) in Bounderby's bank, recapitulating the surveillance he experienced in Gradgrind's school. Bitzer's panoptic, disciplinary lineage solidifies both his own solipsistic Utilitarian code and an agenda of enforcing that legacy on others. When his father dies, he has his mother "shut up in the workhouse" because "all gifts have an inevitable tendency to pauperize the recipient" (88; bk. 2, ch. 1). Bitzer is "self-interest" incarnate, attuned only to the tabular aspects of existence: "His mind was so exactly regulated, that he had no affections or passions" (88). His social consciousness is "the result of the nicest and coldest calculations" (88). When responding to the Coketown workers' desire for "recreations" to alleviate their numbing circuit of regulation, Bitzer remonstrates that " '*I* don't want recreations. I never did; and I never shall . . . ' " (90; bk. 2, ch. 1). He finds validity only in his "great expectations" in Bounderby's bank. With Bitzer, Dickens moves away from the traditional characterization of a "villain." In the ethical realm, Bitzer is more condition than capacity; "volition" is problematic in his case. He lacks any substantive register of "right" and "wrong" outside his "calculations" of what is materially productive for him. In the context of the narrative's echoes of Milton's *Paradise Lost*, Bitzer was not made "Sufficient to have stood, though free to fall" (Milton 3.99); he is more institutional effect than "individual." If any action of his can be seen as "evil," it is one of robotic banality. His portrait is a radical excoriation of Victorian disciplinary procedures and, in the flow of the novel, a production that will come back (like Victor Frankenstein's "Creature") to haunt its creator, Gradgrind.

Among Gradgrind's myriad symbolic resonances is his role in Dickens's condemnation of the social texts of Utilitarianism and its fellow travelers: "Public Commissions, Bluebooks, Parliamentary legislation—all these, in the world of *Hard Times*—are Gradgrindery" (Williams, *Culture and Society* 94). The institutional discourses of this iconic "Gradgrindery" are links in the chain of a Victorian norming apparatus—an apparatus that inspires the one genuine but fleeting revolutionary moment in the novel: "Utilitarian economists, skeletons of schoolmasters, Commissioners of Fact . . . the poor you will always have with you. Cultivate in them, while there is yet time the utmost graces of the fancies of the affections; or . . . . Reality will take a wolfish turn, and make an end of you" (125; bk. 2, ch. 6). This "wolfish turn" of revolt never occurs, but through the image of Gradgrind, Dickens attacks governmental taxonomies as disciplinary cohorts of Utilitarianism, and as the novel progresses, this critique of social scripting takes a more comprehensive turn.

That is, *Hard Times* begins to question, as does Foucault, the contingency of classification itself: "On what 'table', according to what grid of identities, similitudes, analogies, have we become accustomed to sort out so many different and similar things? . . . there is nothing more tentative . . . than the process of establishing an order among things" (Foucault, *The Order of Things* xix). According to Foucault, there is an arbitrariness to received cultural taxonomies. They do not express "a priori or necessary" assemblages (xix). The power to "order," to choose what gets ordered and how, is the power to control that which is ordered. These taxonomies act as ideological instruments of a social power base in their ability to legitimate and exclude, to "determine averages" and "fix norms" (Foucault, *Discipline and Punish* 190).

A questioning of such taxonomies that fix norms is dramatically enacted when Louisa Gradgrind visits Stephen and Rachael. It his her first personal encounter with the Hands, and through her, the narrative elaborates a whole new social ecology:

> For the first time in her life, she was face to face with anything like individuality in connexion with them. She knew what results in work a given number of them would produce . . . . She knew them in crowds passing to and from their nests, like ants or beetles . . . . But, she had scarcely thought more of separating them into units, than of separating the sea itself into its component drops.
>
> (120–21; bk. 2, ch. 6)

This "table" of Utilitarian taxonomies, with its dehumanizing "order of things," is a touchstone of the narrative's distrust and critique of institutional discourses. The Hands are not just economic subalterns "of which vast fortunes were made" (121) but are *sui generis*, members of a separate identity stratum. Dickens's analysis is in accord with Foucault's elaboration of disciplinary taxonomies: "The first of the great operations of discipline is, therefore, the constitution of '*tableaux vivants*', which transform the confused, useless or dangerous multitudes into ordered multiplicities" (*Discipline and Punish* 148). Dickens, through the thoughts of Louisa, assails such "ordered multiplicities" as illusory, relative constructs. Such Utilitarian taxonomies are delineated as primal agents in norming the Victorian proletariat. *Hard Times*, as George Bernard Shaw maintains, presents Dickens "declaring that it is not our disorder but our order that is horrible" (29).

Beginning with the Fleet prison scenes in *The Pickwick Papers*, Dickens's questioning of the "order" of Victorian society is particularly focused on prisons and prisoners (Wilson 14). Natalie McKnight maintains that "Like Foucault, Dickens feared the increasing dominance of imprisoning structures, of 'discipline mechanisms' in society . . . " (16). *Hard Times* is very concerned with such "imprisoning structures." The novel "represents a system of disciplinary scrutiny" (Northcutt Malone 15) that is evident from the novel's opening in Gradgrind's classroom. The prison motif is extensive and

Coketown is imaged in such terms: "All the public inscriptions in the town were painted alike . . . . The jail might have been the infirmary, the infirmary might have been the jail, the town-hall might have been either, or both" (17; bk. 1, ch. 5). The interchangeability of the "jail" with other Coketown institutions symbolizes how "the authority that sentences infiltrates all those other authorities that supervise, transform, correct, improve" (Foucault, *Discipline and Punish* 303). This interchangeability or non-distinction between Coketown's "jail," "infirmary" and "town hall," represents Dickens's realization that civic sites are not ideologically disconnected in performing legal or medical functions. Rather, Dickens's cogent analysis places them as disciplinarily co-valent in Coketown's institutional network; each is among the "authorities that supervise" and "transform" (303).

The disciplinary operations of Coketown even extend to that ostensible location of solace, the church. The workers, though "called away from their own quarter" by the churches' "barbarous jangling of bells" (18; bk. 1, ch. 5) on Sunday, do not respond and regard the churches as "something with which they have no manner of concern" (18). They appear to regard this "calling" as an interpellative move (Althusser 244–45) of the Coketown disciplinary apparatus summoning them to another site for transformation. On a historical line with the Hands' reluctance for religious "guidance," Foucault records that "in the nineteenth century, when the rural populations were needed in industry, they were formed into 'congregations', in an attempt to insure them to work in the workshops; the framework of the 'factory-monastery' was imposed on the workers" (*Discipline and Punish* 149–50). Though the Coketown Hands' resistance to the "factory-monastery" is by default, by non-engagement, it is still resistance. This section marks a distinctive moment of revolt by the Hands against norming procedures, a moment when the narrator's description of oppression agrees with the Hands' recognition of that condition. It also correlates with Friedrich Engels's definitive, contemporary (1845) study of the English working class in which he argues that "Money is the god of this world; the bourgeoisie takes the proletarian's money from him and so makes a practical atheist of him. No wonder, then, if the proletarian retains his atheism and no longer respects the sacredness and power of the earthly God" (143). Harold Perkin's assertion in *The Origins of Modern English Society: 1780–1880*, complements Engels's analysis: the "majority" of people in Victorian industrial cities were "as contemporaries put it, 'pagan' " (200).

However, in *Hard Times*, the "practical atheist" revolt is a faceless one. It is a generalized function of the narrative; it is not voiced by any specific characters, but rather just ascribed to the "labouring people" (18; bk. 1, ch. 5). Given the workers' disdain for the ostensible "sacredness" of the Coketown religious apparatus and the narrative's congruence with Engels's analysis, it is not unreasonable that the reader would expect Dickens to extend this moment of resistance and create characters of the working class who stridently voice the "death of God" among the Victorian proletariat, especially in the personae of Stephen Blackpool and Rachael, but just the opposite is the case. Stephen and Rachael voice an idealized form of religious acceptance that continually looks to "Heaven" to give them " 'peace and rest' " (124; bk. 2, ch. 6). Their conception of religion actually reinforces their resignation to the social inequities that their class endures.

The class structure of *Hard Times* is unique; Dickens does not deploy his usual cast of middle-class characters. Rather, the reader encounters the upper-level bourgeoisie, M. P. Gradgrind; the industrialist/banker Bounderby; the residual aristocrat, Mrs. Sparsit, and the Carlyean dilettante, Harthouse. Uncharacteristically for Dickens, the novel foregrounds the proletarian couple, Stephen and Rachael.

The disciplinary " 'microphysics of power' " (Foucault, *Discipline and Punish* 29) that invests the lives of Stephen and Rachael through Bounderby's mill and the cultural extensions of Gradgrind's Utilitarianism conforms in miniature to D. A. Miller's assessment that "Few of course would dispute that, with Dickens, the English novel for the first time features a massive thematization of social discipline ... " (*Novel* ix). In inaugurating the theoretical connections between Foucault and Dickens in the brilliant "The Novel and the Police" (1981), Miller extends the disciplinarity found in Dickens to elaborate a nineteenth-century, disciplinary "rise of the novel": "And the novel? May we not pose the question of the novel—whose literal hegemony is achieved precisely in the nineteenth century—in the context of the age of discipline. I have been implying, of course, that discipline provides the novel with its 'content' " ("Novel" 18). *Hard Times* certainly displays this infusion of disciplinary "content" with its focus on both the Utilitarian and Industrial agendas to create mechanical "selves" of "regulated actions" (53; bk. 1, ch. 11). Though *Hard Times* exemplifies the "thematization of social discipline," the novel does not isolate Stephen and Rachael's political resonances in a disciplinary matrix, rather it dialogically plays discipline off of received conceptions of "class" to augment its portrait of the disciplinary city.

The 1851 British Census contextualizes the world of Stephen and Rachael: "The masses, therefore, of our large and growing towns—connected by no sympathetic tie with those by fortune placed above them—form a world apart ... divided from the rest as if they spoke another language or inhabited another land" (qtd. in Perkin 202). Dickens emphatically locates Stephen and Rachael in a social fabric that reflects the Census's analysis of proletarian "disconnection," of existing in "another land." This awareness of a drastic class schism in England was a Victorian fixation. The 1851 Census actually echoes Benjamin Disraeli's earlier cultural analysis in *Sybil* (1845), where he sees Victorian England as " 'Two nations . . . who are as ignorant of each other's habits , thoughts, and feelings, as if they were . . . inhabitants of different planets . . . ' " (96; bk. 2, ch. 5). John Barton, the embittered, Chartist weaver in Elizabeth Gaskell's *Mary Barton* (1848), voices the outrage of the proletariat at the inequities between these "two nations" of the rich and the poor: "we pile up their fortunes with the sweat of our brows; and yet we are to live as separate as if we were in two worlds . . . " (45; ch. 1). *Hard Times* continues this cultural motif when Stephen notes the "impassable world" (116; bk. 2, ch. 5) between Bounderby and his workers.

In this subaltern "world," Dickens provides Stephen and Rachael with a separate "language" that underscores their marginality. It seems that more than an attempt at verisimilitude was involved in having Stephen Blackpool and Rachael speak in a Northern English dialect—their discourse acts as a sign of the other, moral "land" that they inhabit; it separates them, just as Sleary's idiolect does, from the formal and statistical ideology of the Gradgrind realm.

In Stephen and Rachael's struggle to endure the inequities and "muddle" of their existence, it is their ethical codes and conversations that sustain them. They comfort each other with genuine sentiment, but too often rely on nostrums: " 'thy word is a law to me' " Stephen tells Rachael, " 'a bright good law' " (51; bk. 1, ch. 10). Rachael, Stephen's "Angel" (68; bk. 1, ch. 13) of solace tells him to " 'Let the laws be' " and Stephen responds: " 'Let all sorts alone. 'Tis a muddle, and that's aw . . . . I come to the muddle many times and agen and I never get beyond it' " (51). Certainly the pathos of Stephen and Rachael is affecting, but their conversations exhibit an attenuated awareness of being characters in the "prevalent fiction" (84; bk. 2, ch. 1) of laissez-faire circumlocution regarding reform of industrial practices: the mill-owners declaim that they are "ruined" when "inspectors were appointed to look in to their works; they were ruined when such inspectors considered it doubtful whether they were quite justified in chopping up people with their machinery . . . " (84). Though sincere, Stephen and Rachael's reflections on their existence are not cogent instances of social awareness.

However, Stephen and Rachael are not equal in their levels of subjection. Rachael and Stephen's ostensible wife appear exemplars of what Sandra M. Gilbert and Susan Gubar in *The Madwoman in the Attic* (1979) diagnose as "extreme images of 'angel' and 'monster' which male authors" (17) attach to women characters. The "monster" of *Hard Times* is Stephen's dissolute wife, a "disabled, drunken creature" (52; bk. 1, ch. 10) who prevents any legal union between Stephen and Rachael. Rachael is Stephen's "angel," providing emotional and domestic comfort for him. In so doing, Rachael is doubly-repressed in both class and gendered passivity—a condition that seems to preclude any possibility for an oppositional voice. This exclusion is reinforced by the narrative's allowance for a development of Stephen's political consciousness—a development singularly delineated in Stephen's two meetings with his "owner," Bounderby.

In Stephen's first encounter with Bounderby, when Stephen futilely tries to find a navigable path through Victorian divorce laws in order to disengage himself from the "moral infamy" (52; bk. 1, ch. 10) of his wife, he utters his subjected " "tis a muddle' " four times, including what is perhaps his "muddle" *magnum opus*: " ' 'Tis just a muddle a'toogether, an' the sooner I am dead, the better' " (58; bk. 1, ch. 11). In this scene, the mechanical laments of Stephen dramatize a Foucauldian docile body "that may be subjected, used, transformed and improved" (*Discipline and Punish* 136) to increase its utility.

In his second meeting with Bounderby, however, a seeming "new" Stephen emerges. Stephen confronts Bounderby regarding the conditions of the Hands, declaiming that they should not be regarded as "figures in a soom or machines" (116; bk. 2, ch. 5). This scene is an oppositional bookend to the first meeting and it is Stephen's most defiant moment in the novel. Two problems adhere to this situation however: Stephen and the other Hands *are* regarded as "figures" in the disciplinary city and the ultimately docile Stephen cannot produce an alternative social program:

> "Of course," said Mr. Bounderby. " Now perhaps you'll let the gentleman know, how you would set this muddle (as you're so fond of calling it) to rights." "I donno, Sir. I canna be expecten to't. 'Tis not me as should be looken to for that, Sir." (115; bk. 2, ch. 5)

The lives of Stephen and Rachael are somewhat a study in the nineteenth century's increasing normalization of the underclass. The Luddite "Hands" of 1812 that the reader encounters in Charlotte Bronte's *Shirley* (1849) retain an active oppositional voice to the factories of the nascent industrial paradigm that have displaced them from their individualized village employment: "Misery generates hate: these sufferers hated the machines which they believed took their bread from them; they hated the buildings which contained those machines; they hated the manufacturers who owned those buildings" (62; ch. 2). The workers actively rebel and the factory's " 'hellish machinery is shivered' " (64; ch. 2). It is the physical enclosure of the factory that frames the outrage of the Hands. By 1854, both physical and psychological enclosure are consolidated for industrial operatives such as Stephen and Rachael.

In a Foucauldian context, Dickens's portrayal of Stephen and Rachael can be read as an original spin on the "two nations" of the Victorian industrial paradigm. For *Hard Times* confronts a world where

> Division of labor and the reorganization of the work-force into units of mass production created factories; the application of technology to industry and the

harnessing of steam and water power produced modern manufacturing. At the
same time, increased production evolved a new people who made their living
from it.   (Cazamian 14)

These "new people," "evolved" from the artificial selection of technology,
represent a new form of subjectivity, one "fabricated" by the "specific
technology . . . called 'discipline' " (Foucault, *Discipline and Punish* 194).
Stephen and Rachael are not mechanical disciplinary products such as Bitzer
and M'Choakumchild, but their lives, in a Foucauldian context, are "fabricated" in the "disciplinary space" (145) attendant to industrial sites such as
Bounderby's mill. They are subject to the same modality of power as Gradgrind's students, a force immanently carried through Coketown society via
tabular regulation. Like the smallpox of the dispossessed street sweeper Jo
in *Bleak House*, which moves on to the upper-class Jarndyce household, so
too Gradgrind's directive to "Never wonder" filters through the unnatural
fogs of Coketown to infect Stephen and Rachael. However, it is not their
"sentiments" that are elided. In the wake of disciplined lives, they genuinely
"never wonder"; they never escape the "muddle" of their subjection.

They comfort each other with stoic moral platitudes that lack any philosophical deep structure—and from beneath this acceptance of suffering, there
emerges a model of docility: the normalized subject. Stephen and Rachael
are not a failure of character development, but a recognition, an intentional
depiction by Dickens of "docile bodies"; that is, the narrative constructs not
just a set of people who only find a "muddle" in negotiating the struggles
of life, but are only capable of such elementary reactions—such that they do
not just lack any substantive resistance but are *incapable* of it.

The representation of Stephen and Rachael's as members of a factory
underclass reflects "the functioning of a power that is exercised on those
punished—and in a more general way, on those one supervises, trains and
corrects . . . the colonized . . . those stuck at a machine and supervised the
rest of their lives" (Foucault, *Discipline and Punish* 29). Dickens's critique
of this disciplinary "supervision" and training follows a consistent line
throughout *Hard Times*. However, that fusion of disciplinary and industrial
oppression diagnosed by the novel bifurcates when an ideological template
is placed on it: for the critique of the attrition of "individuality" in factory-
prisons and Utilitarian schools (particularly in the first half of the novel) is
abruptly attenuated in a contrapuntal, hegemonic "fog" in the novel's second
half with the narrative's sudden fear of collective revolt by the Coketown
workers (bk. 2, ch. 4). Thus, a torsion of ideological registers along class and
institutional lines occurs as the novel progresses; that is, despite *Hard Times*'s
originality in diagnosing the disciplinary scripting in Coketown (an industrial
realm usually associated only with economic/class oppression), the novel's

treatment of the workers, en masse, lacks a platform of resistance that the narrative itself invokes. The proletariat of Coketown reside in a "labyrinth of narrow courts . . . shouldering, and trampling, and pressing one another to death" (48; bk. 1, ch. 10). The Hands are without any substantive avenues of redress for their conditions. Though the workers are involved in "Uniting, and leaguing, and engaging to stand by one another," their efforts against the "united masters" (87; bk. 2, ch. 2) are without effect. If *Hard Times*, as Edgar Johnson maintains, exemplifies "Dickens's violent hostility to industrial capitalism and its entire scheme of life" (2: 802), then where is a viable method of resistance? What the reader receives instead are the theatrical polemics of the union leader, Slackbridge.

Dickens's turn to concessionism appears in almost the exact center of the novel, in Slackbridge's speech to the Hands. The scene is an ideological pivot point in the novel, a hinge on which swings Dickens's Liberal apologism; it is a thematic rupture, decentering the ideological structure of the narrative. The prior anti-institutional invectives, the Radical rebellions against disciplinary normings, now stand as contrapuntal themes. The only potential agent of collectively organizing any change in the Hands' lives, Slackbridge, is represented as an opportunistic demagogue.

Slackbridge is associated with the image of fire, an image that is connected to revolution in Dickens's novels, perhaps most dramatically in the Gordon Riots of *Barnaby Rudge*. His initial description continues this trope: "He had declaimed himself into a violent heat, and was hot" (105; bk. 2, ch. 4). His railing is set beneath the glow of a "flaring gaslight" and he has to "quench his fiery face" with water. The narrative turns admonitory in its tone, warning that in such a volatile gathering it was "irrational" to "pretend that there could be smoke without fire" (106; bk. 2, ch. 4). There is an earlier textual cross-reference to this phrase. When Louisa looks out at the chimneys of the Coketown factories, she exclaims to her father, " 'There seems to be nothing there but languid and monotonous smoke. Yet, the night comes, Fire bursts out father!' " (76; bk. 1, ch. 15). The capitalization of "Fire" signals the symbolism of the line; that is, accounting for the Dickensian symbology of fire, it would appear that the "smoke" of the workers' agitation by Slackbridge is a precursor to the "Fire" of an "irrational" revolution.

Slackbridge's inflammatory "unreason" subverts the workers' "safe solid sense" (105; bk. 2, ch. 4). A political stress appears to fall on this "sense" of the workers; it is a value that is transmuted into "delusions" (106; bk. 2, ch. 4) as they listen to Slackbridge's "irrational" call for collective action. Considering the text as a continuum, this is the point at which the ideological pattern of the novel unravels. At this crucial juncture of the narrative, when a platform of possible collective resistance for the workers is presented, there is a sudden drop into a conservative abysm. The anti-institutional, anti-capitalist arc of the novel is submerged. The reader has followed an oppositional ideological thread only to be led into a labyrinth.

The Slackbridge episode is also a fulcrum in the progress of the plot. Stephen refuses to join his fellow workers in the Union on the strength of an ill-explained "promise" to Rachael to "avoid trouble" (122; bk. 2, ch. 6). Thus, the action that precipitates both Stephen's pariah status and his eventual martyrdom is "never satisfactorily accounted for" (Monod 449). The apparent moral stand by Stephen lacks any discernable rational basis and acts more as a plot device to ensure Stephen's isolation from both sides of the Coketown class structure. It is as if Dickens fixates on echoing the Stephen of the New Testament, the first Christian martyr. In so doing, he sacrifices coherence to typology. This urge for sacrifice is one of the mysterious aspects of *Hard Times*. The reader is never quite sure why Stephen refuses to join the union and assure his outcast status.[1]

The conservative Slackbridge sub-plot reaches its dramatic flashpoint when Stephen is falsely accused of stealing money from Bounderby's bank. Already rejected "by the prejudices of his own class" (121; bk. 2, ch. 6) for not joining the Union, his social martyrdom is completed when he is criminalized by the Bounderby circle and leaves Coketown. Slackbridge reappears to continue his denunciation of Stephen, the " ' proscribed fugitive' ": " 'O my fellow men, behold what a traitor in the camp of those great spirits who are enrolled upon the holy scroll of Justice and of Union, is appropriately capable!' " (188; bk. 3, ch. 4). Stephen is transformed by Slackbridge into a Miltonic serpent, a " 'viper' " who must be " 'cast out' " from the Eden of the Union. In conjunction with Slackbridge's earlier rant, this Grand Guignol scene remands the oppositional arc of the novel to a separate ideological "space"; where Dickens could have pushed the narrative into a mode of active reform, he enigmatically defers to a phobic burlesque of class revolt. It would appear that the whole Slackbridge masque provides a requisite sacrifice in Stephen Blackpool to legitimate the "debunking" of collective proletarian action.

The resolutions of the novel, correspondingly, are individuated. Stephen's flight from Coketown ends in his overtly symbolic fall into an abandoned mine, "the Old Hell Shaft" (203; bk. 3, ch. 6). Despite his role as the "Christian" emblem of the novel, Stephen's fall into "Hell" is congruent with the ironic Satanic imagery that Slackbridge attaches to him. He is lifted from the shaft but his injuries are mortal. Though Stephen links his impending death with the mine's lineage of killing workers " 'wi'out need' " (207; bk. 3, ch. 6), he still sees the industrial oppression responsible for those deaths as " ' Aw a muddle!' " He goes to his "Redeemers' rest" (208; bk. 3, ch. 6) with a stoicism that is admirable but docile.

Humphry House argues that Stephen Blackpool's life "could have been the material of genuine tragedy, but the "result is nothing but a slow record of inglorious misery and defeat" (206). In contrast to House, William J. Palmer, in *Dickens and New Historicism* (1997), opens a much more incisive gateway for evaluating Stephen's fall: it is "Dickens's metaphor for what happens to the disenfranchised, the 'other,' of society" (4) who are caught in "implacable" (4) engines of social control such as the Gradgrind/Bounderby binary. This assessment comports with the institutional fabric of *Hard Times* and its emphasis on the "utilitarian rationalization" of "political control" (Foucault, *Discipline and Punish* 139) found in British Victorian culture.

In the Gradgrind circle, the "Utilitarian/Reason" imperative is brought to an ironic conclusion after Gradgrind's son, Tom, is exposed as the actual thief of Bounderby's bank. Bitzer intends to take Tom to Bounderby for the anticipated reward of Tom's position at the bank. Gradgrind attempts to dissuade his creation by asking him if his heart has any potential for compassion: " 'It is accessible to Reason, sir," returned the excellent young man. "And to nothing else . . . . I am sure you know that the whole social system is a question of self-interest . . . . I was brought up in that catechism . . . as you are aware' " (218; bk. 3, ch. 8). The division of Gradgrind's Utilitarian kingdom is complete. However, Bitzer's "rational" denial of his creator is ironically circumvented by the imagination of Sleary as he foils Bitzer and escorts Tom to a successful escape from the authorities. Thus, in one of Gradgrind's more vulnerable moments, he is saved by the personification of that which he always worked to destroy, Imagination. As Sleary tells him, " 'there is a love in the world; not all Thelf-interetht after all . . . that hath a way of its own of calculating or not calculating' . . . " (222; bk. 3, ch. 8). Sleary, in his Circus identity and enactment of a non-self-absorbed "Fancy," embodies *Hard Times*'s recurrent theme of Imagination "triumphing" over a Utilitarian calculus (as with Sissy Jupe); in fact, one might characterize Sleary as confronting the Utilitarian world of Gradgrind from the framework of Mikhail Bakhtin's conception of the "carnivalesque," a localized cultural expression where "The behavior, gesture, and discourse of a person are freed from the authority of all hierarchical positions (social estate, rank, age, property) . . . " (Bakhtin 123)—a condition that is the polar opposite of Gradgrind. Gradgrind, like the pecuniary and haughty Paul Dombey, ends reduced and reformed in Gradgrind's case, by the sentiment and Imagination he so deprecated in Sissy Jupe and Sleary. He finishes his life in an ironic reversal of his prior raison d'être, "making his facts and figures subservient to Faith, Hope, and Charity" (225; bk. 3, ch. 9).

Another ironic counterpoint in Gradgrind's "reformation" is the course of his son's life. Tom, in the end, is an unreclaimed casualty of Gradgrind's discipline of "Reason." Tom's early statement (40; bk. 1, ch. 8) that " 'I wish I could collect all the Facts . . . and all the Figures, and all the people who found them out; and I wish I could put a thousand pounds of gunpowder under them, and blow them all up together'," is symbolically realized when he robs Bounderby's bank—an act that "blows up" Gradgrind's world and assures Tom's solitary death in exile.

Louisa also endures a solitary end. If there is a tragic figure in *Hard Times*, it is Louisa. Her marriage to the boorish, elderly Bounderby is forced on her by Gradgrind's petitions to see such a union through the " 'strong dispassionate ground of reason and calculation' " (74 ; bk. 1, ch. 15). This scene definitively stages the extent of Gradgrind's incorporation of his own disciplinary psychology: Gradgrind is more than willing to use his exchange-value ideology to prostitute his daughter in order to further enhance the "cashnexus" (Lindsay 313) of his partnership with Bounderby. Louisa, like her brother, Tom, has recognized that her father's training has denied her a life of any " 'aspirations and affections' " (77; bk. 1, ch. 15), but she dutifully resigns herself to the "dispassionate" role of "Mrs. Bounderby."

Louisa's subsequent "fall" stems from an ironic tragic flaw. Despite Louisa's "infidelity" with Harthouse, it is her sacrificial fidelity to her father's idea of social order that places her in such an untenable situation in the first place. In an agonizing moment of recognition she exclaims: " 'I curse the hour I was born to such a destiny' " (164; bk. 2, ch. 12). She never recovers from her contractual marriage to Bounderby: "Herself again a wife—a mother—lovingly watchful of her children, ever careful that they should have a childhood of the mind no less than a childhood of the body . . . . Did Louisa see this? Such a thing was never to be" (226; bk. 3, ch. 9).

The institutional linkages of the novel are completed when Louisa's "husband," Bounderby, is seen "making a show of Bitzer to strangers, as the rising young man, so devoted to his master's great merits" (225; bk. 3, ch. 9). Sissy Jupe, Bitzer's institutional counterpart, avoids becoming a prop in the disciplinary structure of Coketown and inherits the prototypical Dickensian happy marriage, reinscribing the Dickensian convention of a "plot of moral causality" (Morris 11).

The concluding ideological "causality" of *Hard Times* is a somewhat "muddled" affair. In *Dickens's Class Consciousness: A Marginal View* (1991), Pam Morris argues that a "fusion of desire with hate, identification with alienation, invests every aspect of Dickens's texts with a dialogic tension" (10). *Hard Times* evidences this ideological "tension," a mixture of vitriol and compromise in which overarching ideological perspectives lose continuity: for in confronting Victorian power structures along an extended anti-disciplinary arc, the novel, as if writing against itself, leaves the much-assailed political apparatus of Coketown unchanged.

There is certainly currency in Raymond Williams's view that Dickens saw reform at a local, individual level, not through Chartist uprisings (*Culture and Society* 94–95). But such a scheme seems insufficient when considering *Hard Times*'s condemnation of disciplinary and laissez-faire excesses. This condition is indicative of Dickens in many of his novels; he appears a Jacobin in his assault on institutions, and by implication, the society that produces them, but he backs away from revolution (the revolutionary tenor of the anonymous Narrator of *Bleak House* is a notable exception). Though *Hard Times* is an ideologically disordered novel, it is a work that astutely explicates the oppressive dynamic of Victorian institutional networks.

NOTES

1. See George Ford and Sylvère Monod's Norton Critical Edition of *Hard Times* (1966) for both a reproduction (252), and a discussion (278–9) of a passage that Dickens deleted concerning Stephen's promise. In this section, Rachael's sister is seriously injured in a factory accident and Stephen has a John Barton-like outburst against such injustices (252). Rachael, however, convinces Stephen that such anger can only " 'lead to hurt' " and so Stephen promises to follow Rachael's plea to " 'Let such things be' " (252), that is, not to get involved with any collective workers' actions. In his discussion of the passage, Nicholas Coles agrees with Sylvère Monod (451) in arguing that the omission does "damage to the internal coherence of the novel" (178).

WORKS CITED

Althusser, Louis. *Lenin and Philosophy and other Essays*. 1969. Trans. Ben Brewster. New York: Monthly Review P, 1971.

Bakhtin, Mikhail. *Problems of Dostoyevsky's Poetics*. 1963. Introduction. Wayne C. Booth. Trans. and Ed. Caryl Emerson. Minneapolis: U of Minnesota P, 1987.

Bronte, Charlotte. *Shirley*. 1849. Ed. and Introduction Andrew and Judith Hook. Harmondsworth: Penguin, 1974.

Cazamian, Louis. *The Social Novel in England 1830–1850: Dickens Disraeli Mrs Gaskell Kingsley*. 1903. Trans. Martin Fido. London: Routledge, 1973.

Checkland, S.G. *The Rise of Industrial Society in England: 1815–1885*. New York: St. Martin's, 1964.

Coles, Nicholas. "The Politics of *Hard Times*: Dickens the Novelist versus Dickens the Reformer." *Dickens Studies Annual* 15 (1986): 145–79.

Dickens, Charles. *Hard Times: An Authoritative Text.* 1854. Ed. George Ford and Sylvère Monod. Norton Critical Edition. New York: W. W. Norton, 1966.

―――. "On Strike." 1854. *Miscellaneous Papers.* Vol. 1. London: Chapman and Hall, 1961. 453–76.

Disraeli, Benjamin. *Sybil, or the Two Nations.* 1845. Ed. and Introduction Thomas Braun. Harmondsworth: Penguin, 1985.

Engels, Friedrich. *The Condition of the Working Class in England.* 1845. Trans. Florence Wischnewetzky. Ed. Victor Kiernan. Harmondsworth: Penguin, 1987.

Foucault, Michel. *Discipline and Punish.* 1975. Trans. Alan Sheridan. New York: Vintage, 1979.

―――. *History of Sexuality: Volume I: An Introduction.* 1976. Trans. Robert Hurley. New York: Vintage, 1990.

―――. *The Order of Things: An Archaeology of the Human Sciences.* 1966. no trans. New York: Vintage, 1994.

Gaskell, Elizabeth. *Mary Barton: A Tale of Manchester Life.* 1848. Ed. and Introduction Stephen Gill. Harmondsworth: Penguin, 1975.

Gilbert, Sandra M. and Susan Gubar. *The Madwoman in the Attic: The Woman Writer and the Nineteenth-Century Literary Imagination.* New Haven: Yale UP, 1979.

Gissing, George. *Charles Dickens: A Critical Study.* 1903. New York: Haskell House, 1974.

Holloway, John. "*Hard Times*: A History and a Criticism." *Dickens and the Twentieth Century.* Ed. John Gross and Gabriel Pearson. London: Routledge, 1962. 159–74.

House, Humphry. *The Dickens World.* 1941. London: Oxford UP, 1972.

Jackson, T. A. *Charles Dickens: The Progress of a Radical.* 1937. New York: International Publishers, 1987.

Johnson, Edgar. *Charles Dickens: His Tragedy and Triumph.* 2 vols. New York: Simon, 1952.

Kaplan, Fred. *Dickens: A Biography.* New York: William Morrow, 1988.

Lindsay, Jack. *Charles Dickens: A Biographical and Critical Study.* New York: Philosophical Library, 1950.

McKnight, Natalie. *Idiots, Madmen, and other Prisoners in Dickens.* New York: St. Martin's, 1993.

Malone, Cynthia Northcutt. "The Fixed Eye and the Rolling Eye: Surveillance and Discipline in *Hard Times*." *Studies in the Novel* 21.1 (1989): 14–26.

Marx, Karl. *The Economic and Philosophic Manuscripts of 1844.* 1844. Ed. and Introduction Dirk J. Struik. Trans. Martin Milligan. New York: International Publishers, 1964.

Marx, Karl and Frederick Engels. *The Communist Manifesto.* 1848. Introduction Francis B. Randall. Trans. Samuel Moore. Ed. Joseph Katz. New York: Washington Square, 1964.

Miller, D. A. "Discipline in Different Voices: Bureaucracy, Police, Family and *Bleak House.*" *Representations* 1 (1983): 59–89.

———. "The Novel and the Police." 1981. *The Novel and the Police.* Berkeley: U of California P, 1988. 1–32

———. *The Novel and the Police.* Berkeley: U of California P, 1988.

Milton, John. *Paradise Lost. Complete Poems and Major Prose of John Milton.* Ed. and Introduction Merritt Y. Hughes. New York: Macmillan, 1957. 211–469.

Monod, Sylvère. *Dickens the Novelist.* Introduction Edward Wagenknecht. Norman, OK: University of Oklahoma P, 1968.

Morris, Pam. *Dickens's Class Consciousness: A Marginal View.* New York: St. Martin's, 1991.

Palmer, William J. *Dickens and New Historicism.* New York: St. Martin's, 1997.

Perkin, Harold. *The Origins of Modern English Society: 1780–1880.* London: Routledge, 1969.

Ruskin, John. "The Nature of Gothic." *The Stones of Venice.* vol. 2. New York: Merrill and Baker, 1851–53. 151–230.

Shaw, George Bernard. *Shaw on Dickens.* Ed. and Introduction Dan H. Lawrence and Martin Quinn. New York: Ungar, 1985.

Tambling, Jeremy. "Prison-bound: Dickens and Foucault." *Essays in Criticism* 6 (1986): 11–31.

Williams, Raymond. *Culture and Society: 1785–1950.* London: Chatto & Windus, 1958.

———. *Marxism and Literature.* London: Oxford UP, 1977.

Wilson, Edmund. "Dickens: The Two Scrooges." *The Wound and the Bow: Seven Studies in Literature.* New York: Oxford UP, 1965. 3–85.

"Like or No Like": Figuring the Scapegoat in *A Tale of Two Cities*

Mark M. Hennelly, Jr.

The "sacrifices and self-immolations on the people's altar" in Dickens's A Tale of Two Cities *(1859) significantly restage many of the scapegoat paradoxes biblically represented in Leviticus' pronouncement of scapegoat ritual, pictorially dramatized in Holman Hunt's Victorian canvas* The Scapegoat *(1854), and recently clarified by René Girard's account in* The Scapegoat. *An interdisciplinary reading of the novel, which involves both deconstruction and myth criticism, seems best equipped to honor these paradoxes. Leviticus relevantly emphasizes motifs of substitution and sacrifice, besides various Oedipal crimes, while Hunt's controversial painting graphically illustrates and illuminates a series of scapegoat ambiguities, especially those dealing with the problems of supplementarity and the* Sonnenuntergang *or final setting of the Sun and Son. Girard's leads help enlighten what he terms the four "stereotypes of persecution," which also occur in the novel: a culture polluted by "loss of differences"; specific crimes like "parricide and incest"; the stigmatizing "signs of a victim"; and purifying punishment through "collective murder." Such insights coordinate and clarify the novel's general concern with wasteland sameness and difference as personified in Carton and Darnay, located culturally in England and France, and represented semiotically and rhetorically by the "sign of the cross." They also again help coordinate both Oedipal motifs and scenes of writing in the text. Finally, they point to Carton's related roles as the medieval "Knight of the Cart" and the biblical Paraclete*

Dickens Studies Annual, Volume 30, Copyright © 2001 by AMS Press, Inc. All rights reserved.

who supplements "the Resurrection and the Life." In this context scape-
goat paradoxes can ultimately shed their shadowy light on the paradox
of Carton himself.

> And Aaron shall lay both his hands upon the head of a live
> goat, and confess over him all the iniquities of the children
> of Is'rā-el, and all their transgressions in all their sins, put-
> ting them upon the head of the goat, and shall send him
> away by the hand of a fit man into the wilderness.
> —Leviticus 16:21

> And we are put on earth a little space,
> That we may learn to bear the beams of love.
> —William Blake, "The Little Black Boy"

> The principle of mimetic desire, its rivalries, and the inter-
> nal divisions it creates are identical with the equally mimetic
> principle that unifies society: the scapegoat.
> —René Girard, *The Scapegoat*

Leviticus's classic representation of the scapegoat ritual, cited above, especially emphasizes motifs of *substitution* and *sacrifice*, besides atonement,
the head as the source of logic and "capital" punishment, and wasteland
symptomology. It also implies the dialectics of sameness-difference, inside-
outside, and discrimination-indiscrimination. Leviticus subsequently pro-
scribes a lengthy list of transgressions, including endogamous relations with
"near of kin," exogamous relations with "a bondmaid," and the worshiping
of totemic "idols" and "molten gods" (18:6;19:4,20) like the golden calf,
thereby linking such Oedipal acts with scapegoat mythology. Charles Dickens's *A Tale of Two Cities* (1859) significantly refigures these same scapegoat
motifs in its many "sacrifices and self-immolations on the people's altar"
(362;III:10).

The value of a scapegoat reading proves, I think, as paradoxical as the
scapegoat itself. On the one hand, it can clarify and coordinate many of the
apparently contradictory elements in the novel while, on the other, it can
uncover significant depth and complication in a work often regarded as that
most abominable literary scapegoat, the *high school classic*. To appreciate
these values, however, requires a likewise paradoxical, interdisciplinary methodology, which, like the undersea school in Wonderland, teaches the mystery
behind the looking glass of history and the ritual behind rhetoric. More paradoxically, such a comparative method must accommodate both deconstruction
and myth criticism in a cultural context. As William Doty hypothesizes,
arguing that "Myth follows a deconstructive rather than syllogistic logic,"

To deconstruct a mythic text would similarly be to expose the structures by which it works, to lay out the possible alternative futures to which its gestures might lead, to show how its expression is molded and shaped by its cultural contexts—including the ways its mythemes and its language are grounded in its cultural worldview.   (242,236)

Such "alternative futures" can even herald the awakening of "a new Heaven and new Earth," which Carlyle traces to "The first preliminary moral Act, Annihilation of Self (*Selbst-tödtung*)" (186;II,8) in *Sartor Resartus* and which Sydney Carton ultimately discovers through his scapegoat acts of substitution and sacrifice in *A Tale of Two Cities*.

In restaging and displacing this primary Victorian culture value of self-sacrifice, William Holman Hunt's controversial canvas *The Scapegoat* (1854) pictorially and memorably performs such a "far, far better thing." In fact, in this provocative painting begun on the wastes of the Dead Sea and *displayed* in the Royal Academy in 1855, Hunt, whom Dickens once addressed as "a brother-artist" (*Letters* 8:555), most clearly *illustrates* and illuminates the Levitical motifs which so inform the novel. Only Chris Brooks, though, has noted any similarity: "Hunt's hallucinatory image of a final desolation is Sydney Carton's equally hallucinatory vision of the spiritual wasteland that is the underlying reality of the City of Man" (134).[1] I emphasize *displayed* and *illustrates* above to designate verbally the way Hunt's representation itself visually performs a scapegoat role. It *splits* even while *spreading out* meaning and also takes pains to *clarify* some first principle with the solar light of pure reason, even while it seems obscurely haunted by the absence of that first principle. *The Scapegoat* represents or personifies scapegoat phenomenology both in the figure of the goat with its (di)splayed feet and horns and in the frame's eerily illuminated, golden hue. This "frame" features illustrations of illuminating stars and a paschal candle besides complementary "inset" texts serially relevant to *A Tale of Two Cities*: Leviticus 16:22—"And the Goat shall bear upon him all their Iniquities unto a Land not inhabited," which obscurely clarifies the Crucifixion; and Isaiah 53:4, which clearly foreshadows the Redemption. At the same time, the goat, like the frame, is ornamented with a crown or band of red wool (not unlike the "little red caps" of the revolutionary "Redheads" [306;III:4,318;III:5]), which will transform to white—ritualistically equivalent to pure gold—if the offering is accepted (Isaiah 1:18). The beast also seems to face, and give an outer face to, the unmasked skull of its supplanted predecessor; and it appears literally bathed or baptized, not in the blood of the Lamb, but in the same eerie luminosity of its frame.

The exterior source of this ambiguous golden light is the sun *hanging* in the upper left corner of the canvas, which itself is cloven by a shadow and also supplanted by its reflected double in the Dead Sea and which further

reflects what Gillian Beer calls the symptomatic Victorian fear of "the down-
ward motion of *Sonnenuntergang*, the final setting of the sun" (172). J. Hillis
Miller relevantly clarifies this "theme of the second sun": "Quite often this
subsidiary focus involves some secondary light-source, made by human beings or signifying them. The light is a mock human sun, usually emanating
with a red glow from the earth or from some human enclosure" (*Illustration*
131). Coincidentally, Carlyle's analysis of "the symptom of imminent down-
fall" in *The French Revolution*, clearly a precursor text for Dickens, invokes
the same mocking figure, which also recurs throughout the novel: "Time of
sunniest stillness; . . . the new Age of Gold? Call it at least, of Paper; which
in many ways is the succedaneum of Gold" (28–29).[2] Finally, through the
center of Hunt's particular second sun obtrudes yet another predecessor's set
of cloven or split horns, themselves also reflectively doubled on the watery
waste.

Ford Madox Brown noted of this figural canvas that "Hunt's *Scapegoat*
requires to be seen to be believed in. Only then, can it be understood how,
by the might of genius, out of an old goat, and some saline encrustations,
can be made one of the most tragic and impressive works in the annals of
art" (Wood 44). We might further note the abyssal series of romance substitutions the canvas represents and the way the redemptive scapegoat, like Carton, sacrificially replaces Logos as a kind of afterWord or supplemental
anecdote. This itself may even imply the way that Derrida's "White Mythology" of western metaphysics disseminates its own destruction through the
darker metaphors and mythologies of apocalyptic writing, its engraved *Göt-
terdamerung*. Similarly, the incarnate and even "parricidal" Son replaces
the celestial Sun, which Dr. Manette early in the text identifies and deifies as
the "Gracious Creator of Day" (48;I:3). In the same way, the unwilling
victim, the goat with the demonic horns, cloven hooves, and forked tongue
of "the Father of Lies" (326;III:8)—with shaggy hair-shirt and traditional
iconography of lechery—replaces, in fact figuratively "pierces," the side of
the willing victim, *Agnus Dei*, the bloodied Lamb. But at the same stroke, it
also replaces the just as willing victimizers, the sins of the Israelites. In fact,
Isaiah 53:5, the verse following the framing text, reads: "But he was pierced
for our offenses, crushed for our sins," which itself prefigures the Lamb's
breaking open of the sixth seal, causing the sun to turn "black as sackcloth
of [goat's] hair" in Revelation (6:12).

As figured by Hunt, the scapegoat thus becomes a double and double, an
ambiguous mixture of sameness and difference as it represents *both* sin *and*
salvation. Paradoxically, it has (e)*scaped* the fate of its pure double sacrificed
as a "sin offering" on the Day of Atonement (Meisel 83), and yet its "impu-
rity" marks it for synecdochic punishment in order to purify the people. And
the thorny *crux* it "bears" on its crowned head, crucially doubled on the

water, "recalls to life" *both* the Demon's horns *and* the Divinity's cross. Later, our major task will be to see how the scapegoat's *iterum mori*, its penitential pilgrimage to crucifixion, is critically branded by what René Girard calls the four "stereotypes of persecution" in the "rite of the scapegoat": a culture *plagued* or *polluted* by "generalized loss of differences"; specific crimes like "parricide and incest"; the stigmatizing "signs of a victim"; and purifying punishment through "collective murder" (12–44). We will also see how these stereotypes appear in Sydney Carton's scapegoat drama, which ultimately replaces the "Evangelical" letter of the law in Leviticus and Hunt with the branding "beams of love" favored by Blake in "Little Black Boy."

First, though, we need to explore the significant scapegoat roles of sameness and difference. In *A Tale of Two Cities*, Barsad becomes "a Sheep of the Prisons," and "Sheep was a cant word of the time for a spy" (327;III:80). It is thus also a *word*, echoing so many other noted words in the text like "the word 'ACQUITTED' " (109;II:3), figuratively related to sacrificial victims. In fact, *Satan* itself "means the *accuser*" (Girard 196) in Hebrew, which not only clearly links the Sheep Barsad with the Satanic but also unclearly confuses the traditional Biblical discrimination between pastoral sheep and goats when the Son of Man "shall set the sheep on his right hand, but the goats on the left" (Matt.25:33). At the same time, though, it foreshadows Barsad's ultimately helping the Paschal Lamb Carton to become a scapegoat.

After the first paragraph's celebrated comparisons and contrasts of England and France, other less celebrated similarities and differences follow in the next four paragraphs which more significantly prefigure the text's scapegoat mythology. Most notable is the narrative historian's testimony that "Christian pastors" are inspiring France to human sacrifices and burnt offerings for the crime of having "not kneeled down in the rain to do honour to a dirty procession of monks." Such a representation relevantly illustrates Girard's account of chiastic role-reversals in scapegoat myths: "Christianity suffered persecution while it was weak and became the persecutor as soon as it gained strength" (204).

Other such illustrations also "frame" the text, foreshadowing the guillotine's "moveable framework" and the "hangman's" gibbet as more representations of the scapegoat's crucifixion. For example, "that magnificent potentate, the Lord Mayor of London" provides another surrogate, deputized, and displaced source of Power, but this "illustrious creature" is, in turn, also "despoiled" when "the mail was robbed," indicating that *postal* circuitry darkly underwrites the "rite of the scapegoat" and other "divine rights." The repeated "year of Our Lord," 1775, recalls that every year *Anno Domini* falls similarly *after* Christ's scapegoating, but falls differently further and further away from the "original" model that Leviticus's scapegoat precedes and at the same time previews. As we will see, it also implies older dying and reviving gods like those illustrated in the French *Tarot de Marseilles* and its *Le Pendu* (Card XII, "The Hanged One"), which scapegoated face card the novel often seems to personify. For example, this particular card (and its successor "Death," XIII) figuratively represents the marquis's ritualistically "hanged" executioner (200–01;II:15) and becomes Carton's actual trump card when he tellingly teases Barsad, "I play my Ace" (333;III:8) in the pivotal "A Hand at Cards" chapter. Even the "Cock-lane ghost"—"supernaturally deficient in originality"—parodically personifies haunting, absent origins as a problematic cock-and-bull story. The compared "faces" of the twin monarchs on both sides of the Channel further call into question the figure of personification or *prosopopoeia*, which, as Miller defines it, literally gives "a human face or a mask to something or someone" (*Ariadne's Thread* 184). Such a replacement-figure puts on its "best" face with those more terrible twins Fate and Death, the "Woodman and that Farmer" who destroy "marked" victims and construct "rude carts" to bear more scapegoats worthy of Leviticus, like *Cart*on, to sacrifice during their Reign of Terror. We will later have more to say about these *carts* in connection with Lancelot, the scapegoat "Knight of the Cart." Here we can simply note again the significance of prosopopoeia, of "faces" as *prima facie* illustrations of unlikely "likenesses." These likenesses may mask unlikeable qualities as in that Everyman, the Marquis Evrémonde, "with a face like a fine mask" (140;II:7), but may also mask both likeable and like qualities as in the illustration "The Likeness" (105;II:3). In the repeated dummy-subject construction invoked in the opening, "it is likely enough," as likely as the chiaroscuro fancy that "the highwayman in the dark was a City tradesman in the light."

Girard's commentary on the "mimetic desire" of scapegoat persecution suggests that it stages a complex juridical contest between doubled *accusers*, *advocates*, (false) *witnesses*, and, of course, scapegoat *defendants*. His contention that "all the characteristics of the great crisis that provoke collective persecution are discernible in the French Revolution" (20) suggests again that the various "trials" in *A Tale of Two Cities* involve and implicate these same different juridical contestants. And, in fact, Miss Pross's diagnosis of Doctor Manette's amnesia, his "not knowing how he lost himself, or how he recovered himself" during the ancien régime's persecution, relevantly counters Mr. Lorry's cautionary question as "to whether it is good for Doctor Manette to have that suppression always shut up within him" with her own symptomatic sympathy: "Touch that string, and he instantly changes for the worse. Better leave it alone. In short, must leave it alone, like or no like" (128;II:6).

Significant in this exchange between Pross and Lorry are grounds-of-knowledge issues between two friends who similarly revere Manette but dissimilarly read his disease, tropes representing inside-outside paradigms, and the "string" or clue (Book Two is titled "The Golden Thread") linking these scapegoat paradigms. Also important, however, is Miss Pross's zeugmatic construction of "like or no like" with its ambiguous syntax and implied paradox that *better* is "better" than *best*, that the memorable "best of times" in the opening sentence gives way to the just as memorable "far, far better thing" itself in the final sentence.[3] In fact, degrees of comparison and contrast, of similitude and dissimilitude, are compulsively compared and contrasted, especially in that most memorable contradiction "the superlative degree of comparison." But if zeugma (abab) becomes one favorite rhetorical figure for interrogating "like or no like," mirroring chiasmus (abba) reflects the other—"John Solomon, or Solomon John" (326;III:8)—as Sydney Carton reveals to his literal mirror-double Charles Darnay in accounting for his own symptomatic drunkenness: "I care for no man on earth, and no man on earth cares for me" (115;II:4). Both figures recall to life textual *shapes*, *arrangements*, and *patterns* and thereby also repeatedly refigure different dialogic relationships. For Girard, such doubling of sameness and difference becomes further relevant in "the theme of twins or fraternal enemies who illustrate the conflict between those who become undifferentiated in a particularly graphic fashion" (31). For example, the text graphically doubles those titular sibling rivals England and France (redoubled in Carton and Darnay) as Tellson's being "a French House, as well as an English one" (50;I:4), Darnay "passing and repassing between France and England" (95;II:3), and even Miss Pross cooking "half English and half French" (129;II:6) dinners.

As already implied, chiasmus often seems more emblematic and enigmatic as the sign of the cross, which first iconoclastically appears in the narrative reflection that in London "thieves snipped off diamond crosses from the necks of noble lords at Court drawing-rooms" (37;I:1). By Book III, "the mark of the red cross is fatal" to the Evrémond brothers (and their descendants), to these "lords" who have betrayed the scapegoat-model of their Lord and Savior. As Madame Defarge's own brother intones, "I mark this cross of blood upon you, as a sign" (356,361;10). Such a bloody figure itself semiotically links the cross of Christ (and the Blessed) with the mark of Cain (and the Beast) in a way which illustrates Girard's discussion of the ambivalence of differentially stereotyping and stigmatizing the scapegoat:

> In order to blame victims for the loss of distinctions resulting from crisis, they are accused of crimes that eliminate distinctions. But in actuality they are identified as victims for persecution because they bear the signs of victims. . . . At first sight the signs of a victim are purely differential. But cultural signs are equally so. There must therefore be two ways of being different, two types of differences. (21)

In other words, both class and cruelty differentially distinguish the Evrémond's, yet each similarly also bears both signs of blood. And Girard would add that stereotyping any scapegoat, whether named "Jacques" or "Monseigneur as a class" (263;II:24), paradoxically involves labeling as the same all those who question one's own difference, besides ultimately invoking "the primitive double sense of cursed and blessed" (61).

Other signs of the scapegoat's cross, which the text "cross-examin[es]" (103;II:3) and "cross-question[s]" (275;III:1), include that "distressful emblem of a great distress": a "Cross and a new large figure of Our Savior on it" (147;II:8). This grave marker is ironically placed at the marquis's chateau where "the figure on the Cross might have come down, for anything that" (157;II:9) the marquis would know of it—at least until he himself is scapegoated and buried beneath it. In fact, even when the brothers "crossed the road from a dark corner" (361;III:10) to imprison Dr. Manette and bury their secret crime, they literally face the moral crossroads which has plagued the family romance since Oedipus, and which particularly plagues the critical *decisions* of Lucie's father Dr. Manette, lover Darnay, and friend Carton, recalling Girard's reminder that "*decision* has a sacrificial character (*decidere*, remember, is to cut the victim's throat)" (114).

Also figuratively crucial (and clue riddled) are the metatexual and labyrinthine cross-stitchings of Time the Weaver, of the little seamstress who dies with Carton, and especially of Madame Defarge's "fatal register" (362;III:2). She even paradoxically practices post-structural *erasure* by employing unerasable "ink" in order to place scapegoats *sous rature*: "It would be easier for the weakest poltroon that lives, to erase himself from existence, than to erase one letter of his name or crimes from the knitted register of Madame Defarge" (202;II:15). The rape of her peasant sister further implies exogamous crossbreeding, which Leviticus forbids with slaves; but according to the Old Testament prophet, the infraction or mixup is actually only venial when the "victim" is unmarried and unpromised. Besides replicating the beast-with-two-backs, X is also for kissing, though the kiss may be la guillotine's Judas-"kiss" (302;III:4) of betrayal as much as the "kisses" (403;III:15) of peace that sacrificing Carton and the sacrificed seamstress, substituting for Lucie, finally exchange. Moreover, X identifies the alcoholic proof of different *spirits*, from the vintages spilled during the "wine game" (60:I:5) to the transubstantiated blood spilled during Carton's "rite of the scapegoat," which itself becomes proof of his transfigured spirit risen above the crossbeams of his "scaffold" (404;III:15). Together, all these signs signify *In hoc signo vinces*. Bearing the sign of the cross—and thereby becoming a scapegoat, again like Blake's little black-sheep "lamb," who bears the solar beams of divine love but eclipses them with human love—transforms the collective and individual spirits. It brings both closer to the desired *Thing itself*, the *enigmatic X*, with its own promise of real Presence or, at least, the re-membered image and represented likeness of self-presence. No wonder Derrida playfully writes that "chiasmus is authorized, even prescribed, by the ambivalence of the *pharmakon*" (127) as scapegoat.

Before purification can occur, a "persecution text" like *A Tale of Two Cities* usually documents, dramatizes, and diagnoses the four problematic stereotypes of the scapegoat's "persecution complex." And for the post-structuralist Girard, it becomes significant that myth criticism *seems* to be a casualty of the deconstructive assault on "origins" and "essentialism": "as a community moves away from its violent origins, the sense of ritual weakens and moral dualism is reinforced." This critical, epistemological exile reflects "the disintegration of the primitive notion of the sacred"—"that very primitive dual quality of the sacred which unites blessed with cursed"—so that "a philosophy of the mixture . . . is impossible." In fact, as we have suggested, the scapegoat myth itself deconstructively represents the *essential* " 'original' chaos," not the " 'primordial' lack of differentiation" (30). It seems, then, that culture has paradoxically scapegoated the myth of the scapegoat, particularly its *via negativa* or mythic "way of negation" in culturally constructed and compulsively repeated scapegoats like the parodic "Old Un"—"Old Nick" (318;III:7). His familiar double names suggest both the Freudian *un*canny, in which the prefix (Girard's "purely linguistic scapegoat," [4]) identifies the *or*iginal solar ore's scapegoating of repressed difference and *arc*hetypal Otherness, and the related stigma or cruel cut of the scapegoated Beasts of Genesis and Revelation. In fact, these scapegoat figures of Christianity, like crossbred Χριςισσ Himself, are figuratively placed under erasure and semiotically *X'd out* by the new cruciform, La Guillotine: "It was the sign of the regeneration of the human race. It superseded the Cross. Models of it were worn on breasts from which the Cross was discarded, and it was bowed down to and believed in where the Cross was denied" (302;III:4).

Such revelations suggest another problem in *A Tale of Two Cities*, namely, that almost every character at every level of dramatic importance seems a "scapegoat" of some kind or other—from the holy innocent killed by monseigneur's carriage and his hanged father Gaspard to that vitiated victim monseigneur himself. In fact, *incriminating* scapegoat-*crimes* not only breed indiscriminate persecution through "inveterate hatred of a class" (391;III:14), but discriminating Girard's "scapegoat effects" from other categories of violence in *A Tale of Two Cities* becomes problematical and a problem Girard generally explores. This is especially true when he again implies that postmodern readers tend to discredit the scapegoat-historian's "magical thinking" and so read persecution texts ironically (rather than literally) against a narrator like Guillaume de Mauchaut who actually believed that Jews were responsible for poisoning water supplies during the Middle

Ages and that executing these scapegoats would end the plague through a contagious cure (114–19). In so doing, postmodern readers make a scapegoat of Guillaume himself.

Something like this problem of ironic projection occurs in the novel when that prophetic Recording Angel, the mender of roads, takes over as "narrator" through his "countryman's story" of Gaspard who, after murdering the marquis, is hoisted above the town fountain in a "lofty iron cage" and "left hanging, poisoning the water." Whether the road-mender "recounted faithfully," or not, his narrated scapegoating seems problematical in Hayden White's metahistorical sense of the way "realistic" histories written between "the French Revolution and World War I" reflect "ideological disputes" that trap "the historical imagination" somewhere "between metaphor and irony" (45–47). In other words, does "poisoning the water" here represent "actual" contamination from either the victim's body-secretions or the soldiers fouling the well while erecting "a gallows forty feet high"? Or does "poisoning the water" render metaphorical this traditional crime in persecution texts for the rationalized "purpose" of later storming the Bastille and indiscriminately scapegoating all authority figures? Does the "narrator's" exclamation, "How can the women and the children draw water!" (199–201;II;15), privilege the literal reading, or does it metaphorically imply a wasteland clash between the pure water, women, and children and the "poisonous" public execution? And what of Dickens's primary narrator here? Does that narrative voice present the other narrator "innocently" or ironically?

Indiscriminate scapegoating presents a related problem for the reader of *A Tale of Two Cities*, one that involves discriminating between ambiguous "victims of all degrees" (376;III:13), who seem to be as attracted to scapegoating as to Loadstone Rock. As Julia Kristeva describes the scapegoat's abject ambiguity,

> His abjection is due to the permanent ambiguity of the parts he plays without his knowledge, even when he believes he knows he knows. It is precisely such a dynamics of reversal that makes of him a being of abjection and a *pharmakos*, a scapegoat who, having been ejected, allows the city to be freed from defilement. The mainspring of the tragedy lies in that ambiguity.   (84)

Girard, however, discriminates "a scapegoat *in* the text" from a "scapegoat *of* the text" and a *scapegoat* from a *pharmakos* (119–24), by which *he* means a "guilty" *victim* of persecution like Oedipus from an "innocent" victim like biblical Abel. *Pharmakos* also seems similar to *martyr*, etymologically a *witness* in or to some cause, like the seamstress dying with Carton, who plays the "heroic victim of an unjust act of violence" (202). In his classic example of structuralism, *Anatomy of Criticism*, the myth-critic Northrop Frye further discriminates the *sparmagos* "or the tearing apart of the sacrificial victim," as Gaspard "will be torn limb from limb by four strong horses" (200;II:15), from the *pharmakos* "or sacrificed victim, who has to be killed to strengthen others," whether "the mob" or "the tyrant-leader." In fact, "in the most concentrated form of the demonic parody," like the novel's parodies of the apocalyptic beast, the tyrant and victim ultimately "become the same. The ritual killing of the divine king in Frazer, whatever it may be in anthropology, is in literary criticism the demonic or undisplaced radical form of tragic and ironic structures" (148–49).

We could further discriminate willing scapegoats—Frye's heroic "*eirons* or self-deprecators*" (172–75) like Carton and Christ—from unwilling scapegoats destined for "innocent atonement" (360;III:10) like Darnay and John the Baptist and even distinguish different modes of violence that, at least *ironically*, imply scapegoat-persecution. These latter include the rape of Madame Defarge's sister, Manette's false imprisonment, the marquis's vehicular manslaughter, the bereaved father's diminished capacity and (justifiable?) homicide against the marquis, Madame Defarge's vendetta of "family annihilation" (388;III:14), and The Vengeance's inciting the mob to indiscriminate retribution against all authorities, expatriates, "traitors," and "strangers." We might finally discriminate between our putative sympathy for the scapegoat Carton and our apathy if not antipathy for the scapegoat Darnay, even though these twin-figures *both* willingly and sacrificially return to France for a higher cause. "We" thus seem to find scapegoats everywhere but in the mirror so that Girard—with Baudelaire and Eliot—incriminates even "us" (and himself): "*Hypocrite lecteur, mon semblable, mon frère* (41).[4]

The related first persecution stereotype, the cultural crisis of contagious sameness, strongly suggests wasteland mythology: "In many myths the wretched person's presence is enough to contaminate everything around him, infecting men and beasts with the plague, ruining crops, poisoning food [and water], causing game to disappear, and sowing discord around him" (Girard 36). In *A Tale of Two Cities*, the "seasons of pestilence" and "wild infection" (310;III:6) breed such sameness so that again "the contagion of the scapegoat" (Girard 105) plagues the text primarily through substitutional figures of metonymy and homonymy like those linking the serial "echoes" of the Angel, of angelic Lucie the "golden-haired doll" (121;II:5), of her doll-like daughter "little Lucie," and of little Lucie's littler "doll" (240;II:21). Girard, in fact, discusses similar "echo[es]" (129) in the biblical incest-conflict between Herod and his half-brother Herod over his sister-in-law Herodias, which concludes with the scapegoating of John the Baptist (Mark 6:17–28). Such contamination seems especially crucial in Darnay's first trial scene, "A Disappointment" (95–109;II:3), where the expression on

Lucie's face is "unconsciously imitated by the spectators" and the "great majority of the foreheads there, might have been mirrors reflecting the witness" (102). Again, the illustration "The Likeness" visually represents the verbal repetition of the word *like* throughout this chapter, particularly and proleptically in "how very like each other" (104–05) Darnay and Carton appear. And yet the text can also metatexually play with its own visual and verbal mirrors: "so like each other in feature, so unlike each other in manner—standing side by side, both reflected in the glass above them" (108), which mixes the metaphor of its own rhetorical investment into the monstrously crossbred, "chiastic zeugma" of Stryver fitting his evidence like a "suit of clothes": "now inside out, now inside in" (106).[5]

Later, the *danse macabre* of the Carmagnole produces a related kind of double *panic attack* and visitation of The Great God Pan (or homogenized All) as "Men and women danced together, women danced together, and men danced together," representing "how warped and perverted all things good by nature were become" (307;III:5).[6] In scapegoat mythology, the in-crowd and the outsider ultimately become the same—first through common *Angst* and then through uncommon anomie and at-onement. "The paranoiac suspicion of a crowd tormented by the plague" and the dove-tailing or serpentforking of "the marginality of the outsider with the marginality of the insider" (Girard 25–26) become, in *A Tale of Two Cities*, "the universal watchfulness" (275;III:1) which panoptically plagues not only the revolutionary mob but also their sacrificial victims, just as it does in the opening of *Little Dorrit*, Dickens's previous "persecution text."

Again, then, the text projects a monotone "wilderness of misery and ruin," one synecdochically represented by the monseigneur's morally as well as monetarily bankrupt estate: "a crumbling tower of waste, mismanagement, extortion, debt, mortgage, oppression, hunger, nakedness and suffering"—"There is a curse on it, and on all this land" (155;II:9). Little wonder that the pandemic "leprosy of unreality disfigured every human creature in attendance upon Monseigneur" (137:II:7). In England, the "lifeless desert" of Carton's surroundings and the *taedium vitae* of his soulscape are similarly dis-eased, deserted, and disfigured: "Waste forces within him, and a desert all around him" so that even potentially penitential waters seem more poisonous than purifying: his "pillow was wet with [only] wasted tears" (121–22;II:5).

Fred Kaplan has documented Dickens's "notion of himself as physician" and "Christ-like healer" (181); and it is not until Carton appropriates the "healing office" (404;III:15) of the previous Wasteland Physician, Dr. Manette, that he ironically plays both *pharmakon* (antidote) and *pharmakos* (scapegoat), those related mixtures which alone can cure the epidemic of sterile sameness as often signified in "the frequent references to *poison*"

(Girard 16) in scapegoat rites. Manette's recovered memorial describes his earlier attempts to heal Madame Defarge's sister with pharmaceutical mixtures: "I opened some of the bottles, smelt them, and put the stoppers to my lips. If I had wanted to use anything save narcotic medicines that were poisons in themselves, I would not have administered any of those" (352;III:10). Years later, "the chemist" citizen similarly cautions the strange "citizen" Carton regarding the potent drugs of *his* "healing office": "You will be careful to keep them separate, citizen? You know the consequences of mixing them?" (342;III:9). Such a warning reflects the wasteland fear of illogically mixing "the likely and unlikely elements" (Girard 29) in scapegoat mythology, which mixture the unlikely "resurrection man" Carton himself ultimately preaches, practices, and personifies. Derrida also plays with such motifs throughout "Plato's Pharmacy," mixing together the supplementary "dissymmetry" of antidotes, scapegoats, sun gods, tricksters, and writing performances. And Derrida relevantly emphasizes the *unsubstantial* (Girard would say *discarnate*) ability of each "antibody" (123), like the increasingly spectral Carton, to kill (and be killed), cure, and anecdotally lead Logos astray: "The *pharmakon* would be a *substance*—with all that word can connote in terms of matter with occult virtues, cryptic depths refusing to submit their ambivalence to analysis, already paving the way for alchemy—if we didn't have eventually to come to recognize it as antisubstance itself" (70).

This reference to "alchemy" further recalls those "unbelieving chemists who had an eye on the transmutation of metals" (136;II:7) and the "golden giant" who "had a golden arm starting out of the wall of the front hall" of the Manettes' Soho residence and who had figuratively "beaten himself precious, and menaced a similar conversion of all visitors" (123;II:6). The relevance of this enigmatic scapegoat and scapegoating "figure" occurs throughout the text's pervasive imagery of gold, like that in Hunt's *The Scapegoat*, and its own relationship to *conversion, transformation*, and *transfiguration*. Mixing alchemical and fairy-tale motifs, the point seems twoedged, the transfiguration double: secular base metal or fool's gold must transform to and through the sacred Philosopher's Stone of golden wisdom; Tellson's institutional love of gold and Newgate's self-serving "transactions in blood-money, another fragment of ancestral wisdom" (91;II:2), must convert to Lucie's individual gold of love and self-sacrifice. And they do in the humble person of Mr. Lorry; but they do not in the proud, golden figures of the lion Stryver and the stone lions personifying the monseigneur.

"The golden thread that [binds] them all together" (240;II;21), versus la guillotine's *decisive* stroke that cuts them all apart, begins and ends with Lucie who bears the golden name and the golden mane—and who is also worshiped as the golden calf when the Carmagnole figures madly "dance about Lucie" (307;II:5).[7] Her golden clue implies not only the stories of Time the Weaver and the Greek Parcae but also, as we will see, the anecdotes of light-haired Guinevere, who is pursued by both sacred and profane love in "The Knight of the Cart," and the Apocalyptic "woman clothed with the sun, and the moon under her feet" (12:1), who, with the help of her scapegoat "man child" (12:5), crushes the Beast in Revelation. The text repeatedly and significantly links scapegoat Carton (and Lucie's son "who bears my name" so that "my name is made illustrious . . . by the light of his" [404;III:15]) with the *Sonnenuntergang* or sad sun, which even in rising seems to be falling and failing: "Sadly, sadly, the sun rose; it rose upon no sadder sight than the man of good abilities and good emotions, incapable of their directed exercise, incapable of his own help and his own happiness, sensible of the blight on him, and resigning himself to let it eat him away" (122:II:5).[8]

At the same time, the text not only links golden Lucy with solar splendor—even at sundown, "Never did the sun go down with a brighter glory on the quiet corner in Soho"—but replacing the literal second sun of *The Scapegoat*, it also links golden Lucy with golden Luna, the figurative "second sun" of sadness on the night before her marriage. After Lucy describes her star-crossed "love for Charles, and Charles's love for me" to her father, this other golden talisman appears: "In the sad moonlight, she clasped him by the neck, and laid her face upon his breast. In the moonlight which is always sad as the light of the sun itself is—as the light called human life is—at its coming and its going" ([*sic*] 216–17;II:17). In obscurely recalling his own dismembered scapegoat past, her father then clarifies Lucie's lunar ascension as scapegoat redeemer: "It is out of the consolation and restoration you have brought to me, that these remembrances arise, and pass between us and the moon on this last night" (219;II:17). Significantly, Manette's healing begins when his "remembrances arise" like the different ascents of sun and moon, thereby healing contagious sameness with *différance*. And yet the physician also heals himself by unearthing the memory of his buried past and admitting that his presently ordered life is a shame and a sham. In this sense, Victor Turner's analysis of self-scapegoating during liminal seclusion seems particularly germane to Manette's paradoxical act of recalling to life—of remembering—his dismembered, imprisoned past: "it is a transformative self-immolation of order as presently constituted, even sometimes a voluntary *sparmagos* or self- dismemberment of order, in the subjunctive depths of liminality" (80).

With this picture of contagious sameness in mind, we can deal more briefly with the other three stereotypes. The second, symptomatic and self-reflecting crimes, again implies an oedipalized text since, besides parricide, they also "always include ritual infanticide, religious profanation, incestuous relationships, and bestiality" (Girard 17). We have already documented the scapegoating infanticide suffered under the wheeling revolutions of monseigneur's carriage and the related religious profanation of the Cross in the worship of la guillotine. This sharp-toothed Dragon of the Apocalypse is aided by the Scarlet Whore Madame Defarge (and her equally sharp knitting needles), figuratively "drunken with the blood of the saints, and with the blood of the martyrs of Jesus" (17:6). Girard also links this motif of bestiality with *monstrous mixtures* (21) as demonstrated, for example, in the *English* "funeral" procession of Roger Cly: "a crowd in those times stopped at nothing, and was a monster much dreaded" (186;II:14), which again previews the text's new scapegoat formula of *like curing like but only with a difference* that replaces the ancient formula of an "I" for an "I."

The overdetermined "Gorgon's Head" chapter (149–59;II:9) further demonstrates that the crimes of truculent masters can be as monstrous as those of turbulent mobs. As the marquis reveals to his nephew Darnay, "Our remote ancestors held the right of life and death over the surrounding vulgar," hanging some victims in the marquis's own bedroom and even stabbing one "for professing some insolent delicacy respecting his daughter—*his* daughter" (153). Scapegoating, the totemic worship of his own "twin-brother" (154) ancestors, and initial rhetorical confusion over the referent of *his* all seem significant here, especially given "his" own insolent violence to Madame Defarge's sister and brother and the fact that Manette believes that the marquis and his own brother were "so exactly alike, that I then first perceived them to be twin brothers" (350;III:10). When the chapter ends with the ritualistic scapegoating of the Marquis for his driver's crimes of infanticide and *driving too fast*, the opening "Gorgon's head" simile bears even richer scapegoat significance. The crime anecdotally and punningly recalls to life Perseus's decapitation of the Gorgon Medusa's head, which *petrified* her spectators by literally *turning them to stone* through the mirror-ruse of likeness:

> [The stone face] lay back on the pillow of Monsieur the Marquis. It was like a fine mask, suddenly startled, made angry and petrified. Driven home into the heart of the stone figure attached to it was a knife. Round its hilt was a frill of paper, on which was scrawled:
> *"Drive him fast to his tomb. This, from* JACQUES." (159)

In a significant sense, this scapegoat is not only tautologically scapegraced with a critical *rite of writing*, but the heartless logic of the personified head is figuratively decapitated and castrated by the myth's lesson, just as the marquis's hard heart equally receives capital punishment.

Related "parricide and incest" operate on both political and psychological levels. Politically, they recall Gaspard, the "hanged man" being "executed as a parricide" because "Monseigneur was the father of his tenants" (200;II:15), the regicide of "the fallen and unfortunate King of France"

(275;III:1), and even (in extratextual history) his "queen's trial" for "having committed incest with her son" (Girard 20). Psychologically, they recall Dr. Manette's confessional revelation to his love-rival Darnay: "mysteries arise out of close love, as well as out of wide division." Explicit in this confession of ambivalent *likeness* is the father's endogamously "close love" for his "daughter Lucie" who remains "such a mystery" (165;II:10) to him that Manette had earlier confused her with her similarly golden-haired mother. Significant in this confession of what even Darnay terms "an affection so unusual" (163:II:10) is the return-to-the-womb phantasy dramatized in Manette's repetition of making "a young lady's walking-shoe" (72;I:6). In fact, the doctor compulsively returns to this fetishistic behavior until Lorry "quite restore[s]" him by ritualistically scapegoating, dismembering, and then burning the offering so that Manette can remember himself:

> In a mysterious and guilty manner, Mr Lorry hacked the shoemaker's bench to pieces, while Miss Pross held the candles as if she were assisting at a murder—for which indeed, in her grimness, she was no unsuitable figure. The burning of the body (previously reduced to pieces convenient for the purpose) was commenced without delay in the kitchen fire.   (235;II:19)

Such a critical passage further suggests a re-membering of related scapegoat transcriptions: writing the story of general hysteria and writing history, if not historical novels. For Derrida (and Plato), the sophistry of writing "historically" in order to record rote memory mimes something technological like the mechanical semaphore of Manette's lifeless tapping-out of dead knowledge: "the substitution of the mnemonic device for live memory, of the prosthesis for the organ; the perversion that consists of replacing a limb by a thing, . . . substituting the passive, mechanical 'by heart' for the active reanimation of knowledge, for its reproduction in the present" (108). For Girard, what makes "the decoding of representations of [scapegoat] persecution" particularly difficult is that this hysterical Oedipal "drama is no more distracting than storms at sea," the same natural metaphor Dickens dramatically traces throughout Book III, "The Track of a Storm." And yet the "memory" or anecdotal rumor of the Mosaic scapegoat story of brothers murdering their father, stealing his wives, and then guiltily worshiping some totem to atone for that sin provides the clue "to man's greatest enigma, the nature and origins of religion" (95). The "only modern author who took these rumors seriously" (88), though, seems to be Freud in *Moses and Monotheism* and *Totem and Taboo*. Still, Dickens's "howling universe of passion and contention" (248;II:21), his historical and hysterical *A Tale of Two Cities*, suggests that he took these rumors quite as seriously.[9]

The third scapegoat stereotype involves the paradox of marking "victims for persecution because they bear the signs of victims" (Girard 21). Such identification marks may appear absolute like Oedipus' limp, but more often they are ambiguous like the overlapping marked foreheads "of the servants of our God" and "the mark of the beast" in Revelation (7:3;19:20). When Blake's Bard of Experience "mark[s] in every face I meet—arks of weakness, marks of woe" (ll.3–4) in "London," he projectively expresses the way the just and unjust, persecutors and scapegoats alike, share stigmata when violence breeds counter-violence. Whether as undecidable, "unintelligible signs" (318;III:13) or an overdetermined, "great diversity of signals" (389;III:14), scapegoat signifiers semiotically stain everybody differently in *A Tale of Two Cities*, from the marquis's characteristic "deepened marks in the nose" (151;II:9) and Dr. Manette's "obliterated marks of an actively intent intelligence in the middle of the forehead" (73;I:6), to Lucie's apocalyptic "forehead strongly marked" (238;II:20) with compassion for Carton.

We can limit discussion, however, to the "red marks" resulting when "a large cask of wine" ominously "tumbled" from "a cart" and "shattered like a walnut-shell," spilling gallons of wine before Defarge's door-post (59–61:I:5). This scene presents a "demonic parody" of Passover and prefiguration of the "great mark of blood" (283;III:1) which appears during the Reign of Terror with its "stain dyeing" everything "all red" (291;III:2) like some sinister Rorschach. The context of these marks itself prefigures scapegoat Carton's ultimate *tumbril* ride as "The Knight of the Cart," his resulting blood-spill, and his spiritual transubstantiation. Such a reading is reinforced by the prophecy of "BLOOD" closing this scene: "The time was to come, when that wine too would be spilled on the street-stones, and when the stain of it would be red upon many there" and by the repeated motif of wine-blood mixtures: "Six tumbrils carry the day's wine to La Guillotine" (399;III:15). The "wine game" played by the thirsty peasants, however, provides more than comic relief before this last judgment. It suggests the fluidity of scapegoat mixtures, but more importantly, it prepares for the actual wine-writing on the wall by presenting a culture much like Babylon's in Daniel 5, which profusely and profanely drank wine from temple vessels.

Repeated diction like *shattered* and *mutilated* suggests that the days of this kingdom are also numbered, and the "irregular stones of the street" which seem "designed" to "lame all living creatures" suggest, again, pandemic wasteland victimization (if not Oedipus' limp). Further, the specific symptomology of *same names* echoed in *Belshazzar* and Daniel's nickname *Belteshazzar* from "Old Scripture" (303;III:4) recall the duplicity and doubling of textual names like the two *Lucies* and *Jerry Crunchers*. And Belshazzar's doubling of his father's crimes, for which Nebuchadnezzar was ingloriously scapegoated—"was made like the beasts" and "driven" into the wilderness—is also repeated in his own scapegoating, which then prefigures the double "father-son" scapegoating of Manette and Darnay in the novel.

But most significantly, the spectral handwriting on the wall in Daniel reappears here in the "tall joker" wearing "a long squalid bag of a night-cap," who "scrawled upon a wall with his finger dipped in muddy wine-lees—BLOOD." Such a scene of writing, often linked with the Platonic "shadow of the prison wall" (371:III:12), occurs frequently in Dickens and becomes a mysterious shadow-play during this wine game: "a gloom gathered on the scene that appeared more natural to it than sunshine." It again recalls Derrida's "graphics of the supplement or of the *pharmakon*" (153), besides his linking writing with play: "The reading or writing supplement must be rigorously prescribed, but by the necessities of a *game*, by the logic of *play*" (64) because "the god of writing," like the dunce-capped Tarot Fool and Recording Angel here, becomes "a sort of *joker*, a floating signifier, a wild card, one who puts play into play" (92). And just as the critical reading of *pharmakeus* Daniel, "master of the magicians," prefigures Revelation, so too Dickens's own spectrally marking "victims for persecution"—"the forehead" of the nursing mother is "stained with the stain"—haunts this text, apocalyptically previewing Manette's writing "mixed with blood" and "secrete[d] . . . in the wall of the chimney" (348;III:10). And so it also challenges our critical reading. In fact, this "story of a haunting Spirit" (343;III:9) continues until Carton's card-game and cart-ride, until the novel's Apocalyptic but always already unfinished finale.

Girard's last stereotype of collective violence and purification recalls to life Carton's related roles as both the medieval "Knight of the Cart" and the biblical Paraclete who follows "the Resurrection and the Life":

> The foundation and structure of every community is based on violence that is and should have remained destructive at its very essence, but by some miracle the community has been able to *ward off* this violence which, for the time being, has become constructive and has achieved a means of reconciliation through some divinely bestowed reprieve.   (94)

In Chrétien de Troyes's *Le chevalier de la charette*, as retold and discussed by Heinrich Zimmer in *The King & the Corpse* (160–79), the Arthurian "community" is held "in exile" by a mysterious knight until a second knight can escort golden Guinevere to the other knight's kingdom and then safely back again to Camelot. The legend centers on the double quests of two knights, Gawain and Lancelot, to achieve this task. The tale is riddled with romance imagery of doubleness, but what concerns us here are the twin trials "of the 'Two Worlds' of Life and Death," that is, "the test[s] of the cart" and of the Castle of Death, which "would seem to represent two stages in some esoteric ritual of initiation." The cart episode tests what suffering or *passion* the knights are willing "to endure in their quest for the queen" since, in order to receive news of her whereabouts, they are required to exchange their noble horses for an ignominious ride in a cart driven by a dwarf. Ananda K. Coomaraswamy's note reads this exchange "metaphysically" as "the exchange of the solar vehicle for the human body" (166) with its attendant humility and shame. Lancelot hesitates only briefly and then braves the scourge of scandal, while Gawain considers "it would be dishonorable to exchange a horse for a cart." Finally, Lancelot faces "his supreme trial" of *crossing* the sword-bridge, "the border land of the kingdom of Death." Although he "prepared himself as best he might," he is still sorely wounded and later even imprisoned in a "lonely tower" before apocalyptically achieving his far better thing, "the epochal restoration of the queen to the world of life." Zimmer concludes by comparing Lancelot's "perilous path" to both Tarot symbology and Christ's Passion when He is "branded and mocked as a criminal before being committed to the gallows and pillory of the Cross." Thus, the supreme lesson of the "test of the cart" becomes that "the fulfillment of perfect love might entail every sort of social disgrace; it was itself the end that rendered noble all the means."

Dickens felt that Tennyson's Arthurian scenario in *Idylls of the King* was "absolutely unapproachable" (Forster 2:352); and it would betray the test of the text to reduce it allegorically to some similar "medieval" model with Manette playing Arthur, Lucy Guinevere, Darnay Gawain, and Carton Lancelot.[10] Still, *Carton*'s "fulfillment of perfect love" through "social disgrace" and all the textual references to the "leading curiosity" of "the horsemen abreast of [the third] cart" over its scapegoat "going to pay the forfeit" (400–01;III:15) certainly recall the mythic "Knight of the Cart," which Carlyle's precursor chapter on "The Tumbrils" (Book 6, ch.3) had already historicized.[11] And the "Two Worlds" suggest not only Dickens's two cities, but again the *crisscrossing* dialectics, or even Joycean "metempsychosis" (287;III:2), between the borders of life and death in both the novel and scapegoat mythology, especially when Carton successfully "pass[es] the barrier and the frontier" (373;III:11) to Paris, his own liminal "place of trial" (344;III:9). Further, Lucy emphasizes and defends Carton's spiritually "deep wounds" (238;II:20) to Darnay, who now views his earlier advocate more as a nuisance, if not a scandal to their household. Ironically, though, Manette's "story of the Tower" (377;III:13), appropriately referenced in the "Fifty-two" chapter, entwines the fate of all Lucie's "lovers" with related Tarot symbology, particularly the twin towers prominently featured in the House of God and The Moon cards (XVI,XVIII). In fact, after Carton's nocturnal wandering in Paris, which also suggests Christ's Passion and the alchemical and Tarot integration of lunar and solar forces, he "crossed the Seine again for the lighter streets," which implies some kind of threshold crossing. Immediately, the towering "cathedral shone bright in the light of the moon," and then "the glorious sun, rising" and spanning in "a bridge of light'' between ''him and the sun,'' vanquishes his night-fears that ''Creation were delivered over to Death's dominion'' (343–44;III:9).

The violent death and rebirth of the Sun/Son recalls both Lancelot and ''the double transfiguration of the scapegoat'' (Girard 51), which develops from the communal accusation of the accursed one to the blessed one's redemption of, and reconciliation with, that same community. Here it becomes the small community of mutual friends redeemed by Carton's willingness, as he early prophesies to Lucie, to ''give his life, to keep a life you love beside you!'' (183:II:13). This development further recalls Girard's focus on ''the notion of scandal or the stumbling block. Derived from *skadzein*, which means to limp, *skandalon* designates the obstacle that both attracts and repels at the same time'' (132). In terms of Carton and Darnay (and Lancelot and Gawain) who ''change places'' (391:III:14), *scandal* again reflects mimetic desire's obsession with twinning, perhaps even in an intrapsychic sense: ''There are always at least two beings who possess each other reciprocally, each is the other's scandal, his model-obstacle. Each is the other's demon'' (172). In fact, each reflects the other side of Lacan's mirror stage—Carton the ideal Imaginary register, Darnay the more ''real'' Symbolic register. Carton represents a kind of scandal in London; Darnay represents a kind of scandal in Paris. Darnay sees Carton as a scandalous intrusion in his family life; Carton silences the scandalous dialogue by giving up his life for his undemonized, friendly foe. As Lorry advises him, ''You know it is a capital crime, to mourn for, or sympathize with, a victim of the Guillotine'' (374:III:12), which advice surely extends to the reader who ''sympathize[s] with'' Carton himself. And although Girard normally eschews psychologizing of any kind in *The Scapegoat*, even he admits that the *scandalous* ''demonic theme'' helps regulate relationships ''between what the French psychoanalysis calls the *symbolic* and the *imaginary*'' (196).

Carton's ultimate decision to sacrifice his physical curse of ''strong drink'' for his spiritual cure of ''a little light thin wine'' (368;III:12) leads to his ultimate role as Second Paraclete who supplants Christ (the First Paraclete) and who Girard argues ''is working in history to reveal what Jesus has already revealed, the mechanism of the scapegoat, the genesis of all mythology, the nonexistence of the gods of violence'' (207). These reflections recall Dickens's own three-year project *The Life of Jesus* (1846–49), a kind of children's tale of Christ, which reflects his belief that ''all my strongest illustrations are derived from the New Testament'' (Ackroyd 504–05).[12] *Paraclete* means *Advocate*, ''whom the Father will send in my name, [and] he shall teach you all things, and bring all things to your remembrance'' (John 14:26), which recalls Carton's own juridical role as advocate for both Darnay and the Gospel. In fact, he bears witness to both as he also bears the different beams of filial and courtly love:

These solemn words, which had been read at his father's grave, arose in his mind as he went down the dark streets, among the heavy shadows, with the moon and the clouds sailing on high above him. "I am the resurrection and the life, saith the Lord: he that believeth in me, though he were dead, yet shall live: and whosoever liveth and believeth in me, shall never die." (342;III:9)[13]

And yet "the inscrutability of Carton" (332;III:8), which reflects the "like or no like" ambiguity of the scapegoat figure itself, finally transcends any paradigmatic role he may seem to play and any past (or present) reading. Perhaps this is because his sacrificial disembodiment reflects "mimetic desire [which] . . . , by definition, [becomes] discarnate. It empties all people, all things, and all texts of their substance" (Girard 166). Consequently, even a reading as relevant as J. M. Rignall's recognition of Carton's "ambiguities" misses the scapegoat connections between his contradictions: "The very step which makes sense of his life is as perverse as it is noble, as much a capitulation to the uncontrollable forces that have governed his life as a sacrifice and a transcendence of them. To seek to escape sacrifice by sacrificing oneself is the expression of a truly desperate desire for an ending" (130–31). Understanding Carton's role as scapegoat also makes his closing redemptive acts of substitution and sacrifice more different and more meaningful than "the suicidal vengeance of the Revolution" (344;III:9), which seems the real differential meaning behind Girard's several analyses of the Gospels.

In this sense, Carton finally substitutes Revelation for Revolution. Whether he pushes his scapegoat role further and also sees himself as substituting for Darnay in Lucie's heart, or dwelling in her heart through his double Darnay, are matters only suggested. But a deconstruction of Dickens's "mythic text," as we heard Doty prefigure, does "lay out the possible alternative futures to which its gestures might lead." Carton's "better thing" may not be the "best" thing or even the Thing itself, but it reveals "the better side of him" (338;III:9). In this scapegoat sense, it does seem better to have loved and lost, though only the *Pharmakeus* Time, that "great magician who majestically works out the appointed order of the Creator" (399;III:15), can anecdotally tell. Still, solar Time, in turn, seems disordered, supplanted, but ultimately transcended by the imitating subcreator or imaginative "second sun" writing the novel. Playing *pharmakeus* and tricky god of writing, Dickens relevantly wrote Wilkie Collins regarding both his novel's foreshadowing character transformations and, conversely, their "backward light." As we have just witnessed, it is this aesthetic process which figures so prominently in the scapegoat drama of *A Tale of Two Cities*:

I think the business of Art is to lay all that ground carefully, but with the care that conceals itself—to shew, by a backward light, what everything has been working to—but only to SUGGEST, until the fulfillment comes. These are the ways of Providence—of which ways, all Art is but a little imitation.
                                                                              (*Letters* 9:128)

NOTES

1. In *Signs for the Times*, Brooks, though, treats the novel (84–95) and the painting (133–36) separately. His religious reading of the novel also mentions the *Sun/Son* pun (93–94) and the Writing on the Wall reference (88) which we pursue in more detail. Coincidentally, the correspondence between Hunt and Dickens concerned scapegoat issues since the painter believed that he was being held up to ridicule in Robert Brough's story "Calmuck" published in *Household Words*, which Hunt feared was a fictional recreation of his relationship with his model, Emma Watkins (*Letters*: 8:543–45, *passim*). For general discussions of *The Scapegoat*, see Landow (101–13), Meisel, Sussman, and Mizruchi (189–92), whose cover reproduces the painting. For a treatment of the scapegoat's role in realist fiction, see Heyns, especially ch. 2 (90–135) which focuses on Dickensian scapegoats like Orlick and Bradley Headstone (and makes some use of Girard) but does not mention *A Tale of Two Cities*. In fact, for Heyns the Dickensian scapegoat is significantly *outside* the main plot: "The scapegoat in Dickens's narratives . . . is always to some extent 'distractingly irrelevant', in not having an unambiguous place in the moral design" (25). Carton's sacrifice may be ambiguous in many senses, but he is an outsider clearly *inside* the novel's "moral design." For relevant accounts of the novel, see Hutter's treatment of "father-son conflict[s]" (448), Manheim's and Gallagher's discussions of doubling, Monod's and Stewart's rhetorical analyses, Baumgarten's and Lloyd's different treatments of writing and language signs, Rignall's focus on violence, and especially Kucich's comparable discussion of "The Purity of Violence."
2. Timko's is the first of six essays devoted to Carlyle's influence on *A Tale of Two Cities* in volume 12 of *Dickens Studies Annual*.
3. Miller relevantly writes that "the comparative . . . suggests an endless process of further refinement, making more spiritual and making keener" (*Topographies* 285).
4. Although he focuses on Darnay, Eigner compares reader sympathy for both Carton and Darnay (especially 149–50).
5. Cayzer relevantly notes that though Stryver has asked Carton to lay aside his wig so that all can compare him with Darnay, the illustration depicts his wig on (141,n.14). In this (non)sense, the *illustration* "The Likeness" proves *unlike* the text, just as the scapegoat "mocks" its model.
6. For a further discussion of this dance of death in Dickens, see Hennelly (especially 233–34).
7. Robson pertinently writes of Lucy, "whose very name suggests 'light'," that her "ability to redeem others depends upon her capacity to love them and sacrifice for them" (313). For a relevant Jungian-mythic analysis of Lucie, see Jacobson.
8. Derrida puns such movements as "these yarns of suns and sons spin[ning] on" (84).
9. Sterrenberg finds that Dickens's mob "yokes together cannibalism, orality, and rebellion" (245).
10. For a reading of Arthurian motifs in *Little Dorrit*, see Hennelly's " 'The Games of the Prison Children' in Dickens's *Little Dorrit*" (especially 197–201).

11. Cates develops another possible pun on the name *Carton*, and one which bears scapegoat implications: "layers of paper which have been treated and pressed" (645–46). I would only add that *Carton's* etymological link to *cart* and *card* also suggest *quatre*, the missing fourth side that completes and supplants all triangular relationships like that between Lucie's three other "lovers."

12. Along with Brooks noted above, Kaplan is one of several critics who have emphasized the role of "the model of Christ" in the novel (415–17). More recently, Meyers analyzes Christian humanism in the text, while Sroka's biblical reading relevantly touches upon "sacrificial 'scape-sheep' whose suffering and/or death bring life to others" (157); and Rosen's more mythic approach mentions "the sacrifice of a man-god whose death and resurrection have delivered the community" (174). For general, booklength discussions of Dickens and religion, see Larson and Walder.

13. For a booklength treatment of Dickens as *Resurrectionist*, see Sanders (especially 166–70).

WORKS CITED

Ackroyd, Peter. *Dickens*. New York: HarperCollins, 1990. Baumgarten, Murray. "Writing the Revolution." *Dickens Studies Annual*. 12 (1983):161–76.

Beer, Gillian. " 'The Death of the Sun: Victorian Solar Physics and Solar Myth." *The Sun is God: Painting, Literature, and Mythology in the Nineteenth- Century*. Ed. J. B. Bullen. Oxford: Clarendon, 1989. 159–80.

Blake, William. "Songs of Innocence and Experience." *English Romantic Writers*. Ed. David Perkins. New York: Harcourt, 1995. 86–99.

Brooks, Chris. *Signs for the Times: Symbolic Realism in the Mid-Victorian World*. London: Allen & Unwin, 1984.

Carlyle, Thomas. *The French Revolution: A History*. Vol. 1. *The Works of Thomas Carlyle in Thirty Volumes*. Vol. 2. London: Chapman and Hall. 1896.

———. *Sartor Resartus*. Ed. Charles Frederick Harrold. New York: Odyssey, 1937.

Cates, Baldridge. "Alternatives to Bourgeoise Individualism in *A Tale of Two Cities*." *Studies in English Literature* 30(1990):633–54.

Cayzer, Elizabeth. "Dickens and His Late Illustrators: A Change of Style: 'Phiz' and *A Tale of Two Cities*." *Dickensian* 86(1990):130–41.

Coomaraswamy, Anada K. "Notes." *The King & the Corpse: Tales of the Soul's Conquest of Evil*. By Heinrich Zimmer. Bollingen Series 11. Ed. Joseph Campbell. Princeton: Princeton UP, 1989.

Derrida, Jacques. "Plato's Pharmacy." *Dissemination*. Trans., intro., and annotat. Barbara Johnson. Chicago: Chicago UP, 1981. 61–171.

Dickens, Charles. *The Letters of Charles Dickens*. 10 vols. to date. Eds. Madeline House, Graham Storey, and Kathleen Tillotson. Oxford: Oxford UP 1965—.

———. *A Tale of Two Cities*. Ed. and intro. George Woodcock. Illust. Hablot K. Browne. Penguin: London, 1988.

Doty, William G. *Mythography: The Study of Myths and Rituals*. N.p.: U Alabama P, 1986.

Eigner, Edwin M. "Charles Darnay and Revolutionary Identity." *Dickens Studies Annual* 12(1983):147–59.

Forster, John. *The Life of Charles Dickens*. 2 vols. London: Chapman & Hall, n.d.

Frye, Northrop. *Anatomy of Criticism: Four Essays*. Princeton: Princeton UP, 1957.

Gallagher, Catherine. "The Duplicity of Doubling in *A Tale of Two Cities*." *Dickens Studies Annual* 12(1983):125–45.

Girard, René. *The Scapegoat*. Trans. Yvonne Freccero. Baltimore: Johns Hopkins UP, 1986.

Hennelly, Mark M., Jr. " 'The Games of of the Prison Children' in Dickens's *Little Dorrit*." *Nineteenth-Century Contexts* 20(1997):187–213.

———. " 'Playing at Leap-Frog with the Tombstones': The *Danse Macabre* Motif in Dickens." *Essays in Literature* 12(1995):227–43.

Heyns, Michiel. *Expulsion and the Nineteenth-Century: The Scapegoat in Realist Fiction*. Oxford: Clarendon, 1994.

The Holy Bible. King James Version. New York: American Bible Society, n.d.

Hutter, Albert D. "Nation and Generation in *A Tale of Two Cities*." *PMLA* 93(1978):448–62.

Jacobson, Wendy S. " 'The World Within Us': Jung and Dr. Manette's Daughter." *Dickensian* 93(1997):95–108.

Kaplan, Fred. *Dickens: A Biography*. New York: William Morrow, 1988.

Kristeva, Julia. *Powers of Horror: An Essay on Abjection*. Trans. Leon S. Roudiez. New York: Columbia UP, 1982.

Kucich, John. "The Purity of Violence: *A Tale of Two Cities*." *Dickens Studies Annual* 8(1980):119–38.

Landow, George P. *William Holman Hunt and Topological Symbolism*. New Haven and London: Yale UP, 1979.

Larson, Janet L. *Dickens and the Broken Scripture*. Athens: U Georgia P, 1985.

Lloyd, Tom. "Language, Love and Identity: *A Tale of Two Cities*." *Dickensian* 88 (1992):154–70.

Manheim, Leonard. "A Tale of Two Characters: A Study in Multiple Projection." *Dickens Studies Annual* 1(1970):225–37.

Meisel, Martin. "Seeing It Feelingly: Victorian Symbolism and Narrative Art." *Huntington Library Quarterly* 49(1986):67–92.

Meyers, Richard M. "Politics of Hatred in *A Tale of Two Cities*." *Poets, Princes, and Private Citizens*. Ed. Joseph M. Knippenberg and Peter Augustine Lawler. Lanham, MD: Rowan & Littlefield, 1996. 63–75.

Miller, J. Hillis. *Ariadne's Thread: Story Lines*. New Haven and London: Yale UP, 1992.

———. *Illustration*. Cambridge: Harvard UP, 1992.

———. *Topographies*. Stanford: Stanford UP, 1995.

Mizruchi, Susan L. *The Science of Sacrifice: American Literature and Modern Social Theory*. Princeton: Princeton UP, 1998.

Monod, Sylvère. "Some Stylistic Devices in *A Tale of Two Cities*." *Dickens the Craftsman: Strategies of Presentation*. Ed. Robert B. Partlow, Jr. Carbondale and Edwardsville: Southern Illinois UP, 1970. 165–86.

Rignall, J. M. "Dickens and the Catastrophic Continuum of History in *A Tale of Two Cities*." *Charles Dickens's* A Tale of Two Cities. Modern Critical Interpretations Series. Ed. and intro. Harold Bloom. New York: Chelsea House, 1987. 121–32.

Robson, Lisa. "The 'Angels' in Dickens's House: Representation of Women in *A Tale of Two Cities*." *Dalhousie Review* 72(1992):311–33.

Rosen, David. "*A Tale of Two Cities*: Theology of Revolution." *Dickens Studies Annual* 27(1998):171–85.

Sanders, Andrew. *Charles Dickens: Resurrectionist*. New York: St. Martin's, 1982.

Sroka, Kenneth M. "A Tale of Two Gospels: Dickens and John." *Dickens Studies Annual* 27(1998):145–69.

Sterrenburg, Lee. "Psychoanalysis and the Iconography of Revolution." *Victorian Studies* 19(1975):241–64.

Stewart, Garrett. *Death Sentences: Styles of Dying in British Fiction*. Cambridge: Harvard UP, 1984. 83–97.

Sussman, Herbert L. "Epilogue: The Scapegoat." *Fact Into Figure: Typology in Carlyle, Ruskin, and the Pre-Raphaelite Brotherhood*. Columbus: Ohio UP, 1979. 137–42.

Timko, Michael. "Splendid Impressions and Picturesque Means: Dickens, Carlyle, and *The French Revolution.*" *Dickens Studies Annual* 12 (1983):177–95.

Turner, Victor. *From Ritual to Theatre: The Human Seriousness of Play.* New York: Performing Arts Journal Publications, 1982.

Walder, Dennis. *Dickens and Religion.* London: Allen & Unwin, 1981.

White, Hayden. *Metahistory: The Historical Imagination in Nineteenth-Century Europe.* Baltimore and London: Johns Hopkins UP, 1973.

Wood, Christopher. *The Pre-Raphaelites.* New York: Crescent, 1981.

Zimmer, Heinrich. *The King & the Corpse: Tales of the Soul's Conquest of Evil.* Bollingen Series XI. Ed. Joseph Campbell. Princeton: Princeton UP, 1971.

Monstrous Displacements: Anxieties of Exchange in *Great Expectations*

Clare Pettitt

Contrary to traditional critical views which characterize it as a return to his earlier, comic style, Great Expectations *represents a development in Dickens's thinking about social issues and an emergent culture of modernity in the 1860s. Using Dickens's interest in contemporary research into disturbances of mind, this essay shows how descriptions of Pip's mental state are used to register anxieties about exchange and displacement, reflecting the larger themes of the novel, and emphasizing Pip's passivity. It is suggested that Dickens represents Pip's education as a modern subject as dependent upon his surrender to an alienated and fragmented sense of selfhood. A detailed examination of the closing chapters of the first volume reveals Dickens's deliberate opposition of oral culture to written culture and a broader discussion follows of the anxieties which Dickens associates with a civilization dependent upon writing and paper exchange. This leads to a brief discussion of J.S. Mill's "On Liberty," which compares the ways in which both Mill and Dickens struggle to balance their support for liberalism and Free Trade with a belief in the sovereignty of the individual. A final discussion of Dickens's appropriation of elements of Mary Shelley's* Frankenstein *shows how Dickens chooses to attribute monstrosity to a culture which privileges consumption over production, and which depends entirely on exchange to create value.*

Dickens Studies Annual, Volume 30, Copyright © 2001 by AMS Press, Inc. All rights reserved.

The publication of *Great Expectations* in weekly parts in *All the Year Round* from December 1860 to August 1861, was met with rejoicing by contemporary critics who saw it as signalling Dickens's return to his earlier comic style after "passing under the cloud of *Little Dorrit* and *Bleak House*."[1] Later critics, too, have seen in *Great Expectations* a move away from the broad social criticism of the preceding novels and a return to a more intimate, personal narrative. In this article, however, I suggest that *Great Expectations* does, in fact, develop the themes of the novels of the 1850s, and that, far from turning his back on social criticism in this novel, Dickens rather begins a remarkable investigation of the mechanisms of market capitalism and the constituents of modernity through the "restlessly aspiring discontented" Pip.[2]

Dickens had separated from his wife in 1858, between writing *Little Dorrit* and *Great Expectations*, and Annie Fields recorded in her diary on 6 May 1860, after dining with him, that "[a] shadow has fallen on that house, making Dickens seem rather the man of labor and of sorrowful thought than the soul of gaiety we find in all he writes."[3] Dickens's own relationship with his role as a "man of labor" was a complicated one. His enjoyment of the fruits of his labor and his pride in his achievements were shadowed by his anxieties about his own class position, and his constant dread of failing to sustain his own levels of productivity. In *Great Expectations*, Dickens may be dramatizing not only the pathological effects of a capitalist restlessness predicated on ideas of expansion and tireless exploitation of resources, but also his uneasiness about his own involvement in the capitalist marketplace.

It is now a commonplace that as labor became more specialized in the nineteenth century, more divisions appeared between people. Joe points this out when he explains his reasons for leaving after visiting Pip in London, he says "one man's a blacksmith, and one's a whitesmith, and one's a goldsmith, and one's a coppersmith. Divisions among such must come"(*GE* 224). But Dickens also shows how divisions manifest themselves within people, as they adjust to a highly competitive environment. The clearest and most famous example of this in the novel is, of course, Wemmick's rigidly divided existence, "the office is one thing, and private life is another"(*GE* 208), he says, but Dickens shows this self-division more pervasively in his portrait of Pip living in terror of his expectations, and alienated from himself. The newly rich Pip feels powerless and vulnerable, describing his relationship to his servant, for example, as "my bondage to that taskmaster"(*GE* 247). Others have already usefully pointed out some of the allusions to Mary Shelley's *Frankenstein* in *Great Expectations*[4]: through his pervasive use of multiple, distorted, and displaced versions of the *Frankenstein* story, Dickens is able to elaborate upon the problematics of identity as a result of capitalist division. The monstrosities which Dickens figures in *Great Expectations* are those of competitive capitalism: the violent division of human sympathy, the promiscuity of exchange, the obscuring of agency, and the transgression of the traditional boundaries of privacy, individual sovereignty, and space.

Pip's actual migration in the text is attended by the bewildering migrations in his dreams, mimicking the transgression of boundaries between people and things which, I suggest, Dickens registers as an inevitable, yet alarming and violent effect of market capitalism.[5] Pip's delirious dreams during the illness he suffers after Magwitch's death form the climactic chorus of an alternative narrative that runs through *Great Expectations*:

> I confounded impossible existences with my own identity;I was a brick in the house-wall, and yet entreating to be released from the giddy place where the builders had set me; . . . I was a steel beam of a vast engine, clashing and whirling over a gulf, and yet I implored in my own person to have the engine stopped, and my part in it hammered off.   (*GE* 458)

The images which appear in this dream I think are significant—bricks, steel beams, engines and hammers: these are the materials of industrialism, and it is within these that the unconscious Pip figures his identity as trapped. His sense of panic and powerlessness in the dream are rendered by the words "entreating" and "implored," and a sense of individuality crushed or blocked is dramatized by Pip's becoming only one brick in a wall, and one part of a "vast engine." In the early 1860s, at the same time that Dickens was writing *Great Expectations*, Karl Marx was using similar images of mutilation and displacement in his now famous protest against industrial capitalism in *Das Kapital*:

> [A]ll means for the development of production transform themselves into means of domination over, and exploitation of, the producers, *they mutilate the labourer into a fragment of a man, degrade him to the level of an appendage of a machine*, destroy every remnant of charm in his work and turn it into a hated toil; . . . they transform his lifetime into working-time, and drag his wife and child beneath the wheels of the Juggernaut of capital. (emphasis mine)
> (482–83)

Dickens and Marx seem here to be confronting the same horror, although it is, perhaps, significant that, while Marx's laborer is the passive and mutilated victim of the industrial process, Dickens complicates Pip's experience in his dream: he is both passive as "a brick in the house wall," and active as "a steel beam of a vast engine." That Pip can be both an active participant and a passive victim at the same time perhaps reflects Dickens's own ambivalent attitude to the self-help culture of the 1860s.

Great Expectations dramatizes Pip's crisis of identity as a direct consequence of his migration from the rural economy of his boyhood to the remorseless capitalist exchange of the city. The coercion of modernity, the

"Juggernaut of capital," is partly figured in the text by the incursions of Pip's involuntary unconscious, and the pain and fear of displacement that Dickens registers there. Yet Dickens does not allow any return for Pip, and it is *only* at the level of the unconscious that Pip's resistance to his experiences in London is possible: it is not Pip's bad faith that produces his dreams, which are less dreams of conscience than the dreamt *consciousness* of the bewildering logic of the "cash nexus" of transferable value. Dreams seem to be important in *Great Expectations* because they represent the beleaguered remnant of private identity in a world which increasingly demands the sacrifice of individuality to public conformity. The very oppositions which Marx claims are threatened by industrial capitalism are those violated in Pip's dreams: what Mark Seltzer has described as "the opposition between the personal and the commercial, between private and public, between persons and material objects"(53).

In view of Pip's vivid dreams, the famous charges made by George Orwell that "Dickens's characters have no mental life"(i, 500), and by G. H. Lewes that Dickens is unable to render the "complexity of the organism,"[6] seem unfounded. In *Great Expectations*, dreams, visions, and anxieties continually invade the narrative and Pip refers often to his "mental life": "my inner self"(*GE* 42), "[m]y state of mind"(43), "[w]ithin myself"(64), and "the innermost life of my life"(236). Peter Brooks, among others, in his well-known psychoanalytic reading of *Great Expectations*, noticed this psychological narrative and has diagnosed the end of the novel as dramatizing, "[t]he return of the repressed—the repressed as knowledge of the self's other story, the true history of its misapprehended desire—[which] forces a total revision of the subject's relation to the orders within which it constitutes meaning."[7] Although Brooks's discussion of the novel is compelling, I am arguing here that the state of hypersubjectivity which Dickens attributes to Pip is actively constituted by the "main plot," the plot which Brooks describes as "centrally, unashamedly, and—at first glance—unsuspiciously concerned with issues of plot and plotting"(114). Pip is coerced by a self-help culture into an active involvement in this capitalist "plot": the mystery plot of his expectations and the "crowd of speculations and anticipations"(285) which attends it, produces the confusion of his identity and his sense of victimization which Dickens dramatizes in the dreams. Furthermore, there is no redemptive recognition or return possible for Pip at the end of the text, enmeshed, as he is by then, in a newly literate and commercial society which excludes the unwritten, the private, and the dreamt.

Dickens was fascinated by dreams and the nature of their relationship to personal identity. In June 1866, Dickens told his friend G. H. Lewes, " 'curious stories of dreams, etc.'—a case of an inconsequential dream seeming to come true in the most minute details, and examples of the strange effect which shock could have on people's behavior and perception of themselves,''[8] and in the Spring of 1870 Dickens had lunch with Lewes and George Eliot and talked of dreams again(Ashton 250). Lewes's professional interest in psychology probably made him an attentive listener. Many of Dickens's friends were psychologists or interested in psychology. Apart from Lewes, he knew John Connolly, William Thackeray, Charles Reade, John Forster, Richard Monckton Milnes, and Brian Procter, among whom were three government lunacy commissioners and one co-proprietor of an asylum,[9] and Dickens was certainly interested in contemporary research into the functions of the mind. In *Great Expectations* he renders psychological phenomena with surprising accuracy, the young Pip is able to "recall . . . what I hardly knew I knew"(*GE* 21), just as G. H. Lewes, in the second volume of his *Physiology of Common Life*, published in 1860, tells us that "we can have a sensation without thinking of that sensation; and in like manner we can think without thinking that we think"(ii, 192). The older Pip in mortal danger, trapped in the lime kiln with the murderous Orlick, is described thus:

> In the excited and exalted state of my brain, I could not think of a place without seeing it, or of persons without seeing them. It is impossible to over-state the vividness of these images, and yet I was so intent all the time, upon him, himself—who would not be intent on the tiger crouching to spring!—that I knew of the slightest action of his fingers.   (*GE* 423–24)

Through Lewes and others, Dickens may have been familiar with the work of Henry Holland, whose investigations into the basis of identity and consciousness seem almost to offer a commentary on Dickens's technique in *Great Expectations*. For example, in his 1840 *Medical Notes and Reflections*, in a chapter entitled, "On Dreaming, Insanity, Intoxication, &c.", Holland writes of:

> that natural function of mind by which we perpetually change our relation to external objects, even when all the senses are open and awake;—at one moment abstracting our consciousness from them altogether;—at another admitting some sensations, while   others are excluded;—these unceasing changes, which in their series make up the chain or circle of life, being sometimes the effect of the will, sometimes wholly beyond its control.   (245)

Dickens's interest in dreams, states of consciousness, identity, and the freedom of will in *Great Expectations* clearly reflects contemporary scientific debate around such subjects. But he uses powerful descriptions of mental states to figure an identity continually under threat of collapse, the "perpetual changes" that Holland describes as natural sense responses to stimuli, becoming, for Pip, a forced defence against the relentless battery of novelty, strangeness, and violence which assails him.

Pip's dream of his transformation into bricks and machinery is the last in the novel, but other dreams are recounted throughout the text. As a child, Pip dreams that he is "drifting down the river . . . to the Hulks"(*GE* 15) to be hanged, and he develops a dread of the file that he steals for Magwitch, "in my sleep I saw the file coming at me out of a door, without seeing who held it, and I screamed myself awake"(79). On the eve of his move to London, Pip dreams again, "[a]ll night there were coaches in my broken sleep, going to wrong places instead of to London, and having in the traces, now dogs, now cats, now pigs, now men—never horses. Fantastic failures of journeys occupied me until the day dawned"(157). In London, Pip "miserably dreamed that my expectations were all cancelled, and that I had to give my hand in marriage to Herbert's Clara, or play Hamlet to Miss Havisham's Ghost, before twenty thousand people, without knowing twenty words of it"(258). And returning to Satis House as a young man, "[a] thousand Miss Havishams haunted me. She was on this side of my pillow, on that, at the head of the bed, at the foot, behind the half-opened door of the dressing room, in the dressing-room, in the room overhead, in the room beneath—everywhere" (304–05). When Magwitch reappears in Pip's life "I had the wildest dreams concerning him, and woke unrefreshed"(343). Like the "bricks and machinery" dream, all these are dramatizations of displacement: the anxiety underlying each one is an anxiety provoked by things being in the wrong places—the file achieves an autonomous identity, Miss Havisham fragments into a multiple image and fills Pip's room, horses are replaced by pigs, and Pip has to take first Herbert's place in marriage, then Mr. Wopsle's in the play. At the "simple" level of plot, in a text which famously divides Pip in two—both the younger "unknowing" and the older "knowing" identity—the dreams allow Dickens to dramatize Pip's unconscious uneasiness which is both expressed and simultaneously repressed in the dreams. But the dreams dramatize more specific uneasinesses, too. Karl Marx writes in a section of *Das Kapital* called "The Fetishism of Commodities," that quantities of value "vary continually, independently of the will, foresight, and action of the producers. To them, their own social action takes the form of the action of objects, which rule the producers instead of being ruled by them"(438). This rebellion of things, which perform their actions independently of the will of the producer, is clearly suggested in Pip's dreamlife over which, although its producer, he has no control. He cannot prevent the file, or the pig, or Herbert's Clara moving autonomously into the wrong place. And furthermore, the displacements and muddling of categories within the dreams also comments on an economy fatally disconnected from the actual scene of production. Pip's bewilderment and loss of self in the dreams echoes his uncertainty about the material source or agency of his wealth and urban identity, which is veiled from him. "In my sleep I saw the file coming at me out of a door, *without seeing who held it"* [my emphasis]: the dreams mimic the attenuation of agency in a capitalist marketplace, the "uncertain[ty]" and veiling of the "agency of production"(Seltzer 51). In Marx's terms it is, in fact, *money* which effects this "veiling" process: "money that . . . actually conceals, instead of disclosing, the social character of private labour, and the social relations between the individual producers"(439). The "social relations" effectively concealed by the veil of money in *Great Expectations*, are, of course, crucial to the novel's uneasy investigation of the power of currency to outrun all social control in a free market economy. Pip's fantasizing of Miss Havisham's agency in the place of Magwitch's reveals the ease with which such veiled and displaced origins can be misattributed. Compeyson, is, of course, a forger and the linguistic games which Dickens plays with Joe's honest *forging*, in the sense of creating use-value, and Compeyson's *forgery*, in the sense of concealing the origin of his writing to fabricate exchange-value, serve to underline the novel's anxious preoccupation with production and agency.

Amanda Anderson has suggested that the only reflective characters in Dickens's narratives are the fallen ones, usually women, whom she describes as "fall[ing] into self-reading."[10] Certainly in *Great Expectations*, Pip's retelling of his life from a vantage point remote from the experiences he relates creates the effect of Pip recovering the innocence of the past in a changed and knowing state. Frequent reminders of this appear in the text: "I knew nothing then"(*GE* 61); "I know what I know of the pain she cost me afterwards"(83); and "Wretched boy!"(239). But Pip's fall is not, as Anderson's argument suggests it should be, a sexual one. It is rather an economic one. It is his inflated expectations which divide him from his community. That Pip is to be "immediately removed from his present sphere of life and from this place"(137), is announced by Jaggers in chapter 18 of the first volume, and this chapter is perhaps worth looking at in some detail.

The chapter starts at the village pub, the Three Jolly Bargemen, where Mr. Wopsle is reading out loud an account of a "highly popular murder"(132) from the newspaper to a group "round the fire"(132). "Of that group I was one"(132) recalls Pip. Sites of reading, in the novel, as has been noticed before,[11] are very carefully described by Dickens, and this scene of communal reading—of the literate in the community using their skills for the benefit of the illiterate—and of the meeting of literate and oral cultures—would have been common practice in the 1820s when the novel is set, and indeed, as David Vincent has shown, continued to be so throughout the century, as "there was no unilinear development in the function of literacy in the industrialising economy"(153). Campaigners for working-class education, particularly the National and British and Foreign Schools Societies, abhorred such practices; indeed, the Chancellor of the Exchequer had said in 1836 that "he would rather that the poor man should have a newspaper in his cottage than that he should be sent to a public house to read it,''[12] yet Dickens relishes the public nature of Wopsle's oral performance to the group "round the fire": "[h]e enjoyed himself thoroughly, and we all enjoyed ourselves" (*GE* 132). Perhaps there are overtones here of Dickens's own reading performances, during which he imagined a similar intimacy with his audience of thousands. He said of his inaugural reading in Birmingham in 1854, that "we were all going on together, in the first page, as easily, to all appearance, as if we had been sitting round the fire."[13] Shared reading and writing can only subsist in an intimate oral space, and it was perhaps the illusion of such a community which gave Dickens such pleasure at his public readings. When Pip writes his first letter to Joe, "[t]here was no indispensable necessity for my communicating with Joe by letter, inasmuch as he sat beside me and we were alone"(46). Pip delivers the letter "with my own hand"(46), and the incident serves to illustrate the low priority of literacy skills in a close-knit oral culture. In fact, Pip's patchy education is typical of the early nineteenth century, as Vincent reminds us; working-class children were sent to school, if at all, only until they were nine or ten, but not apprenticed until they were 14, which shows which skills were considered more important and more difficult to acquire (56). Yet Dickens's nostalgia for a preliterate culture is complicated by Joe's desire to learn to read and write. It is made very clear in this chapter that Joe has been debarred by circumstances from entering a literate culture. His drunken father prevented him from going to school, and his poverty prevented him from ordering an epitaph of his own composition to be carved on his father's tombstone: "poetry costs money"(48), he remarks, significantly, to Pip. Written words and money are, in fact, inextricably linked in a text which figures both as modern systems of exchange predicated upon a space or distance between the producer and the consumer.

The group around the fire in the pub to which Pip belongs is disrupted by the entrance of the "stranger"(133), who cross-questions Mr. Wopsle on what is "distinctly state[ed]"(134) on the "printed paper"(133). He then calls away Pip and Joe from the public house, for a *"private* conference"(135)[my emphasis] which he conducts after "looking over some entries in his pocket-book"(136). Clearly, the status of Mr. Wopsle's "public" text is very different to that of Mr. Jagger's private one. The literate industrialized society to which Jaggers belongs is one in which writing, detached from speaking, can control remotely: "I am instructed to communicate"(137), he tells Pip, and "you are most positively prohibited from making any inquiry on this head, or any allusion or reference . . . in all the communications you may have with me"(137). From this point on, writing and communication for Pip becomes disciplinary: "keep to the record"(138), Jaggers warns him, sharply. Writing is also now tied up with money: Pip is given money in this scene, and he is promised further written instructions, "you shall receive my printed address"(141). Pip's entry into the modern, capitalist world of paper exchange has begun, and it proves most uncomfortable. David Vincent has drawn attention to the way in which "[t]he passage from oral to literate modes of communication relied on and in turn demanded new ways of relating individual and collective forms of identity and behavior"(229). Pip's alienation from the old ways is immediate, he falls into a "confused division of mind"(*GE* 144) and feels it "very sorrowful and strange that this first night of my bright fortunes should be the loneliest I had ever known"(144). In the course of the chapter, Pip has been propelled from the jovial community of the pub, to his "little room": his expulsion from an oral co-operative culture, into a divided and lonely literate urban one, in which he will often be figured reading alone, is prepared in this chapter. Even as Pip distances himself from his childhood, which has been, in fact, a violent and abusive one at the hands of his sister, he begins to rewrite it as idyllic, "furnished with fresh young remembrances"(144). The chapter ends with Joe's pipe smoke curling up around his window, "like a blessing," "pervading the air we shared together." Marx remarked in *Das Kapital* that, "[a] thing can be a use-value, without having [an exchange] value. This is the case whenever its utility to man is not due to labour. Such are air, virgin soil, natural meadows, etc."(425). The air that Pip shares with Joe is perhaps the last pure use-value in the novel, shared, not exchanged. In the next chapter, Pip is already a consumer, prostrating Trabb's boy with "the stupendous power of money"(150), and at the end of the chapter, he leaves the village: "the world lay spread before me"(158). Pip's Miltonic "fall" is into the capitalist and competitive world of London.[14]

David Harvey records that "[i]t was only after 1850,. . . that stock and capital markets (markets for 'fictitious capital') were systematically organized and opened to general participation under legal rules of incorporation and market contract"(262). Humphry House noticed long ago that Dickens's later work reflected this change, "[t]he fortunes of nearly everybody in *Little Dorrit* and *Our Mutual Friend* hang on the big capitalists"(165), he remarked. Dickens shows in these novels, and in *Great Expectations*, in his own words, the "uncertainty of life, some illustration of its vicissitudes and fluctuations,"[15] and how these fluctuations now depended on the decisions of remote capitalists and no longer on individual effort. The new capitalist society which Pip enters thus has the effect of removing personal control, and challenging the integrity of individuals. As Seltzer has suggested, "the double process of systematization and industrialisation, the making of individuals as products of the system, [was] progressively elaborated during the course of the nineteenth century"(131).

Pip's lack of will manifests itself in an "inability to settle to anything"(*GE* 310), and when forced to confront his and Herbert's debts, Pip's fantasy of power is, significantly, an institutional one, "I would sit with his [Herbert's] symmetrical bundle and my own on the table before me among the stationery, and feel like a bank of some sort, rather than a private individual''(276). But, as Marxist critics have pointed out, it is also necessary for competitive capitalism to create and maintain the myth of the individual subject. Terry Eagleton has pointed to the importance of the individual subject, noting the "mysterious inscrutability of such subjects with which capitalism helps to modify its social relations''(52). Dickens uncompromisingly shows, in *Great Expectations*, the ways in which the capitalist society which Pip enters in London transforms him into a modern subject. It is a critical commonplace that Pip invents himself, from the first page of the novel when he "called . . . [himself] Pip, and came to be called Pip''(3). Hillis Miller, among others, has claimed that, "[i]n his relations to other people he must initiate something novel rather than repeating the old''(48). This view has been disputed by Kate Flint, who has argued that Pip is "in many ways extremely passive''(Dickens, *GE*, xii). Through Pip, Dickens shows that active participation in modern society demands a certain passivity, and thus suggests the ways in which capitalist values mass-produce the modern individual identity. The troubled sense of displacement which surfaces in Pip's dream life constitutes a trace of resistance to this manufactured selfhood.

John Reed has argued that the emergence of memoir and autobiography in the Victorian period was a development of Romantic thinking which figured truth as a product of the slowly maturing self (15–25). But *Great Expectations* presents a forceful challenge to such a view, suggesting instead, in a nightmarish vision of environmental determinism, that individuals are constructed and acted upon by "unnatural" environments. Images of torture and aggression run through the narrative, and Dickens makes explicit the damage caused by extrinsic influences. Estella presents an extreme example, "her baby intelligence . . . receiving its first distortions from Miss Havisham's wasting hands" (*GE* 309).[16] But other examples abound, for instance, Dickens makes Pip say of the "degraded and vile sight''(226) of the convicts spitting nut shells about in the coach, "[a]s I really think I should have liked to do myself, if I had been in their place and so despised''(228): the determinism of environment is everywhere figured in *Great Expectations*. Estella talks to Pip, "as if our association were forced upon us and we were mere puppets''(267), and this complicates conventional views of the novel, such as that expressed by John Reed, who claims that, "Dickens's mature novels embody in their narrative methods the drama of the free will opposing necessity''(245). Dickens's mature novels seem rather to explore the coercive social formation of self and to register the psychological pain produced by such violent interventions.

J. S. Mill's essay "On Liberty" had been published just before *Great Expectations*, in 1859. In it, Mill describes precisely the debate which I see as underlying Dickens's novel. In his introductory chapter, Mill says that "[t]he subject of this Essay is not the so-called Liberty of the Will; . . . but Civil, or Social Liberty: the nature and limits of the power which can be legitimately exercised by society over the individual"(69). Mill, a liberal supporter of free trade and democracy, uses this essay to voice his concerns about the increasing social systematization which seemed, in the late 1850s and early 1860s, to be an alarming consequence of industrialization. "Human nature is not a machine to be built after a model, and set to do exactly the work prescribed for it, but a tree, which requires to grow and develop itself on all sides, according to the tendency of the inward forces which make it a living thing" protests Mill (127). At the same time, he applauds "the so-called doctrine of Free Trade, which rests on grounds different from, though equally solid with, the principle of individual liberty asserted in this Essay" (132). Mill and Dickens seem caught in the same nets, here. Both are strong believers in free trade and in the principle of individual liberty, and both are struggling to reconcile the two at a time when human agency, and indeed, identity, seemed dangerously threatened by the emergent commercial culture.

An article in Dickens's *All the Year Round* in March 1860, entitled "France and Free Trade" was enthusiastically supportive of the "delight in enterprise." "[I]t appeared that if trade were good for the merchant, it was even better for the customer; that if it made private fortunes, it also performed a public service; that if it were attractive to individuals, it was also essential to the state."[17] Yet both Dickens and Mill remained troubled by the relationship of the individual to the state. Another article in *All the Year Round*, in 1861, entitled "Convict Capitalists," discussed the problem of forgery, "the fraudulent bankrupt has a use in pointing out the traps and pitfalls of trade; the forging bank-clerk directs the attention of men to the blindness of business professors."[18] The article suggests that the most dangerous of the "traps and pitfalls of trade" is the very anonymity of an exchange system which depends not on gold, but on its representation in writing, so that individuals can assume false "written" identities, effacing their own for criminal purposes. Far from a "natural" system, then, free trade is represented as a threateningly artificial one here. During the same period, Marx was arguing of the mechanisms of free trade, that "Nature has no more to do with it, than it has in fixing the course of the exchange"(442). Maybe it was Dickens's uncompromising exposure of the *unnatural* in modern society in his novels, which made Marx write to Engels that Dickens had "issued to the world more political and social truths than have been uttered by all the professional politicians, publicists and moralists put together"(Ackroyd 757).

Pip is the quasi "son" of a blacksmith, like Daniel Doyce in *Little Dorrit*, the "self-helpful" son of "north-country blacksmith"(Dickens, *LD* 184), and like many of the heroes of Samuel Smiles's *Self-Help*, yet Pip's social progress does not conform to the Smilesian pattern.[19] Pip is, indeed, passive. He produces nothing, he is, purely and entirely, a consumer. George Orwell noticed that Dickens's London was "a city of consumers, of people who are deeply civilized but not primarily useful"(483), and it is as a consumer that Pip's capitalist identity is formed: "I enjoyed the honour of occupying a few prominent pages in the books of a neighbouring upholsterer"(*GE* 218). His mysterious inheritance may confer a "stupendous power"(150) upon him, but it is a circumscribed social power which requires conformity rather than inventiveness, "only it's as well to do as other people do,"(178) as Herbert Pocket explains. His economic power also makes him a potential victim in a competitive and struggling society, as Wemmick points out, "[y]ou may get cheated, robbed, and murdered, in London"(170), and contradicting Pip's naïve idea that such crimes are generally provoked by "bad blood between you and them," Wemmick emphasizes the arbitrary violence of the city, "[t]hey'll do it, if there's anything to be got by it"(170). Pip's entry into subjectivity, then, is as a consumer: an economic subject, whose subjectivity is predicated on his ability to pay.

Joe Gargery is not a subject. As Kate Flint has shown, his role in the novel as "the unquestionable embodiment of moral and social value" depends on his having no "complex inner life"(Dickens, *GE*, xix). Yet I would argue that reading Joe as the unquestionable embodiment of moral and social value, much as we seem to be encouraged to do so by the text, is not, in fact, what Dickens perhaps finally intends us to do. It has already been said that Joe's lack of subjectivity in the text clearly signals Dickens's intention to figure Joe and the forge as representing settled pre-capitalist values—the opposite term to the "guarded and suspicious world"(*GE* 290) of London, where value is in a constant state of flux. By contrast, Joe's value is non-transferrable, as he says himself "I'm wrong in these clothes. I'm wrong out of the forge, the kitchen, or off th' meshes"(225). Joe's static identity in the novel, that of village blacksmith, defines his immoveable "place", both geographical and social. At the end of the novel, Pip notices "[t]here was no change whatever in Joe"(463). Neither do we see Joe ever taking money for his wares: we merely see him "sticking to the old work"(225), and the forge itself becomes symbolic of value unaffected by the fluctuations of the market. Jeff Nunokawa has discussed the effect on Victorian fiction of mid-nineteenth-century anxieties provoked by the speeding up of exchange and commercial imperialism. He suggests that Solomon Gills's shop in *Dombey and Son* was conceived by Dickens as "a sanctuary from the activity of capitalized exchange"(42), although he also argues that Dickens is unable to sustain it as such. Joe's forge is just such another "fantasy of the transcendence of the economic"(42), but the novel does sustain it, precisely because it remains a fantasy, and Pip cannot return, so the novel never asks us to believe in London and the village on the marshes *at the same time*. Jay Clayton, in a recent article, has written helpfully that "*Great Expectations* is a palimpsest of different cultural periods. Raymond Williams has pointed out that no era is ever characterized by a single ideology, and he has proposed dividing cultural beliefs along temporal lines into the 'residual, dominant, and emergent.' "[20] In this reading, the world of Joe's forge is residual, the world of Pip's London is dominant or emergent. Yet the idealization of Joe's forge as both simultaneous with and divided from the urban environment is crucial to a novel which takes the idea of place and displacement as one of its central themes.

David Harvey identifies one of the contradictions produced by capitalism and globalization when he says, "[t]he identity of space was reaffirmed in the midst of the growing abstractions of space"(272). As space was increasingly conquered by new technologies, and the action of capital became more and more attenuated and remote in its effects, a "corrective" value was increasingly attributed to the particularity of space. In *Great Expectations* Dickens dramatizes this contradiction by his contrast of the particular and local space of the village which belongs to Pip, with the alienating and alarming spaces of London. "Ours was the marsh country"(*GE* 3), declares Pip with a confident possessiveness of tone. Pip has intimate knowledge of this country, remembering, even in the dark, that "the beacon by which the sailors steered" was "an ugly thing when you were near it"(7), and always able to find his way across the marshes "I knew them well, and could have found my way on a far darker night"(418). References to "our country"(15 and 75), "our clerk"(24), "our village"(78), and "our own marsh mist"(84) establish Pip's sense of belonging, both to the place and to the community of the village. By contrast, London is represented by images of violence. Smithfield, the first place Pip experiences, and, significantly, a huge market, is a "shameful place, being all asmear with filth and fat and blood and foam"(163), Newgate prison, with its condemned prisoners, "was horrible, and gave me a sickening idea of London"(164), and Barnard's Inn reminds Pip of "a flat burying-ground"(171) where he "nearly beheaded" himself on a window that "came down like the guillotine"(172).

Only a few days after he has left his village, Pip thinks:

> On a moderate computation, it was many months, that Sunday, since I had left Joe and Biddy. The space interposed between myself and them, partook of that expansion, and our marshes were any distance off. That I could have been at our old church in my old church-going clothes, on the very last Sunday that ever was, seemed a combination of impossibilities, geographical and social, solar and lunar.   (183)

Both time and space have expanded between Pip and his old life. Although Dickens seems to be asking us to judge Pip morally wrong for thinking of Joe and Biddy as remote and "so far away"(184), at the same time, the novel

reinforces the enormous distance between "the London streets so crowded
with people and so brilliantly lighted"(184) and "the poor old kitchen at
home"(183–84). So Pip's self-blame in the text for his neglect of home is
mitigated by the novel's structural insistence on the remote relation of the
two. Pip is clearly figured as having crossed a boundary when he leaves the
village for the first time, "with a strong heave and a sob I broke into tears.
It was by the finger-post at the end of the village, and I laid my hand upon
it"(158). Even at the end of the book, when Pip is again banished to the
fallen, capitalist world, Joe and Biddy are represented as so circumscribed
by the village that they are only able to accompany Pip "as far as the finger-
post . . . before [they] say good-by!"(475). The hermetic division between
the two "places" of the novel is structurally essential to Dickens's project
of figuring modernization and its consequence, alienation, and thus the simple
concepts of blame and fault become very difficult to apply to the displaced
Pip. Dickens, in *Great Expectations* and other, later novels, repeatedly questions the possibility of moral agency for individuals in a modern world of
deferral and transferable values.

The remote power of capital is figured most memorably in the novel by
the reappearance of Magwitch, and Pip's discovery that his expectations have
emanated from the other side of the world. As John Carey and others have
noticed, Magwitch's reappearance in the text is accompanied by allusions to
Mary Shelley's *Frankenstein* (101). Yet, the text has already prepared us for
the incursion of Shelley's narrative through previous references to monstrosity. Pip, reflecting on his childhood considers that "I have no particular
reason to suspect myself of having been a monstrosity"(*GE* 67), but "I
considered myself a young monster"(70), Estella calls him a "little coarse
monster"(82), and his details of his trip to Miss Havisham are a "monstrous
invention"(121) while her vanity of sorrow is later described by Pip as "monstrous" (396), and onlookers and officials at Magwitch's sentencing are described as "civic gewgaws and monsters"(453). The first direct reference to
Frankenstein appears when Pip "started a boy in boots"(218), "[f]or, after I
had made the monster (out of the refuse of my washerwoman's family) . . . he
haunted my existence"(218), The "Avenger"(219), or the "avenging phantom"(218) is clearly a recycled version of Mary Shelley's creature. It is Pip's
capital which has created the monster, but the story reverses when Magwitch
reappears. " 'Yes, Pip, dear boy, I've made a gentleman on you! It's me wot
has done it!' "(317).

> "I was making a gentleman. The blood horses of them colonists might fling
> up the dust over me as I was walking; what do I say? I says to myself, 'I'm
> making a better gentleman nor ever *you*'ll be! . . . 'If I ain't a gentleman, nor
> yet ain't got no learning, I'm the owner of such. All on you owns stocks and
> land; which one on you owns a brought-up London gentleman?' " (318–19)

It is Pip who is figured as the created monster here. But Dickens's use of the *Frankenstein* story muddles attributions of monstrosity. Magwitch has been attended throughout the text by images of dogs and savage beasts, "like a wild beast"(321), and Pip's repeated "abhorrence" of him recalls Victor Frankenstein's repulsion from the creature he had made, "[t]he abhorrence in which I held the man, the dread I had of him, the repugnance with which I shrank from him, could not have been exceeded if he had been some terrible beast"(317), "my blood again ran cold . . . I got away from him, without knowing how I did it"(320), and "[t]he imaginary student pursued by the misshapen creature he had impiously made, was not more wretched than I, pursued by the creature who had made me"(337).

Baldick has argued that "[Dickens's] purpose in later works is repeatedly to implicate his readers in the creation of the monstrous, so that the new Dickens monster of *Great Expectations* appears no longer as an alien to be dismissed, but as a presence beneath our skins"(120). I argue that Dickens's muddled attributions of Mary Shelley's story serve to emphasise the distortions produced by capital which, in its unceasing circulation, transfers value backwards and forwards, muddling identities, effacing origins, and implicating everybody. Karl Marx himself figures this monstrosity in *Das Kapital* when he writes:

> By turning his money into commodities that serve as the material elements of a new product, and as factors in the labour process, by incorporating living labour with their dead substance, the capitalist at the same time converts value, i.e. past, materialized and dead labour, into capital and value big with value, a live monster that is fruitful and multiplies.   (468)

The climactic and explicit introduction of the *Frankenstein* narrative at the moment of Magwitch's disclosure is used by Dickens to emphasize Pip's realization that he has been "bought" by Magwitch who views him with "an air of admiring proprietorship"(332).[21] Through Pip's realization, Dickens is able to figure the "fruitful monster" of capitalism that 'makes' and destroys people by remote power. Pip marvels that Magwitch is "so bound up with my fortunes and misfortunes, and yet so unknown to me"(342), but it is precisely this "invisible hand" of capital that Dickens intends to expose. In New South Wales, Magwitch, who is the real Smilesian hero of the novel, is a successful capitalist, " '[i]t all prospered wonderful . . . I'm famous for it' "(318). Through the attenuation of the *Frankenstein* story across space, so that Magwitch the capitalist in Australia can create Pip the gentleman in London, Dickens registers the potential monstrosity of capital without responsibility, Seltzer's "uncertain agency of production," Marx's concealed "social character of private labour," finally become visible, and are abhorrent to Pip. Magwitch has been read as symbolic of the productive working class, "Magwitch differed little from the uncouth monster which respectable society envisaged to itself as the typical 'labouring man,' '' says Jackson, [22] and undoubtedly, as George Orwell also noticed, there is a powerful class antagonism encoded in Dickens's representation of Pip's reaction to him (477). Yet, while Dickens registers some anxiety about the possibility of Smilesian economic transformations resulting in power in the wrong hands, it is the power of Magwitch's money, detached from its source, exchanged and mediated through Jaggers, and precisely not Magwitch's labor, which has directly intervened in Pip's life.[23] Pip is, crucially, bought rather than made.

The return to Satis House and Pip's potential union with Estella of the published ending, allow Pip to travel backwards and to redeem some of the losses of his youth.[24] Dickens's original ending, bleaker and more provisional than the one which he rewrote on Bulwer-Lytton's advice, places Pip in London again, "walking along Picadilly with little Pip"(Dickens, *GE* 481). Pip is clearly still divided from his old life, he and Estella merely "looked sadly enough on one another"(482), and the present exerts no curative power over the past. In both endings, though, Pip lives in exile, working abroad in "the East" for Clarriker and Co., a "partner in the House"(*GE* 476), although "I must not leave it to be supposed that we were ever a great House, or that we made mints of money. We were not in a grand way of business, but we had a good name, and worked for our profits, and did very well"(476). Pip "works for his profits," deliberately eschewing superfluity or excess: having released the monster of capitalism in his text, Dickens now seems anxious to control and circumscribe its power.

Great Expectations is a novel, which, as Kate Flint has put it, "calls into question how one may understand the processes of history themselves, and the extent to which it is possible to play an active part in the shaping of one's own, or society's, future"(ix), and in this, *Great Expectations* resembles the earlier *Little Dorrit*. Dickens, in his later work, is concerned to figure the ways in which subjectivity is constantly distorted by an aggressive and divisive modern culture. Pip's engagement in such a society forces him, paradoxically, into a passive role in *Great Expectations*. The struggle and conflict of the late work is the struggle and conflict of the self-seeking expression in a history which, as Edward Said has said, is "both more inclusive and more dynamic" than ever before (xv). Ultimately, the monster of capitalism engulfs both Magwitch and Pip: both inventor and invented, making the maintenance of a stable individual identity a perilous project in a world of endlessly transferable value.

NOTES

1. "*Great Expectations,*" *Saturday Review* xii, no. 299 (20 July 1861): 69.
2. Charles Dickens, *Great Expectations*, ed. Margaret Cardwell (Oxford: Clarendon P, 1993) 107. All further references to the novel are to this edition and will be given parenthetically in the text.
3. Annie Fields, "Diary entry," 6 May 1860, quoted in George Curry, *Charles Dickens and Annie Fields*, (San Marino: Huntington Library, 1988) 65.
4. Iain Crawford, "Pip and the Monster; The Joys of Bondage," *Studies in English Literature 1500–1900*, 28:4 (Autumn 1988):625–48; and Chris Baldick, *In Frankenstein's Shadow: Myth, Monstrosity and Nineteenth-Century Writing* (Oxford: Clarendon P, 1987), 118–20. For the discussion of Dickens and *Frankenstein*, see chapter 5, "The Galvanic World: Carlyle and the Dickens Monster," 92–120.
5. Clare Slagter, in "Pip's Dreams in *Great Expectations,*" *Dickensian* 83:3 (Autumn 1987):180–183, itemises some of Pip's dreams and points out that they are often narrated at the end of a chapter or number, and suggests that this provides a point of reflection for the reader on the action which has gone before.
6. G.H. Lewes, "Dickens in Relation to Criticism," *Fortnightly Review*, xi, (February 1872): 149. Lewes also complains that in the character of Micawber in *David Copperfield* "one is reminded of the frogs whose brains have been taken out for physiological purposes." 148.
7. Peter Brooks, "Repetition, Repression, and Return: The Plotting of *Great Expectations,*" *Reading for the Plot: Design and Intention in Narrative* (Oxford: Clarendon P, 1984),129. See also Julian Moynihan's classic "The Hero's Guilt: The Case of *Great Expectations,*" *Essays in Criticism* 10 (1966): 60–79.
8. G.H. Lewes, "Journal Entry," (6 June 1866), quoted in Rosemary Ashton, *G.H. Lewes: A Life* (Oxford: Clarendon P, 1991), 234.
9. Information from Helen Small, *Love's Madness: Medicine, the Novel, and Female Insanity 1800–1865* (Oxford: Clarendon P, 1996), 186.
10. Amanda Anderson, " 'The Taint the Very Tale Conveyed': Self-Reading, Suspicion, and Fallenness in Dickens" in *Tainted Souls and Painted Faces: The Rhetoric of Fallenness in Victorian Culture* (Ithaca: Cornell UP, 1993), 66–107, 89. Anderson overstates her argument, however, when she suggests that Dickens displaces all problems of agency onto sexualized female subjects.
11. See Murray Baumgarten, "Calligraphy and Code: Writing in *Great Expectations,*" *Dickens Studies Annual* 11 (1983): 61–72.
12. *Hansard*, 3rd Series, XXXIV (1836), col.625: Select Committee on Newspaper Stamps. Quoted in Vincent 235.
13. Charles Dickens "Letter" to Hon. Mrs. Richard Watson (13 January 1854), *The Letters of Charles Dickens*, eds. Graham Storey; Kathleen Tillotson and Angus Easson (Oxford: Clarendon P, 1993) vii, 244. Quoted in Helen Small, "A Pulse of 124: Charles Dickens and a Pathology of the mid-Victorian Reading Public" in James Raven, Helen Small and Naomi Tadmore, eds. *The Practice and Representation of Reading in England*, (Cambridge: Cambridge UP, 1996), 277.

14. This is not to argue that Pip's rural life on the marshes is an idyllic one. In fact, Pip's childhood is a violent and abused one, becoming idyllic, as Dickens shows clearly, only in Pip's memory once he has left.

15. Charles Dickens, "Speech to the Newsvendors' Benevolent Institution," (20 May 1862) in K.J. Fielding, ed., *The Speeches of Charles Dickens* (Oxford: Clarendon P, 1960), 310.

16. Gail Turley Houston has usefully drawn attention to Pip's admission "[t]ruly it was impossible to dissociate her [Estella's] presence from all those wretched hankerings after money and gentilitythe innermost life of my life" (GE 236) and has pointed out that ". . . in contrast to Dickens's earlier works, in which he represents the heroine as a haven from aggressive economies, in *Great Expectations* both hero and heroine are constructed, that is made economically." Gail Turley Houston, " 'Pip' and 'Property': The (Re)Production of the Self in *Great Expectations*," *Studies in the Novel* 24:1, (1992): 16. I do not have space to discuss Estella's role in Pip's capitalist plot, but there is clearly much to be said on this point.

17. "France and Free Trade," *All the Year Round* (10 March 1860): both quotations 467.

18. "Convict Capitalists," *All the Year Round* no.59 (9 June 1860): 202. This article may have had some influence on Dickens's invention of the Magwitch/Compeyson plot in *Great Expectations*.

19. The recent publication of Smiles's *Self Help* is noticed in *All the Year Round* in 1861. The article, 'Convict Capitalists' starts, "Mr. Smiles's Self-Help is a book that has been extensively sold and adopted as an educational text-book by certain American colleges. Its success has been well deserved. The world can never hear too much in praise of application and perseverance, energy and courage, industry and ingenuity, self-culture and the dignity of work." "Convict Capitalists," 201.

20. Jay Clayton, "Is Pip Postmodern? Or, Dickens at the End of the Twentieth Century" in Janice Carlisle, ed., *Great Expectations* (Boston, New York: Bedford Books of St. Martin's Press, 1996), 623.

21. I do not agree with Iain Crawford that "Dickens's Victorian version of the *Frankenstein* myth denies the original's emphasis upon the sufficiency of the individual will, stresses instead the value of human community and, finally, embraces the supremacy of divine authority." 627.

22. T.A. Jackson, quoted by House, 157. House accepts this part of Jackson's theory as "very plausible."157. See T.A. Jackson, *Charles Dickens: The Progress of a Radical* (London: Lawrence & Wishart, 1937), 188–200.

23. Michael Greenstein has noticed the liminality of challenging characters in Dickens—orphans, bastards, rebels, criminals: "liminal personalities challenge and transform society," but I argue rather that Magwitch's criminality and its association with Pip throughout *Great Expectations* serves rather to symbolise universal implication in a divided and iniquitous society. Michael Greenstein, "Liminality in *Little Dorrit*," *Dickens Quarterly* 7(2) (June 1990): 276.

24. Although Peter Brooks maintains that the 'new' ending does not represent closure as it " 'unbinds' energies that we thought had been thoroughly bound and indeed discharged from the text." Brooks 136.

WORKS CITED

Ackroyd, Peter. *Dickens*. London: Minerva, 1991.

Anderson, Amanda. *Tainted Souls and Painted Faces: The Rhetoric of Fallenness in Victorian Culture*. Ithaca: Cornell UP, 1993.

Ashton, Rosemary. *G.H. Lewes: A Life*. Oxford: Clarendon P, 1991.

Baldick, Chris, *In Frankenstein's Shadow: Myth, Monstrosity and Nineteenth-Century Writing*. Oxford: Clarendon P, 1987.

Brooks, Peter. *Reading for the Plot: Design and Intention in Narrative*. Oxford: Clarendon P, 1984.

Carey, John. *The Violent Effigy: A Study of Dickens's Imagination*. London: Faber and Faber, 1991.

"Convict Capitalists," *All the Year Round*. No.59 (9 June 1860): 201–04.

Crawford, Iain. "Pip and the Monster; The Joys of Bondage." *Studies in English Literature 1500–1900*. 28:4 (Autumn 1988):625–48.

Curry, George. *Charles Dickens and Annie Fields*. San Marino: Huntington Library, 1988.

Dickens, Charles. *Great Expectations*. Ed. Janice Carlisle. Boston, New York: Bedford Books of St. Martin's Press, 1996.

———. *Great Expectations*. Ed. Kate Flint. Oxford: Oxford UP, 1994.

———. *Great Expectations*. Ed. Margaret Cardwell. Oxford: Clarendon P, 1993.

———. *The Letters of Charles Dickens*. Eds. Graham Storey; Kathleen Tillotson and Angus Easson. Oxford: Clarendon P, 1993. VII.

———. *Little Dorrit*. Ed. Harvey Peter Sucksmith. Oxford: Clarendon P, 1979.

———. *The Speeches of Charles Dickens*. Ed. K.J. Fielding. Oxford: Clarendon P, 1960.

Eagleton, Terry. "Power and Knowledge in 'The Lifted Veil.' " *Literature and History* 9(1) (Spring 1983): 52–61.

"France and Free Trade." *All the Year Round* (10 March 1860): 466–72.

"*Great Expectations.*" *Saturday Review* xii, No.299 (20 July 1861): 69–70.

Greenstein, Michael, "Liminality in *Little Dorrit*," *Dickens Quarterly* 7(2) (June 1990): 275–83.

Harvey, David. *The Condition of Post-Modernity: An Enquiry into the Origins of Cultural Change*. Oxford: Basil Blackwell, 1989.

Holland, Henry. *Medical Notes and Reflections*. London: Longman, Orme, Brown, Green and Longman, 1840.

House, Humphry. *The Dickens World*. 1941; Oxford: Oxford UP, 1960.

Jackson, T. A. *Charles Dickens: The Progress of a Radical*. London: Lawrence & Wishart, 1937.

Lewes, G. H. "Dickens in Relation to Criticism." *Fortnightly Review* xi, (February 1872): 141–54.

———. *Physiology of Common Life*. London: Blackwood, 1860.

Marx, Karl. *Karl Marx: Selected Writings*. Ed. David McLellan. Oxford: Oxford UP, 1977.

Mill, J. S. *Utilitarianism, On Liberty, Considerations of Representative Government*. London: Everyman, 1993.

Miller, J. Hillis. *Victorian Subjects*. Hemel Hempstead: Harvester Wheatsheaf, 1990.

Nunokawa, Jeff. *The Afterlife of Property: Domestic Security and the Victorian Novel*. New Jersey: Princeton UP, 1994.

Orwell, George. "Charles Dickens," (1940) in *George Orwell: The Collected Essays, Journalism and Letters*. Eds. Sonia Orwell and Ian Angus. London: Penguin, 1970. i, 454–504.

Raven, James, Helen Small and Naomi Tadmore. Eds. *The Practice and Representation of Reading in England*. Cambridge: Cambridge UP, 1996.

Reed, John R. *Victorian Will*. Athens: Ohio UP, 1989.

Said, Edward. *Culture and Imperialism*. London: Chatto & Windus, 1993.

Seltzer, Mark. *Bodies and Machines*. New York and London: Routledge, 1992.

Small, Helen. *Love's Madness: Medicine, the Novel, and Female Insanity 1800–1865*. Oxford: Clarendon P, 1996.

Turley Houston, Gail. " 'Pip' and 'Property': The (Re)Production of the Self in *Great Expectations*." *Studies in the Novel* 24:1 (1992).

Vincent, David. *Literacy and Popular Culture: England 1750–1914*. Cambridge: Cambridge UP, 1989.

"Servants' Logic" and Analytical Chemistry: George Eliot, Charles Dickens, and Servants

Jonathan Taylor

This essay sets out to investigate the discourse attributed to servants in Eliot's essay "Servants Logic" and to compare this discourse with the meanings encrypted in the butler—the "Analytical Chemist"—in Dickens's Our Mutual Friend. *Eliot accuses servants of failing to comprehend anything which has reference to the world outside their domestic and private contexts. This "servants' logic," however, can be seen as a form of empirical knowledge. Indeed, the servants' questioning of the masters' "universal" propositions, such as that of causality, seems to prefigure twentieth-century physics. Ironically, it is the servants and not the masters who, to use Eliot's own words, can "look to the next century for the triumph of . . . [their] ideas."*

The empirical facts of science act as a kind of poison to the mastery of "geniuses" such as Eliot's Mr. Queasy. Thus, the Analytical Chemist seems to poison his masters both figuratively and literally. The Veneerings' laissez-faire mastery seems to depend on a separation of contexts and discourses between the classes—but upper-servants such as the butler come to deconstruct this opposition. Indeed, the Analytical Chemist seems to portend a revolution in which bourgeois rule will be overthrown in the same way that the middle classes overthrew feudalism. The Analytical Chemist encodes an awareness that his masters will be dislodged philosophically by the same empirical sciences with which they themselves undermined the idea of feudalism. Eliot and G. H.

Dickens Studies Annual, Volume 30, Copyright © 2001 by AMS Press, Inc. All rights reserved.

264 DICKENS STUDIES ANNUAL

*Lewes attempt to use empirical science as a tool of bourgeois mastery;
but, it seems, empirical science has no master.*

> In reasoning with servants, we are likely to be thwarted by
> discovering that our axioms are not there . . . [For them]
> any two or more circumstances which can be mentioned
> will account for a given fact, and . . . nothing is impossible,
> except that they can have been in the wrong.
>   —George Eliot, "Servants' Logic"[1]

I

As a prime example of what she calls "servants' logic," George Eliot complains that servants' "standard measures are of a private kind"—such as "a
good lump" or "a handful" (SL, 392). According to Eliot, servants are
incapable of comprehending any unit of measurement which does not have
reference to something as private as their own bodies. Clearly, Eliot is thus
assuming that her own measurements are public and non-arbitrary—and, of
course, British law supports her in this assumption. The power of the master
over the servant in Victorian society would thus *seem* to be justified by a
hierarchy of discourses, whereby the middle class have recourse to an accepted and universal system of measurement, while the servant class have
reference only to their own, personal measurements. There is, though, no
real difference between "a handful" and the imperial unit of, for instance,
"a foot": both measurements, in fact, depend upon the intensely private
context of the body. In this way, Eliot's essay can be seen as part of a
significant middle-class strategy in the nineteenth century to try and restrict
servants' discourse to the domestic sphere, while portraying "masters' logic"
as a wider "truth" (SL 391).

Eliot's *public* measurements are only perceived as such by her implied,
middle-class readers: these measurements are public only insofar as they are
private to her class. If they are not shared by servants in the essay, Eliot also
unwittingly implies that the servants' own *"standard"* measurements are
private only insofar as they are public to the servant class: if Eliot's humor
is to be shared by her readers, it is evidently necessary that those readers'
servants must also use such measurements as "a good lump" and "a handful." The hierarchy Eliot attempts to establish between public and private
measurements is actually, therefore, merely the opposition between two,
equally private, *class* discourses—between, that is, two equally "context-
bound" discourses, to use Basil Bernstein's term (164).[2] Every opposition
Eliot attempts to set up within her essay conforms to this pattern: every

opposition is constituted not by the difference between public and private assumptions or by the difference between the "carefully-drawn conclusion" and the "bold fallacy" (SL 391), but simply by the conflict between masters' and servants' discourses.

For instance, Eliot declares that:

> The majority of minds are no more to be controlled by strong reasons than plum-pudding is to be grasped by sharp pincers. . . . If our experience of this fact had reference only to the affairs of mankind at large, it would, perhaps, be easier to bear. . . . Unfortunately, our keenest experience of this sort has reference to our own domestic affairs. (SL 391)

Ironically, Eliot's own language is here marked by the domestic: for Eliot, "control" over other minds is analogous to an attempt to grasp "plum-pudding" with "sharp pincers." The analogy unwittingly deconstructs the very opposition it is meant to establish—the opposition between the reasoning master or mistress and the unreasoning servant who cannot think beyond the specificities of the kitchen. The culinary incompetence of Eliot's servants is mirrored by her metaphorical attempt to grasp "plum-pudding . . . by sharp pincers."

Eliot gives two examples of the reasoning master—namely, the "dyspeptic physiologist" and the "genius" (SL 393). Both are male; indeed, the latter uses his wife as a mediator between himself and his cook: Eliot addresses him directly, writing: "You ask your wife with . . . unusual emphasis on 'My dear,' to inquire into the making of the soup. Your wife . . . is rather frightened at the cook" (SL 393). As mediator, the genius's wife, Mrs. Queasy, belongs to neither the drawing-room nor the kitchen. She is neither a reasoning master nor an unreasoning servant. She is excluded from Mr. Queasy's "genius," but, as E. S. Turner observes, the servants can also " 'blind her with [their kind of] science' " (101). Eliot leaves unmentioned in her essay the most obviously problematic confrontation: that between mistress and male servant. If "reason" belongs to the bourgeois male, then the locus of reason within the relationship between mistress and male servant is doubly ambivalent. The issue of gender remains the unspoken text of Eliot's essay.[3]

Though Eliot speaks of the "triumph of . . . ideas" (SL 392), the real subject of the essay is surely the triumph of the master's power within the home. "We may look to the next century for the triumph of our ideas," she declares, "but it is impossible to look there for our dinners. . . . [Here] the immediateness of the success is everything" (SL 392). Eliot *claims* here that intellectual mastery is not her present concern—she is more immediately concerned with her dinner; the fact is, though, that a satisfactory dinner seems to presuppose the triumph of her bourgeois ideas.

This was increasingly true as brute force gradually disappeared from the master-servant relationship during the eighteenth and nineteenth centuries. As Dorothy Marshall writes: ''[During the eighteenth century] physical punishment . . . [of servants] tended to become less frequent . . . [particularly] because a master or mistress with a bad reputation found difficulty in securing good servants'' (24). As Michel Foucault puts it, in the nineteenth century ''punitive practices . . . no longer touched the body.'' According to Foucault, punishment became ''less immediately physical . . . a combination of more subtle . . . sufferings, deprived of their physical display'' (11, 8). Without such display, however, the Victorian master or mistress must seem to possess less and less power. Eliot's Mrs. Queasy only needs to complain too much for Sally to ''give warning.'' Subsequently, the mistress can only retreat ''upstairs'' (SL 394). Sally the cook cannot be forced to make soup without fat, because she will leave her mistress's employment if the means of compulsion become unacceptable. N. N. Feltes cites one woman who, in the same year as Eliot's essay, writes to the *Daily Telegraph* about ''a cook who, at the slightest reproach threatens to leave: 'What is this' [she asks] 'but a species of tyranny that servants, as a class, try at in a variety of ways?' '' (204). Feltes argues that, by the 1860s, ''domestic servants . . . have learned, in E. J. Hobsbawm's phrase, 'the rules of the game' ''; that is, they have ''clearly learned the use, *intra moenia*, of a free labour market''(204).[4] Indeed, as Marshall observes, the nineteenth century made ''things . . . easier'' for servants to find employment: ''there [were] . . . reliable registry offices to be found [and] . . . the use of advertisements for servants became common'' (12). When Mrs. Queasy's cook ''give[s] warning,'' she is actually exchanging the ''private'' discourse of the kitchen for the very public discourse of a ''free labour market.''

Eliot seeks to mystify a master-servant bond based merely on cash payment and free labor forces by an appeal to ''authority and tradition,'' as the ''safe guides of the uninstructed'' (SL 395). ''Tradition'' can refer only to a feudal past, which the Victorian bourgeoisie sought to appropriate to legitimize themselves; in buying mastery with a cash payment, they also sought to buy into a tradition of mastery. ''Authority,'' however, is not only engendered but eroded by a cash payment: without force or even the threat of force, servitude loses its context-bound specificity, and so Sally *can* look ''out of the window'' (SL 394) for alternative employment. For a servant in the 1860s, there is usually a job elsewhere. Simple, physical coercion had once bound the servant to his or her master. Within feudalism, such a confrontational relationship was mediated by the law; as Marshall writes, under Tudor law, ''disobedient servants might be committed to the House of Correction with very little difficulty'' (10). However, as cash payment replaced all other ties under capitalism, it became apparent that a master was *anyone* who has money.

For Eliot, however, the master also has reason, and this acts as a substitute for the legalized brute force of feudal mastery. The exchange between Sally and the dyspeptic physiologist ends with a dismissal of what Eliot calls Sally's *"nonsense"* (SL 393). Eliot tries to uphold a hierarchical division of sense and nonsense. Robbins writes:

> The master's authority [is able] . . . to close off speech, to frame all confronta-
> tion so as to keep his dinner rather than the independent purposes of his kitchen
> staff in sharpest focus. Within such a frame, there can be no "Servants' Logic",
> no ultimate purposefulness that would bestow rational meaning on these actions
> in their own right.   (77)

However, Robbins also goes on to remark upon "just how near Eliot's dialogues come to suggesting the existence of such a logic" (77). Eliot herself
admits that, in a direct confrontation, "carefully-drawn conclusions are quite
powerless by the side of a good bold fallacy" (SL 391). In all of the exemplary
conversations between masters and servants, the masters are defeated by
reasoning servants, whose minds refuse to be "controlled." Even the physiologist's dismissal of his cook's speech as "nonsense" is a form of retreat:
" 'Say no more, I'm in a hurry,' " he says (SL 393).

Despite herself, Eliot constructs dialogues that stage a struggle not so much
between sense and nonsense, but between a middle-class rationalism and a
working-class empiricism; an empiricism in which, as Eliot writes, "conclusions are determined . . . by vague, habitual impressions and by chance associations" and "any two or more circumstances which can be mentioned will
account for a given fact" (SL 392). As Eliot knew well, in *The Critique of
Pure Reason* (1781–87), Immanuel Kant had divided knowledge into two
types: one form "altogether independent of experience, and even of all sense
impressions . . . called *a priori*," and the other "empirical knowledge, which
has its sources *a posteriori*, that is, in experience" (31). Wendell V. Harris
argues that the debate between these two types of knowledge forms "the
basis of the fundamental metaphysical opposition of the nineteenth century."
He continues:

> The essential question that divides . . . [nineteenth-century thinkers] is . . . the
> very old one of whether all understanding of the world as it is and all formations
> of the goals that would make the world what it should be depend on the
> application of logic to careful observations, or on faculties superior to logic
> and observation.   (7)

Harris uses the terms "empiricist" and "transcendentalist" to differentiate
between the two positions. Eliot's rationalism, however, undermines such
categorization by being at once empiricist and transcendentalist. In her essay

"The Future of German Philosophy" (1855), she is evidently in accord with the philosopher Otto Gruppe whose work she is reviewing. Gruppe, she says, "renounces the attempt to climb to heaven by the rainbow bridge of 'the high *priori*' road" nevertheless, she does assert that, "the uphill *a posteriori* path . . . will lead . . . to an eminence whence we may see very bright and blessed things on earth" ("Future" 153). For Eliot, in "Servants' Logic," the path to this "eminence" would seem to entail a certain authoritarianism: servants must be "guided" by "a mild yet firm authority . . . without urging motives or entering into explanations" (SL 395). This is precisely the kind of authoritarianism which Harris identifies as typical of the nineteenth-century transcendentalist, for whom "Seers of special insight are required . . . to lead . . . [while] others . . . follow. Thus, there are times at which dissent ought not to be tolerated" (12). What legitimizes such authoritarianism for Eliot is her "reflection that the life of collective mankind is slowly swayed by the *force* of truth" (SL 391; my italics). Universal truths, in contradistinction to "nonsense" and "twaddle" (SL 391), do exist for the Eliot of "Servants' Logic." Her amusement at the servants' belief that "an effect may exist without a cause" (SL 392) depends upon the law of causality being universal and absolute. For Eliot, such truths possess a force which will eventually sway mankind and bring about "blessed things on earth" ("Future" 153). Eliot elevates reason to an almost divine status—thus transferring absolute authority from God to her thinkers.

This move may originate with Plato's (in)famous demand for "communities [to] have philosophers as kings" (153), but, more immediately, Eliot seems to be continuing the project of the Enlightenment and, in particular, Kant's *Religion Within the Limits of Reason Alone*. Of this, Sylviane Agacinski writes: "For Kant . . . only the law of Reason can impose absolute and universal obligations on *humanity,* and nothing else could be truly sublime. . . . Reason—as the faculty for knowledge of the unconditioned absolute . . . [is] the only true master" (142). Agacinski, however, overstates the case. For Kant, reason only perpetuates itself as an externalized master insofar as it seeks its own effacement: as Agacinski herself implies, Kant believes that through "genuine education" the universal "moral law . . . [becomes] turned inwards" (142, 136)—and thus each becomes his or her own master. Kant's scheme attempts, through education, to overcome an externalised, intersubjective relationship to reason; Eliot, on the other hand, concludes that such a relationship is necessary to the master-servant hierarchy: "wise masters and mistresses," she says, "will not give [their servants] . . . reasons" (SL 395). Nevertheless, it is also clear that, if Kant is wrong in "identifying the true with the universal" (142), to use Agacinski's phrase, then Eliot's withholding of reason from servants *and* Kant's system of education both constitute arbitrary exercises of power by the masters and/or educators of reason.

In "The Future of German Philosophy," Eliot seems to equivocate over the possibility of discovering absolute and universal laws: "The language of all peoples soon attains to the expressions *all, universal, necessary,* but these expressions have their origin purely in the observations of the senses. . . . To isolate such expressions, to operate with them apart from experience, to exalt their relative value into an absolute value . . . is an attempt to poise the universe on one's head" (151). For Eliot, the terms "necessary" and "universal" are *necessary* merely for the values they bestow on human knowledge—a human knowledge which, despite such terms, is still contingent on observation. However, if the principle of causality, for example, were to have its origin "purely in the observations of the senses," it seems peculiar that Eliot should not allow servants, who have based their opinions empirically on "two or more circumstances" (SL 392), to question the principle. Since servants' logic is seen to be derived from "private" contexts and "circumstances," Eliot's dismissal of it is ironic given the wish she expresses elsewhere to derive "the abstract . . . from the concrete" (150). The definition of the "boundary of . . . [human] knowledge" seems to be that which excludes all knowledge of servants—and thus principles which are empirically contingent for masters are absolute and universal laws for their servants. Eliot's inconsistency arises, of course, from her attempt to keep quite separate, in different essays, her empirical philosophy and analysis of domestic affairs. The servants in "Servants' Logic" highlight her inconsistency by exhibiting the empirical attitude she elsewhere declares as her own.

Kant asserts that the judgments which "are necessary, and in the strictest sense universal" originate from "a faculty of knowledge *a priori*"; he writes: "That in the sphere of human knowledge we have judgements which are necessary, and in the strictest sense universal, consequently pure *a priori*, it will be an easy matter to show. . . . If we cast our eyes upon the commonest operations of the understanding, the proposition, 'Every change must have a cause,' will amply serve our purpose" (32). Kant, it seems, stands behind Eliot as she claims authority over the servant who believes that "an effect may exist without a cause" (SL 392). If, as she seems to assume, this law is universal, the servant is simply in the wrong. Nevertheless, given Eliot's disavowal of *a priori* knowledge, her assumption of the universality of causality is at least as "nonsensical" in Kantian terms as the servants' provisional avowal that "an effect *may* exist without a cause." Even Kant acknowledges that, without universal *a priori* laws, "the very notion of a cause would entirely disappear" (32). The servants' questioning of causality is subversive only in Eliot's a posteriori system.

Indeed, what also makes it so politically subversive is that the relationship between cause and effect is hierarchical, and represents a philosophical ideal of the master-servant relationship: ideally, the master should represent the "cause" of the servant's servitude and his or her work.[5] As masters, the physiologist and the genius in Eliot's essay expect that their "orders" should be sufficient cause for their cooks to squeeze the spinach thoroughly and to "send up . . . soup free from fat" (SL 394). Eliot's masters and mistresses, however, do not possess sufficient power over their servants, physically or philosophically, to enforce this rigid form of causality. For Eliot's servants to claim that "an effect may exist without a cause" or that "like causes will constantly produce unlike effects" (SL 392) is, then, to question the very authority of the master over the servant and over what the servant produces.

In this respect, Eliot's servants function as physicists; their strange ideas about causality come from the fact that they "see . . . deeply into the causes of things" (SL 394). According to A. D. Lindsay, Kant relies too heavily on "the finality of Newtonian physics" (xx)—and the same criticism could be levelled at Eliot; on the other hand, the servants' questioning of causality seems to foreshadow major trends of twentieth-century physics—namely, quantum and chaos theories. As Oliver Lodge argues, the "basis of . . . the doctrines of Relativity and Quantum" can be traced back to the work, in the 1860s and 1870s, of Clerk Maxwell; in particular, Lodge singles out "the extraordinary Memoir" (251) published by Maxwell in the very year of Eliot's essay, 1865. Robin Gilmour writes:

> Maxwell argued that the laws of matter at the molecular level could have only a statistical validity, not mechanical certainty. Since neither they nor their encounters can be observed, he said . . . "molecular science teaches us that our experiments can never give us anything more than statistical information, and that no law deduced from them can pretend to absolute precision."[6]   (138)

Lodge argues that such contingency may even foreshadow Werner Heisen-[berg's twentieth century "doctrine of uncertainty," (1925) whereby "all events are made up of immense numbers of . . . minutiae"[7](262). Heisenberg's doctrine can be used, he says:

> to seek . . . physical justification for the admission of an element of contingency amid physical phenomena. . . . It is held that strict determinism vanishes from physical science, or that the law of causation may have gaps in it, when we come to deal with the smallest particles. . . . The discovery of the quantum is supposed to affect the deterministic philosophy in a revolutionary manner.
> (262–63)

Servants such as Eliot's cook Sally come to deconstruct the strict causal sequence upon which Eliot's Newtonian logic relies by their reference to the "immense numbers of . . . minutae" which constitute and modify the relation of causes and effects. When, as Eliot writes, servants "presuppose . . . that like causes will constantly produce unlike effects'' (SL 392), they are justified in retrospect by twentieth-century physics. Sally has reference to other causes of her servitude besides her present mistress and master: she talks of other masters, such as '' 'Mr. Tooley' '' (SL 394), and even threatens the self-mastery of resignation. She suggests the multiplicity of causes and effects modifying any hierarchical relation; though Eliot and Mrs. Queasy would have us believe otherwise, her oblique references to Tooley, resignation, and Mr. Queasy's '' 'constitution' '' (SL 394) are certainly not nonsensical irrelevancies to the state of the soup—they are all minor causes in themselves. Ironically, it is not Eliot but her physicist-servants who, in a sense, "may look to the next century for the triumph of . . . [their] ideas'' (SL 392).

II

Mr. Queasy, who is "a genius" (SL 393), complains about the soup because the dyspepsia—or "the interesting facts in animal chemistry," to use Eliot's phrase—comes between him and his work. The long-established hierarchy is here reversed: as Eliot remarks, rather than being able to "evolve" a "momentous theory," Mr. Queasy is himself the subject of a process of "evolution of fatty acids" (SL 393); rather than science being mastered and shaped by Mr. Queasy and his theory, the "facts" of science are mastering him. Just six years before Eliot's essay, the genius who *did* evolve a momentous theory of evolution, Darwin, had demonstrated that mankind was a product of nature; never again could science believe itself to be the absolute master of nature. In failing to locate absolute mastery in the reasoning bourgeois male, Darwinian nature becomes as poisonous of Mr. Queasy's form of scientific mastery as is Sally's soup. What poisons mastery is the independence of the scientific *facts* of nature—and thus of Sally's soup—from any kind of hierarchical control; empirical scientific facts come to subvert Mr. Queasy's theory and his power.

The independence of soup and other foods from the stringent demands of consumers increasingly became a subject of public concern during the nineteenth century. In 1820, an analytical (rather than animal) chemist called Friedrich Accum had pointed out that food might always be a kind of poison. As Michael Cotsell writes:

> [It was] Accum . . . whose *Treatise on Adulterations of Food and Culinary Poisons* (1820) first drew public attention to the facts of food adulteration. He believed that "In reference to the deterioriation of almost all the necessary views and comforts of existence . . . that *in the midst of life we are in death.*"
>
> (26)

Victorian servants involved in the preparation or the serving of food might, therefore, always be poisoning their masters. In this sense, it does not matter whether Sally is consciously "putting arsenic in food" (SL 393) or not.

Cotsell cites Accum as the primary model for the butler in Charles Dickens's *Our Mutual Friend* (1864–65)—a novel contemporaneous with Eliot's essay. The Analytical Chemist, as the butler is known, presides over the Veneerings' dinner parties and announces that " 'dinner is on the table' " as if to say " 'Come down and be poisoned.' " (51). Through the work of people like Accum, the middle class had become more aware of food adulteration, and more fearful of the control its servants had over that food and wine: the Analytical Chemist embodies those anxieties as does Ally in Eliot's essay.[9] By 1857, Louis Pasteur had demonstrated that the fermentation process is engendered by living micro-organisms. The Analytical Chemist represents, then, an awareness, on the part of his masters, that the very micro-organisms which are fermented into wine might poison—that the distinction between, for instance, wine and poison is, in a sense, non-existent; significantly, the Analytical Chemist "always seem[s] . . . to say, after 'Chablis, sir?'—'You wouldn't if you knew what it's made of' " (*OMF* 52).

The threat of poison is as constant at the Veneerings' as it is at the Queasy's. As Deborah A. Thomas observes, "the . . . people who dine repeatedly with the Veneerings seem resigned to habitual dyspepsia" (8). Twemlow is "susceptible to east wind" (*OMF* 52), and "Lady Tippins lives . . . in a chronic state of inflammation arising from the dinners" (*OMF* 683). Yet, if, as Thomas suggests, "the mercenary feast . . . is . . . provided to enrich, aggrandize, or otherwise promote . . . self-interests" (7), then it seems clear that the more one is able to eat—and thus the more one is able to overcome digestion—the greater one's aggrandizement. Whilst Twemlow is eventually forced to take "two pills" as a " 'precautionary measure in connection with the pleasures of the table' " (*OMF* 684), Lady Tippins seems to assert her pre-eminence over the other guests during the meal by making "a series of experiments on her digestive functions [which are] . . . extremely complicated and daring" (*OMF* 53). It seems that, unlike Eliot's Mr. Queasy, Tippins is not mastered by facts of animal chemistry; rather, she attempts to prove mastery over dyspepsia and such facts in her own scientific "experiments." In contrast, the Lammles' disgrace and disempowerment is consummated by the Veneerings' eating "upon" them (*OMF* 683) in a near-cannibalistic gesture of mastery. This is not, however, merely a competition between guests at the table. It is also a way of validating mastery over the non-guests: namely, the cooks who produce the food and the retainers who serve it up. If the words " 'Come down and be poisoned' " are a challenge to mastery, Lady Tippins is willing to meet such a challenge like a "hardy battle cruiser" (*OMF* 53).

Mastery is here both subverted and perpetuated through an uneasy stand-off. In order to avoid a full-scale confrontation, the servants refuse to take responsibility for the poison in the food: Sally, Eliot's cook, "fires up" (SL 393) with indignation at the merest mention of arsenic, while the Analytic Chemist can safely acknowledge the fact of poison without taking responsibility for the cooking. Likewise, the masters—Queasy and the Veneerings, respectively—avoid confrontation and thus assertion of their power by the very way they seek to *prove* that power: that is, by consuming everything their servants provide them to eat or drink. Dining well is a sign of mastery because of the contrast with those who do *not* dine so well—and, indeed, with those who are starving. The "circumstance that some half-dozen people had lately died in the streets of starvation" (*OMF* 186–87) is separated from the world of the Podsnaps and Veneerings by its utter *other*-ness: giving "a dinner upon . . . whatever befals" (*OMF* 683) is thus a way of overcoming the poor precisely by ignoring them. This kind of laissez-faire mastery is purely self-assertive, depending as it does not on intervention but distance. Podsnap, for instance, seeks to prove his mastery by "putting" such things "behind him" (*OMF* 187): "I do not admit these things. . . . If they do occur (not that I admit it), the fault lies with the sufferers themselves. It is not for *me* . . . to impugn the workings of Providence (*OMF* 188). These "things"—the Victorian "facts [of] . . . starvation" (*OMF* 187)—will not, however, go away.[10]

The spatial division between the ruling class and the lower classes is fundamental to the plan of *Our Mutual Friend,* where the Veneerings are separated from the river by " 'a goodish stretch' " (*OMF* 60) and Lizzie Hexam is " 'removed' " from Eugene Wrayburn by being a " 'working girl' " in the Paper-Mill (*OMF* 761). The eminently Victorian institution of the factory express mastery by segregation—and, during the Victorian age, it is into such institutions that the individualized feudal relationship between master and servant gradually vanishes, becoming a generalized, class (non-) relation.

In a chapter entitled "The Widening Gulf," Turner argues that it was particularly during the early part of the nineteenth century that servants "were relegated to basements"—and "to this submerged plane the self-respecting mistress did not dream of descending" (101). Furthermore, by being "idle" and keeping away from "household chores," the mistress, argues Turner, tries to "deepen the chasm" between herself and her servants; she makes "a virtue of aloofness" (101). Through a peculiarly domestic version of laissez-faire, the bourgeoisie seeks to establish authority by a mode of retreat.[11]

This rule by distance, however, is undermined by the upper servant, with whom the master must come into at least some contact. One such servant is, of course, the butler. When waiting on the Veneerings, the Analytical Chemist represents the collision of one space with another. In this sense, the novel's most dangerous character is not part of the proletariat, but is in a liminal position *between* proletariat and bourgeoisie. The danger lies in the fact that the servant might, by working, throw into relief the idleness of his masters. This, in part, explains why the duties of the Victorian butler were relatively light in front of the guests. The Analytical seems merely to announce dinner, serve the wine and pass on messages. As Turner writes, "the butler [was] . . . as often as not . . . kept for ostentation;" (158) indeed, at the Veneerings', the "four pigeon-breasted retainers in plain clothes" simply "stand in line in the hall" (*OMF* 49). The position of such immobile retainers is paradoxical in the extreme: though they must not appear too much like their hardworking fellow-servants, neither must they appear too much like their idle masters. The retainer is, on the one hand, the *mutual friend* of both masters and servants and, on the other, the friend of neither.

Indeed, throughout the nineteenth century, the distance between the servant and his master only increases; as Robbins writes, "[After] the symbolic *volte-face* of 1848, the bourgeoisie backed away from its identification with the servant figure as it achieved hegemony and began to fear the militant masses beneath it" (81). This fear is at work when Frances Power Cobbe argues, in 1868, for the replacement of "the whole patriarchal idea of service . . . with . . . a contract."[12] What Cobbe is advocating is precisely the kind of non-relationship which exists between the Analytical and his masters. When he speaks, it is to announce dinner to *everyone*—so individual contact is avoided; and personal communication is only necessitated by the written messages (*OMF* 59, 693) he passes on to Mortimer and Eugene. In this respect, the Analytical seems to point up the specifically *written* aspect of Cobbe's contractual account of service. For Dickens, however, writing momentarily brings master and servant together upon receiving his message, Eugene and the Analytical speak "in confidence" and "in responsive confidence" (*OMF* 693). *Pace* Derrida, writing here constitutes a moment of almost intimate closeness—a closeness that is obviously disruptive of class hierarchy. Also, the messages function as literal invitations to a world outside the world of domestic hierarchy: they are invitations to risk that power in an empirical engagement in the world of the poor and starving. Mortimer's story of the "Man from Somewhere" (*OMF* 48) gains empirical specificity when he receives his message and leaves the Veneerings'. The messages, like the wine, are a kind of poison to a generalised laissez-faire mastery.

Otherwise, the Analytical remains invisible on a personal basis to his masters: he can only ever be seen and heard by everyone at once. When he attempts to attract Mortimer's personal attention, Mortimer "remains unconscious" of him "in spite of all the arts of the chemist" (*OMF* 59); "everybody looks at him" (*OMF* 58) except Mortimer. The Analytical fascinates the guests *collectively*—and does so despite *and* because of their wish to ignore him. As Dickens puts it: "everybody looks at him [but] . . . not because anybody wants to see him" (*OMF* 58). He is so fascinating because he appears so meaningless: he possesses what Timothy Clark calls "the fascination of a world without interiority" (23). No one, not even Dickens, has access to his interior meanings: he only "*seem*[s] to say . . . 'You wouldn't if you knew what it's made of' " (*OMF* 52; my italics); and he is only "*like* a gloomy Analytical Chemist" (*OMF* 52; my italics). Like one of Maurice Blanchot's corpses, he is "altogether similarity and also nothing more" (258).

Like so many others, George Eliot criticizes Dickens for merely "rendering the external traits" of his characters ("Natural History" 271). This is never more true than with the Analytical Chemist. Surely the point, though, is that the servant—and particularly the visible, upper-servant—is *denied* any internal traits by such employers as the Veneerings. His meaninglessness is imposed upon him because of the Veneerings' avoidance of any kind of individualized master-servant relationship: to his employers, he is less than human. Indeed, because of this lack of any kind of humanizing recognition, he becomes not just an "Analytical Chemist" but an "Analytical Machine" or "Analytical Engine"—the name Charles Babbage gave, in 1834, to a projected "general purpose programmable computing machine" (Sussman 4). The machine could be programmed with punched cards—like the Analytical Chemist, it is constituted for its masters by their orders; both Analytical Chemist and Analytical Engine are thus denied self-consciousness and self-motivation by their masters. However, it is this very absence of interiority that so fascinates the masters—and so the servant / machine also comes to be constituted by their masters' anxieties. The Analytical Chemist's meaning seems to his masters to be necessarily "diabolical" (*OMF* 305): it is inevitable that he "object[s] as a matter of principle to everything that occurs on the [Veneerings'] premises" (*OMF* 159).[13] Since the masters' power depends upon denying consciousness to the servant / machine, it is evident that any sign of consciousness or independence will be deeply troubling; but even if there are no such signs, the masters will neurotically detect them anyway.

It is hardly surprising that the Analytical Chemist might be analogous to the Analytical Engine in the sense that, in the nineteenth century, servants were fast becoming indistinguishable from "the workman" who is, as Marx observed, "an appendage of the machine" (87). For the bourgeoisie, servants could, ideally, be just machines: after all, domestic appliances such as the "dumb-waiter" were at their most popular during the 1860s. The process of becoming increasingly machinic is part of the process by which the servant becomes increasingly "other"—and this *other*-ing of servants is marked, in turn, by their decline in status during the nineteenth century. As Turner puts it, "In the nineteenth century the servant's status steadily slumped. Lord Chesterfield had viewed menial servants as his 'equals in Nature . . . inferiors only by the difference of our positions'; but the employers of the nineteenth century would have none of this'' (100). Servants, it seems, are gradually subsumed into a proletariat to which they themselves do not feel they belong. The erosion of the distinction between paid labor and domestic servitude is reflected by an increasing slippage between the two terms on the part of the ruling class: as Feltes points out, ''the [parliamentary] Act of 1867 was . . . the last to be entitled a 'master and servant act,' '' after which ''employer'' and ''employee'' (202) became the usual terms.

The Analytical Chemist certainly does not seem to consider himself a proletarian. On the contrary, he is willing to defend his higher status in an assertive manner, in complete contrast with his employers' laissez-faire. This is apparent in the duel he has with the truly proletarian ''Coachman'' who enters with a message during one of the dinners:

> The Analytical is beheld in collision with the Coachman; the Coachman manifesting a purpose of coming at the company with a silver salver . . . the Analytical cutting him off at the sideboard. The superior stateliness . . . of the Analytical prevails over [the Coachman, who] . . . retires defeated. (*OMF* 693)

The Analytical here occupies a peculiar role whereby he is sole poisoner *and* sole defender of his masters against a potentially insurgent proletariat.

In fact, the Analytical has more claim to a feudal tradition and aristocratic pre-history than do his masters. Marshall points out that, during feudal times, ''the great [domestic] officials such as the steward, the comptroller, and the clerk of the kitchen [were] in many cases . . . drawn from the nearer kinsman'' of aristocratic householders; and she goes on to connect the duties of such officials with those of the ''modern butler'' (5). In the case of the Analytical, these aristocratic traces take the form of the ''Analytical solemnities'' (*OMF* 258) that the ''bran-new'' (*OMF* 48) Veneerings so desire. On coming into power, the bourgeoisie seeks to naturalize itself by assuming the trappings of the feudal aristocracy it has deposed. All the ''new'' things the Veneerings have bought, such as ''their carriage,'' their ''coat-of-arms'' (*OMF* 48) and the Analytical Chemist himself, are signifiers of an aristocratic lineage. As G. K. Chesterton remarks of the Analytical: ''The truth about servants . . . is simply this: that the secret of aristocracy is hidden even from aristocrats. Servants, butlers, footmen, are the high priests who have the real dispensation'' (213).

The Analytical does indeed function like a ''priest'': when he ''concedes'' the ''chalice'' (*OMF* 56, 53) to those at the table, he seems to be officiating at a kind of secular Eucharist. In so doing, he ''concedes'' or ''proffer[s]'' not only the chalice but also power. After all, Christ and his priests are servants: during the Last Supper, Christ washes the feet of his disciples.

What the Analytical dispenses, though, is an *illusory* power: the wine is only Champagne and Chablis and nothing more. The cup-bearer himself does not believe in the transcendental nature of the wine: he is quite aware what the Chablis is "made of" (*OMF* 52). Since, as Thomas Thomson writes, chemical "analysis [is] the art of determining the constituents of which every compound is composed" (190), it is clear that, by definition, analysis is deconstructive. Chablis and Champagne are used at the Veneering dinners as the indicators of social status they have been for centuries; yet the Analytical Chemist is subversively aware that Chablis is merely a compound of other substances.

It is this subversive knowledge of what the Chablis is "made of" which makes the butler seem "like a gloomy Analytical Chemist" (*OMF* 52). Historically speaking, it was quite conceivable that such knowledge would be within the Victorian butler's reach. "From time to time," writes Turner, "the butler withdrew to the cellars in order to perform rites of rectification and purification"; some butlers, indeed, were even called upon to "brew beer" themselves.[14] Nevertheless, it is ironic that this vestigial aristocrat and priest should be associated with the very modern science of analytical chemistry in whatever form. The Analytical haunts the Veneering dinners as a Banquo-like ghost—as a ghost, that is, of extinct aristocratic and priestly hierarchies. He is thus witness to the precariousness of any class of masters, while also serving as a reminder to his new masters how they deposed the previous hierarchies, philosophically and scientifically speaking. Since the bourgeoisie abandons its "revolutionary self-image" at the moment of its "arriving in power," as Robbins argues (81), it becomes afraid of the revolutionary progress of history it has in part unleashed. Therefore, when the Analytical Chemist first seems to say, " 'Come down and be poisoned, ye unhappy children of men' " (*OMF* 51), it is as if he is announcing the Last Judgement to his bourgeois masters. If, as Cotsell writes, " 'children of men' " is the biblical phrase for all those destroyed by the Deluge (26), the Analytical seems to be announcing a second Deluge—a second revolution. Either Mme. de Pompadour or Mme. du Barry is said to have prophesied the French Revolution of 1789 with the words "Après nous, le Deluge" and the Analytical Chemist seems to echo these words.

George Eliot, on the other hand, seems unable to decipher such cryptic warnings in her servants. Her declaration that "we may look to the next century for the triumph of our ideas" is, for all its flippancy, part of bourgeois philosophical agenda which attempted to appropriate a potentially-revolutionary future in the name of the bourgeoisie: part of this attempt was made through science. Ironically, the new masters of the nineteenth century often saw science as *their* weapon. As Gilmour observes, the Victorians' faith in science was largely based upon the "hero-worship" of certain scientists;

"the ambition . . . behind . . . the writings of Huxley and Tyndall," Gilmour asserts, "was to challenge the *de facto* priesthood for cultural leadership (134–35). The bourgeoisie attempted to construct what Galton called a "scientific priesthood" (135)—a priesthood of which Dickens's Analytical Chemist is a member. This secular priesthood was to replace its Christian predecessor; as Beatrice Webb writes, at this time "the men of science were routing the theologians [and] confounding the mystics" (130).

However, the Victorian bourgeoisie's perception of sciences like chemistry was inherently contradictory, for while it seemed ready to accept the empiricism of science, it was unwilling to lose sight of its transcendental purpose. Even if science was no longer engaged on "the never-ending search for the philosopher's stone and the elixir of life" (20), as Charles-Albert Reichen puts it, scientists were themselves *believed in* as never before. By the mid-nineteenth century, science was believed to have the potential, as Gilmour writes, "to solve the problems of life" (134)—a more generalized, though equally transcendental purpose as that of searching for the philosopher's stone. The kind of Positivist stance which Eliot displays in "The Future of German Philosophy" masks transcendentalism with an apparent acceptance of the empirical methods of science. It is Positivism which lies behind Eliot's assertion that "the uphill *a posteriori* path . . . will lead . . . to an eminence whence we may see very bright and blessed things on earth." Eliot attempts to combine the a posteriori or empirical methods of science with a Positivist and, ultimately, bourgeois notion of progress.

Despite this attempt, however, the alliance between science and the new bourgeois masters was always threatened by that empiricism. Demanding the kind of Positivist "Philosophy of Science" first proposed by Auguste Comte, Eliot's partner, G. H. Lewes declares in his *Biographical History of Philosophy* (1857) that,

> The *speciality* of most scientific men, and their incapacity of either producing or accepting general ideas, has long been a matter of complaint. . . . Moreover, the evil of speciality . . . [also] affects the very highest condition of Science, namely, its capability of instructing and directing society.   (654)

Lewes complains that scientists challenge the very possibility of general or universal ideas: they fail to sanction the universalizing doctrine of the bourgeoisie and thus refuse to help it to instruct and direct society. Lewes fails to acknowledge Kant's warning that, once empiricism is accepted as the only form of knowledge, "universality . . . [becomes] only an arbitrary extension of validity."[15] The increasing speciality of scientists is part of empiricism's move away from such universalism. Though the establishment of the Chemical Society in 1841 and the Royal College of Chemistry in 1845 would seem to suggest the increasing social authority of Victorian science, these institutions actually fostered what Lewes sees as the anti-social evil of speciality. Moreover, science's capability of practically instructing society was further undermined as it moved away from what Gilmour calls "that monument to applied science" (113)—the Great Exhibition of 1851. The Analytical Chemist represents cryptically the kind of *pure* and *specialized* science Lewes and the bourgeoisie were coming to fear.

Of all the sciences, analytical chemistry is the most subversive of Lewes's philosophy of "general ideas"—and of any Positivist philosophy which exhorts science towards transcendental ends. Specialization is inherent within it: analysis, by its very nature, is simply the process of separating out smaller elements—not the discovery of a general idea or *elemental* truth. Indeed, the development of empiricism in chemistry depended upon the very deconstitution of general ideas; as Reichen writes: "The alchemist . . . of the Middle Ages . . . thought in terms of the accepted philosophical notions of the era. . . . Slowly [however] the practice of chemistry began to move away from the search for the philosopher's stone to more practical and reasonable goals" (26). In the end, that is why the new bourgeois order is so nervous of a science for which it is in part responsible. Lewes and others try to re-impose a moral and philosophical discourse onto chemistry. The pure empiricism of modern analytical chemistry is poison to any form of transcendentalism; and any class seeking to establish hegemony must move away from analytical chemistry. For Lewes and Eliot, this retreat is disguised by their apparent acceptance of empiricism. Marx compares modern bourgeois society to a "sorcerer who is no longer able to control the powers of the nether world whom he has called up by his spells" (85–86). He refers, of course, to the powers of the proletariat, but he might just as well be speaking of that modern-day sorcerer, the Analytical Chemist.

NOTES

With thanks to Dr. John Schad for his help with this article.

1. "Servants' Logic," in *Essays of George Eliot,* ed. Thomas Pinney (London: Routledge and Kegan Paul, 1963) 392. All further references to this essay appear parenthetically in the text, prefixed with the abbreviation "SL."

2. Bruce Robbins points out the similarity between the discourse that Eliot attributes to domestic servants and the "context-bound" language Basil Bernstein attributes to the working class in general: see *The Servant's Hand: English Fiction from Below* (Durham: Duke UP, 1993) 89, Bernstein writes:

Forms of socialization orient the child towards speech codes which control access to relatively context-tied or relatively context-independent meanings.

Thus . . . elaborated codes orient their users towards universalistic meanings, whereas restricted codes orient, sensitize, their users to particularistic meanings. . . . One of the effects of the class system is to limit access to elaborated codes.

Bernstein's distinction between "universalistic" and "particularistic" meanings seems, though, merely to recycle Eliot's patronizing account of her servants' logic. Despite his efforts "to avoid implicit value judgments about the relative worth of speech systems," Bernstein admits that "in complex industrialized societies [a restricted code's] . . . differently focused experience may be disvalued, and humiliated" (Bernstein 176). Bernstein states what Eliot implies—namely that the discourse of the ruling middle class is "universalistic": its assumptions and conclusions are presumed to be universally true.

3. It is also the unspoken text of Bernstein's paper.

4. He is quoting from E. J. Hobsbawm, "Custom, Wages, and Work-Load in Nineteenth Century Industry," *Labouring Men* (1968) 345.

5. Georg Wilhelm Friedrich Hegel implies this direct form of causality in his "Master-Slave Dialectic" (1807). For Hegel, the master unequivocally causes the other's slavery by overpowering that other during a "life-and-death struggle"—causation is here constituted by brute force. *See Phenomenology of Spirit,* trans. A. V. Miller (Oxford: Oxford UP, 1977) 114. Eliot would have been aware of Hegel's work through her partner, G. H. Lewes.

6. Gimour is quoting Clerk Maxwell, "Molecules," *Nature,* VIII (1873) 440.

7. Heisenberg argued that it was impossible to measure the speed of an electron as it orbited the atom at the same time as its position, and vice versa.

8. All further references to this novel appear parenthetically in the text, prefixed with the abbreviation "*OMF.*"

9. In order to impress on his cook the importance of thoroughly squeezing spinach, Eliot's dyspeptic physiologist tries to find an analogy for the harmful effect of leaving water in the greens; he says: " 'I tell you, there must be no water. Suppose it was arsenic.' " In response, "Sally departs, muttering, and spends that morning . . . under a sense of injury from false imputations" (SL 393). In other words, it is the bourgeois master's own neurotic anxieties which first conjure up the possibility of poison—and only subsequently does the servant herself come to be dangerously fixated on the subject of arsenic.

10. In *Chartism* (1839), Thomas Carlyle writes that it is "vain . . . to think that the misery of one class . . . can be isolated." See *Critical and Miscellaneous Essays IV,* The Works of Thomas Carlyle, XXIX (London: Chapman and Hall, 1899) 168. Carlyle too is concerned with the "*facts*" which Podsnap's kind of mastery attempts to ignore. As he warns the Victorian masters of laissez-faire: "The haggard naked fact speaks to us: . . . Are these millions guided? . . . Fact searches for his third-rate potato, not in the meekest humour . . . and does not find it" (Carlyle 1556–56). The "naked fact," it seems, still speaks despite the ruling classes seeking spaces in which, like Podsnap, they can make laborers and "misery . . . go out of sight," as Carlyle puts it. Significantly, Carlyle adds that, "a . . . briefer method" of achieving this disappearance "is that of arsenic";

poisoning in this class relation is mutual, it seems. See Carlyle 129–30. Dickens, of course, was very heavily influenced by Carlyle's writings.

11. This is, in a sense, analogous to the point Foucault makes in *Discipline and Punish*. Foucault argues that the techniques of discipline inherent within Jeremy Bentham's Panopticon are primarily isolation and surveillance—and such techniques are clearly used within the domestic space as well. As with laissez-faire mastery, the Panopticon's "strength is that it never intervenes." He writes: "The Panopticon assures the automatic functioning of power . . . [and] sustain[s] . . . a power relation independent of the person who exercises it. . . . The inmates [are] . . . caught up in a power situation of which they are themselves the bearers" (Foucault 201, 206). The connection with laissez-faire is confirmed by the fact that those in power do not even need to be *in* the Panopticon—so constant surveillance is no more necessary than intervention. As Foucault writes, "the inmate must never know whether he is [actually] being looked at . . . but he must be sure that he *may* always be so" (Foucault 201; my italics).

12. See "Household Service," *Fraser's* 77 (Jan. 1868) 124. This article is quoted in Feltes, 205.

13. Likewise, in *The Difference Engine* (New York: Bantam, 1991) by William Gibson and Bruce Sterling—a recent fictional account of Babbage's Engines—Babbage's co-inventor, Ada Byron [*sic*], makes explicit this fascination with that which lacks or borders on consciousness:

> An Engine [could be said to] *live* . . . and could indeed *prove* its own life, should it develop the capacity to look upon itself. The Lens for such a self-examination is of a nature not yet known to us; yet we know that it exists, for we ourselves possess it. (Gibson and Sterling 422)

Herbert Sussman points that these words "echo the actual words of [the historical] Ada Byron Lovelace in her published *Notes* on the Babbage Engine" (Sussman 17). In 1843, she wrote that,

> In enabling mechanism to combine together *general* symbols, in succession of unlimited variety and extent, a uniting link is established between the operations of matter and the abstract mental processes. . . . Thus not only the mental and material, but the theoretical and the practical in the mathematical world, are brought into more intimate and effective connection with each other. We are not aware . . . that anything partaking of the nature of what is so well designated the *Analytical* Engine has been hitherto proposed . . . as a practical possibility, any more than the idea of a thinking or of a reasoning machine. (Quoted in Sussman 17)

14. Turner 163–64. However, Turner goes on to note: "As the nineteenth century progressed, butlers were called on less often to show their expertise in the cellar. . . . Perhaps the middle-class palate was becoming more fastidious. . . . Many gentlemen declined to give their butlers unrestricted access to the cellar." Turner claims that this was "not *so much* because they were afraid of unskilled doctoring of their wines but because they thought the stocks would last longer if the butler

was deprived of the key" (my italics)—but it is clear even from this statement that the threat of such doctoring played a part in the increasing restrictions on the butler's role.

15. Kant 31. Though, for Lewes, "positive Science . . . [is] advancing on a straight road, every step . . . being that of inalienable truth" (Lewes 664), Kant's warning, as has been seen, is borne out in the twentieth century by Heisenberg's doctrine of uncertainty.

WORKS CITED

Agacinski, Sylvanie. "We Are Not Sublime: Love and Sacrifice, Abraham and Ourselves." In *Kierkegaard: A Critical Reader.* Ed. Jonathan Ree and Jane Chamberlain. Oxford: Blackwell, 1997.

Bernstein, Basil. "Social Class, Language, and Socialization." In *Language and Social Context.* Ed. Pier Paolo Giglioli. Harmondsworth: Penguin, 1972.

Blanchot, Maurice. *The Space of Literature.* Trans. A. Smock. Lincoln and London: U. of Nebraska P, 1982.

Carlyle, Thomas. *Chartism.* In *Critical and Miscellaneous Essays IV*, The Works of Thomas Carlyle, XXIX. London: Chapman and Hall, 1899.

Chesterton, G. K. *Criticisms and Appreciations of the Works of Charles Dickens.* London: J. M. Dent and Sons, 1992.

Clark, Timothy. "Dickens Through Blanchot: The Nightmare Fascination of a World Without Interiority." In *Dickens Refigured: Bodies, Desires and Other Histories.* Manchester: Manchester UP, 1996.

Cotsell, Michael. *The Companion to "Our Mutual Friend."* The Dickens Companions 2. London: Allen and Unwin, 1986.

Dickens, Charles. *Our Mutual Friend.* Ed. Stephen Gill. Harmondsworth: Penguin, 1985.

Eliot, George. "The Future of German Philosophy," "The Natural History of German Life," "Servants' Logic." In *Essays of George Eliot.* Ed. Thomas Pinney. London: Routledge and Kegal Paul, 1963.

Feltes, N. N. " 'The Greatest Plague of Life': Dickens, Masters and Servants." *Literature and History* 8 (1978): 197–213.

Foucault, Michel. *Discipline and Punish: The Birth of the Prison.* Trans. Alan Sheridan. Harmondsworth: Penguin, 1991.

Gibson, William and Bruce Sterling. *The Difference Engine,* New York: Bantam, 1991.

Gilmour, Robin. *The Victorian Period: The Intellectual and Cultural Context of English Literature, 1830–1890.* London: Longman, 1993.

Harris, Wendell V. *The Omnipresent Debate: Empiricism and Transcendentalism in Nineteenth-Century English prose.* DeKalb: Northern Illinois UP 1981.

Hegel, Georg Wilhelm Friedrich. *Phenomenology of Spirit.* Trans. A. V. Miller. Oxford: Oxford UP, 1977.

Kant, Immanuel. *Critique of Pure Reason.* Trans. J. M. D. Meiklejohn. Ed. Vasilis Politis. London: J. M. Dent, 1993.

Lewes, George Henry. *The Biographical History of Philosophy: From Its Origin in Greece Down to the Present Day.* London: Parker, 1857.

Lindsay, A. D. "Introduction to Kant's *Critique of Pure Reason.*" In *Critique of Pure Reason.* Trans. J. M. D. Meiklejohn. London: J. M. Dent and Sons, 1969.

Lodge, Olive. "Science in the 'Sixties." In *The Eighteen-Sixties: Essays by Fellows of the Royal Society of Literature.* Ed. John Drinkwater. Cambridge: Cambridge, UP, 1932.

Marshall, Dorothy. *The English Domestic Servant in History.* London: The Historical Association, 1949.

Marx, Karl and Friederich Engels. *Manifesto of the Communist Party.* Harmondsworth: Penguin, 1967, 1987.

Plato. *Republic.* Trans. Robin Waterfield. Oxford: Oxford UP, 1994.

Reichen, Charles-Albert. *A History of Chemistry.* London: Prentice-Hall, 1962.

Robbins, Bruce. *The Servant's Hand: English Fiction from Below.* Durham: Duke UP 1993.

Sussman, Herbert. "Cyberpunk Meets Charles Babbage: *The Difference Engine* as Alternative Victorian History." *Victorian Studies,* 38:1 (1995): 1–20.

Thomas, Deborah A. "Dickens and Indigestion: The Deadly Dinners of the Rich." *Dickens Studies Newsletter,* 14:1 (1983)7–12.

Thomson, Thomas. *The History of Chemistry,* Vol. II. New York: Arno Press, 1975.

Turner, E. S. *What the Butler Saw: Two Hundred and Fifty Years of the Servant Problem.* London: Michael Joseph, 1962.

Webb, Beatrice. *My Apprenticeship.* Cambridge: Cambridge UP, 1979.

Hetty and History: The Political Consciousness of *Adam Bede*

Eleni Coundouriotis

Adam Bede *may be regarded as Eliot's response to Macaulay's immensely popular* History of England. *Eliot's novel does history by deploying irony to fracture and trouble the unitary voice of the narrative of progress characteristic of Macaulay's Whig history and to pit competing historical explanations against each other. Differences of class and gender generate contradiction in the novel despite the characters' consent to a national historical narrative. In an attempt to define Eliot's realist project against Macaulay's novelistic history, I turn to Fredric Jameson's analytical term "strategies of containment" and mount a critique of Jameson's analysis of realism. If we read Eliot as a critic of her times, it becomes difficult to follow Jameson's assumption that the novelist undertakes strategies of containment to achieve ideological closure in the novel. The story that Eliot tells is one in which she comments on her contemporaries' ways of constructing their historical narratives and the closure they enact through such narratives to guarantee social stability. Eliot's treatment of Hetty brings to light the narratives that her contemporaries try to silence and hence the tragic outcome of her plot disrupts the vision of social order restored at the end of the novel.*

Rural settings such as Hayslope (the setting of *Adam Bede*) are at the heart of Eliot's imagination of the English nation. As Elizabeth Helsinger argues, Eliot's rural settings elicit nostalgia by foregrounding personal stories as

---

quests for national identity. The rural scenes, Helsinger says, are "at the center of a nationalizing culture as touchstones of moral sense and social stability" (218). But whereas Eliot on the one hand looks at the past to imagine possibilities of community for the future, she is also examining critically the way in which her own period misremembers this past. In *Adam Bede*, she develops her double task as a realist: to create a coherent and total fictional portrayal of a specific time and place in the past (the conventional " 'tis sixty years since" of Scott's *Waverley*) and also to undermine this coherence in order to examine the ideological assumptions of her own contemporaries' historical memory of that past. Eliot's historiographic ambitions were shaped by her reaction to the dominant historical paradigms of her time. Writing in the late 1850s, she inevitably wrote history in the context of Thomas Babington Macaulay's immensely successful *History of England*. Macaulay (who died in 1859, shortly after the publication of *Adam Bede*) had given history not only a wide audience but great narrative authority that novelists like Eliot sought to reappropriate for the novel.[1] Eliot saw herself as intervening in her society's incomplete and misguided historical memory. In *Adam Bede*, she fractures the unitary voice of the narrative of progress advanced by Macaulay and pits contradictory historical explanations against each other.

Eliot's task is in important ways metahistorical; her novel comments on already widely disseminated narratives of history. According to Jerome Buckley, "By the time of the Exhibition (1851) faith in the Macaulyan progress had engendered a confident complacency" (36).[2] Discontent with this intellectual climate pushed Eliot to use the novel, as Rosemarie Bodenheimer argues, to do "real" history (10). Eliot shows that the semantic closure imposed by Whig history severely restricted the capacity of historical discourse to engage in a critical appraisal of the present. By 1859 when *Adam Bede* was published, the wide dissemination of Whig history had produced a powerful association between the notions of progress and social stability: Britain's social stability (always a relative term measured in comparison to revolutionary France and its aftermath) provided a powerful affirmation of the progressive character of those changes that gave Britain its technological superiority. Yet, in addition to the widely recognized impact of the "growth of population" and the "industrial revolution" in the period from 1792 to 1832, a "political counterrevolution" took place, according to E. P. Thompson, in which "the English ancien regime received a new lease of life" (197). The reparation of Arthur's moral authority at the end of *Adam Bede* (where he appears physically diminished, but his well-being affectionately and respectfully desired by Adam and Dinah) dramatizes what Thompson identified as "the new lease of life" of the English "ancien regime."

Margaret Homans reads Eliot's refusal to "expel" the aristocracy and the working classes from the novel symptomatically. Eliot includes both the aristocracy and the working classes, according to Homans, in a diminished state and subordinated to a "vision of all-comprehending middle class ascendency" (157). Thompson's argument about the resurgence of aristocratic culture at this time shifts our reading of *Adam Bede*. Aristocratic and working-class culture are foregrounded in the novel because Eliot perceived that the middle class adopted and appropriated aristocratic and working-class attributes in an aesthetic recasting of itself that helped it achieve hegemonic status.

Adam Bede marks Eliot's effort to speak not only against the rhetoric of progress, but to address the ideological closure that she perceived to be its silent legacy. Whig history, according to Eliot, did not adequately address the counterrevolution that gave the gentry, such as Arthur, renewed authority.[3] Macaulay's work was the reigning alternative to reaction. However Macaulay perceived both his legislative career and his work as a historian as an effort · to discredit the alarmist fears of reaction. As Herbert Butterfield concluded, Macaulay's closure of the historical narrative in response to present needs became a constitutive element of Whig history (11–12).

Macaulay's history addressed the interrelation between the astonishing material progress of recent years and the political institutions of the nation. His argument implicates the character of political institutions in the construction of national character, but his emphasis lies in the immediate concern to stabilize the existing political institutions (most notably Parliament) in face of pervasive social displacement and upheaval. Whig history, "written from the point of view of the winners" (Arac in "Tradition," 14), sought to correlate its own assertion of ever greater social stability (stemming from a parliamentary government that is responsive to the country) with the dramatic technological advances of the age. The past is interpreted by Whig historians under the strong influence of the current political landscape.

What Macaulay's narrative accomplishes is in many ways similar to what Fredric Jameson describes as "strategies of containment" in *The Political Unconscious*. The *History* is novelistic in Jamesonian terms as it attempts to enact closure. What I would like to uncover in Eliot's novel is its political consciousness which means that if we extend Jameson's assumptions about the novel to Eliot it is impossible for Eliot to tell the story she wants: how a particular type of ideological closure (typified by the belief in progress advanced by Whig history) shaped her society's selective memory of the past and propagated a kind of censorship of the discourse of change, making difficult the realization of radical social reform. Eliot's text functions less like a novel in Jameson's terms and more like his description of criticism. Jameson's "strategies of containment" function as the focal point for an exegesis of interference that seeks to dismantle the novelist's effort to enact closure. The critic's imperative to totalize, according to Jameson, seeks to dismantle the coherence of the novelist's strategy of containment (52–53). Assuming that Eliot is not seeking closure but critiquing the closure of another narrative (that of Whig history), Jameson's description of the novelist's function does not apply. Yet his description of the critic's function is closer to what Eliot accomplishes. I will turn first to Eliot's construction of her contemporaries' historical point of view that energizes the nostalgic return to a rural past and then, in an attempt to define further her realist project, to the Marxist theories of totality and representation in the works of Jameson and Georg Lukacs.

A critical commonplace about *Adam Bede* needs to be challenged. Eliot does not depict "provincial England *before* the modern fragmentation became evident" (Auster 59, emphasis added).[4] In her historically specific depiction of the early 1800s, she is at pains to show a moment when the pastoral life and the recognizable beginnings of "modern fragmentation" existed simultaneously and contiguously.[5] The historical lesson to be learned, therefore, is that the adverse conditions of the present (1859) stem from the inability of the pastoral world of Hayslope to address the realities of Stonyshire, the mill town. And this is not only a problem of the past because the memory of places such as Hayslope persists in the present as powerful descriptions of national character. Historical memory selectively privileges one aspect of the past (Hayslope) over the other (Snowfield). In addition, Eliot demonstrates that the exclusive association of the past with the country and the present with the city underpins the tendency to ignore the protoindustrial past. Historical change becomes manifest in the delineation of geographically distinct areas.

As a consequence of this spatial organization of the historical imagination, causal relations over *time* are played down. The city-identified narrator is separated from the world of the novel not only by the time difference of sixty years, but also by geographical location.[6] In so far as the troubling sphere of Snowfield must be disconnected from Hayslope in order to reaffirm the social order present in the beginning of the novel, the ending represses not only geographical links but links between the present and the past. The ending of the novel gives no indication of how one social reality evolved into another because the place (Snowfield) in which these links between past and present are most powerful is relegated to the margins of historical memory.

Nowhere is the narrator's own urban, or modern, orientation more evident than in the much-discussed personification of Old Leisure (ch. 52). Old Leisure seems curiously out of place in Eliot's representation of the past. He is introduced as a paean to a quality of life most characteristic of the past and lost to the present:

> Surely all other leisure is hurry compared with a sunny walk through the fields from 'afternoon church,'—as such walks used to be in those old leisurely times,

when the boat, gliding sleepily along the canal, was the newest locomotive wonder; when Sunday books had most of them old brown-leather covers, and opened with remarkable precision always in one place. Leisure is gone—gone where the spinning-wheels are gone, and the pack-horses, and the slow waggons, and the peddlars who brought bargains to the door on sunny afternoons. (557; ch. 52)

This description is occasioned by the Poysers' walk home from church, but Old Leisure is strangely incompatible with our impression of the Poysers or of Adam who is accompanying them. As Raymond Williams aptly remarked, Eliot's personification, far from portraying an abstract figure of generalized well-being, is instead "a class figure who can afford to saunter, who has leisure precisely in the sweat of other men's work" (*Country* 178).We may add to this, however, that Old Leisure is no longer compatible with the characterization of Squire Donnithorne, who is actively reorganizing his estate for his greater profit and cannot be imagined "sauntering by the fruit-tree wall, and scenting the apricots when they were warmed by the morning sunshine, or sheltering himself under the orchard boughs at noon, when the summer pears were falling" (557; ch. 2).

Rather the personification of Old Leisure encapsulates a nostalgia that is peculiar to Eliot's own time and that shapes the past as the opposite of the present.[7] This idealization comes from an urban and contemporary point of view and does not belong in the least to the past it purportedly represents. We are told that, "[Old Leisure] only read one newspaper, innocent of leaders, and was free from that periodicity of sensations which we call post-time." Furthermore, "excursion trains, art museums, periodical literature," features that typify the narrator's sense of her modernity and contrast with Old Leisure, anchor the narrator's perspective squarely in the city (557; ch. 52). Old Leisure is arguably the stuff of collective memory and not of the self-conscious and critical examination of the past.

As Deirdre David has stated, Old Leisure "argues that negative social and historical change has taken place" (213). But Eliot also dwells on those aspects of the present idealization of the past that (like the personification of Old Leisure) sustain a continuity of values between the two historical moments even as they speak of changed social circumstances. This continuity, Eliot indicates, stands in an unresolved tension with the sense of rupture from the past so that both (continuity and rupture) contribute to an essentially contradictory memory of the past. Eliot's realistic portrayal seeks, therefore, to represent (and bring to consciousness) the incompatibility between the insistence on the continuity of the constitutive values of society (the class structure and the patriarchical family are two examples) and the reality of society's economic and industrial transformation in the last sixty years.

The developments in the novel that culminate in the happy ending map a trajectory opposite to the course of historical events. This movement "against history'' has its analogous geographical shift: instead of the narrator's own experience of a shift of focus from the country to the city, the novel enacts the closing of Hayslope's borders and Dinah's entrapment within those borders. In the course of the story, Dinah's world of hunger, oppressive labor, and spiritual need does not significantly impinge on Hayslope's integrity. Instead, Dinah is retrieved from the mill town into the total and meaningful world of the pastoral community.

Despite the inconsistencies that clearly situate Old Leisure as a literary figure of 1859, the personification has served as the key evidence to those who argue that Eliot was committed to the idea of a pastoral past. David, who has developed the most interesting argument along these lines, seeks to demonstrate "Eliot's implicit desire for a world unmolested by disruptive historical change" by describing it as a "strategy of containment"(211). Using Jameson's term (which I also deploy at length later in the essay), David argues that Eliot's portrayal of Hayslope "virtually literalizes her strategy of containment" so that she may suspend the realm of history entirely and tell a story whose historical implications are erased (212–13). David describes Eliot's representation in the following terms: "In this ideal place untainted by ideology . . . time is so fixed that it becomes atemporal: it is always a sunny summer morning and the fruit is always fragrantly ripe." "Disruptive change" is relegated to the world outside Hayslope (212). Eliot is able to suspend ("contain") the potential challenge which Hetty's tragedy brings upon the stable social order of Hayslope. Hetty's murder, trial and subsequent death all take place outside Hayslope. According to David, Eliot, therefore, has structured the drama's resolution in such a fashion as to close Hetty off from the renewed foundations of a stable and harmonious Hayslope.

But, as I have been arguing, the degree of closure that Hayslope achieves as a community is not endorsed by Eliot. In other words, Eliot is not simply giving shape to a fantasy of an "ideal place untainted by ideology"; rather she tells a story that depicts the enactment of ideological closure by a community over a period of known, historical time. Therefore, she sees the history of the past sixty years as a matter of increasingly narrowed experience. The rapid changes in the conditions of life have resulted in the loss, rather than the gain of possibility, including discursive possibility.

The cause for such a narrowing is, in part, the inability of the nation to imagine an alternative social order to the one that governs the relation between Adam and Arthur. The happy ending shows the narrowing of social possibility that results when the imperative of historical narrative is to show a legacy of social continuity despite the actual experience of profound change. The typification of Adam in *Adam Bede* is itself only a compensatory myth for the reality of his social (and political) impotence which, while not fully evident when looking at Hayslope in isolation, has come into full view over

time with the obsolescence of his artisan status. I will examine the representation of work in the novel further, but let me first turn to look at how Macaulay
imagines historical continuity.

Eliot's focus on the recent past creates the possibility for a very different
evaluation of the present than Macaulay's treatment of the more distant past.
The bulk of Macaulay's *History* (left unfinished at the time of his death)
covers a period of a mere seventeen years, from 1685 to 1702. The first two
volumes, which were the most widely read, end with the enthronement of
William. In contrast, the recent past referred to by Eliot coincides with the
period around Macaulay's birth, a period that Macaulay's broader historical
scope includes in the present, not the past. The decline to which Eliot gives
voice belongs, in Macaulay's scheme of things, to the present; for Macaulay,
this is the period that bears the fruit of the Revolution of 1688 and confirms
the progressive course of history. In the third chapter of his *History* (the
"State of England in 1685"), Macaulay seeks to establish progress as an
indisputable and self-evident fact.[8] In terms of my comparison of the *History*
to *Adam Bede*, Macaulay's most telling juxtapositions of past and present
address the status of the country gentleman and the condition of the industrialized North. For Macaulay, the change in status of the country gentleman
encapsulates more than any other change the greater affluence and cultural
refinement of the nation in the present:

> The modern country gentleman generally receives a liberal education, passes
> from a distinguished school to a distinguished college, and has every opportunity
> to become an excellent scholar. He has generally seen something of foreign
> countries. A considerable part of his life has generally been passed in the
> capital; and the refinements of the capital follow him into the country. There
> is perhaps no class of dwellings so pleasing as the rural seats of the English
> gentry.   (1:249–50)

His counterpart at the time of the Revolution, on the other hand, was "a poor
man" who often "had received an education differing little from that of (his)
menial servants" (1:250). An index of his poverty was his lack of opportunity
for travel: "he was generally under the necessity of residing, with little interruption, on his estate" (1:251). By contrast, Eliot registers additional changes
since the turn of the century, organizing her novel around a past-present
comparison that covers the period of the last sixty years.

Macaulay addresses the impact of the recent past in his allusions to the
changes wrought by industrialization. His description of the conditions in
what had become during the late eighteenth and early nineteenth century the
protoindustrialized North, can be read as a response to the "condition of
England" critics. Once again, Macaulay structures his comparison by shifting
the focus to the period roughly two hundred years ago. The North, which

had a naturally inhospitable and infertile terrain, was literally a savage land in the seventeenth century; industrialization, Macaulay tells us, civilized it (1:223). Even when taking the difficult issue of child labor under consideration, Macaulay sees improvement in the present conditions. He refers explicitly to the legislation passed to limit child labor, and compares the present situation to the conditions of the children who worked on the farms. He does not discuss, however, the abuses of the early years of industrialization that led to the reforms (1:327). This is consistent with the general organization of the chapter in which Macaulay does not differentiate between the present and the recent past.

In the third chapter of the *History*, Macaulay gives the impression that change had been occurring gradually over a period of some two hundred years. The technique of comparing past and present (two fixed moments in time) serves to obscure the varying speed of change and most significantly the catastrophic experience of the early industrial period, Macaulay's recent past. In effect, Macaulay gives the impression that changes have been occurring gradually and diminishes their immediate disruptive impact while using the protracted time-frame to create a momentum of inevitability and necessity for the desired reforms. He shapes a pragmatic and politically astute strategy for the liberal advocacy of reform that must stem a strong tide of reactionary feeling.

Despite the closeness of their specific political affiliations, Eliot creates a fictional discourse that disturbs the cohesiveness of Macaulay's position. Her past and present comparison lays stress precisely on the abruptness of the changes of the last few years. This abruptness and its far-reaching implications distinguish the period of the last sixty years as unique in Eliot's eyes. It is as if Eliot, sympathizing with Macaulay's intent, remains dissatisfied with his strategy and the price paid by arguing away the real extent of the trauma of their contemporary history.

For Eliot, the differences between 1799 and 1859 are marked without ambiguity in the changes that characterize the conditions of work. Adam's artisan status speaks most eloquently to this effect:

> To "make a good job" of anything, however small, was always a pleasure to Adam; and he sat on a block, resting on a planing-table, whistling low every now and then, and turning his head on one side with a just perceptible smile of gratification—of pride, too, for if Adam loved a bit of good work, he loved also to think, "I did it!" And I believe only the people who are free from that weakness are those who have no work to call their own   (340; ch. 27).

Adam derives his sense of self-worth and dignity from his work as a craftsman which is implicitly compared in the final sentence to a factory worker. Eliot is interested in showing how this sense of self determines Adam's interactions with the upper classes to which he must eventually sell his services. For example, Eliot recounts Adam's confrontation with Squire Donnithorne over the price of a frame he made on Miss Liddy's order. Adam's assurance in the value of his work safeguarded him from the Squire's power as purchaser. Thus, "hav(ing) work to call (his) own" Adam goes to the extreme of offering to give the frame away for free rather than accept a price lower than the one he set (290; ch. 21). Eliot makes clear that the Squire is resentful of Adam's self-assertion, but at the same time Adam prevails and receives his price. As an independent artisan, he can determine the price of his labor and goods.

Adam's carpentry, however, can also be compared to Dinah's preaching. The two occupations pertain to distinct geographical localities, each of which is vying for representational space within the novel. The marriage of Dinah and Adam enacts a resolution in the tension between these two alternatives and banishes Snowfield out of view. The various circumstantial reasons for which Dinah stopped preaching after her marriage (including the historical fact that women preachers were prohibited) are not adequate responses to her initial hesitations to leave Snowfield. As she explains to Adam, these hesitations gave rise to a vision in which "It seems to me as if you were stretching out your arms to me, and beckoning me to come and take my ease, and live for my own delight, and Jesus, the Man of Sorrows, was standing looking towards me, and pointing to the sinful, and suffering, and afflicted" (553; ch. 52). When Adam comes to meet Dinah, their union is a foregone conclusion, as if Dinah is powerless to do otherwise. Yet even as Eliot couches Dinah's decision in the language of divine ordinance, the import of this decision is limited to the personal happiness of two individuals rather than the wider social implications of Dinah's work in the cotton-mill town (576; ch. 54). In the end, we come to feel that the distance that divides the materially comfortable Hayslope (the place that is kept in full view of the reader) and the cotton-mill is quite arbitrary.

Eliot's attitude to recent historical changes takes shape in her contextualization of the novel's setting. In her conversation with Mr. Irwine, Dinah explains the transformation of Snowfield since the establishment of the cotton-mill. But despite the particular instance of Mr. Irwine's memory of Snowfield before the cotton-mill, the characters in the novel exhibit very little consciousness of the past. They are aware of present historical events such as the wars with France, but do not speak of their own community's origins. In fact, we are led to believe that the Poysers have always belonged on the Hall Farm, "the old place where [Mr. Poyser] had been bred and born" (393; ch. 32). The Poysers' sense of independence and proprietorship is shored up by their agreement with Squire Donnithorne that allows them to manage the farm as they please. The narrator, however, provides us with some background against which we can place the Poysers' sentimental belief in their right to the farm:

> It was once the residence of a country squire, whose family, probably dwindling down to mere spinsterhood, got merged in the more territorial name of Donnithorne. It was once the Hall; it is now the Hall Farm. Like the life in some coast-town that was once a watering-place, and is now a port, . . . the life at the Hall had changed its focus, and no longer radiates from the parlour, but from the kitchen and the farmyard. (116; ch. 6)

The Poysers are part of a specific juncture in the Hall's history and represent at once the Hall's fall in status and its rejuvenation. The Hall Farm resonates as a valued symbol of cultural authenticity; Eliot historicizes this symbol and shows that it represents a type of life no longer available in her time.

The Hall Farm is a symbol of prosperity despite its dilapidated structure. The Hall, transformed into a place of work, is a place of plenty and well-being which significantly registers the recent inclusion of working people within the nation's prosperity. But, all the same, the Poysers' presence on the Farm rests precariously on the changing economy of agriculture. The focus here is on a historical moment that demonstrates the opening of possibility while it foreshadows the curtailment of a better future. From the moment when Squire Donnithorne plans to change the types of work done on the farm for his greater personal profit, the Poysers' presence on the farm is threatened. Mrs. Poyser's tirade against the squire demonstrates that their stay on the farm is conditional on the type of work they are required to do. Thus she refuses to undertake the conversion of the farm to a full-time dairy and challenges the Squire to turn them out. Her resistance to the squire clearly dates the novel's action to a period before the total ascendancy of the new economic powers, but it also reveals a clearly articulated awareness of the conditions to come. Mrs. Poyser forcefully tells the squire, "we're not dumb creaturs to be abused and made money on by them as ha'got the lash i'their hands, for want o'knowing how t'undo the tackle" (394; ch. 32). At stake here is the entire way of life that the Poysers represent and the concomitant broadening of prosperity across class lines that their arrival on the Hall Farm had announced. Squire Donnithorne's profit motive clashes with the conditions of living that have made the Poysers into a symbol of the pastoral and its implied social stability. If class conflict arises, therefore, Eliot depicts the squire as the instigator.

Despite Squire Donnithorne's threats and the imminent instability they suggest, the outcome of the novel reinforces the existing social order, and does so contrary to our own knowledge that the way of life portrayed in the novel came to an end. The novel's conclusion, however, relies in large part on a circumstantial development; it is only the squire's timely death that removes his threats. Furthermore, when Arthur inherits the estate, he must redress the instability caused by his own behavior. For all its apparent similarity to the order that existed during his childhood, the order established by

Arthur at the conclusion of the novel is different. Now it is an order established out of reaction to the imminent threat of disorder. Despite the favorable outlook on which the novel ends, it marks the beginning of the type of hardening of social possibility with which Eliot is concerned.

In addition to placing Hayslope in relation to its past, Eliot keeps her reader continuously aware of the more worldly context within which the events of the novel unfold. The period is one of continuous war against France, first against revolutionary France and then against Napoleon. The contemporary attitudes toward the French help Eliot organize her perception of the imminent narrowing of social possibility. Historians have documented how the patriotic feelings aroused by these wars helped the cause of reaction against the French revolution and against the agitation of reform in England (Thompson 197–98). While the habit of contrasting the national character of the Englishman with his French counterpart is not new to this period, it now became the basis on which to demonstrate why English history was marked by peaceful change and would never succumb to the violent revolutionary changes of France.

Adam is most closely identified with the racial ideal. As Eve Kosofsky Sedgwick has noted, his name combines Biblical and Saxon references to place Adam at the center of his culture's value system (142). But Eliot also establishes Adam's paradigmatic Englishness in reference to the French. The anonymous traveler who comes to Hayslope in the beginning of the novel comments, upon noticing Adam, that "we want such fellows as he to lick the French," and the reply he receives is "He's an uncommon favorite wi'the gentry, sir" (61; ch. 1). Adam is not only the quintessential Anglo-Saxon; he is also the guarantor of social stability. His superior abilities, coupled with his readiness to conform, flatter the gentry's sense of their authority and encourages their paternalistic sense of obligation. Social harmony is the natural extension of national character and is, therefore, essentially unchangeable. Mr. Craig, the Donnithorne's gardener, is the only one to break rank with the consensus against the French: "There's them at th' head o' this country as are worse enemies t'us nor Bony and all the mounseers he's got at's back" (566; ch. 53). But he is quickly silenced by Mr. Poyser's mainstream opinion, "The war's a fine thing for the country, an'how'll you keep up prices wi'out it? An'them French are a wicked sort o' folks, by what I can make out; what can you do better nor fight'em?" (566; ch. 53). As farmers, the Poysers are direct beneficiaries of the protected grain markets the war ensures.

Instead of thinking through Mr. Craig's implication that the French are being scapegoated to cover up for domestic tensions, Mr. Poyser uses the dominant rationalization in favor of the war (that the French are intrinsically evil) to shore up the existing economic order which happens to be in line with his immediate interest. Eliot, in her role as realist observer, documents

how Mr. Poyser contributes to the closure of any remaining discursive open-
ings through which the revolutionary impulse of the French could be brought
to bear on Mr. Poyser's own countrymen—especially, as we shall see, on the
social realities of the neighboring Snowfield.[9]

Eliot unambiguously characterizes Mr. Poyser's neighboring Snowfield, a
place of which his niece can speak, as a place of hunger. By contrast, Dinah
describes Hayslope as a place "wherein they eat bread without scarceness"
(133–34; ch. 8). We have only to think of Carlyle's sympathetic account of
the Manchester Insurrection ("insurrection never so necessary," *Past and
Present* 21) to realize the imminent danger of revolution in England. Eliot
also shows how limited the framework for discussion of events such as the
French Revolution is when confronted by the kind of consensus to which
Mr. Poyser gives voice.

The "happy" ending of the novel must be seen within the context of these
increasingly narrowed discursive possibilities that have their origin in the
period depicted in the novel and continue to delimit the nature of reform in
Eliot's day. She sets herself the ambitious task of at once recreating the past
as it exists in the memory of her contemporaries and of undermining this
portrait by deploying a highly disruptive tragic strain in her story. The
"happy" ending rounds off the portrayal of those years as idyllic. But while
Adam and Arthur renew their particular social contract on the basis of an
ethic of personal attachments and commitments, Hetty is excluded from the
same ethic. As Sedgwick argues, Hetty in her capacity as woman enables the
men to reaffirm their bond despite their class difference: "in the presence of
a woman who can be seen as pitiable or contemptible, men are able to
exchange power and to confirm each other's value even in the context of
the remaining inequalities in their power" (160). Sedgwick also notes the
"thoroughness of [Eliot's] feminist analysis" (140); as feminist readers,
therefore, we are compelled to address the disruptive energy bound up in the
unsatisfactory resolution of Hetty's lot. Hetty disrupts the affirmation of the
"happy" ending and is the point of departure from which we can identify
and reconstruct Eliot's critical perspective on her contemporaries' historical memory.

Seeking to modify the sense of rupture with the past that organizes the
thought of the rhetoricians of progress, Eliot shows that the beliefs about
national character embodied in her characterizations of Adam and Arthur
have helped assure the continuous supremacy of a moral order based on a
hierarchical class structure.[10] Furthermore, this order has prevailed despite
the intensification of class conflict in response to industrialization and urbanization. The most outstanding feature of recent history, according to the logic
of *Adam Bede*, is a legacy of continuity: the fundamental values that organize
the social structure have remained unchanged. Reading the novel, we should

be struck ultimately with the unresponsiveness of social "form" to the changes in economic conditions. Eliot does not play down the extent of the changes that have taken place. Those clearly contribute to her portrayal of the pastoral Hayslope as a lost world. Instead, the uniqueness of her insight lies in her insistence that despite such momentous changes, the fundamental class distinctions that determine authority have not only persisted but hardened into place.

The enthusiastic response to *Adam Bede* at the time of its publication provides ample proof of the powerful resonance that the belief in a pastoral past had on the mid-century imagination. Like others, Ann Mozley in her unsigned review for *Bentley's Quarterly Review* (July 1859, qtd. in Carroll 86–103), focused on the scene of the country dance at Arthur's birthday party and praised Eliot for recuperating a lost pleasure: "That merry stamping, that gracious nodding of the head, that waving bestowal of the hand, where can we see them now?" (Carroll 99). The overall consensus on the novel was that its characters (especially all the subordinate characters) were very convincing. In fact, Eliot's choice of depicting farmers and artisans was perceived as original (*Saturday Review* Feb. 26, 1859, in Carroll 73).[11] Most importantly perhaps, Eliot's seriousness won her a new audience not habituated to reading novels (Mozley in Carroll 87).

But opinion was equally unified in condemning the "excesses" of Eliot's story. For example, a writer for the *Saturday Review* praised the way Eliot integrated her characters into a "connected whole," but condemned Hetty's child murder for being "as superfluous as it was arbitrary" (Carroll 75). E. S. Dallas writing for *The Times* seconded this opinion by concluding that, "there is not much of a story" (Carroll 80).[12] While Eliot's efforts to portray the "common" people were very well received, there was little engagement with the story proper.

In fact, Eliot's early readers understood her avowal of realism as a posture of broad tolerance toward all aspects of her subject matter. E. S. Dallas compared her to Thackeray because both, he claimed, showed their readers that "we are all alike, that our natures are the same" (Carroll 79). He went on to distinguish Eliot from Thackeray by pointing out that Thackeray showed how we all shared a partially evil nature, while Eliot "finds good" in all her characters and "lets them off easy" (Carroll 79). Where *Adam Bede* is concerned, it would be more appropriate to rephrase this formulation and ask whether it is not Eliot's opinion that society shelters the likes of Adam and Arthur (thus "let[ting] them off easy"), while it tragically abandons the likes of Hetty.

Hetty's exile and solitary death facilitate the novel's happy resolution. Yet the reader's dissatisfaction with such a state of things may arise as an independent judgment regardless of the "objective" circumstances presented by the novel. As Susan Morgan has noted, "when I think of what we, as opposed to Adam, have learned, I think uneasily of what to make of Hetty." Thus the "harmony with which the novel ends is again shown to be limited, to depend on its own illusions of an ordered universe" (Morgan 270). Arthur is ultimately rewarded for his penitence by being able to preserve his estate in the form that most flatters his self-conception as benevolent squire. While Arthur cannot be held accountable for Hetty's act of infanticide, his efforts on her behalf are an acknowledgment of his complicity in her fate. Despite the fact that he saves her from execution, Hetty dies and never returns to the community. Whether or not Hetty is saved from execution is only important in the plot for the extent to which it restores Arthur in the reader's estimation. The reader's consent to the story's resolution, therefore, amounts to an endorsement of Arthur's privilege. If Hetty and Arthur were considered on equal moral ground (in terms both of class and gender), then Arthur, like Hetty, should have died while away and not returned to his previous position. But Arthur and Hetty are not social equals. Eliot records what in all likelihood would have happened given the prevailing values and lets this "objective" picture speak of the inequities.

In an attempt to understand further how Eliot deploys the ending of *Adam Bede* to highlight the incompatible historical memories of her contemporaries, it is worthwhile to return to Jameson's analytical term, "strategies of containment." Within the Marxist theory of interpretation that Jameson puts forth in *The Political Unconscious*, strategies of containment function as the focal point for an exegesis of *interference* that seeks to dismantle the novelist's effort to enact closure. Jameson retrieves the concept of totality as elaborated by Georg Lukacs and calls for its use as a methodological tool of narrative analysis. As I mentioned in my introductory remarks, the critic's "imperative to totalize," therefore, seeks to dismantle the coherence of the novelist's strategy of containment (52–53). By totality, Jameson is not referring to the closed system of the novel, but to the infinitely expandable context within which the novel, as a purportedly closed semantic system, can be placed; the critic's "imperative to totalize" aims to explode the text's self-imposed semantic limits. Jameson here relies mostly on Lukacs's elaboration of totality in *History and Class Consciousness* where Lukacs placed the category of totality at the center of his effort to understand reified realities through theory. Jameson transposed this method to a theory of narrative (54). As argued very convincingly by Jameson in his earlier *Marxism and Form*, Lukacs's entire thought may be understood as a hermeneutics.

In so far as I do not find that Jameson's assumptions about the novel in *The Political Unconscious* apply to *Adam Bede* and what I am trying to define as a critical, historical realism, I think it is fruitful to return to Lukacs's earlier, pre-Marxist elaboration of the concept of totality in *The Theory of the Novel.* Here Lukacs shows that the novel itself posits a totality and not as semantic closure but, paradoxically, as the intimation of meanings unavailable to direct representation. Thus the novel, a "created totality," uses *irony* to intimate that which is absent from immediate experience:

> The irony of the novel is the self-correction of the world's fragility: inadequate relations can transform themselves into a fanciful yet well-ordered round of misunderstandings and cross-purposes, within which everything is seen as many-sided, within which things appear as isolated and yet connected, as full of value and yet totally devoid of it .... Thus a new perspective of life is reached on an entirely new basis—*that of the indissoluble connection between the relative independence of the parts and their attachments to the whole.*
> (emphasis added, *Theory* 75)

Irony, therefore, opposes its own meaning to the appearance of fragmentation; it provides an alternative order of coherence to challenge the apparent autonomy of the first order. In fact, fictional representation, much like "theory" in Lukacs's later Marxist thought, is an interpretive method. The difference between the two, realist narrative and theory, is that theory aims to overcome dissonance by explicitly synthesizing an alternative explanation of things while narrative can only achieve an approximate statement of the condition of dissonance itself. The synthesis aimed at by Lukacsian critical theory is also invoked by Jameson as the final step of the hermeneutic process following the necessary first step of the text's deconstruction.

If Eliot is not engaged in an act of ideological closure (such as the one suggested by David, or that of Macaulay's *History*) but seeks to uncover such an act by means of her story, then we must take issue with Jameson's basic assumptions about the realist novel in *The Political Unconscious.* Jameson's definition of the "political unconscious" seems to preclude the possibility of a realist novelist consciously uncovering the language of class conflict in their representation of daily life. Jameson explains, "It is in detecting the traces of that uninterrupted narrative (class struggle), in restoring to the surface of the text the repressed and buried reality of this fundamental history, that the doctrine of the political unconscious finds its function and its necessity" (20). While it is beyond argument that the task of representation has political implications, it is also possible that the novelist is using his or her fiction to "restor[e] to the surface" a political context that has been buried within the dominant mode of thinking about historical discourse. In other words, to generalize that all realist narratives attempt to repress (by means of totalizing narratives) rather than illuminate the political implications of their representations is to underestimate their complexity. Jameson's theory gives us no means to assess what Jonathan Arac has termed the "historical-political *consciousness* actually available" in a novel, or its explicit political content (*Critical* 276, emphasis added). On the basis of this assumption, Jameson steps in to demystify the literary work through his own act of interpretation. Instead we must confront Eliot's own claims that she is explaining the world to us. Her story is a *created totality* (as Lukacs defines the term in *The Theory of the Novel*) that uses irony to interfere in the discourse current among her contemporaries. Eliot's portrayal of Hetty anchors Eliot's project of interference and uncovers what Helsinger calls "the risks of history" in the novel, subverting the vision of harmonious social evolution that the novel seems to endorse (219).

Hetty deeply affects the personal histories of the other characters, but the disruptive implications with which her tragedy is ripe remain unfulfilled. There is a lingering sense in *Adam Bede* that the most momentous changes are taking place on a register that is imperceptible to the characters in the novel. In part her tragedy stems from her faith in Arthur. But, in this respect, she is far from the exception in her community. When Hetty sets off to find Arthur at his regiment, she acts on the most widely held assumption of her community: a willingness to believe in Arthur's moral superiority exclusively on the basis of his high rank in society. For example, early in her characterization of Adam, Eliot points out that he " . . . was very susceptible to the influence of rank, and quite ready to give an extra amount of respect to every one who had more advantages than himself, not being a philosopher or proletaire with democratic ideas . . . " (209; ch. 16). This predisposition, compounded with evidence of Arthur's genial personality, grows into a strong faith that Arthur would shape a better future for the entire community. "Every tenant," Eliot tells us, "was quite sure things would be different when the reins got into his hands" (130; ch. 7). Indeed, despite the ensuing tragedy, Arthur's personal character secures the novel's happy ending. The particular confluence of issues of character and class determine the social contract that is renewed by the novel's ending. Therefore, it is important to examine the enabling conditions that preclude dislocation and secure the continuity of a particular type of social organization.

From the beginning of the novel, Eliot is at pains to show that Arthur's conduct would never be shameless. "His own approbation was necessary to him," she tells us, "and it was not an approbation to be enjoyed quite gratuitously; it must be won by a fair amount of merit" (169; ch. 12). And again, "Nature has taken care that he shall never go far astray with perfect comfort and satisfaction to himself; he will never get beyond that borderland of sin, where he will be perpetually harassed by assaults from the other side of the boundary" (171; ch. 12). Arthur's standards for his own conduct may be high, but society at large is also willing to judge him leniently because, in Eliot's view, people are seduced by the appeal of Arthur as a symbol of the nation's well-being:

he was but twenty-one, you remember; and we don't inquire too closely into character in the case of a handsome generous young fellow, who will have property enough to support numerous peccadilloes—who, if he should unfortunately break a man's legs in his rash driving, will be able to pension him handsomely; or if he should happen to spoil a woman's existence for her, will make it up to her with expensive bon-bons, packed up and directed by his own hand.   (170; ch. 12)

Eliot's irony is directed here at the social consent to the authority that rests in propertied privilege. It is the same consent that will ratify the happy ending and ignore the injustice done to Hetty. In the end, Eliot isolates Arthur from his class by way of his self-imposed exile and demonstrates that his personal suffering is not insignificant.

During Arthur and Adam's second meeting in the woods (the one after Hetty's trial), their respective moral positions are about to be reversed for the second time. While Arthur's wrongdoing had given Adam the morally superior ground, Arthur's ability to appease Adam's lingering anger (and thus contain its socially disruptive potential) returns him to the morally superior position:

Adam was forcing Arthur to feel more intensely the irrevocableness of his own wrongdoing: he was presenting the sort of resistance that was the most irritating to Arthur's eager, ardent nature. But his anger was subdued by the same influence that had subdued Adam's when they first confronted each other—by the marks of suffering in a long familiar face.   (512; ch. 48)

Arthur's susceptibility to the memory of their childhood bond helps him attain Adam's forgiveness: "it was impossible for [Adam] not to feel that this was the voice of the honest, warm-hearted Arthur whom he had loved and been proud of in the old days" (512; ch. 48). The moral sway of personal attachments effaces the sense of class injury so that, as part of their forgiveness of each other, they restore their labor relation; Adam promises to continue as overseer of the Donnithorne estate (516; ch. 48).

In their first confrontation in the woods when Adam had just learned of Arthur's relationship with Hetty, Adam accused Arthur of using the influence of his status to gain sway over Hetty. Until the moment he forgives Arthur, Adam insists on seeing the tragedy in terms of a class injury. Thus during the trial, he demands that Arthur also be held responsible for the infanticide. It is important to remember that Arthur and Adam's fondness for each other before the crisis derived in large measure from their mutual contentment in the class-determined roles that they enabled each other to play out. Their expectations for the future were shaped in large part by Arthur's ambitions to reform the estate. The disruptive effect of Arthur's liaison with Hetty is not limited to the personal lives of these characters but reveals the larger moral bankruptcy of Arthur's class and his own inability to achieve even the preconditions for the reform which he has promised.

While everyone in the community admires Arthur, Hetty's infatuation with Arthur has been attributed to her vanity and egoism. As Henry Auster concludes, "Her disgrace, misfortune, and banishment are the natural consequences, as George Eliot sees it, of the frivolous egoism and indifference that had originally set her apart from the life around her" (129). Eliot makes it quite clear, however, that Hetty falls in love with Arthur's status and is thus no different from the others in her community. What distinguishes Hetty is her strong impulse to escape the tedious, tiring life of a dairy maid. Her awareness of her own beauty and of Arthur's susceptibility to it gives her hope that she can belong in the gentry because, quite simply, she looks the part. When she secretly tries on the earrings Arthur gave her, for example, we are told that "she was not thinking most of the giver," but admiring the transformation in herself which made the possibility of an escape from her tedium seem real (295; ch. 22). Her vanity is a direct reflection of her personal revolt against her social status. Hetty's claims to higher social standing on the basis of her looks are confirmed by Mrs. Irwine who remarks at Arthur's birthday party, "What a pity such beauty as that should be thrown away among the farmers, when it's wanted so terribly among the good families without fortune!" (319; ch. 25). The effect of this comment on Arthur is to legitimize his attraction for Hetty and encourage him to act upon it despite the fact that there is no intention on his own or Mrs. Irwine's part to lift Hetty out of her class.

Hetty's looks propel her upward mobility. The rebuff of Hetty's claims, however, reveals a more complicated picture: class distinctions in Eliot's England are upheld on the basis of a "natural" hierarchy that is not accountable to change. It is precisely at the moment of *reaction*, when the natural authority of the gentry is asserted against imminent change, that Hetty's claims are rebuffed. Her aestheticized view of class distinctions lead her to illusory hopes, but at the same time it betrays a perception that class distinctions are already arbitrary to a significant degree. As we saw, the moral code that governs the relation between Arthur and Adam is based on their consent to a social structure they have learned as children; childhood memory ratifies their class relation and lends it the appearance of the natural order of things.

Mediated through its aftermath (the reconciliation of Adam and Arthur, the marriage of Adam to Dinah), the tragedy of *Adam Bede* lends itself to a powerful reconfirmation of the social order. Barbara Hardy was able to speak of the novel's depiction of a "tragic regeneration" (43) that comes as a result of a "moral pattern which shows the pain as productive" (32). The implications of Hetty's tragedy are contained within the perception that it brings about a greater good. Eliot does not espouse this reading of events, but sees it instead as a function of a historical memory that seeks to suppress any inconsistencies. To this end, Hetty's suffering is marginalized in the novel, and Arthur's suffering is pivotal to the novel's resolution.

The reaffirmation of the existing social order which takes place at the end of the novel is staged as a *reaction* to the potential of disruptive change. Adam and Arthur both agree to fall back on their old relation. The novel depicts a particular juncture at which the authority of class stalled the process of change. The history of the ensuing sixty years, however, saw the dramatic economic transformation of society (whose beginnings were encroaching on the borders of Hayslope) and an unequal response in terms of class relations. The persistent moral authority of the upper classes (if only as cultural icons to be imitated by the middle class) is at odds with the economic realities of the nation, according to Eliot. The novel speaks directly to Eliot's present by depicting a moment when the divergence between cultural values and economic reality is taking hold. Ultimately, therefore, the kind of continuity for which Eliot argues (and tries to make visible) creates a much greater historiographical challenge than either the narrative of progress or the narrative of reaction.

NOTES

1. In "History versus Fiction: Thackeray's Response to Macaulay," Jane Millgate discusses extensively the competitive relationship between the novel and history in the middle of the century. The shift by midcentury from a perceived generic continuity between history and the historical novel to the greater authority of history proper is illustrated by an anecdote that G. Otto Trevelyan narrates in the biography of his uncle. As proof of Macaulay's celebrity, Trevelyan notes that once, when Macaulay was in Scotland toward the end of his life, he became surrounded by an admiring throng. A young woman bystander, not recognizing Macaulay, asked who he was, upon being told it was the author of the *History*, she exclaimed, "Oh, I thought it was only a romance" and proceeded to "add herself to the group of starers" (2:399).

2. With the exception of "a powerful minority of sceptics and prophets [who] scorned the 'visibility of progress,' " such events as "the Great Exhibition of 1851 proclaimed it triumphantly, and even in the 1860s when elements of doubt were penetrating many favorite orthodoxies, the sense of improvement remained" (Briggs 2). Asa Briggs substantiates this statement by quoting from Macaulay's *History of England* which he called "the most important and influential English history book of the nineteenth century." For Briggs, Macaulay unambiguously asserted the progressive course of English history in the last one hundred and sixty years (2).

3. My reading of Eliot is opposed to Terry Eagleton's assessment of Eliot's ideological complicity with her times. Eagleton claims that Eliot "recasts historical contradiction into ideologically resolvable form" and does so most powerfully in *Adam Bede*. Her "realism," furthermore, "involves the tactful unraveling of interlaced processes, the equable distribution of authorial sympathies, the holding of competing values in precarious equipoise" (114). Instead I argue that Eliot confronts an existing tendency to "recast historical contradiction into ideologically resolvable form" in the reigning cult of progress. She opposes to its historical narrative, her critical estimation that progress and destruction take place side by side. Furthermore the simplicity, or what Eagleton calls the "transparency," of the rural in Eliot's novel, is something she deliberately complicates by pointing repeatedly to all the truths it leaves out (112).

4. Another critic who overlooks the ways in which Eliot portrays the past as already fragmented (because he focuses on Loamshire as a total and independent world) is Philip Fisher. In *Making Up Society*, he discusses Eliot's opposition of nature and society as the contrast between the woods where Hetty and Arthur make love and where Hetty murders her child and the community of Hayslope which constitutes society in its totality in Fisher's analysis.

5. As Mary Jean Corbett argues, "*Adam Bede* is not the apotheosis of a premodern rural life, but the image of a world that cannot actualize the values that small-town society traditionally and mythically embodies" (293).

6. Corbett has argued convincingly that Eliot's project to historicize the pastoral and reveal that it is a product of the urban imagination was set out in her essay on Riehl. In the essay, Eliot, according to Corbett, "demystif[ies] the established literary convention for seeing rural life, the pastoral . . . She thus aligns herself with the verities of the natural historian against the misrepresentations of the 'urban imagination' " (289).

7. Walter E. Houghton extensively describes the association between a prevailing sense of lost leisure and the accelerated pace of everyday living in the Victorian era (6–8). Houghton also sees Eliot's description of Old Leisure as a reflection of a prized Victorian attitude, "earnestness." Old Leisure lacks earnestness, according to Houghton: "He was not, as one would say, taking life seriously. And that means, we see, that intellectually he has no concern whatever with ideas . . . he is, indeed, **happy** in his inability to know the causes of things" (218–19).

8. See John Clive for a discussion of the influence of Scott in the pioneering "social history" of the third chapter of Macaulay's *History* (119).

9. The relevance of the French Revolution for England was put most forcefully by Carlyle. In *The French Revolution*, Carlyle justifies the outbreak of the revolution on the basis of the material suffering of the French people and the moral bankruptcy of its natural leadership, the aristocracy. In *Past and Present*, moreover, an equally threatening imbalance is shown to pervade the English situation:

Shall we say then that the world has retrograded in its talent of apportioning wages to work, in late days? . . . Never till now, in the history of the Earth which to this hour nowhere refuses to grow corn if you will plough it, to yield shirts if you will spin and weave in it, did the mere manual two-handed worker . . . cry in vain for such "wages" as he means by "fair wages," namely food and warmth!   (26–27).

If the cause for insurrection is actual hunger (and it is not possible to deny the legitimacy of such a cry), then by allowing such conditions to take hold of the country, the English make the possibility of revolution likely.

10. See Mark Warren McLaughlin for a reading along these lines. McLaughlin, however, neglects to tie his discussion of class issues to gender. He focuses on Adam without treating gender. Homans, who insists on reading class through gender, chooses Dinah as her main focus, a heroine who becomes a transcendent, classless symbol of domesticity. I would argue that Dinah is part of the consensus narrative that Eliot shows her society investing in while Hetty's exclusion is there to trouble the consensus narrative.

11. Pinney and Knoepflmacher have treated extensively Wordsworth's influence on Eliot's commitment to apply her realism to the common people. Eliot has argued her own position on this score in "The Natural History of German Life" where she observes "how little the real characteristics of the working classes are known to those who are outside them, how little their natural history has been studied" (*Essays* 268).

12. Dickens was one of the few contemporary readers to be truly impressed and moved by Hetty (see his comments in Carroll 75).

WORKS CITED

Arac, Jonathan. *Critical Genealogies: Historical Situations for Postmodern Literary Studies*. New York: Columbia UP, 1987.

———. "Tradition, Discipline, and Trouble." *Profession* (1990): 12–17.

Auster, Henry. *Local Habitations: Regionalism in the Early Novels of George Eliot*. Cambridge, Mass.: Harvard UP, 1970.

Bodenheimer, Rosemarie. *The Politics of Story in Victorian Social Fiction*. Ithaca and London: Cornell UP, 1988.

Briggs, Asa. *The Age of Improvement: 1783–1867*. London: Longmans, 1959.

Buckley, Jerome Hamilton. *The Triumph of Time*. Cambridge, Mass.: Harvard UP, 1966.

Butterfield, Herbert. *The Whig Interpretation of History* (1931). New York, London: W. W. Norton, 1965.

Carlyle, Thomas. *The French Revolution*. 3 vols. New York: G. P. Putnam, 1902.

————. *Past and Present* (1843). New York: New York UP, 1965.

Carroll, David, ed. *George Eliot, The Critical Heritage*. New York: Barnes and Noble, 1971.

Clive, John. *Macaulay, The Shaping of a Historian*. New York: Knopf, 1973.

Corbett, Mary Jean. "Representing the Rural: The Critique of Loamshire in *Adam Bede*." *Studies in the Novel* 20.3 (1988): 288–301.

David, Deirdre. *Intellectual Women and Victorian Patriarchy*. Hamsphire: Macmillan, 1987.

Eagleton, Terry. *Criticism and Ideology* (1976). London: Verso, 1978.

Eliot, George. *Adam Bede* (1859). New York: Penguin, 1985.

————. *Essays of George Eliot*. Ed. Thomas Pinney. London: Routledge and Kegan Paul, 1963.

————. *Middlemarch* (1871). London: Pan Classics, 1973.

Fisher, Philip. *Making Up Society: The Novels of George Eliot*. Pittsburgh: Pittsburgh UP, 1981.

Hardy, Barbara. *The Novels of George Eliot: A Study in Form*. London: Athlone, 1959.

Helsinger, Elizabeth K. *Rural Scenes and National Representation: Britain, 1815–1850*. Princeton: Princeton UP, 1997.

Homans, Margaret. "Dinah's Blush, Maggie's Arm: Class, Gender, and Sexuality in George Eliot's Early Novels." *Victorian Studies* 36.2 (1993): 155–78.

Houghton, Walter E. *The Victorian Frame of Mind 1830–1870*. New Haven: Yale UP, 1957.

Jameson, Fredric. *Marxism and Form*. Princeton: Princeton UP, 1971.

————. *The Political Unconscious: Narrative as a Socially Symbolic Act*. Ithaca, NY: Cornell UP, 1981.

King, Jeannette. *Tragedy in the Victorian Novel*. Cambridge and London: Cambridge U P, 1978.

Knoepflmacher, U. C. *George Eliot's Early Novels: The Limits of Realism*. Berkeley and Los Angeles: U of California P, 1968.

Lukacs, Georg. *The Historical Novel*. Translated by Hannah and Stanley Mitchell. Introduction by Fredric Jameson. Lincoln and London: U of Nebraska P, 1983.

————. *History and Class Consciousness* (1923).Trans. Rodney Livingstone. Cambridge, Mass: MIT P, 1967.

————. *The Theory of the Novel* (1920). Trans. Anna Bostok. Cambridge, Mass.: MIT P, 1971.

Macaulay, Thomas Babington. *The Works of Lord Macaulay* (Edinburgh Edition), 8 vols. New York: Longmans, Green, 1897.

McLaughlin, Mark Warren. "*Adam Bede*: History, Narrative, Culture." *Victorians Institute Journal* 22 (1994): 55–83.

Millgate, Jane. "History versus Fiction: Thackeray's Response to Macaulay." *Costerus* 2 (1974): 43–58.

Morgan, Susan. "Paradise Reconsidered: Edens without Eve." In Jerome J. McGann, ed. *Historical Studies and Literary Criticism*. Madison: U of Wisconsin P, 1985, 266–82.

Pinney, Thomas. "The Authority of the Past in George Eliot's Novels." *Nineteenth-Century Fiction* Sept. 1966: 131–47.

Sedgwick, Eve Kosofsky. *Between Men: English Literature and Male Homosocial Desire*. New York: Columbia UP, 1985.

Thompson, E. P. *The Making of the English Working Class*. New York: Vintage, 1963.

Trevelyan, G. Otto. *The Life and Letters of Lord Macaulay* (2 vols). New York: Harper, 1876.

Williams, Raymond. *The Country and the City*. New York: Oxford UP, 1973.

————. *Culture and Society, 1780–1950* (1958). New York: Columbia UP, 1983.

"The Good Angel of Our Lives": Subversive Religion and *The Woman in White*

Carolyn Oulton

The Woman in White *is largely concerned with the issue of religious experience. Specifically, it questions manly Christianity as a viable ethos, insofar as it seeks to locate separate and distinct virtues in each gender. The novel systematically subverts the idealization of feminine weakness, which exposes the female protagonists to manipulation by unscrupulous authority figures. Furthermore, in embracing the tenets of manly religion the central male protagonist, Walter Hartright, is seen to assume an inappropriate degree of moral authority at the expense of his female counterparts. Hartright repeatedly defines virtue in terms of his own active resolution, recognizing Laura's influence in purely symbolic terms. But in transcending such simplistic precepts, it is she who is seen to undergo the most meaningful religious development in the novel.*

The Woman in White is, of course, concerned with female resistance to pre-scribed social roles. But Wilkie Collins's first major novel also explores women's religious experience, implicitly questioning the validity of Walter Hartright's manly Christianity, that seeks to contain religion within a rigid moral framework. The manly ideal, most famously propounded by Charles Kingsley and in Thomas Hughes's novel *Tom Brown's Schooldays,* was a pervasive one. The *Dictionary of Phrase and Fable* defines manly Christianity in terms of "Healthy or strong-minded religion, which braces a man to face the battle of life bravely and manfully." This circular definition—in which

Dickens Studies Annual, Volume 30, Copyright © 2001 by AMS Press, Inc. All rights reserved.

manly religion develops and perpetuates manliness—reveals the shared assumptions inherent in this ideal. Where evangelicalism stresses the internal conflict between conscience and temptation, manliness regards life itself as a battle to be fought with valor.

Notably Allen Warren describes its glorification of rigorous engagement with the elements, so central to Hartright's experience in South America:

> There is firstly the close connection between manliness and good health, both physical and moral. . . . There was a widely held belief that a healthy physique was more important than a veneer of social culture. Linked to these concerns was the value of a simple and Spartan life away from the debilitating materialism of the city. . . .   (Mangan and Walvin 99)

However, the detractors of this religious ideal, which they dubbed ''muscular'' Christianity, perceived a glorification of violence in its emphasis on fighting. This inconsistency in the ideal of masculinity is pinpointed by Shirley A. Stave, in her analysis of Hartright's position at the beginning of *The Woman in White*:

> On the one hand, maleness/masculinity is typically associated with authority, with the power to speak and act, with Law, with reason, with the establishment of civilization. On the other hand, it is identified with physical strength, brute force, that which is untamable and uncontrollable, the antithesis of civilization.
>   (Stave 288)

In *The Woman in White* the manly Christian approach is seen to be ultimately untenable, not least because it transfers religious experience to the realm of physical action. Available only to men, it necessarily undervalues the religious lives of women and renders them vulnerable to false judgments. *The Woman in White* demonstrates the limitations of this ethos in regulating and explaining the religious experience of the female Broad Church protagonists, Marian Halcombe and Laura Fairlie. The central but elusive Laura, is perhaps an unlikely symbol of rebellion, being memorably uptstaged by her more robust sister and by the troubling presence of Anne Catherick. But in a novel preoccupied with the ideal of manliness, her feminine experience provides a crucial counterweight to the pronouncements of its male hero. In this context, Laura is as subversive a force as the more celebrated Marian.

The major conflict in the novel takes the form of a battle of wits. Sir Percival and Count Fosco conspire to appropriate Laura Fairlie's fortune, while she and her sister Marian must resist them, through vigilance and cunning. This conflict taking place in the domestic sphere, does not involve immediate physical danger, thereby rendering bodily strength almost irrelevant. Count Focso himself decries violence and displays of temper as a means of coercing Laura, and sets out to defraud her by means of superior intelligence.

Manly religion is therefore shown to be inadequate to the exigencies of Marian's and Laura's situation. As women, they are not able to enact such a role, and when Marian attempts to do so, the removal of her restrictive outer garments leads her, symbolically, to take a fever. There are socially prescribed limits to her sphere of action and in overstepping them, she plays into the hands of her male enemies, as she is later to do in rescuing Laura from the lunatic asylum by illicit means.

Walter Hartright, the manly Christian of the novel, fails to recognize the limitations of his religious position. His preamble begins, however unintentionally, by highlighting a contradiction in the religious code he has embraced. One of the buzz-words of this ideal was "endurance," and he begins by enlisting it on the feminine side, using his wife's patience as a foil to his own more active virtue. Ignoring the moral courage of Marian and Laura, he remarks somewhat complacently that "This is the story of what a Woman's patience can endure, and what a Man's resolution can achieve" (33). Simultaneously celebrating patience as a virtue and subordinating it to resolution, Walter is setting up the dichotomy between male and female that is integral to the manly ideal. In order for Walter to enact the roles of manly Christian, he must be counterpoised by complementary but negative virtues, located in the female characters. As Charles Kingsley outlines it in his novel *Yeast*, the manly Christian possesses intellect and courage and turns to a woman for the gentleness which would be inappropriate in himself. His knight teaches the heroine "where her true kingdom lay—that the heart, and not the brain, enshrines the priceless pearl of womanhood before which gross man can only inquire and adore" (88). However, in associating endurance with patience, Walter is already betraying the inadequacy of a religious ethos that locates specific and separate virtues in each gender.

This apportioning of characters according to gender is questioned in the presentation of the characters themselves. Walter himself has been used to be "admitted among beautiful and captivating women much as a harmless domestic animal is admitted among them" (89). In other words, he is obliged to abandon his masculinity in the presence of his pupils, effectually becoming sexless. Pesca is of small stature and first appears as a comically feminized character, yet it is he who is able to unnerve the count in his role as Secretary of the sinister Brotherhood. The implications of a religious ideal based on gender difference are confronted directly in Walter's reaction to Marian and Laura, as will be seen.

Marian herself is reminiscent of the ideal of manly Christianity. Her masculinity is initially signaled in the references to physical traits such as facial hair; moreover she is described on more than one occasion as possessing supposedly masculine qualities, such as intelligence and courage. But as a woman, Marian is debarred from action. Having been insulted by Sir Percival, she records in her diary:

> If I had been a man, I would have knocked him down on the threshold of his own door.... But I was only a woman—and I loved his wife so dearly!... She knew what I had suffered and what I had suppressed.... (268)

It is this combination of forcefulness and self-control that makes the strength of her character, but a consciousness of her negative status as a woman leads Marian to equate self-control in herself with helpless passivity. Her lack of both fortune and physical attractiveness does allow her a certain licence, and she uses this freedom to approximate herself to the emblem of manly religion, feeling, for instance, that she is in competition with Sir Percival for the guardianship of Laura's welfare. But her power is limited, as she is forced to give way to male counterparts, and the restrictions on her behavior lead to her neurotic contempt for herself as "only a woman." Fulfilling all the necessary criteria for a "manly" hero, she constantly preempts rejection from this role by belittling her own moral status. She outmaneuvers the count and manages to overhear his conversation with Sir Percival, by climbing out of a window in her underwear, only to insist that "My courage was only a woman's courage" (341–42).

Walter perpetuates such assumptions by emphasizing his own growth into a manly Christian. The providential nature of his deliverance from death is made clear by Marian's dream at Blackwater Park, in which he tells her that he will miraculously be saved on three separate occasions. She then sees him escape disease, hostile Indian arrows, and shipwreck. It is within this wider providential context that the characters develop their several views of religion. As in Marian's vision, Walter endures various hardships in Central America and then returns to face the count and Sir Percival. From this point onwards he presents himself as having undergone a religious experience through physical exertion:

> From that self-imposed exile I came back, as I had hoped, prayed, believed I should come back—a changed man. In the waters of a new life I had tempered my nature afresh. In the stern school of extremity and danger my will had learnt to be strong, my heart to be resolute, my mind to rely on itself. (427)

It is significant however that the dream predicting these events is accorded to Marian rather than to Walter himself. Walter's allusions to providence as beckoning him onwards on an unknown journey, stress the inconsistency of his own assumption of authority. Religious truth is not so easy of definition. Running parallel to the enaction of manly religion is an alternative set up by these two sisters.

Marian's passionate and instinctive faith informs her love for her sister, through whom much of her religious ideology is mediated. Laura herself becomes a truly religious figure, embodying active virtue and not simply abstract purity, when she offers mutual forgiveness to a man she now knows to be corrupt. The integrity sustained by both sisters throughout their ordeal at Blackwater Park is shown to be more valuable by far than mere bodily courage.

Marian's religion is romantic and immediate. On meeting Walter again in Limmeridge churchyard, Marian becomes a mediator between him and God, praying, "Father! help him in his hour of need" (431). This is the only moment in Collins's major fiction when a character appeals directly to God as "Father," and it serves to emphasize both Marian's feeling of closeness to God and the idea of his immediate presence in the novel. It is this direct relationship with God that Walter appears to have lost, coming to use religion as a form of self-aggrandizement when Marian's prayer is instinctive and selfless.

However, on Walter's return from South America, Marian is displaced, as he takes over the responsibility for outwitting the count. Marian is now compared to Laura in the descriptions of her wasted arms and haunted eyes, and his reaction to her is notably insensitive. She admonishes him to remember her courage when "the time comes," which in his narrative he claims to have done—in fact, he will not allow her to accompany him to Count Fosco's house, insisting that she stay with Laura. Ignoring her active role in protecting her sister hitherto, Walter now insists on presenting her in mystical terms, as a "good angel." This terminology suggests that Marian is a spectator rather than an active participator in events. In relegating her to the sidelines, Walter imbues her with symbolic purity only at the cost of her active resolution.

This need simultaneously to adore and dismiss qualities such as innocence and purity is shown by both Walter and Marian in their understanding of Laura. Walter encapsulates this inconsistency when he refers to her love for him as "her sacred weakness" (149). Marian too makes Laura a repository for the virtues which she herself disclaims:

> Everybody thinks me crabbed and odd (with perfect justice); and everybody thinks her sweet-tempered and charming (with more justice still). In short, she is an angel; and I am—Try some of that marmalade, Mr Hartright, and finish the sentence, in the name of female propriety, for yourself. (61)

It is this misrepresentation by both Marian and Walter that misleads readers and even whips them into fury with Laura herself. Susan Baleé, who makes a convincing case for the strongminded Marian as subverting the idea of the helpless spinster, contrasts her favorably with her married sister. According to this view, Marian's resolution is emphasized by Laura's weakness, and Laura herself, "who retains her role as angel in the house throughout, is a pathetic character" (204). Nina Auerbach memorably and somewhat subjectively refers to Laura as "nebulous," "incompetent," "vapid," and infantile in the course of three pages in which her character is not even under discussion! (135–38). Sue Lonoff offers the milder view that "Collins tries to emphasise Laura's spiritual qualities; he has Walter praise her integrity and her quiet resolution. But Marian is so markedly superior in force of personality . . ." (143) [that Fosco's positive assessment of her is justified]. Meanwhile Mark M. Hennelly, Jr. dismisses Laura altogether as a "passive damsel in distress" (103). This dismissive, or even hostile, response owes little to the character of Laura herself and a great deal to her presentation by other characters in the novel. As Catherine Peters (who likewise sees her as more childish than angelic) concedes, "Those who seek to exploit her, and those who love her, equally deny her full status as an adult" (222).

Before Laura's marriage, Marian herself adopts the position of "manly" protector of her sister. Every time Laura displays resolution, Marian insists that it is the first occasion on which their roles have been reversed, and perceives the situation as unnatural and unpropitious.

Laura is, in fact, the central religious figure in the novel, partly in her role as mediator of spiritual values (the moral status of each major protagonist is tested specifically in their response to her); furthermore it is Laura whose understanding of religious precepts undergoes the greatest change. At the beginning of the novel her very innocence renders her virtuous behavior less impressive, her secluded existence and watchful sister precluding the threat of temptation. It is her ordeal at the hands of her husband and Count Fosco that invests her with moral authority, allowing her to confront and withstand corruption, where formerly she had been oblivious to its existence.

Laura's complex response to religion has been too long overlooked by those who take at face value the descriptions of her by other characters. The insistence that she remain innocent, as has been suggested, does not initially permit her to develop an active faith. Even Anne Catherick, whose simplicity permits her to see visions as Marian does, dreams of Laura in company with an angel marrying Sir Percival standing by a devil. In this simplistic view of a completely pure Laura, the angel is insufficient to save her and is seen to be weeping.

Laura has been brought up in a sheltered environment, in which her accession of knowledge is regarded as "profanity"; this in itself is shown to be damaging. Her nervous gestures betray the difficulty with which she sustains her angelic image, and yet she is not equipped to deal with life outside Limmeridge. As Philip O'Neill puts it:

> It is Laura's tragedy that she too easily accepts appearance for reality and does not recognise the danger of always accepting things at face value. This does not mean that she belongs to the corrupt world of appearance but rather represents the Edenic world where appearances and reality do coincide. (100)

This is the danger of her upbringing, that she is not able to distinguish between truth and falsehood. Her code of morals is noble, but inadequate to the situation in which Sir Percival places her. In confessing to him that she loves another man, she gives him an opportunity to force her into marriage by praising her rectitude and insisting that he will try to be worthy of it.

Ultimately, Laura must adopt a more complex religious stance, through an encounter with "fallen" human nature outside Limmeridge. Her marriage to the villainous Sir Percival forces her to come to terms with a world less heroic than she had assumed it to be. Throughout her vicissitudes she retains her own goodness, but she finds it necessary to conceal the realities of her relationship with her husband for as long as possible. Not only does she seek to preserve Marian's view of her as untainted; she has learned to be self-sufficient and wants to protect her sister's peace of mind. This growing awareness of corruption, as Sir Percival repeatedly accuses her of ignoble behavior, allows her to show true Christian mercy and humility. Her experience at Blackwater Park allows her to show a more mature commitment to religious principles than has hitherto been practicable. Her sacrifice of herself in marriage was undoubtedly noble, but her last conversation with her husband is more admirable yet. Leaving him to go to London, she says unaffectedly, "Will you try to forgive me, Percival, as heartily as I forgive you?" (Collins 408). This practical demonstration of Christian virtue has a marked effect on the sanctimonious housekeeper, whose citing of religious precepts is temporarily quelled. She admits that:

> I thought of saying a few comforting and Christian words to the poor lady, but there was something in her face, as she looked after her husband when the door closed on him, that made me alter my mind and keep silence. (409)

Significantly, Laura makes no reply when Mrs. Michelson recovers sufficiently to inform her that we all have our cross to bear. Mrs. Michelson, the widow of a clergyman, represents a comic version of what was Laura's own reliance on simplistic precepts before her marriage. Laura now affects her to the point where she begins to question her own maxims, and cannot concentrate on her husband's collection of sermons. Inspired by Laura's example in enacting the religious ideal on a personal level, she starts to imbue practical acts of charity with religious worth, taking over the nursing of Marian. Trite proverbs are now replaced with "hope" and "belief" in a practical religion, as she writes:

The precious blessings of religious consolation which I endeavoured to convey were long in reaching Miss Halcombe's heart, but I hope and believe they came home to her at last. I never left her till her strength was restored.   (419)

Laura is shown at this point to inspire religious feeling in others not only through her symbolic purity, but also through her response to adversity. Marian's perplexed references to her will-power and resilience make it clear that she finds this aspect of her sister's personality threatening. But the passive resistance shown by Laura is an appropriate and practicable female alternative to manly Christianity. She is able to defend herself against the machinations of her husband and the count, by refusing to betray her own principles. Keeping within the bounds of propriety, she stymies the plan to rob her by refusing to sign a document she has not read, and of which she might be ashamed. In so doing she redefines feminine virtue, emphasizing the positive value of inaction as passive resistance to corruption, while feminine submission becomes a self-control capable of turning the other cheek. Jenny Bourne Taylor notices this relationship between passive resistance and self-control, though she rather unfairly attributes it solely to Marian: "It becomes a subtle form of female resistance—the way that patience can be turned into resolution". (125). Nor will Marian and Walter acknowledge this transition as it applies to Laura, and attempt to reinstate her in her former simplistically innocent role. No compromise is allowed, because in upholding the ethos of specifically manly Christianity, Walter requires the defenseless counterpart without which his role as protector would become redundant. It is essential to his religious understanding that Laura should maintain a passive innocence seemingly without effort. Only by containing his wife's purity within his own more active virtue, can he envisage a balance between the complementary positive and negative elements of religion. Barbara Fass Leavy explains this complex issue in terms of a "splitting in the Victorian mentality which, in order to protect its feminine ideal, had to keep her free of, on one side, the sexuality and intellect of one sister, and, on the other side, the maturity that comes from a confrontation with pain and suffering" (130). Laura's increased maturity is pointedly ignored by her husband and sister, who attribute any change in her to the effects of a mental collapse.

In adopting such a rigid view of religion, Walter becomes brutalized and loses the "feminine" sensitivity which had been so obvious in him during his time at Limmeridge. In assuming the ethos of manly Christianity, Walter has lost the power he previously possessed to empathize with Laura in particular, and he is no longer personally receptive to religious influences. This loss of receptivity is masked by his citation of providential deliverance as a sign of special favor.

From thousands on thousands of miles away—through forest and wilderness, where companions stronger than I had fallen by my side, through peril of death

> thrice renewed, and thrice escaped, the Hand that leads men on the dark road
> to the future had led me to meet that time.   (Collins 435)

Significantly, he perceives a link between his deliverance from death and
Laura's vulnerability—now that she is divested of her identity, he is able to
fight on her behalf in the manly tradition. In locating strength in himself
rather than in God, he further loses his humility and even the sense of humor
on which it was based. According to Collins, it is in this arrogation of power
and moral judgment that the primary danger of manly Christianity lies.

At the temporal level, it is also potentially damaging to individuals. Laura's
position as the mediator of religious values places her under enormous pressure, as the figure of female virtue who must inspire the more active characters. She is a symbol of religious purity, and as such she must live up to the
expectations of those around her in order to provide a focus for their faith.
Marian declares quite specifically that she believes in Laura as she believes
in her religion (97). It is the stress of these expectations that is betrayed in
her longstanding nervous habits, the contraction round her mouth and her
restless hands. Walter takes on the same nervous twitch in his face as he is
forced to leave her, a link with the sensitive Laura that is wrongly interpreted
by Gilmore as a sign that he is losing his moral character. Before he leaves
Limmeridge Walter senses "something wanting. At one time it seemed like
something wanting in her: at another, like something wanting in myself, which
hindered me from understanding her as I ought" (77). He later comes to
connect this "lack of something" with Laura's resemblance to Anne Catherick, which is strengthened by her ordeals in the later stages of the novel. But
in coming to embody the manly Christian hero, he has lost his "feminine"
powers of intuition, and fails to comprehend that he himself perpetuates the
likeness by imposing such a stringent role on her. The appearance of something "lacking" in Laura is traceable to the onus she is under to repress
aspects of her character which are incompatible with her angelic status. On
his last night at Limmeridge Walter comes close to comprehending this repression, if only in relation to her love for him:

> The cold fingers that trembled round mine—the pale cheeks, with a bright red
> spot burning the midst of them—the faint smile that struggled to live on her
> lips and died away from them while I looked at it, told me at what sacrifice of
> herself her outward composure was maintained.   (143)

Similarly, Marian can acknowledge her sister's self-control only in the specific terms of her love for Walter. She is surprised by the "passive force"
she displays and does not see it as extending beyond the sphere of her relations
with Walter and Sir Percival.

She is repulsed by the idea of Laura's future role as the sexual partner of

Sir Percival, and describes her as having lost her innocence when she has had this side of marital relations explained to her. However this encounter seems never to have taken place, as Sir Percival himself implies in his declaration that she is not likely to have children. Laura's innocence is essential to her emblematic religious role, and Sir Percival's exclusion from the possibility of redemption is made clear when he refuses to believe in it. Accusing her publicly of having had improper relations with Walter before her marriage, he tells the count that he believes in "nothing about her but her money" (353–54). This cynicism emphasizes Sir Percival's corruption and reminds the reader of the symbolic purity of his wife, in relation to whom he is tested. But this mystical status means that Laura cannot be allowed to deviate from the parameters that have been set up for her. Unlike Marian, she cannot indulge in displays of temper, nor is she allowed to betray imperfections by representing herself in a diary. After her marriage she maintains a steady reserve, refusing to divulge the humiliations inflicted on her by her brutal husband, for fear of distressing her sister.

Only on the borderline between sanity and insanity can she emulate marginalized figures such as Anne Catherick, becoming at once a more complex and more threatening figure. This disintegration of social identity does not simply disempower Laura by reducing her to "a persecuted alien" with a "death wish" (Knoepflmacher 62) as her detractors often suggest. Released from the confines of her emblematic purity, she is able to relinquish responsibility for sustaining the others' belief. As Catherine Peters suggests:

> The fear of losing complete possession of oneself is a fundamental one; but it often carries with it a secret sense of exhilaration. To be another person, for a while at least, can be liberating as well as terrifying.   (212)

Appearing by her own gravestone, she takes on a ghostly dimension, and Marian seeks to spare Walter the sight of her face. Walter later recalls Laura's appeal to be taken seriously in language that seems to condemn her for making it: "I raised her head, and smoothed away the tangled hair that fell over her face and kissed her—my poor, faded flower! My lost, afflicted sister!" (Collins 499). This declaration employs the evangelical language of ineluctable damnation, at the moment of Laura's only rebellion.

In becoming a manly hero Walter has been obliged to substitute assertiveness and self-preservation for humility and self-denial. He comes to rely more on himself than on God, revelling as he does in his newfound physical and mental prowess. It is no coincidence that he begins to make judgments about other characters at this point, pondering with satisfaction that it is not for him to say that the count will escape judgment, and describing Laura as a "lost sister." In mediating his religious beliefs through his own resolution, and through Laura's perceived patience, Walter comes to fulfil the ideal of manliness in its specifically religious sense. However, in so doing he embraces a religious code that is not simply inadequate but potentially damaging. Too liberal an adherence to the manly Christian code induces Hartright to assume an inappropriate degree of spiritual authority and renders him insensible to his wife's religious development. *The Woman in White* suggests that the scope of this manly ideal should be extended, allowing female characters to participate in the inner renewal, or development through experience, that Collins regarded as essential to religious experience. It was a theme to which he would return in later novels, through the more ambiguous figures of Magdalen Vanstone and Lydia Gwilt.

WORKS CITED

Auerbach, Nina. *Woman and the Demon: The Life of a Victorian Myth.* Cambridge, Massachusetts: Harvard UP, 1982.

Balee, Susan. "Wilkie Collins and Surplus Women: The Case of Marian Halcombe." *Victorian Literature and Culture* 20 (1992): 197–215.

Buckley, Jerome H., ed. *The Worlds of Victorian Fiction.* Cambridge: Harvard UP, 1975.

Collins, Wilkie. *The Woman in White.* Middlesex: Penguin, 1974.

Hennelly, Mark M., Jr. "Reading Detection in *The Woman in White.*" In *Wilkie Collins: Contemporary Critical Essays.* Ed. Lynn Pykett. Hampshire, UK: Macmillan, 1998.

Kingsley, Charles. *Yeast.* Stroud: Alan Sutton, 1994.

Knoepflmacher, U.C. "Wilkie Collins's Cinderella: The History of Psychology and *The Woman in White.*" In *The Worlds of Victorian Fiction.* Ed. Jerome H. Buckley. Cambridge: Harvard UP, 1975.

Leavy, Barbara Fass. "Wilkie Collins's Cinderella: The History of Psychology and *The Woman in White.*" *Dickens Studies Annual* 10 (1982): 91–141.

Lonoff. Sue. *Wilkie Collins and His Readers: A Study in The Rhetoric of Authorship.* New York: AMS, 1982.

O'Neill, Philip. *Wilkie Collins: Women, Property and Propriety.* London: Macmillan, 1988.

Peters, Catherine. *The King of Inventors: A Life of Wilkie Collins.* London: Secker and Warburg, 1991.

Pykett, Lynn, ed. *Wilkie Collins: Contemporary Critical Essays.* Hampshire Macmillan, 1998.

Stave, Shirley A. "The Perfect Murder: Patterns of Repetition and Doubling in Wilkie Collins's *The Woman in White." Dickens Studies Annual* 25 (1996): 287–303.

Taylor, Jenny Bourne. *In the Secret Theatre of Home: Wilkie Collins, Sensation Narrative and Nineteenth Century Psychology.* London: Routledge, 1988.

Warren, Allen. "Popular Manliness: Baden-Powell, Scouting and the Development of Manly Character." In *Manliness and Morality: Middle-class Masculinity in Britain and America, 1800–1940.* Manchester: Manchester University Press, 1987.

A Forgotten Collaboration of the 1860s: Charles Reade, Robert Barnes, and the Illustrations for *Put Yourself in His Place*

Simon Cooke

Charles Reade enjoyed manipulating his illustrators. Believing that artists should be subservient, he routinely imposed authorial control over his collaborators. Expecting to be obeyed, he bullied his illustrators into giving him precisely the effects he demanded. More challenging, however, is the partnership between Reade and Robert Barnes, the artist employed to illustrate the serialized version of Reade's lurid attack on trades-unionism, Put Yourself in His Place. *Barnes's illustrations are important, for they combine a careful adherence to Reade's directions with a more personal and imaginative response. Highlighting Reade's emphasis on melodrama and realism, and always insisting on the fiction's curious combination of theatricality and journalism, the artist further develops his own, more sensitive interpretations of character, the class conflict, and emotional relationships. Infusing a note of psychological complexity, he visualizes the characters not only as melodramatic types, but as individuals of sensibility. Barnes's illustrations are thus presented as complex mediations in which the text is both respected and extended, confirmed and enhanced. Largely overlooked, the illustrations strongly suggest that the best response is produced not when the artist is controlled, but when he is free to interpret. At once faithful and imaginative, Barnes's designs are models of sixties illustration, and bear comparison with the best of Millais.*

Dickens Studies Annual, Volume 30, Copyright © 2001 by AMS Press, Inc. All rights reserved.

Charles Reade was fascinated by the engravings which routinely accompanied the serialized novels of the 1860s. His interest, as a discerning connoisseur (Compton Reade 2: 305), was partly a matter of personal taste. He enjoyed looking at good examples of black and white, and used his *Picture Book* (ms, now in the Parrish Collection, Princeton University) to collect graphic designs by J. D. Watson, Fred Walker, and Ellen Edwards. More important, he was deeply concerned with the functions of illustration: what it could do, and how it should be used. His views on this subject were forceful, if not particularly original. Reaffirming the position of Dickens and Trollope, his central belief was that illustrators should always be the subordinates of authors, producing images that clarify, focus, and generally "promote" the characteristics of the text (Trollope 1: 199). As he explains in a letter to Ticknor and Fields (the American publishers who were struggling to find a designer for *It is Never Too Late To Mend*), the artist must always "draw in the same Key" and must never miss the "point" of the author's intention (2 November 1855, Burns, *Charles Reade* 151).

This philosophy pervades Reade's critique of the composite text and is realized in his dealings with the artists who illustrated his own set of novels. Indeed, he did his best to manipulate their activities. Sometimes a bully, and always strident and obtuse, he was determined to take control and force the designers to provide him with exactly what he wanted. He imposed an iron grip on the work of Matt Stretch, one of the artists entrusted with the illustration of *Good Stories*. Stipulating what he should illustrate and which qualities should be stressed, his directions were specific and his judgments outspoken (Parrish 269). He was almost as forceful in his dealings with Edward Hughes (Nowell-Smith 94), the illustrator of "A Terrible Temptation" (*Cassell's Magazine* 1871), and was downright insulting to Charles Keene, whose illustrations for "A Good Fight" (*Once a Week* 1859) he tersely condemned as "paltry" (Pantazzi 44). Always aiming to impose his will, no matter how "impracticable" (Burns, *Charles Reade* 151) his demands might be, Reade was generally regarded as a hard taskmaster.

However, the desire to control was not always realized as completely as he might have wished. More complicated is the collaboration with one of the most interesting practitioners of sixties black and white, Robert Barnes (1840–95).[1] Principally known as an "Idyllic" designer of rural scenes and quaint interiors (Goldman 137–38), Barnes provided a series of striking designs for Reade's Sensational attack on the unions, *Put Yourself in His Place* (*The Cornhill Magazine* 1869–70). This collaboration is problematic because it embraces authorial control while also demonstrating its limitations. By all accounts, Barnes was difficult to manage, for although his images are responsive to the author's demands, underscoring key elements in his text, he makes his own visualizations as well. Oscillating between illustration and interpretation, observance of authorial desire and his own imaginings, he clarifies the novel while simultaneously enriching and extending it.

The result is a composite text of unusual depth and complexity: a dense interplay of image and word in which the illustrations, in the form of full-page designs and initials, confirm and expand the written material. Yet, perhaps surprisingly, this "important" collaboration (Goldman 138) has never been analyzed. The illustrations are mentioned by Reid (257) and again by Goldman (138), both of whom are impressed by the "sustained" quality (Goldman 138) of the artist's "bold" (Reid 257) and vigorous designs. But neither of these comments constitutes a critique and, in contrast to the attention directed at his work for Hardy's *The Mayor of Casterbridge* (*The Graphic* 1886), which Arlene Jackson has examined at length (96–105), Barnes's images for Reade are virtually a critical blank. This article sets out to provide a detailed account of their multifaceted partnership. I will focus on how Barnes was manipulated by Reade's directions, and how, despite authorial instructions, he manages to re-visualize. In Reade's own terms, I will examine how the artist "takes up the tale," "speaks" for the author, and "for himself" (Reade to Ticknor and Fields, 2 November 1855, Burns, *Charles Reade* 151).

Reade's intention to manipulate Barnes is evidenced from the very beginning of their relationship, in January of 1869 (ms letter from Reade to Smith, 16 January 1869, Murray Archive, John Murray, London). Introduced to the artist by George Smith, who may have selected Barnes on the basis of his faithful illustrations for a novel by Frederick Greenwood, *Margaret Denzil's History* (*Cornhill Magazine* 1863–64), Reade immediately took control of the situation by organizing a series of "consultative" meetings between himself and "his" designer. In this he was greatly encouraged by the *Cornhill's* proprietor. Anxious to appease the author, whom he had tried to employ since the launching of *The Cornhill* in 1859 (Smith 2: 10–11), Smith allowed Reade to manipulate Barnes, prepare him for the first instalment (March 1869) and generally determine how the illustrations should proceed.[2]

Reade's primary aim was to identify areas of correspondence between the artist's visual style and his own. As noted earlier, Reade believed successful illustration could only proceed from the equivalence of image and word; upholding this belief, he actively sought those elements of Barnes's art that chimed with his own and, appropriately directed, could help to interpret the central concerns of *Put Yourself in His Place*. This process was far from problematic, for Barnes was in many ways an ideal collaborator, with a range of interests which well-equipped him to illustrate Reade's lurid text. For example, Reade must have noted that Barnes was adept at representing the bourgeois idyll (as it is shown in his work for *The Leisure Hour*, 1864, *London Society*, 1862–65 and elsewhere), while also being concerned (in

Pictures of English Life, 1865, and *The British Workman*, 1869–71) with the proletariat. Able to shift seamlessly between classes, between bourgeois interiors and images of (sentimentalized) poverty, Barnes was not likely to be troubled by the alternation between masters and men (or, more accurately, respectable middle class and agitator) which structures the author's text. His experience as the illustrator of Wood's (Ellen Price's) *Oswald Cray* (*Good Words* 1864–65) had also equipped him with a knowledge of the racy conventions of Sensational prose, and Reade could be confident of his understanding of this type of novel.

But Reade was most interested in two primary elements lying at the heart of Barnes's design: the commitment to "realism" (as it is manifested in the exactitude of his drawing and its Pre-Raphaelite attention to detail), and the fascination with melodramatic gesture (Goldman 138). As far as Reade was concerned this combination of realism and theater was vital because it exactly matches the fusion of opposites that would form the central device of *Put Yourself in His Place*. Focusing on this sharing of interests, Reade realized he could use the artist's fascination with these qualities as a means of elucidating his own. This is precisely what he did. Directing Barnes towards the combinations appearing in the text, he imposed authorial control while also exploiting his illustrator's interests. Indeed, he did his best—short of selecting what Barnes should illustrate, and there is no evidence to suggest he ever went this far—to direct his partner toward the visualization of these key ingredients. This process took the form of practical preparations in the weeks before the first instalment, to be published in March 1869, was handed to the artist.

To focus Barnes's mind on melodramatic gesture, Reade provided him with advance details of the most striking incidents, and insisted he should emphasize the novel's rhetorical business. Believing that the best illustrations "present a stage situation" which could easily be "transplanted to the theatre" and form a striking "tableau" (Burns, *Charles Reade* 347), he highlighted this concern as the primary means of expressing what he elsewhere describes as "dramatic power" (Parrish 269). He was equally determined to focus Barnes's mind on the novel's factual basis. Having spent some years researching the industrial conflict in Sheffield (Compton Reade 2: 194; Burns, "Sheffield Flood" 687–88), he insisted the illustrations should reflect a parallel knowledge. A stickler for verisimilitude, who fervently believed in the value of "diligence and research" (ms letter to Ticknor and Fields, 21 July 1855, Huntington Library), Reade wanted the designs to be based on a close observation of the novel's "real" setting. To that end, he took his illustrator on a reconnaissance trip to Sheffield where, on 19 and 20 January 1869, they conducted research by looking at the buildings and the condition of the people. Of course, this was bound to be superficial; but it provided the artist with journalistic opportunities to observe the manners, customs, and settings of the urban proletariat. Directed to "cull" the "Truth" (ms letter to Smith, 19 January 1869, Morris L. Parrish Collection, Princeton University, published with permission of the Library), Barnes was empowered to fill his mind with images of industry—images which formed a strong contrast to the idealized versions of the rural poor appearing in *Pictures of English Life* and (the author hoped) provided him with a visual frame of reference for use in the illustrations.

So Barnes was carefully directed as to what the author expected of his work for *Put Yourself in His Place*. Highlighting the nexus of theater and verisimilitude, Reade challenges his artist to revisualize the "melodramatic realism" (Burns, "Cloister & Hearth" 76) located at the heart of his (and all) Sensational novels. Barnes's response was rigorously professional: faithfully adhering to the author's directions, he underscores the fiction's Sensational paradox, giving equal emphasis to the notations of the stage and to the author's obsession with the "documentary evidence" (Swinburne 301) of the every-day. This combination occupies a central part of the illustrations, although (as we shall see) it is only a part of his overall response.

Barnes foregrounds the interest in gesture by showing the characters as if they were literally actors—thespians who move in a series of stage-like spaces and, at moments of great emotional intensity, freeze into gestural tableaux. He particularly stresses moments of conflict and recoil, when the personae are forced to respond to a moment of surprise or an unexpected meeting. This visualization crystallizes the directions in the text, and amplifies the characters' dramatic emotions by showing their gestures with an almost schematic precision. For example, in the meeting between Mrs. Little and Dr. Amboyne, the artist highlights their feelings of surprise by visualising a classic "start": a moment of melodramatic recoil in which the characters stare at each other's faces while the doctor raises his hands and Mrs. Little begins to raise hers (*Cornhill* 19: fp [facing page] 513; fig. 1). Described by Reade as a climax of "astonishment" (19: 520), the incident's theatricality is under-scored by the composition's static power. The illustrations further provide distinct representations of the emotionalized conflict between Henry and the agitators. Thus, in the confrontation between Henry and his tormentors Tucker and Simmons, the artist stresses once again the gestures of re-coil—with the workmen stepping back, with upraised arms, from Henry's cool and intimidating gaze (20: fp 257).

The most powerful designs, however, are those representing the sufferings of Grace. These take the form of veritable show-stoppers, gestural tableaux in which Grace's role as a melodramatic heroine is emphasized by the images' obsessive mapping of her inner despair. So, when she thinks she has lost her father's approval she is shown kneeling in front of Carden in a gesture of

Fig. 1. "It was the Woman He Had Loved, the Only One."

pleading (20: fp 641): an image sharply recreating the author's insistence on her looking into her father's face, with eyes "imploring, streaming . . . . wild" (20: 658). Grace's despair on losing Henry (or thinking she has lost him) is likewise conveyed by the melodramatic gestures of hiding the face (21: fp 386), drooping (initial letter, 386) and couch-bound prostration (21: fp 257; fig. 2). Attitudinizing wherever she can, the Grace of the illustrations is indeed a product of the stage, a character whose essential theatricality is vividly conveyed by Barnes's dense and melodramatic designs.

Yet this emotionalized turmoil is framed by a rigorous observation of Readian "facts." For although Barnes presents the characters as melodramatic actors, their settings are "realistic." Remembering what he had seen in Sheffield, the artist is careful to reproduce the urban milieu. This is partly visualized in the form of tangible exteriors—a good example being the crowded yard outside Cheetham's workshop (19: fp 385)—although it is clinched by the careful replication of the workshops' interiors. Barnes treats these interiors as catalogues of things, Pre-Raphaelite spaces containing all sorts of industrial gear, from grindstone and gearing to treadle and forge (19: fp 641; 20: fp 278). Developing the author's spare descriptions, he stresses the materiality, the "thingness" of their contents. He also recreates the details of the middle-class interiors, so underscoring the contrast between the comfort of the Cardens, and the rudimentary world of Henry and the workers.

In both domains the illustrations act as a registration of the "real", that roots the fiction in the contemporary world and, as Reade intended, provides a graphic equivalent to his journalistic treatment of detail, characters, and events (see Burns, "Sheffield Flood," 687–88). Finely balanced against the illustrations' emphasis on rhetorical gesture, the details of each scene provide a sort of validation, in effect a "making real" of what is otherwise theatrical. In fact there are numerous designs in which reality and theater are fused in a perfect equilibrium. When Grace collapses in Henry's workshop (*Cornhill* 20: fp 129; fig. 3), the illustration combines a distinct tableau with details of unusual clarity. Showing Henry as he leans over the prostrate Grace, holds her hand and looks at the "sight of her helpless condition," it gives equal emphasis to the "white heat" of the forge (20: 150), the tools placed on its rim, the monumental anvil in the far background, and the bellows.

Designed as a mediation between the melodramatic moment of emotional crisis and the hard facts of the here and now, this image typifies the re-visualisation of Reade's "melodramatic realism." The overall effect is one of intensification, of focusing the reader's mind on passionate events taking place in material settings. Condensing Reade's theater of the real, the artist reaffirms what contemporary reviewers described as the novel's combination of "dramatic positions" and "naturalness" (" Put Yourself," *Examiner* 11 June 1870: 373), "startling incidents," and "forcible descriptions" ("Put

Fig. 2. "A Sigh of Horror was Uttered on the Veranda"

Fig. 3. '' He Then Darted Back to Her''

Yourself,'' *Saturday Review* 11 June 1870: 778). Barnes's designs are conceived, in short, as powerful instruments, striking examples of black and white that infuse the text with the emotionalized physicality of propaganda. They may even have helped to make the novel a "great sensation" (Coleman 312), which, if Coleman is to be believed, ultimately led to the author receiving death-threats from Sheffield trade-unionists (321).

More telling from an artistic point of view is the author's approval of Barnes's work. Although he checked every proof before it was published (see ms letter from Reade to Smith, February 1869, Murray Archive), Reade had to admit that Barnes had generally adhered to his brief. As the author remarks in a letter to Smith, in which he evaluates "Honest Work," the design for the opening number (*Cornhill* 19: fp 257; fig.4), the effect is a good combination of drama and fact. He expresses minor concern about the lack of detail in the treatment of the foreground, but overall he proclaims himself "satisfied" (ms letter to Smith, 8 February 1869, Murray Archive). Yet Reade also recognized the artist's desire to experiment. Looking at "Honest Work," he particularly highlights the lack of an exact correspondence between the image and the scene it is supposed to present (ms letter to Smith, 16 February 1869, Murray Archive), but accepts the design (actually a conflation of two situations: *Cornhill* 19: 274; 19: 390) as being fundamentally true to the text. Perhaps surprisingly, Reade is tolerant of his artist's manipulations, and (in contrast to his tyrannies elsewhere) allows that "Honest Work" has "been changed (very happily) by Mr B" (ms letter to Smith, 16 February 1869, Murray Archive). Recognizing Barnes had given him what he wanted, Reade appears to accept that the result of this artistic freedom might well be an enhancement of the text—a grafting on of new ways of reading.

Indeed, "Honest Work" (fig. 4) epitomizes the artist's approach. Produced, as Reade might remark, in the "best possible spirit" (ms letter to Smith, 16 January 1869, Murray Archive), it acts as a faithful illustration and as a visual link between unconnected scenes. At once a complement to the text, it opens up new territories of imaginative response. This interpretive approach is more generally developed in illustrations which foreground aspects of the novel that are latent or half-submerged. Focusing on subtexts, selecting and rearranging material, highlighting aspects of style and drawing out themes, Barnes greatly expands the often limiting terms of his original instructions from Reade.

The illustrator is particularly interested in the development of Reade's middle-class characters. Minimizing the novel's "venomous" attack on the unions (Brantlinger 51), it foregrounds its central concern with the drama of the middle class. This interest is important, for Reade's characters are poor material. Usually condemned as conventionalized types, and always displaying what Burns had described as an embarrassing "lack of psychological

Fig. 4. "Honest Work"

depth'' (Burns, ''Cloister & Hearth'' 80), the characters' primary expression, as we have seen, is realized in the form of melodramatic gesture. However, Barnes revisualizes these personae as individuals of feeling and complexity. Adding another dimension to the characters' theatricality by providing a series of illustrations running in parallel to the images of stage-like excess, he rewrites the personae as individuals of psychological resonance.

This deepening is partly achieved by enhancing the author's portraiture. Developing the terse directions given in the text, he endows the characters with facial detail which, as Arlene Jackson remarks, is ''highly individualised'' (96). As in his later work for Hardy's *The Mayor of Casterbridge*, distinctive faces are used to suggest distinctive states of mind. His technique is exemplified by the illustration showing the face of Mrs. Little (fig. 1). This carefully develops the outer signs of suffering; conventionally described as having a worn but ''beautiful'' face (*Cornhill* 19: 520), she is revisualized as a troubled ascetic with an aging complexion—witnessed by unflattering lines (20: fp 1)—and black and piercing eyes. Reade's description would barely suggest her troubled past; but Barnes's portrait, with its unidealized directness, certainly does. The psychological profiles of Grace, Henry and especially Jael are likewise suggested by their distinctive faces, and this effect is enhanced by the consistency of detail so that portraits remain the same over the period of serialization (March 1869–July 1870). By looking at Barnes's designs we gain a sense of looking through an album of faces that we ultimately know, and read, as tangible manifestations of plausible characters (see 19: fp 257; 20: fp 129; 20: fp 385) .

This individuation takes us some of the way, but the characters' complexity is particularly suggested through the working of the gaze. Adhering to the mid-Victorian belief, as voiced by theorists such as Lavater (53–58) and Bell (101–02), that the eye was the window of the soul, the artist endows the personae with types of ''significant'' gaze which poetically suggest their traits of mind and emotional condition. Developing, modifying, and rearranging the author's mentions of the look, as well as providing new information of his own, he invests the personae with a depth of feeling that is either lacking or undeveloped in Reade's text. Barnes's versions of Reade's dramatis personae are thus infused with a new intensity; compelled to gaze, glance, peer, stare or squint, their inner lives are inscribed in their look and the way they look at each other.

The process of manipulating the ''significant gaze'' is typified by the emphasis on the ''look'' of Jael Dence. Barnes uses this look to highlight the character's inner conflict between duty and love. When she appears in ''Honest Work'' (*Cornhill* 19: fp 257; fig. 4), her status as a trustworthy servant is clearly shown by Barnes's replication of her huge ''orbs'' (19: 274) and ''candid'' look (19, 272). Yet the illustration also shows her looking intently at Little's turned back. This is not at all the "shy glance" (19: 390) of Reade's "demure" character, but a "look of concentration" (19: 272) which foregrounds her attraction to and desire to be noticed by the man who will eventually become her mistress's lover. What Barnes does, in other words, is rearrange the details of Jael's gaze so that miscellaneous descriptions from the text are recombined to create a focused representation of the conflict between serving Grace and falling in love with Little. Compelled to scrutinize the intimacy of Henry and Grace as they work (ironically enough) on a carving of her head, Jael's turmoil is elegantly evoked, within the frame of a single illustration, by the workings of her honest but obsessive gaze.

Looking similarly acts to focus Grace's emotional conflict as she falls in love with Little. Using the gaze as a sort of chart, Barnes demonstrates how Grace progresses through a series of overwhelming feelings. When she first appears she is endowed with an inward look of concentration (19: 257; fig.4), so stressing her interest in her work while also suggesting a sort of coy awareness of Little as he bends over her. This gives way to intense representations of tenderness (when she looks at the picture of Henry's mother, 20: fp 385), pleading (in her gazing at her father, 20: fp 641), despair (21: fp 258; fig. 2), registered in her downcast gaze, and finally terror, as it is registered in the fixed gaze of her staring eyes (22: fp 1). Highlighting Grace's look as the index of her soul, Barnes cleverly provides a portrait of mind, a series of focused representations which greatly extend the idea of this character as just another beauty. Although he shows her as a melodramatic type, whose emotions, as we have seen, are given a vivid if simplified representation in the showing of her attitudes, Barnes's emphasis on her gaze infuses the character with another level of meaning. At once a gesturing actress, Grace can also be read as a character of intense and internalized feeling.

So can the character of Little. Endowed with varieties of gaze that extend or (on a few occasions) contradict the author's descriptions, Barnes's characterization is a radical transformation of the author's original. Reade's Henry Little is passionate and impulsive; possessing a piercing gaze and "black eye" (19: 390), his tendency to extremes is stressed by his gazing at his lover's face (20: 150), and by his "angry" (20: 278) confrontation of his enemies at the forge. Barnes's Little, on the other hand, is far more restrained. Adopting a reflective sort of look (Collins 360), his gaze is self-absorbed rather than passionate, introspective rather than energetic. When he takes tea with his mother and Jael, for instance (20: fp 513; fig. 5), his gaze is abstracted, implying a stillness of mind. A self-directed expression is similarly used to imply his inwardness when he explains his inventions (21: fp 1), and when he contemplates his mother examining the wooden bust (20: fp 1). He is equally cool when he gazes at the prostrate Grace; lacking the tears described in the text, his look is restrained, and, by its very undemonstrativeness,

Fig. 5. "I am a General Leading My Amazons"

far more convincing as a representation of mind than Reade's sentimental excess (20: fp 129; fig.3). Indeed, Barnes's revisualization of Little greatly deepens his psychological authenticity. Converted from a "resourceful hero" into a thinker (Burns, "Cloister & Hearth" 78), the character is validated by Barnes's providing him with an added sense of self-possession and gravitas.

Freed from the melodramatic trappings of eyes which flash "black lightning" (*Cornhill* 19: 387)—the only visualized "flashing" of the eyes being reserved for the climactic rescue (22: fp 1)—the Little of the illustrations has a depth beyond the original letterpress. His self-directed gaze works in another sense as a reassignment of class: for although Little is supposed to be an able workman, albeit with a wealthier background, Barnes accentuates his look as a signifier of bourgeois restraint. Keeping his gaze to himself, Barnes's Little is configured as a John Halifax who is motivated by the "refined" emotions of the "respectable" middle class, and is always a gentleman. This point is interesting, for, as Jane Seel has established, Barnes was himself self-made, and came from humble stock.[3] Born of a shoemaker and an illiterate mother, he may have identified with the fiction's toiler in art, validating his own station in life by making his counterpart as respectable as possible. There is certainly a close resemblance between Little's solemn looks and Barnes's intent gaze, as it is shown in a photograph of the artist in his twenties (fig. 6, collection of Jane Seel). As dark and introspective as his creator, Little is perhaps a portrait of the artist as a young man, with the artist's powerful eye and habit of inward analysis.

We can be sure, as these detailed examples have revealed, that Barnes uses the "significant look" to focus attention on the personae's inner lives. By highlighting the gaze, the artist cleverly develops the characters of Henry, Grace, and Jael, infusing them with a depth and complexity which is otherwise lacking in the emphasis on theater. The gaze acts, in other words, to stress the introspective. It is equally useful as a means of visualizing the characters' emotional relationships.

Barnes manipulates the "look" as a sign of the interconnectedness between the main players. More particularly, it works as a token of difference, with middle-class characters adopting one way of looking at each other, and workers another. Within the bourgeoisie the intent gaze always suggests intimacy, or the desire to be intimate. In "Honest Work", Grace and Little are drawn together as they scrutinize her attempts to carve (19: fp 257; fig. 4). Described by Reade as a "pretty picture" of "mischievous" love (19: 390), Barnes's design is a moment of overwhelming intensity in which the characters' fascination with each other is elegantly shown by the shy interaction of looks. The intimate relationship between Grace and her father is similarly visualized when she glances up at him and pleads with him about the possibility of marrying her hero (20: fp 641). These characters are united, in short, by a

Fig. 6. Carte de visite portrait of Robert Barnes, circa 1868. Unknown photographer.

loving gaze: a visual engagement that links their faces and (as in Barnes's nexus of looks in *Pictures of English Life*) draws them together. However, this type of harmonious gaze is markedly at odds with the look attributed to the proletariat. For while the bourgeoisie are unified by the look of love, the workers'/agitators' gaze is literally repulsive, and pushes the characters apart. Thus, in "Mind Thyself" (20: fp 257), the glaring eyes of Little and Simmons (20: 277) create a moment of recoil which is only counterbalanced by Henry's coolness. Likewise in the illustration showing the blown-up Little hanging from the window (19: fp 385; fig.7), the artist places the strongest emphasis on the disconnected staring of the terrified workmen. Described only as characters "running wildly in the yard" (19: 405), Barnes's workmen enact a chaos of discontinuous gazing in which the looks emanate in all directions and give a visual representation of chaos.

Alternating between these moments of desperation and calm, Barnes's treatment of the gaze is systematically organized. His illustrations of the bourgeoisie show scenes of intense contemplation, of looking at a beloved, or gazing around the family home, while the images of workmen are always a combination of aggressive and formless looks that split the composition apart. This contrast is stressed by the contrast between types of illustration, there being a calculated clash between the pyramidal and static designs associated with the hermetic world of the bourgeoisie (see 19: fp 257; fig.4), and the open, discontinuous, and dynamic designs which encode the restless, disrupted, and disruptive world of the proletariat. (21: fp 129; 20: fp 257; 19: fp 385, fig. 7).

Barnes's analysis of the class-struggle is realized, then, as a contrast between types of gaze and their formal organization. More importantly, Barnes emotionalizes the conflict of interests, presenting it as an opposition of loving and lovelessness, harmony and the shapelessness of discord. This preserves the essential conflict of *Put Yourself in His Place*—it being interesting to note that Barnes is no more sympathetic to the workers than Reade—but recasts it as a parable of love and hate.

Such emotionalism is central to the artist's interpretative designs, for the illustrations inject a note of sensibility into the reading of Reade's lurid tale. As we have seen, Barnes expands the characters by visualizing shades of feeling, by developing their psychological profiles and by revisualizing their relationships. All of this stands in Romantic counterpoint to Reade's vituperative attack on the unions. At the same time, his illustrative designs are faithful replications of the author's emphasis on realism and theater, and highlight the fiction's dynamic fusion of the two.

Barnes's designs for *Put Yourself in His Place* might thus be described as a complex combination, a dialectic in which the text is both respected and expanded, reaffirmed and overlaid with an interest in feeling and character

Fig.7. "Death by Suffocation at his Back, and Broken Bones Awaited Him Below"

which cleverly develops the novel's emotional content. The end result is a tangible enhancement of Reade's tale, a fluid mediation between Sensationalism and the Dickensian novel of feeling. Boldly visualized and powerfully focused on the fiction's key elements, Barnes's illustrations are a valuable addition, a secondary text empowering us to read and mentally extend the world of the novel. More than this, Barnes's collaboration with Reade clearly demonstrates how the author gained his best results not by imposing a tyrannical hold on his artist's activities, but by influencing his work while allowing him plenty of room for maneuver. Enjoying this arrangement, Barnes produced what are arguably his best designs, and certainly the richest illustrations for a fiction by Reade.

So the collaboration between Reade and Barnes can be viewed, finally, as a great success. Conceived as fusion of image and word, its complex interactions produced one of the outstanding composite novels of the time. Working as a paradigm of sixties illustration, which can be viewed as a bold alternation between the imaginative responses favored by Rossetti and the faithful illustration of Millais, the embellished version of *Put Yourself in His Place* is undoubtedly one of the richest of the *Cornhill's* serializations. Although overlooked, it deserves to be interpreted as a text of equal standing with the work of Trollope and Millais, as it appeared in *Framley Parsonage (Cornhill*, 1860–61), and *The Small House at Allington (Cornhill*, 1862–64). It is all the more annoying to find that Barnes's designs for Reade were never republished in full; the illustrations were entirely missing from the first book edition (1870), and were only republished in part in subsequent imprintings (1871, 1876, 1885). Without these outstanding designs, Reade's text is impoverished: for *Put Yourself in His Place* is an illustrated novel which richly deserves the closest attention.

NOTES

1. Robert Barnes, ARWS, was a successful artist who illustrated a wide range of periodicals and books in the 1860s and '70s and later turned to painting. He exhibited at the Royal Academy, London, the Royal Scottish Society of Painters in Watercolours, London and Edinburgh, and the Royal Society of Arts, Birmingham. Details of Barnes's publications are given in Goldman 139–40; 270–73; and in Houfe 54.
2. Details of the business arrangements between Reade and Smith are recorded in *The Cornhill Ledger*, 1868–69 (Smith Elder Papers, National Library of Scotland, Edinburgh). The terms agreed were generous, for Reade was paid £153.17.0 for each instalment of *Put Yourself in His Place* (15–24). This favorably contrasts with the £63.10 paid to Ainsworth for each part of *The Bramleighs of Bishops's*

Folly (2). Barnes's fee is not recorded, although it would be reasonable to assume that he was paid the going rate of £10 to £15 per cut.

3. This fact has been established by Mrs. Jane Seel, Barnes's great-granddaughter. Meticulous research by Seel has also established that Barnes was the father of sixteen children and lived in affluent homes in Berkhamstead, Redhill, and Brighton. Many of his works, along with a series of documents, letters, and photographs, are still in the family. I am indebted to Mrs. Seel for her enthusiastic assistance in the preparation of this article.

WORKS CITED

Manuscript and Archive Sources

Charles Reade's *Picture Book and Dictionary*, ms. Morris L. Parrish Collection of Victorian Novelists, Manuscripts Division, Department of Rare Books and Special Collection, Princeton University Library.

Ms. letter from Reade to George Smith, 19 January 1869. Miscellaneous Correspondence (additions made 1969–81). Morris L. Parrish Collection of Victorian Novelists, Manuscripts Division, Department of Rare Books and Special Collections, Princeton University Library.

Ms. letters from Reade to George Smith, January-February 1869. Murray Archive, John Murray, London.

Ms. letter from Reade to Ticknor & Fields, 21 July 1855. The Reade Collection, The Huntington Library, San Marino, California..

Smith, George. *Recollections of a Long and Busy Life*. 2 vols, ts. Smith Elder Papers, National Library of Scotland, Edinburgh.

The Cornhill Ledger, 1868–69, ms 23189. Smith Elder Papers, National Library of Scotland, Edinburgh.

The Jane Seel Collection, England.

Printed Works

Bell, Charles. *The Anatomy and Philosophy of Expression*. Sixth Ed. London: Bohn, 1872.

Brantlinger, Patrick. " 'The Case Against Trades Unions in Early Victorian Fiction." *Victorian Studies* 13:1 (September 1969): 37–52.

British Workman The (1869–71).

Burns, Wayne. *Charles Reade: A Study in Victorian Authorship*. New York: Bookman, 1961.

———. *"The Cloister and the Hearth*: A Victorian Classic Reconsidered." *Nineteenth Century Fiction* 2 (1947–48): 71–82.

———. "The Sheffield Flood: a Critical Study of Charles Reade's Fiction." *PMLA* 63 (1948): 686–95.

Coleman, John. *Charles Reade*. London: Treherne, 1903.

Collins, Charles Allston. "On the Expression of the Eye." *Macmillan's Magazine* 14 (September 1866): 357–63.

Goldman, Paul. *Victorian Illustration*. Aldershot: Scolar, 1996.

Greenwood, Frederick. *Margaret Denzil's History. The Cornhill Magazine* 8–10 (1863–64).

Hardy, Thomas. *The Mayor of Casterbridge. The Graphic Magazine* (1886).

Houfe, Simon. *The Dictionary of Nineteenth Century Book Illustrators*. Woodbridge: The Antique Collectors' Club, 1996.

Jackson, Arlene. *Illustration and The Novels of Thomas Hardy*. London: Macmillan, 1981.

Lavater, J.C. *Essays on Physiognomy*, abridged from W. Holcroft's translation. London: Robinson, n.d.

Leisure Hour The (1864).

London Society (1862–65).

Nowell-Smith, Simon. *The House of Cassell*. London: Cassell, 1958.

Pantazzi, Sybille. "Author and Illustrator: Images in Confrontation." *Victorian Periodicals Newsletter* 9 (1976): 39–49.

Parrish, M. L. *Wilkie Collins and Charles Reade: First Editions Described with Notes*. New York: Burt Franklin, 1968.

Pictures of English Life. With eight illustrations by Robert Barnes. London: Sampson Low, 1865.

Reade, Charles. *A Good Fight. Once a Week* (July-October 1859).

———. *Good Stories*. New York: Harper, 1884.

———. *It is Never Too Late To Mend*. Boston: Ticknor & Fields, 1856.

————. *Put Yourself in His Place*. *The Cornhill Magazine* 19–22 (March 1869–July 1870).

————. "Put Yourself in His Place." *The Examiner* 11 June 1870: 373–74.

————. "Put Yourself in His Place." *The Saturday Review* 11 June 1870: 777–78.

————. *Put Yourself in His Place*. London: Smith Elder, 1870.

————. *Put Yourself in His Place*. With four illustrations by Robert Barnes. London: Smith Elder, 1871; 1876.

————. *Put Yourself in His Place*. With eight illustrations by Robert Barnes. New ed. London: Chatto and Windus, 1885.

————. *A Terrible Temptation*. *Cassell's Magazine* (1871).

Reade, Compton. *Charles Reade: A Memoir*. 2 vols. London: Chapman & Hall, 1887.

Reid, Forrest. *Illustrators of the Eighteen Sixties*. London: Faber & Gwyer, 1928.

Swinburne, Algernon. *Miscellanies*. London: Chatto & Windus, 1886.

Trollope, Anthony. *An Autobiography*. 2 vols. London: Blackwood, 1883.

————. *Framley Parsonage*. *The Cornhill Magazine* 1–3 (1860–61).

————. *The Small House at Allington*. *The Cornhill Magazine* 6–9 (1862–64).

Wood, Ellen (Ellen Price). *Oswald Cray*. *Good Words* (1864–65).

Seeing Dickens: Dickens Studies 1999

Michael Lund

In the past, readings of Dickens generally uncovered an artist ahead of his time, a genius understanding social evils and conceiving aesthetic entities grandly and intricately constructed. They put before our eyes the Dickens we have come to recognize as the familiar subject of classroom discussion and scholarly agreement. Some contemporary critics, however, turn art from an agent of illumination into an object for analysis, an artifact of the past which we, with our own enlightenment, can use to understand history and, it is hoped, to envision a wiser course into the future. Still, there are new scholars who assert that some aspects of Dickens's art have remained unnoticed, misunderstood, or undervalued for years and purport to open up these areas to our old eyes. And some critics insist that much of what we have known about Dickens and his age needs revision in light of later study. A final group of studies argue that completely new ways of seeing are now available to literary scholars. Elements of Dickens's world are emerging, that is, and becoming visible for the first time because of new kinds of sight.

I. Previewing Dickens

In "The Blind Daughter in Charles Dickens's *Cricket on the Hearth*," Elizabeth G. Gitter turns a postmodern eye on a character who cannot see in order to gain perspective on Dickens's time, on his art, and on our own critical practices. These acts provide a model for this essay, which hopes, as a preview

---

of what is to come, to determine what scholars are now seeing in Dickens's work and in the phenomenon of literature generally.

The concluding scene to Dickens's 1845 tale has been praised as effective closure, but Gitter points out that one character, Bertha, "remains alone, excluded from the celebration of satisfied desire represented by the ending." Such a handicapped person could not aspire to romance: "Irredeemably ineligible for marriage, she exists outside the conventions of narrative closure" (675). Playing music for the others who dance, however, she is still "necessary for the final *pas d'ensemble*; without her, there can be no fairy-tale ending" (675). Necessary to art, Gitter says, Bertha underscores limitations to social understanding in the world this art reflects. Thus, while she is the product of Dickens's genius, this character now can also be used to highlight what we, privileged by history, believe are social failings hidden from Dickens's view.

The blind did not possess subjectivity in Dickens's day, or, in fact, for a good while thereafter, Gitter reminds us: "the blind awaken in us a sense of 'disquieting strangeness' because, exposed and yet not seeing themselves exposed to the other's gaze, they have (as we imagine them) no shame, no modesty . . . " (685). Instead they become material for others' expression of self, for the disguising of sins, especially by the father: "the blind girl is the daughter who cannot see the sins of the father. She is the child who is too innocent to feel or to provoke shame" (683). Bertha, according to Gitter, is both an object on which the father's flaws are projected and a perfect mirror for a man's best notion of himself, for he can create himself by what he tells her of himself.

Cures for blindness occurring as early as the eighteenth century would affect how blind people were thought of in Victorian and Modern societies. While restorations of sight were rare in real life, the miraculous cure became an event in fiction, one that Dickens was aware of and drew on to round off his story of an amiable carrier and his young wife. Bertha's function, then, is to aid Dickens in a novelist's work. Even more unsettling to Gitter, Dickens's use of the character "invites his sighted readers to laugh at the spectacle of [Berta's] ridiculous behavior, to participate in the sadistic pleasures of teasing the blind" (680). Why, asks Gitter? In part, she concludes strongly, so men can be morally restored: "Sightless and partnerless, playing her harp so that others can dance, she is the suffering servant who allows Dickens in the end to turn a blind eye to incestuous wishes and guilty desires. Through her he is able to make light of darkness" (686).

This kind of corrective reading of Dickens, of course, differs from many studies of the past, which uncovered an artist ahead of his time, a genius understanding social evils and conceiving aesthetic entities grandly and intricately constructed. Such deconstructive exercises turn art from an agent of illumination into an object for analysis, an artifact of the past which we, with our own enlightenment, can use to understand history and, one hopes, to chart a wiser course into the future. Reading what has been written about Dickens in the year 1999 has challenged me to review how I have seen Dickens in my own teaching and scholarship over the past quarter century. And it forces me to examine values in the entire enterprise of literary study, previewing what we are all likely to see in Dickens in the future.

II. Recognizing Dickens

Many works from 1999 put before our eyes the Dickens we have come to recognize as the familiar subject of classroom discussion and scholarly agreement. Ruth Glancy's *Student Companion to Charles Dickens*, for instance, fulfills the promise of the series in which it is offered, "to meet the needs of students and general readers for accessible literary criticism on the American and world writers most frequently studied and read in the secondary school, community college, and four-year college classrooms" (vii). More than readings of individual texts (although those are there too), Glancy's text offers students such things as a two-page definition of the term "Dickensian" (23–25), generous discussion of the forces of Victorian publishing, and a succinct "Life of Charles Dickens" tied to his major writings.

Glancy's discussions of individual novels are broken down into sections like "Historical Background," "Stylistic and Literary Devices," "A Feminist or Psychoanalytical or Marxist Reading of . . . ," so that the work as a whole introduces contemporary approaches to literature as well as developing a comprehensive view of Dickens's achievements. While the more frequently taught Dickens novels get detailed analysis, Dickens's "Other Novels from *Dombey and Son* (1848) to *The Mystery of Edwin Drood* (1870)"—which, besides *Dombey and Son*, include *Little Dorrit*, *Bleak House*, and *Our Mutual Friend*—are presented in a single chapter.

The most complete of the works recognizing a familiar Dickens in 1999 is *The Oxford Reader's Companion to Dickens*, edited by Paul Schlicke and written for both general reader and specialist by an international team of more than sixty scholars. (The challenges and rewards of editing the volume are the subject of Schlicke, "Editing.") Because its primary goal is "to illuminate the active interrelation between the man, his writings and activities, and his time" (viii), this 654–page volume becomes a substantial guide to Victorian life in its variety and multiplicity, with entries, for instance, on Chartism, London (15 pages, double-columned, fine print, subdivided), public health, and transport (roads, coaches, railways, omnibuses, cabs). Here is a sampling of discoveries (or recoveries):

- Dickens's wrote under the pseudonym "Tibbs" (see *Bell's Life in London*), as well as Boz.
- Capital offenders who could read a verse from the Bible were able to "escape the gallows on their first felony conviction" (66).
- "His cellar at Gad's Hill Place, auctioned off on 13 August 1870, comprised dozens of cases of Iberian sherry and vintage port, French claret and champagne, 40 bottles of red burgundy, a selection of German hocks and Moselles, 11 dozen bottles of Highland whisky, 28 dozen bottle of French brandy, 17 bottles of the Regency favorite, curaçao, and a sampling of liquors and cordials" (201).
- "The Portuguese version of *Hard Times* (1988) ensured that all of the novels have been filmed at least once" (233).
- Between 1983 and 1986 *A Christmas Carol* was translated into the following South African languages: Zulu, Tsonga, Tswana, Xhosa, and Venda (568).
- The development of magic lanterns in Dickens's day made possible "dissolves from one image into another and the simulation of such effects of movement as the passing of clouds" (364).
- "Readers who want a quick fix [on the value of Victorian money] which will most often give them some guidance will, however, get a *very approximate* notion of present-day [1997] values if they multiply Dickens's figures by 70" (383).

Of course, this only suggests the range of material.

Material on each individual Dickens's title (and the magazines he edited or published in) is neatly set off on separate pages, with a gray rather than white background to the black text, making it easy to find and read as a unit. Considerable space is allowed for David Paroissien to consider issues of Dickens's characterization, of limited interest to most forms of contemporary criticism but certainly central to Dickens's enduring popularity, if not also, in unacknowledged ways, to his high place in academic literary history. There is also, of course, appropriate attention to current critical interests, for instance, issues relevant to the history of the book: publishing, copyright, composition, editions, illustration, magazines, newspapers and the British press, modes of production, readership, reviews and reviewing, and serial literature. The section on "criticism and scholarship" will serve upper-level undergraduates and beginning graduate students well in its succinct overview of Dickens studies. Also helpful for students are sections on "novelists and the novel before Dickens and during Dickens's lifetime." Finally, there are engaging pictures and illustrations, maps, a 15-page, double-columned listing of Dickens's characters (in case you get confused about who appears in which book), and a handy time-chart to connect Dickens's life, work, and times.

A work similar to *Student Companion to Charles Dickens* and *The Oxford Reader's Companion* is Leon Litvack's *Charles Dickens's Dombey and Son. An Annotated Bibliography*. Its three sections deal with, (1) the text—editions, composition, etc. (one interesting sign of the times: electronic editions are also mentioned); (2) studies (reviews and criticism); and (3) biographical studies and bibliographies. The review of "Criticism, 1900–1998" (222 pages, by far the largest section of the book) makes one wonder how anything more could be said about one novel. That *Dombey and Son* is one chosen from so many others as an object of continual reassessment, however, tends to confirm Litvack's argument that it represents a powerful literary achievement.

A helpful introduction, which points readers toward specific entries (numbered for easy finding), concludes by noting that "Even after 150 years of scholarly and critical endeavor, there is considerable potential for further investigation of this novel and the issues it raises" (xxxiv). So wide is the umbrella under which this survey is conducted, and so many the categories included, that one turns with some curiosity to see what might be left for section 2.7: "Miscellaneous." There an essay by Geraldine Bussey in a 1952 issue of *Punch* perhaps provides a model for all of us Dickensians. It recounts the story of a father who disturbs his family with violent reactions while reading *Dombey and Son*. In some desperation the wife returns the book to the library before its due date, even though her husband had not finished reading it. As he "prepares his pipe, tobacco, and slippers" to continue reading, however, she is struck with regret. But a crisis is avoided "when the father reveals that he has that day bought a *Dombey and Son* of his own" (351).

Along with the volumes of Schlicke, Glancy, and Litvack comes Edgar Rosenberg's critical edition of *Great Expectations*, which is founded on an assertion that this novel might well stand first among readers worldwide and that "the opening of the novel is one of the most celebrated in fiction" (xii). "Launching *Great Expectations*" tells the familiar story of the novel's birth with new detail and in a lively manner, including appropriate attention to the role of serial fiction in the new journal, *All the Year Round*. In a detailed analysis of Lever's *A Day's Ride*, Rosenberg not only identifies merits and demerits of Lever's art, but also places that story within the full context of literary publishing in Victorian England. "Writing *Great Expectations*" is equally detailed and informative: "one look at the manuscript page of *Great Expectations*, as I have suggested, should be enough to convince anybody of the nervous pains Dickens took with his chapters, his paragraphs, his sentences" (431). Despite its title, "Putting an End to *Great Expectations*" quite rightly insists that more will be written about this one subject, even as the "Selected" bibliography runs to seventeen pages of tightly squeezed commentary on important studies, helpfully divided into fourteen sections.

Dickens's first readers were handicapped, Rosenberg argues at one point, in understanding Dickens's grand scheme in this novel because of its initial weekly publication. Rosenberg refers to the " 'naive' reader of *All the Year Round*" as opposed to the " 'advanced' reader of the volume" (406); and he dismisses a version many Americans read: "*Harper's* [serial version of *Great Expectations*], of course, is textually insignificant, except as a literary curiosity" (xiv). Rosenberg's criticism, however, assumes the importance of authorial intention: "when Dickens sat down to write *Great Expectations* at the end of September 1860, he fully planned to publish the book in monthly parts and . . . its issuance in weekly numbers was an accident of the trade, ultimately irrelevant to the conception and scaffolding of the book—a fiat by the editor-publisher of *All the Year Round*, not the biographer of Pip's fortunes" (410). Literary history is not now seen as simply a matter of the author's desire, however. The form in which any work appears contributes to its reception, to its integration with the culture which surrounds it, and to its future effect on that culture. Anyone who has taught a Dickens novel in installments over many weeks' time knows the rewards of extended anticipation and delayed gratification. And attention to detail, moving ten pages at a time, can often generate an even greater grasp of the "organic structure" (409) Rosenberg is determined to assert for this novel.

In addition to expanding his own earlier study of the novel's two endings, Rosenberg includes a new piece by Jean Callahan, "The (Unread) Reading Version of *Great Expectations*." It is one of five reading texts Dickens prepared but never performed, most probably because it was so long. Callahan finds "Dickens simply ignored the degree to which his alterations violated the original logic of his text" (551), and "it shows how resolutely Dickens sweetened away the less-than-universal truths of class, and any suggestion that these truths might shape and be hidden in the deepest parts of the psyche" (553). While he finds the reading version "structurally coherent" (554), he also notes that the process involved "the purging of all feminine influence in Pip's story" (555).

III. Uncovering Dickens

Other work on Dickens asserts that aspects of his art have gone unnoticed, misunderstood, or undervalued for years and purports to open up these areas to our old eyes. Not surprisingly, 1999's issues of the *Dickensian* by and large fulfill this goal. David Parker, for instance, says in those pages that, while no exact model for Wemmick's cottage in *Great Expectations* exists, we "have overlooked an institution that dominated the suburb [of Walworth] throughout Dickens's adult life, an institution that embodied Wemmick's architectural and horticultural tastes, but on a grander scale. The Royal Surrey Zoological Gardens . . . '' (130). Also interested in the workings of the creative impulse in Dickens, Gilian West (''Little Dorrit'') identifies historical sources for *Little Dorrit*, famous, actual residents of debtors' prisons, including William Combe (imprisoned from 1799 to 1823) and John Thomas Serres (in prison on and off from 1795 to 1825). In another piece, Gilian West argues analogously that ''the tragedy of Dombey is founded on the history of Christopher Huffam'' (''Huffam'' 6), Dickens's godfather, who generally has been thought unimportant in Dickens's life.

Rather than historical places or figures as sources for Dickens's work, Peter Merchant traces possible influences from Ruskin's *Unto This Last* and Eliot's *Silas Marner* to *Great Expectations*. Especially intriguing is an argument that derives from the fact that Eliot's short novel was published on 2 April 1861, and ''the pivotal thirty-ninth chapter of *Great Expectations*,'' when Magwitch appears at Pip's door, was issued on 11 May: ''What appears possible is that a scene which Eliot had set before her readers just a few short weeks (at most) before Dickens completed chapter 39 of *Great Expectations* oddly lodged inside his own 'work in progress', like Eppie providentially entering Silas's cottage, an uninvited but inspirational guest'' (136).

Rather than arguing that elements of specific texts have been overlooked in Dickens studies, Philip V. Allingham says, also in the *Dickensian*, that it is time to review the author's theory of short fiction: ''After a century of neglect, Dickens's short fiction seems ready for critical re-appraisal which will go beyond its relationship to his novels and define those qualities which distinguish it from his other work; to establish, in short, Dickens's aesthetic of the short story'' (146). This could be done, Allingham points out, by re-reading Dickens's works and by examining the values revealed in his role as editor. He concludes that Dickens valued short fiction's ''power to move (whether to tears of laughter or of sympathetic, sentimental response, or to goosebumps and dread) a readership far vaster than that which he reached with his full-length novel published in monthly parts'' (151–52). Linda Hughes and I reconsider Dickens as editor of Gaskell's *North and South* in *Household Words* (96–123).

Rodney Stenning Edgecombe (''Personification'') proposes a refinement in our understanding of Dickens's style. In his use of personification, says Edgecombe, Dickens ''rid the trope of its sculptural, static quality, and instead of loading *ad hoc* figures with painterly emblems, use[d] less tangible, less predictable modes of embodiment'' (231). He sees bad art in those Dickens characters who ''are always staging themselves, slipping into allegorical functions, and appropriating personification as a means of self-advancement'' (237). Francesco M. Casotti, in an article that would also have fit nicely in *Dickens, Europe and the New Worlds* (discussed below), finds, judging from the availability of editions in Italian, that "Dickens is well known and widely read in Italy" (22) and is, in fact "a permanent feature of the Italian cultural background" (22).

But the most pages in this year's *Dickensian* are appropriately devoted to Leon Litvack, whose well-documented, two-part article also looks at Dickens in his relationship to "new worlds." Seeking sources for the dark tones in *Great Expectations*, he reexamines "a nation which had embarked on a conscious programme of colonial expansion, which would eventually transform Britain into a worldwide empire" (24). While the essay might seem a radical act of post-colonial criticism, its conclusions are less revolutionary: "The far-flung outreaches of empire like Australia appear at the edges of texts like *Great Expectations*; but because of their peculiarly powerful influence, attention to them, particularly in terms of what is unsaid and occluded, is an interesting, even exciting area of exploration" (27).

Specifically, Litvack reviews what was published about prisons, transportation, and Australia in *Household Words* and other prominent mid-Victorian publications by writers like Samuel Sidney and Caroline Chisholm because, he argues, within the pages of *Great Expectations* there is insufficient presentation of Magwitch's life. Litvack notes, for instance, that a revealing article on convicts and prison reform appeared in the same issue of *All the Year Round* in which Magwitch appears before Pip (113). This material provides a larger context within which Magwitch's life would have been understood by Victorian readers: "The image which emerges from the treatment of Australia in *Household Words* is multivalent, encompassing farming life, bush life, and convict life. It is depicted as a fluid, dynamic society, where 'mateship' governed social allegiances and codes of behaviour, and where English class barriers could be bridged" (46). Magwitch's conjuring up an image of Pip when he is alone in Australia, then, could be a product of this immigrant experience.

A great deal of the collection, *Dickens, Europe and the New Worlds*, edited by Anny Sadrin, would fit into this same category of critical studies, new looks at neglected aspects of Dickens's world. In this volume, for instance, Paul Schlicke provides a reconsideration of "A Lazy Tour of Two Idle Apprentices," which he finds "a particularly good example of the kind of interior journey into the uncanny at which Dickens is particularly adept, and travel is an integral component of that journey" (194). Although the work is generally ignored now, Schlicke insists it "repeatedly infuses the journalistic account of a holiday in unfamiliar locations with more than a whiff of surrealism, and prepares the ground for the decidedly uncanny tales that appear along the way" (198).

"A Lazy Tour" is now available, by the way, in the third volume of *The Dent Uniform Edition of Dickens' Journalism*, edited by Michael Slater. The focus of this volume, says Slater, is "on Dickens the masterly journalist rather than Dickens the masterful editor" (xiii). A succinct introduction to the volume connects the writing he was doing for the magazine to events in his personal life and his other professional projects. The collection is not complete, but includes "the great majority of the single-authored articles and essays" Dickens contributed to *Household Words* (ix). In making selections, the editor has "used much the same selection criteria as in the preceding volume of this edition" (xviii), and a complete listing of Dickens's writings for the magazine is included in an appendix.

K. J. Fielding, with Shu Fang Lai, cautions in *Dickens, Europe and the New Worlds* against assuming that Dickens the novelist, essayist, and editor was equally accomplished in all fields. Fielding insists that "Dickens was not particularly well informed about the latest advances in science, and it is ludicrous to suppose that he was or could have been" (206). The impulse to credit a single author with omniscience is an inspiration to sloppy scholarship: "So much is easily available, with some effort, in well-edited and well-indexed information, that should be investigated before general ideas are hopefully let loose like Miss Flite's caged birds" (209).

Another of the products that have come from Dickens Project meetings, these essays in *Dickens, Europe and the New Worlds* show how fruitful a thematic conference can be. Even though some essays contradict each other, the whole takes up a single subject and rotates it through an entire circuit so that it is seen from nearly every conceivable angle. In some ways, the editor's building of the volume echoes Malcolm Andrews's point about Dickens as author. Andrews is interested in "the polyphonic voice that is exercised in his fiction and in his reading performances" seen against "attitudes within Victorian culture towards the constitution of the self" (147). Dickens was willing "to experiment with a kind of self-annihilation and to make a public exhibition of it" in his public reading (153). Dickens, then, according to Andrews, tore "himself to pieces, in order to fuse thousands of strangers into one community" (154). Robert M. Polhemus sees Dickens's voice not as fragmented, but as transformed by James Joyce: "Dickens serves as a Victorian bridge in the history of the novel in English for Joyce to unite his imaginative, post-Freudian 'work in progress' to key patterns, moments and figures of puzzling sexual regeneration that renew and animate the Scriptures ... " (284). And Neil Forsyth considers words of Dickens translated into images, concluding that David Lean's version of *Oliver Twist* "eliminates the plot-nonesenses [of Dickens's original] and focuses for the most part where the novel's main interest lies: on Oliver's helplessness, on his relations with the authorities, then with Fagin and the London boys, and then with Sikes and Nancy" (259).

Matthias Bauer, on the other hand, offers a Dickensian model for our contemporary reading of a volume like Sadrin's, suggesting that we can entertain and hold in one framework many voices. Studying the use of foreign languages in *Little Dorrit* (especially the elusive "Altro"), he concludes: "By becoming like a child, each individual who interacts and communicates with other individuals has the chance to strike upon a natural form of understanding and thus rediscover a state before the division of tongues" (161). Roger D. Sell argues for a "mediating" criticism of Dickens's achievements, one that links different visions or interpretations rather than locking in on just one: "Our minds really can work in several different ways at once . . . . No single world can monopolize truth and wisdom" (299). Sylvère Monod concurs, stating in "Translating Dickens into French" that this lifetime project has yielded great rewards: "Modern criticism by and large recognizes that each new generation of readers has a right to new versions of the great classical works" (232).

Ronald R. Thomas's "Spectacle and Speculation: the Victorian Economy of Vision in *Little Dorrit*," pursues the theme of this review essay, seeing Dickens. He points to parallels between the two cities of Venice and London in Dickens's novels and in the cultural consciousness of Victorians, as both places were great centers of commerce at certain moments in history. Important symbols connected to these cities in *Little Dorrit* are a prison, palace, and bank, representing great wealth as well as great failure. Thomas notes: "Both [London and Venice] defeated their rivals by making wealth and power dependent upon successful speculation about the price of goods rather than on the acquisition and domination of land and people" (40). Thomas then sees Dickens offering a warning to his age from the lessons of history through his novel's central male character.

Dominic Rainsford, "Crossing the Channel With Dickens," rethinks the apparent contradiction in the novels between often traumatic crossings of the British Channel and the frequently calm life on the Continent. Reviewing magazine pieces and novels which talk about crossing, he concludes: "Crossing the Channel is a standing joke, a farcical unnecessary obstacle [in Dickens's work]. By flagrantly exaggerating its significance, Dickens simply emphasizes that he considers the societies on either side to be equally accessible to his imaginative powers, and equally fit objects for his social criticism and concern" (12). Anny Sadrin's argument, wondering why Dickens chose Dijon as place for Edith Dombey's and Carker's rendezvous, follows a similar line: he "never made adultery the central subject of his plots," but may have been trying it out indirectly, unwilling to offend his readers: "We sense the novelist's relish in creating the atmosphere of scandal and debauchery, indulging in false suspense, trying his hand at a new form of writing" (19).

Michael Hollington also considers Dickens's view of the Continent. Presentation of Paris boulevards in *Household Words* reveals Dickens's fascination with "the tangles of modern cities, where high and low, human and animal have got mixed up'' (31), in part because the paving of streets undertaken during mid-century first produced mud rather than eliminating it, as desired. Lawrence Frank also finds Dickens, through his interest in archeology and mesmerism, moving away from the material present, transforming Rome in *Pictures from Italy* into "a metaphor for the romantic mind" (48). Reviewing the author's travels in Italy, Tore Rem finds that Dickens maintained a critical distance from his own country's sense of "national identity" and entertained— "for an Englishman at the time—a rather unusual openness to what Europe represented" (131).

Dickens's view of America, according to Patrick McCarthy, was incomplete because of the physical limitations he faced in travel: "Offended by vulgarity and rawness, praised beyond mortal due and alternately crushed and insulted, rushed and rushing along, he had no time to see the broader horizons of America or to see his limited self seeing America" (75–76). Nancy Metz finds his description of the United States owed as much to the words of other travel writers as it did to his own senses: "even in the descriptive and dramatic scenes, where one might expect Dickens to rely primarily on his personal observations and experiences, a closer reading of the context almost always reveals the extent to which these experiences are mediated through published accounts" (83). Jennifer Gribble finds Dickens's criticism of the new world an indirect "indictment of mid-Victorian imperialism." She says of Jarndyce's giving up Esther to Woodcourt, providing her a little Bleak House: "The apparent pastoral of the happy ending shows the new world founded on the unacknowledged and irresolvable feelings of the old, and driven by the essential selfishness of libidinal energies" (98). John C. Hawley, however, concludes that in Dickens "the world is the same everywhere. More importantly, humanity is the same as well" (186). Only "in the world of the imagination" might Dickens find something better (192).

Brian Cheadle traces an evolution rather than a fixed portrait in Dickens's representation of an English center and a colonial periphery. He agrees that Dickens challenged Victorian complacency in early works but recognized all systems as containing contradiction: "The notion that *Oliver Twist* is single-mindedly dedicated to cultural cleansing thus needs to be qualified. Even at this early stage of Dickens's career the novel reflects a centre divided against itself" (103). In later novels "Dickens begins to figure the colonial periphery more consistently as a cornucopia rather than a receptacle" (108). And Dickens "becomes fascinated by characters who return unbidden from the periphery to challenge the centre . . . "(110). By the end of his career, Cheadle believes, Dickens and his readers "have reached a point where civilisation and savagery, centre and periphery are becoming hardly distinguishable, though the tensions of the agitated exchanges remain as strong as ever" (111).

This kind of careful adjustment of Dickens's place in cultural history is continued in John O. Jordan essay, "Dickens and Diaspora." Acknowledging how postcolonial authors make use of Dickens, he sees the Victorian master's writing "as a form of cultural capital exported from Britain to the world in the form of radio scripts, films, theatrical and television adaptations, school syllabuses and curricula, as well as printed texts, and consumed, rejected, appropriated or transformed by local Anglophone elites" (240). In some senses, argues Jordan, Dickens "is identified more with 'literature' than with Englishness" (242); and in a number of cases of postcolonial literature "it is through imaginative literature of the highest order that one comes to terms with the world and eventually exercises control over it" (243). Dickens is, then, "not simply a canonical author with a fixed position in literary history. He is also a living and ever-changing text, as important to late twentieth-century writers in the Anglophone diaspora as he has always been for those closer to the metropolitan centres" (250).

Scientific views of change in human nature over time and the question of character development in fiction are linked by Victor Sage. He argues that Dickens's view of human identity was more complex than emerging tenets of Social Darwinism. Citing Dickens's "journalistic campaign on behalf of Owen in the sphere of natural history," Sage says that the author of *Our Mutual Friend* remained "outside those optimistic mid-century paradigms of growth and development which are such an important common feature in the discourse of both biology and aesthetic realism" (224).

James Buzard sees the tension in Dickens between England and other cultures represented in the very form of *Bleak House*. In this novel, he argues, "the voice that tries to convince us it has travelled from the claustral inside of its culture *out* [the omniscient narrator] is paired with one that speaks of a journey from the bleak outside of culture *in* [Esther]" (122). But the novel cannot bring into a harmonious whole elements outside the limit of Dickens's cultural frame. Esther and Woodcourt's marriage "is a union that bears out what the novel was always suggesting, that the greatest extent to which the circle of duty could expand and remain meaningful—remain a 'place'—was to the borders of the nation" (123–24). Sara Thornton, studying "the notion of foreignness in the Dickensian text" (169) through the figure of Hortense, arrives at a similar conclusion: "If in *Bleak House* we see an England engaged thus in an act of self-perpetuation, it is important to recognize that Britannia has not used her own progeny to effect change, but has brought in an immigrant worker to do the dirty work, so to speak. The change is of course no change at all, but a means of maintaining the status quo with new energy from the world outside" (179).

The question of Dickens's distance from central mores of his culture is more complex, according to Patricia Plummer (the final essay in *Dickens, Europe and the New Worlds* considered here). While "in *Oliver Twist* Dickens is obsessed with Otherness"—Nancy, Sikes, Fagin—the "marginalised characters command significantly less space within the literary landscape of *David Copperfield''* (273). However, in his last novel, Dickens returns to an exploration of the boundaries of gender and race, drawn to Helena Landless as "a character who in a way foreshadows the current preoccupation with multiculturalism and collapsing of fixed gender identities" (280). The author's attraction to such figures justifies continuing critical scrutiny, concludes Plummer: "It is this notion of instability that makes for the enduring appeal of Dickens's novels" (280).

Rodney Stenning Edgecomb ("Middle-Class Erasures") also sees distance between Dickens's novels and the voice of the growing Victorian middle class. He asserts that Dickens viewed the middle class as deliberately ignorant of social realities: "Even though Dickens never pulled down the temple, he went further than Thackeray in mocking the pillars of a repressive society— Podsnap a telamon and Mrs. General a caryatid" (288). Indeed, to Edgecomb, Victorian convention in Dickens tore down as much as it built up: "Middle-class piety tries to mask working-class needs with its own vision of decency . . . and it decreases [sic] the evolution of time just as much as it decreases 'offensively' vibrant lively objects" (292).

Mark M. Hennelly, Jr. is similarly interested in Dickens's characters in relationship to Victorian conventions, especially those related to sexuality and motherhood. Looking at the opening of *Oliver Twist*, in which Oliver is born and his mother dies, Hennelly notes that the doctor does not know—and Dickens cannot narrate—what the midwife understands. *David Copperfield* might have been written, then, as Dickens himself noted, to " 'show the faults of mothers, and their consequences' "; but *Twist* "seems penned differently and perhaps less blindly to 'perform other feminine offices for the promotion of her recovery' . . . [w]hether the referent of the feminine pronoun here is Nancy, or Rose, or Agnes, or even Charlotte subjugated (and presumably prostituted) by the aptly named *Claypole* . . . " (99).

John Bowen also points us to things we have always known are there in Dickens's world, but which deserve another look. His *Other Dickens: Pickwick to Chuzzlewit* is "a reading in sequence of all the novels and some of the minor writing published by Dickens between 1836, when the first installment of *Pickwick Papers* appeared, and the final episode of *Martin Chuzzlewit* in 1844" (2). He argues that the main achievement of all this is changed readers: "His writing, which almost exactly spans the Reform Acts of 1832 and 1867, is often close to that of contemporary radical discourses" (24). Bowen explores, then, Dickens's "representational radicalism" (29), an unrestrained manner of presenting the world.

Bowen repeatedly takes stances which include paradox: the interpolated tales in *Pickwick*, for instance, "remain both part of the novel and [have] nothing at all to do with it" (71). In general, his approach is to lay bare the oppositions in Dickens's art. He does intend not to resolve them, but to let them exist together in their own natures, without insisting they be put to rest in any fixed scheme. *Oliver Twist*, for instance, is "all homes and journeys, a pattern of repetitions and attempted repetitions, of substitutions and displacements, where each figure, place, or journey seems to echo and invoke a double" (93). The elements of *Nicholas Nickleby* cannot, says Bowen, be absolutely categorized: "There are many such instances, in which Dickens moves with astonishing facility between plots and genres of discourse or creates complexly hybrid scenes and idioms to bring them together" (122). Indeed, Bowen can be eloquent in presenting contradiction, as when he says *The Old Curiosity Shop* in the pages of *Master Humphrey's Clock* is "a house of the living dead, Dickens's house that he is required to build, in response to public demand, around the absent body and ever-present little name of Nell, a book which is also a clock that both measures and arrests time in narrative, which is also a shop that sells everything and nothing, which is also a tomb and a waxworks exhibition of a 'waxworks child' and a crypt and a funeral procession" (156).

A central claim of Bowen's book is that *Martin Chuzzlewit* is "one of the most important of all nineteenth-century novels" (183) because here "Dickens gives us one of the first and most prescient of modern novels, and a key harbinger of modernism" (184–85). Bowen explores in detail the novel's pursuit of these Victorian and post-Victorian themes: "the nature of a commodified and self-commodifying culture and the role of finance capital within it; the possibilities of secrecy, surveillance, and detection within modern urban space; the radical autonomy of the self and its capacity for re-invention within such a world; the genealogy of ethical behavior in such conditions" (184). Accepting what has been called a faulty plot, Bowen wishes us to turn toward its virtues: "The energies of the book seek to evade the bindings of plot in order to permit the many extraordinary events and encounters of the text, not just those between fictional characters, but between fictional readers and fictional characters (who may also be things), fictional things (which may also be characters), humans, readers, monsters, and everything beyond and in between" (216).

A danger of Bowen's approach, however—an approach constructed on contradiction and paradox—is visible when he says that *Barnaby Rudge* "takes witnesses, participants, narrators, and readers of historical events to places and states of mind not assimilable to the orthodoxies of historical fiction and its criticism" (159). The resultant reading of the novel, thus similarly uncategorizable, can be hard to assimilate, hard to hold in memory, hard to fix into critical history. Even so, this book could trigger a productive reconsideration of literary history and the history of the novel genre.

If Bowen flirts with separation from conventional critical method, John Glavin's *After Dickens: Reading, Adaptation and Performance* revels in it.

"Why not," he asserts at the beginning, "transgress, then, not only the binding of theory and the boundaries of text but the boundaries that separate academic departments and the bindings that enforce the disciplines of critique?" (7). He seeks, for instance, the untold story of Miss Barbary in *Bleak House*: "we can still read inside *Bleak House* a novel which insists on our resistance, which time and again implores us to look where it mutely points, away from what it seems to say" (46). Glavin's approach, thus, is to focus, not on the novels of Dickens, but on what various individuals and groups have made or might make of them: "We've got to get up off our knees from venerating the fetishized text—or down off the high horse from which we beat it, degraded and dethroned—and return to the fundamental understanding that we are writers too" (7). Those who come "after Dickens"—recasting, staging, performing his works—are Glavins's subject: "If a novel, a poem, a play is to be read at all, it's got to be retrieved, put back together, refurbished" (2). And those who witness such adaptations also become subjects: "the spectator must permit the adaptation to take him or her as its target. In effect, the spectator must permit the self to be adapted also" (36).

Glavin's argument asserts, among other things, that "from the start Dickens was in not quite equal parts thrilled (less) and (more) frightened by the stage' (11); he maintained a "*childish* rejection of thought" (16); he preferred speech ("the weapon against the world Dickens's child-heroes most skillfully deploy" [20]) to writing; he "thoroughly loathes and fears (and inevitably, therefore, envies) theatre" (63); the actor "embodies everything that Dickens, terrified, denies: the stage, the body, desire itself" (102); Dickens's novels after the mid-1840s are haunted by "deep-seated patterns of grief" (150), as "ordinary happiness is for Dickens literally unimaginable" (151); "keeping to the truth, Dickens's novels repeatedly insist, can and will do only enormous harm" (132); and, most telling, "Virtually everything in Dickens turns on shame" (22).

This final idea, the force of shame, Glavin explains through a refinement of the concept of narcissism. Glavin notes that "the male body in Dickens is routinely, and successfully, voyeurized" (72); and public scrutiny undermines individual masculine identity. Glavin is quick to assert that, "in thus connecting heterosexuality to shame and homosocial agamy with self-pleasuring as-upon theatre, I am not *outing* the novel or Dickens. Narcissism is from the start Dickens's essential subject" (93). This is narcissism as defined by Heinz Kohut, an appreciation of one's own abilities that lies behind "creativity, empathy, transcendence and wisdom" (118–19); and it "drives Dickens's freakish, anti-referential, and entirely inimitable prose" (119). Glavin asserts Dickens's "willed and chosen withdrawal from, and subsequent subversion of, any sort of natural or social order which might claim the power or might to impose itself on the supremely, agonizingly, narcissistic self" (121).

Finally, to abide by his own insistence that we articulate what comes "after Dickens," Glavin offers a "How To Do It" guide for adapting *Little Dorrit*, which he explains is now "a play about Arthur Clennam" (167) with Amy Dorrit played by a broom. And then in this strange book's strange "Coda," Glavin adapts a 1986 adaptation of *Our Mutual Friend* in a text titled "Come Up and Be Dead."

IV. Re-visions of Dickens

If some recent Dickens studies argue that significant parts of his achievement have failed to get adequate attention, other scholars insist that much of what we have known about Dickens and his age needs revision in the light of later study. We have seen orphans in Dickens novels since initial publication, for instance, but Baruch Hochman and Ilja Wachs believe we have failed to recognize what they call the "orphan condition" as the source of his entire world: "Dickens has the capacity to irradiate every moment in the world he creates with an energy of meaning perhaps unparalleled in nineteeth-century fiction. The source of this capacity is, finally, a mystery, but we believe that our focus in this study on the never-absent figure of the abandoned child sheds some light on it" (22). Admitting that "our reading affirms a very traditional view of Dickens" (25), Hochman and Wachs offer their interpretations against "the tendency in postmodernist interpretations . . . to lose track of the vital centers of gravity of the works that are studied" (216)—in this case, Dickens the individual man. The book proceeds through detailed studies, especially of the titular heroes Oliver Twist and David Copperfield, as well as *Bleak House*'s Esther Summerson, *Great Expectations*'s Pip, and numerous characters from *Little Dorrit*. Rather than clutter each chapter with footnotes, they provide "A Bibliographical Overview" in a separate section, surveying work that provides "biographical evidence" of Dickens's relationship to orphanhood, "historical background" on the orphan theme (the reality of orphanhood in Victorian England), and "Dickens discourse in recent decades" (201).

The authors set out their methodology in their analysis of *Oliver Twist*. Dickens's novels after *Oliver*, they point out, also "preserve the paranoid plot and its sense of a world polarized between wicked, often grotesque figures who pursue and persecute the protagonist, and the innocent protagonist who undergoes supreme suffering" (54). Their approach is perhaps most insightful in the case of *Bleak House*, where Hochman and Wachs take on the rich subject of the novel's two narratives: "To give form to what Esther cannot integrate in consciousness, he creates an extraordinary medium through which to project the impulses and imaginings that must be contained in the course of her struggle. His medium is, of course, the third-person narrative voice, whose venting of everything that inhabits the orphan condition is one of the miracles of Dickens's art'' (86). The book's treatment of *Little Dorrit*'s Flora Finching is also provocative: ''Flora's mode of thinking bears a close resemblance to features of Dickens's own creative process'' (161). *Great Expectations* ''constitutes Dickens's most sharply focused treatment of the orphan condition,'' and it ''seems to master the disintegrative energies that shape *Little Dorrit*'' (166). Hochman and Wach's see the latter as a significant failure on Dickens's part, citing ''the absence in the novel of representations of constructive psychic process or of any sense of a positive generativity'' (163). (Nancy E. Linda, however, sees the orphan or abandoned child situation in that novel differently: ''For Arthur and Amy, both 'soul-murdered' former children, the modest ending of the novel is a personal triumph'' [143]).

Hochman and Wach's reliance on the ''orphan condition'' as the foundation of Dickens's art is perhaps too dependent on one underlying assumption: ''we must assume that the blacking experience grafts back onto some other, earlier, still more traumatic, thoroughly infantile experience, or fantasy, of abandonment'' (49). Yet the authors admit that ''the material directly available from the hard biographical sources [concerning early infantile experience] is very like the evidence we have garnered from the novels themselves . . . . This material must be interpreted to reach the position we argue in this study'' (202). And sometimes it seems that Dickens is being faulted for not following the direction the ''orphan condition'' would require: ''although [David Copperfield] does write his memoir, he does not imbue it with the energy and the outrage that we might have expected to 'get into' the life of an orphaned and abused Dickensian hero—a hero whose very initials echo, by inversion, Dickens's own, and point directly back to Dickens himself . . . '' (66).

Douglas Steward also considers Dickens's ''infatuation with the orphan'' (29) in arguing that we should revise or reject Freudian/Oedipal understandings of *Great Expectations*: ''Repression [of Pip's guilt] would be the more normal process in Freudian terms, but *Great Expectations* constitutes, with all its self-reproach, a literary autoflagellation that attests to Pip's masochism even as he writes'' (41). If masochism comes from guilt at privilege (capitalism) in this novel, thinks Steward, then it differs significantly from sadism, by which ownership/capital is established/continued over things (and women). Dickens's work then can be seen as deconstructive of an exploitative order.

Where Steward, like Hochman and Wachs, reassesses a familiar subject in Dickens's world (the orphan), Deborah Vlock places Dickens's exploration of all subjects within a larger frame, the context of Victorian popular entertainment. She finds Victorian theater underlying much in nineteenth-century culture: "the tropes of the theatre gave voice to other forms of artistic and popular expression; people read novels, newspapers, social criticism—indeed, just about everything worth reading—through the lens of popular performance" (3). Her aim is to see and hear Dickens's novel more as Victorians did, imagining the nineteenth-century reader—"not as isolated, curled up on a window seat in the privacy of the sitting room"—but instead "sitting in a theatre, the imagination's playhouse, with a book in one hand and an eye and ear on the stage" (192). To document this cultural context informing Dickens's world Vlock has explored such things as Victorian melodrama, acting manuals of the period, works of journalism, theater and opera criticism, and accounts of theater audiences. She also traces British attitudes toward theater through preceding centuries up to the time of Dickens's publication. One conclusion about this machinery of popular entertainment is clear: it "served a common deity: the god of social regulation, of power delegation, of labor division and cash disbursement" (57).

Since the novels of Dickens and his contemporaries were read aloud in parts, and popular entertainment borrowed from them and informed them, Vlock uses in her analyses the term "imaginary text," meaning a " 'reading space' located outside of the actual narrative embodiments of Victorian novels, and inside the field of sociodramatic possibilities—of idioms and gestures and a whole range of signifiers—established by popular entertainments" (6). Also key to her study is what she calls "the pattered voice," a "verbal gesture historically linked to performance and subversion" (38), which has both male and female forms and changes according to class. It is characterized by "eccentric lexicons and/or its verbal excess, logical discontinuities, and rapid, repetitive delivery" (40). This voice, Silas Wegg's in *Our Mutual Friend*, is subversive.

While clearly written, Vlock's book seems redundant in places, repeatedly referring back and forward to its other chapters. Part of the reason for repetition, however, is that her task is a daunting one: to recreate something that never existed in print, as her book does, but which was made up of sound, which existed fleetingly within the medium of the human voice. She achieves her goal, however, in many cases, providing "close textual readings, in which the spoken voice inspires or haunts the written" (100). Especially in her exploration of "spinster patter," Vlock makes us revise key Victorian stereotypes.

The language of spinsters in Victorian fiction and popular entertainment, says Vlock, reveals a significant social concern: "The popular notion of the English spinster or widow was of a woman with a spectacular verbal deformity, a soul sister to the dwarf, the bearded lady, the human pig" (169). She is "carnivalesque" and, in her sexual identity especially, threatens the bourgeois community. Vlock considers in detail, for example, Flora in *Little*

Dorrit: "she is, despite the novelist's best efforts to conceal it, a spinner (spinster) of stories, a speaker of strange and resonant tongues, disruptive, exciting, disconcerting" (187).

Vlock's book, then, situates itself along the contradiction between theatrical novels and the novel form's antagonism to drama as something inherently false, as something that must be stringently controlled (evidenced by Dickens's own strict marking of his reading texts). It is true, she notes, that theater is subversive: "theatres encouraged erotic and social acts which were unacceptable outside of their walls" (78). And Victorian novel readers carried that subversive attitude into Dickens's and others' novels because their " 'reading' skills were cultivated in the theatre, the place where words spawned worlds of action, where voices could inspire sexual fever and acts of insurrection" (91).

Mary Lenard also sees Dickens's work within a larger Victorian context, sentimentalism. She believes that "feminized, sentimentalist social reform discourse in nineteenth-century British literature is culturally important and needs to be studied" (10) as a framework within which Dickens's popular fiction especially should be reevaluated. While Dickens's borrowed from the style women writers used in opposing Utilitarianism and laissez-faire capitalism (77), says Lenard, he "tried to claim artistic superiority over women sentimentalist writers . . . by constructing them as imitators of his own works" (83). When Dickens accused women writers Frances Trollope and Harriet Beecher Stowe of plagiarism, then, it was "in order to claim himself as the 'owner' of that cultural space and thereby exclude the female social reform writers who shared it with him by discrediting them" (93).

Like the sentimentalism of many Victorian authors, another context within which Dickens's work can be seen is the discourse of nineteenth-century science. Daniel Hack sees Dickens's intent in his use and defense of spontaneous combustion in *Bleak House* as an effort to combat the authority of scientific inquiry: "Dickens uses the spontaneous-combustion incident to investigate and manipulate . . . distinctions between events and symbols, bodies and signs, empirical investigation and textual interpretation, and scientific and literary authority" (135). The spontaneous combustion episode, which generated energetic response, is seen by Hack "as part of the novel's more general argument against the silencing or discrediting of individuals lacking what those in positions of authority deem sufficient cultural capital" (146). Hack explores a fascinating situation in the monthly advertiser running contemporaneously with Dickens's story for the original Victorian audience, a debate about the contents of an imported pale ale. He sees this part of Dickens's original serial text also as evidence of a larger cultural debate about authority. In the end, in Dickens's novel the interpreter of texts rivals the scientist as cultural authority.

Rather than studying Dickens's art in relationship to scientific inquiry, other scholars place Dickens's work in the context of legal processes during the Victorian period. In an examination of the legal principle of equity and the novel *Bleak House*, Dieter Paul Polloczek reasserts the place of literature in a culture, our own, where classic works are being marginalized. Noting that "criticism in the nineties has predominantly attempted to illuminate and articulate possibilities for the notion of the marginal" (453), he links that effort to ancient ideas of equity: "Equity is known as a maxim applied and instituted in the majority of Western legal systems ever since Aristotle formulated it as a correlative, in the context of Greek tragedy, to the consideration of mitigating (or sometimes exacerbating) circumstances that connect criminal action with tragic error" (458). And he concludes that "literature's relation to hegemonic discourse corresponds to equity's task of introducing particulars into the law's generality" (459). In *Bleak House* in particular "the text participates in, and is meant to influence, symptoms of what many of Dickens's contemporaries perceive as the role of the law in social and psychological disintegration" (463). Thus, "What makes modern literature an appropriate site for equity's persistence is its specific ability to reconfigure the traditional tropes of supplementary relationship, such as the general-particular, the generic-singular, and the dominant-marginal" (476).

Kieran Dolin's *Fiction and the Law: Legal Discourse in Victorian and Modernist Literature* also explores the relationship of Dickens's art to the legal tradition of equity, noting that "*Bleak House* is a product of legal history, as well as literary history" (80). This book explores shared elements of the novel genre and the law: "an evidentiary model of narration, a plot concerned with the commission and rectification of crime and civil wrong, and the adoption of a critical tone with respect to official agencies of law" (2). Noting that early novelists included lawyers, Dolin reminds us that that law and the novel have in common a "concern with ethics, their ideal of an enriched humanity in contrast to the denuded functionalism of rational-scientific legal discourse, and their commitment to the Enlightenment project of emancipation through dialogue" (9). Dolin's study "focuses especially on the legal trial, in which the 'endeavor to obtain a hearing' is formally undertaken, and in which some resolution to the conflicting visions of reality represented by different characters and their actions and languages is attempted" (19).

In the chapter specifically about Dickens, Dolin links narrative technique with the pursuit of legal principles: "Esther's narrative, like the plot of the novel, opposes the hermeneutic failure of Chancery . . . . What an evidentiary analysis of her narrative adds to the critical understanding of the novel is a sense of the importance of the individual witness" (86). Even in Victorian England's Court of Chancery, says Dolin, the principle of equity is not lost, although it is obscured: "Against this [the "dead hand" of the court of

Chancery], Dickens set the 'progress' of Esther Summerson and, through her, the reclamation of the ideals of equity. The upshot of this two-fold presentation is to override any static assumptions underlying the " 'Condition of England,' to insist on the necessity of change by using the temporal properties of narrative" (95). Dolin concludes that *Bleak House* is "a critical intervention in debates about social organization, rather than as a linguistic, revolutionist or pessimistic attack on all social structures" (78).

Victorian discoveries about heredity provide the framework within which Goldie Morgentaler recasts Dickens's achievements. In a book that is clearly focused and would be particularly accessible to students, she observes that, for Victorian authors in general, "tracing resemblances between generations became a way of internalizing the godhead, locating not only the power of creation but also the ability to determine and predict future conduct within the invisible and mysterious processes of biological inheritance" (22). Especially early in his career, then, "Dickens tended to define positive moral qualities as being hereditable, but he was extremely reluctant to ascribe a hereditary basis to evil" (x). Morgantaler makes this case with *Oliver Twist*: "Heredity is the natural equivalent of portraiture, preserving family features over the course of generations and maintaining them intact despite the passing of time" (41). Thus, the novelist can work as portrait painter, identifying and preserving self. After Darwin's *Origin of Species* in 1859, however, in important works (*Great Expectations* and *Our Mutual Friend*) Morgentaler finds that "heredity very nearly disappears as a factor in the formation of the self" (xi) and the issue of identity becomes problematic in Dickens's world.

By 1846, says Morgentaler, Dickens saw egotism and narcissism at work in individual destinies more than the inheritance of moral virtues. Women can found dynasties, but here Dickens's limited women to their biological function. While *Dombey and Son* challenges bloodline and genealogy, it "ends by resurrecting heredity as a positive force in human life" (62). In *Great Expectations*, however, "Dickens's new post-Darwinian understanding of human nature" (78) means "the individual tries to fashion himself on any model which chance provides, being drawn particularly to those models bearing the stamp of social approbation" (77). In *Little Dorrit* Dickens "has moved towards a more complex understanding of hereditary influence, namely that it constitutes a condition which is only partly deterministic" (97–98). And in *Our Mutual Friend*, "when Dickens jettisons heredity, what he replaces it with are metaphors of disintegration and dispersal" (175). Dickens was not happy with this situation, according to Morgentaler, and returned to the question of heredity in his last, incomplete novel, *The Mystery of Edwin Drood*.

An important element of Morgentaler's argument links heredity and class in Dickens: "What is on the surface—that is, the social world of class division and man-made demarcations—is contradicted and obliterated by the sub-merged and unacknowledged effects of heredity which homogenize social gradations into a single biological entity'' (122). In *Tale of Two Cities*, ''Dickens's use of the term 'race' reverts to its older meaning of a limited group of people descended from a common ancestor (OED), thus a hereditary aristocracy may be a race'' (143). Such portraits as Riah's in *Our Mutual Friend* ''suggest that heredity, when applied to race in the nineteenth century, had a homogenizing effect, highlighting the qualities of permanence and uniformity while scanting those of change and diversity'' (156).

Andrew Sanders's *Dickens and the Spirit of the Age* perhaps does the most of the 1999 studies in contextualizing our author. His aim is to place Dickens's work and thought in response to four characteristics of a new world: ''its political and technological enterprise; its urbanization; its new definitions of social class and social mobility; and, finally, its dynamic sense of its distinction from, and currency with, the preceding century'' (4). This is a particularly profitable enterprise, says Sanders, because ''Dickens was an embodiment of the spirit of an age that remains substantially and often uncomfortably familiar'' (16). Sanders uses contemporary sources (letters, non-fiction, other documents of the times) to explain Dickens the man, as well as Dickens's work as the product of that man. He compares, for instance, Dickens in London to Dickens in America, to Marx in London, and to Baudelaire in Paris.

Both Dickens the man and Dickens the writer were reflections of larger social forces, Sanders insists: he ''embodied [his age's] essentially rootless dynamism and its receptivity to innovation'' (43); and the ''England of the 1830s was particularly propitious for the steady rise in literary renown on which he began to calculate'' (37). His daily life and work were embodied in the site of a modern age, the city: ''Dickens's style is commonly awkward, inexact, and flabby when he describes farmland, or grass or flowers; it is precise, vivid, and energized when he attempts to delineate the life of a London street'' (82). And many of his admirable characters find their place in an emerging, competitive, more open society.

Despite being intricately situated within a modern environment, Dickens's art was significantly shaped, Sanders shows, by the literary conventions of an earlier time: ''Dickens's deep respect for, and creative roots in, the comic fiction of the eighteenth century led him steadily to transform and adapt the conventions and the fluid narrative structures established by Fielding and Smollett and, to a lesser degree, Sterne and Goldsmith'' (161). In works like *Barnaby Rudge*, however, Sanders finds ''those aspects of the culture of eighteenth-century England which most vexed the progressive Dickens: its supposedly complacent acceptance of social stratification and of class privilege . . . '' (169). If the world that shaped his predecessors needed change, the artists of that time remained themselves models for the later Dickens.

Hogarth was an inspiration, "an essentially urban artist, one who had made art out of a close observation and analysis of often unpleasant metropolitan truths, and yet one who never eschewed comedy" (173–74).

If Dickens's art grows from the past, Sanders nevertheless feels his fiction reaches into the future: "It remains surprisingly illuminating to a larger, and far from exclusively British, world which his twentieth- and twenty-first-century readers have inherited" (153). One important reason for the relevance of Dickens's novel is a fundamental principle of Dickens's thought, progress: "The progressivist Dickens rejected what he saw as the limiting social values of a dead era; the novelist Dickens took what he needed from the fiction of the past and remade it for the modern world" (186). Dickens's style as well as his vision belong in our own time, Sanders concludes, perhaps more than some other Victorian authors: "his experiments with a fictional form that reflects as well as represents the restless, thronged rhythms of urban life seem to render him increasingly distinct from those of his nineteenth-century contemporaries who insisted on the unique, and narrow, virtues of psychological realism" (186).

The question of Dickens and the ideology of his age is also taken up John Farrell, especially the notion that, to achieve selfhood, Dickens's characters must separate themselves from their society. Farrell challenges that idea, which would put Dickens at odds with his contemporaries, by discussing "partnerships" in the novels: "There are relationships and revelations at work in Dickens's great fiction that the war between system and self, important though that is, does not exhaustively determine" (764). Society is not always antagonistic to the individual, Farrell argues; in fact, there is in Dickens a "sense of social being as the essential transfiguring power that initially converted a world of matter into a world of meaning" (771). Exploring the interrelationship of three men—Bradley Headsone, John Harmon, Eugene Wrayburn—each of whom is "partnered" with another character—Farrell finds Dickens's "construction of the modern self's emergence as a site of narrative choices, possibilities, and constraint" (778). He finds the material world can add to an individual's assertion of identity: "If the body is for Dickens the self's figurative projection of identity in the material world, the props are acquisitions from the material world that supplement the self's expressiveness" (791). For instance, "The crutch-stick becomes the expressive site of their [Sloppy/Jenny Wren] partnership, each using its handle as a locus of self-identity while, in the same act, changing the crutch itself from a sign of deformed humanity into a sign of shared life" (793).

V. New Ways of Seeing

If much work on Dickens asserts that aspects of his art have been unseen or neglected in the past, a final group of studies argue that completely new ways of seeing are now available to literary scholars. Elements of Dickens's world are emerging, that is, and becoming visible for the first time because of new kinds of sight.

Nancy Armstrong, for instance, claims that our multimedia age can recognize the power of photography in defining literary realism. Seeing the portrait of Lady Dedlock in *Bleak House* as a fading mode of representation, she argues that nineteenth-century novelists had to accept photography's "definition" of images to reach large audiences, which led to a shared idea of reality (46). Dickens's art, then, did not pretend to represent reality, but photographic images: "realism refers neither to things themselves nor to the writing that records their vicissitudes as such, but to things as they have been captured and reproduced within the photographic frame" (46). The creator of Lady Dedlock "based identity on the sequential displacement and retrospective accretion of images" (52). Dickens and his contemporaries, however, understood what they were doing—"deliberately transforming [an] object into a photographic referent with a precise location in a social space" (51)—and thus, created "a highly organized field of vision" (51). Her conclusions about how Victorians saw their world call for a change in theory, not just a revised understanding of Dickens: "if novel theory today fails to acknowledge realism's visual sophistication, it is because that theory shares modernism's iconophobia" (38).

John R. Reed's essay on "literary description" is a useful complement to Armstrong's argument. "Description has long been undervalued as a narrative device," says Reed; and his ultimate subject is that technique in fiction in general. Noting that Jacob's Island, a real place in London, is mentioned in *Oliver Twist*, Reed argues that its description is an agent for social change: "The fictional narrative becomes the energizing vehicle that carries and lends force to the description of the real place that then transfers that energy to the real world by way of the reader's reception of it" (265). Asking "what role does the description of a real location play when it appears in a work of fiction?" Reed concludes that Dickens at least "believed that he could persuade his readers to actual changes in their lives through the power of his representations" (23).

Rather than Dickens's technique, Hilary M. Schor's *Dickens and the Daughter of the House* takes a familiar topic of his fiction and argues persuasively that it be seen in a different way. She admits in the beginning that "The Dickens novel has seemed a . . . machinery for the entrapment and consumption of gullible girls, and the novelist's wickedness has seemed inarguable" (1). Yet, the more she reads Dickens, the more she finds that daughters are a central value and a powerful force in his fictional world: daughters are "transmitters, not only of material property, but of ideology, memory, and faith" (4). Nancy in *Oliver*, for instance, "dominates the second half of the novel, disrupting the expectations of others, generating new plots of her own" (22), even if she herself disappears within her own "complicated" story (24). This makes Schor's one of those rare scholarly books that inspires us to rethink not just a single author but the period in which he worked. In nineteenth-century England, she reminds us, "the work of the daughter [is] to gather memory, and to convey the past, at the same time that it is her job to stand on the bridge of culture, the moment of reproduction that insures the transmission of value" (43). And this may well be true in many of the novels of Trollope, Wilkie Collins, and Elizabeth Gaskell.

Schor finds Dickens's daughters must leave their father's house in order for a story to be told, that is, for the novel to exist: "To move the plot forward, to do the work of narrative and inheritance, the daughter must move outside the father's house" (4). Thus, Dickens's novels cannot come into being without daughters. In *Little Dorrit*, for instance, Schor notes of Amy that, "for all her narratorial meekness, she is the only character to speak, uninterrupted, for two chapters, and to make so powerful a claim for herself and her way of seeing" (142). And even if a woman's transgression initiates plot, the resolution may be just: "If the role of the adultery plot in all these novels has been to adjust the balances of social order, and return everyone to a rightful (righted, written) place within plot and history, the daughter's story has been the fulcrum of that balancing act . . . " (98).

In its more radical application, this critical approach can arrive at unsettling, provocative conclusions: "In the end, David [Copperfield] may be his own Scheherazade; he may be a dispossessed daughter; he may be a woman writer; he may, after all, be the heroine of his own life" (13). Or this: "In *Bleak House*, the daughter stages her own revolution: her recapture of weapons of writing, which in this novel are the weapons of property. *Bleak House* is the novel the orphan daughter writes to reclaim her property; more than that, it is the autobiographical fiction the bastard daughter writes to ask, 'who killed my mother?' " (101).

Schor relies heavily on the word "uncanny" to describe the daughter's power in Dickens's world, suggesting an undeniable force that is at the same time inscrutable: a woman's "magical quality, at once reproductive and already dead, is the source of the daughter's terrifying and promising uncanniness, and it is, somehow, enough to send a strong man reeling" (46). Dickens's daughter is a material being, but she is also connected to, possessing, the past, a thing of no substance: "The female body is sexually charged; it is vulnerable; it is impregnable. And that, of course, is the secret of Nell's body—that she is, at the age of fourteen, on the verge of menstruation, of which the blood that falls from her feet at every step is a hint" (41–42). This famous and seemingly vulnerable daughter's power exists not just within the world of the novel but in the structure of Victorian literature.

That Nell's birth comes with her mother's death—that she recreates her mother—means "Nell represents the perfect moment of narrative, when origin and end (mother and daughter) come together" (41). Along with such uncanny daughters, Schor also considers the "dark heroine" in Dickens's novels like Edith Dombey, who hint at stories about women Dickens could not tell. The letter Edith has for Florence is a female narrative, unread and as yet unknown to Dickens's readers, that points toward "the texts that might represent more fully both the power and the pathos of being in an economy that traffics in women, and that does not (yet) let them out of the shadows of representations" (69).

Schor's analysis of *Bleak House* is particularly convincing, as she measures's Esther's narrative role: "her power, at this moment, as narrator, is almost entirely unlike her powerlessness as *character*" (119). Esther's is above all the story of a daughter: "The attempt to bring the mother back to life, to hear the words she never says to her daughter, is the most powerful motive for fiction in every Dickens novel from *Oliver Twist* to this one, and this novel is merely the one that gives it the most piercing voice" (122). The mother's gift is the right "to scribble, write, crease, direct, dictate; to devise and bequeath; to rewrite and revise; the courage not to stop that process of writing and rewriting that is duplicated in every reader's baffled reading and rereading of *Bleak House*" (123). Amy Dorrit is linked to Esther in Schor's reading. Despite the fact that the titular heroine of *Little Dorrit* can be said to be disappearing, vanishing, taking as little as possible to live, she seems to own the narrative at the end as her name is entered into the marriage books: "for all the novel's renunciatory urgency, it seems to present itself as female property, as a text that belongs (like all true narratives, at least in this book) to women" (148).

Schor makes a similar observation about *Great Expectations*, noting that Dickens's second ending at least does give Estella her own voice. In *Our Mutual Friend* "Bella resists this plot [marriage] heroically and resolutely: indeed, she reclaims the language of heroines like Edith Dombey or Estella Havisham, insisting that by knowing her own value she will at least sell herself intelligently in the marriage market" (180). Perhaps the most affirmative of all the stories of Dickens's daughters is the one told of Jenny Wren: "Dickens could never imagine a female enfranchisement; he wants to enclose ever fair heroine in a gold bower . . . . But the weirdness of Jenny Wren . . . seems to offer some other account of property and persons for Dickens. In that alternate account, one in which the heroine has a house that is less bleak and in which she can sign her name to her own (however antic and crooked) story, it is the heroine who gets to write after it, for herself, 'the end' " (207).

The line of argument throughout the book is strong, if sometimes circuitous. So careful to get it all right is Schor that she begins many paragraphs with "but," reversing or refining a point she had just made in the preceding paragraph. Thus, she takes her intricate logic one step further to yet a finer expression of her interpretation. I expect others scholars will proceed down these arduous paths of understanding now made available by this and other recent studies of Dickens.

Indeed, as Elizabeth Gitter explains in the essay with which this review began, we learn new ways of seeing as we move into the future, and the concepts of blindness and sight themselves alter as we travel. Consciousness and subjectivity are seen in people who had been, in some sense, invisible and themselves without vision. My conclusion about "Dickens Studies 1999" is that Dickens's sight remains worthy of exploration—his words are still inimitable—and that the current generation of scholars has eyes open to the past and to the future, sight repeatedly widened by the visions of others to our common interests.

WORKS CITED

Allingham, Philip V. "Dickens's Aesthetic of the Short Story." *The Dickensian* 95 (Summer 1999): 144–53.

Andrews, Malcolm. "Charles Dickens and his Performing Selves," In *Dickens, Europe and the New Worlds*. ed. Anny Sadrin. London and New York: Macmillan and St. Martin's. 146–54.

Armstrong, Nancy. "Fiction in the Age of Photography." *Narrative*. 7(1): 37–55.

Bauer, Matthias, "Foreign Languages and Original Understanding in *Little Dorrit*," *Dickens, Europe and the New Worlds*. 155–68

Bowen, John. *Other Dickens: Pickwick to Chuzzlewit*. Oxford. Oxford UP.

Buzard, James. " 'Anywhere's Nowhere': Dickens on the Move," *Dickens, Europe and the New Worlds*. 113–27.

Casotti, Francesco M. "Italian Translations of Dickens." *The Dickensian* 95 (Spring 1999): 19–23.

Charles Dickens' Great Expectations, ed. Edgar Rosenberg. New York and London: W. W. Norton.

Cheadle, Brian. "Dispatched to the Periphery: the Changing Play of Centre and Periphery in Dickens's Work." *Dickens, Europe and the New Worlds*. 100–12.

The Dent Uniform Edition of Dickens' Journalism, Volume 3. "Gone Astray" and Other Papers from *Household Words* 1852–59. Ed. Michael Slater. Columbus: Ohio State UP.

Dickens, Europe and the New Worlds, ed. Anny Sadrin. London and New York: Macmillan and St. Martin's Press.

Dolin, Kieran. *Fiction and the Law: Legal Discourse in Victorian and Modernist Literature*. Cambridge: Cambridge UP.

Edgecomb, Rodney Stenning. "Middle-Class Erasures: The Decreations of Mrs. General and Mr. Podsnap." *Studies in the Novel* 31(3): 279–95.

———. "Personification in the Late Novels of Dickens," *The Dickensian* 95 (Winter 1999): 230–40.

Farrell, John P. "The Partners' Tale: Dickens and *Our Mutual Friend*." *ELH*. 66(3): 759–99.

Fielding, K. J., with Shu Fang Lai, "Dickens's Science, Evolution and the 'The Death of the Sun.' " *Dickens, Europe, and the New Worlds*. 200–11.

Forsyth, Neil. "No, but I Saw the Film: David Lean Remakes *Oliver Twist*." *Dickens, Europe and the New Worlds*. 251–66.

Frank, Lawrence. "*Pictures from Italy*: Dickens, Rome, and the Eternal City of the Mind." *Dickens, Europe and the New Worlds*. 47–64.

Gitter, Elizabeth G. "The Blind Daughter in Charles Dickens's *Cricket on the Hearth*." *Studies in English Literature 1500 1900*. 39(4): 675–89.

Glancy, Ruth. *Student Companion to Charles Dickens*. Westport: Connecticut: Greenwood.

Glavin, John. *After Dickens: Reading, Adaptation and erformance*. Cambridge: Cambridge U. P. Cambridge Studies in Nineteenth-Century Literature and Culture 20.

Gribble, Jennifer. "Borrioboola-Gha: Dickens, John Jarndyce and the Heart of Darkness," *Dickens, Europe and the New Worlds*. 90–99.

Hack, Daniel. " 'Sublimation Strange': Allegory and Authority in *Bleak House*." *ELH*. 66(1): 129–56.

Hawley, John C. " 'A Far Better Rest I Go To': Dickens and the Undiscovered Country," *Dickens, Europe and the New Worlds*. 181–93.

Hennelly, Mark M., Jr. " 'Deep Play' and 'Women's Ridicules' in *Oliver Twist*: Part V." *Journal of Evolutionary Psychology*. 20(1–2): 92–102.

Hochman, Baruch, and Ilja Wachs, *Dickens: The Orphan Condition* Madison, Teaneck, and London: Farleigh Dickinson UP.

Hollington, Michael. "Dickens, *Household Words* and the Paris Boulevards," *Dickens, Europe and the New Worlds*. 22–33.

Hughes, Linda K., and Michael Lund. *Victorian Publishing and Mrs.Gaskell's Work*. Charlottesville: U. P. of Virginia, 1999. Victorian Literature and Culture Series.

Jordan, John O. "Dickens and Disaspora," *Dickens, Europe and the New Worlds*. 239–50.

Lenard, Mary. *Preaching Pity: Dickens, Gaskell, and Sentimentalism in Victorian Culture*. New York: Peter Lang,1999. Studies in Nineteenth-Century British Literature 11.

Linda, Nancy E. "The Acquisition of a Future: Arthur Clennam's Developmental Task in *Little Dorrit*," *The Dickensian* 95 (Summer 1999): 138–43.

Litvack, Leon. *Charles Dickens's Dombey and Son. An Annotated Bibliography*. New York: AMS Press.

Litvack, Leon. "Dickens, Australia and Magwitch Part I; The Colonial Context," *The Dickensian* 95 (Spring 1999): 24–50.

Litvack, Leon. "Dickens, Australia and Magwitch Part II; The Search for *le cas Magwitch*." *The Dickensian* 95 (Summer 1999): 101–27.

McCarthy, Patrick. "Truth in *American Notes*," *Dickens, Europe and the New Worlds*. 67–76.

Merchant, Peter. "From Eliot to Dickens: The Descent of the Stone Slab in *Great Expectations*." *Dickens, Europe and the New Worlds*. 132–37.

Metz, Nancy. "*The Life and Adventures of Martin Chuzzlewit*: Or America Revised." *Dickens, Europe and the New Worlds*. 77–89.

Monod, Sylvère. "Translating Dickens into French," *Dickens, Europe and the New Worlds*. 229–38.

Morgentaler, Goldie. *Dickens and Heredity: When Like Begets Like*. New York: St. Martin's. [2000]

Oxford Reader's Companion to Dickens. Ed. Paul Schlicke. Oxford: Oxford UP.

Parker, David. "Wemmick's Cottage." *The Dickensian* 95 (Summer 1999): 128–31.

Plummer. Patricia. "From Agnes Fleming to Helena Landless: Dickens, Women and (Post-)Colonialism." *Dickens, Europe and the New Worlds*. 267–82.

Polhemus, Robert M. " 'Doveyed Covetfilles': How Joyce Used Dickens to Put a Lot of the Old World into the New." *Dickens, Europe and the New Worlds*. 283–93.

Polloczek, Dieter Paul. "The Marginal, the Equitable, and the Unparalleled: Lady Dedlock's Case in Dickens's *Bleak House*." *New Literary History*. 30(2): 453–78.

Rainsford, Dominic. "Crossing the Channel With Dickens." *Dickens, Europe and the New Worlds*. 3–14.

Reed, John R. "Dickens on Jacob's Island and the Functions of Literary Description." *Narrative*. 7(1): 22–36.

Rem, Tore. "*Little Dorrit*, Pictures from Italy and John Bull." *Dickens, Europe and the New Worlds*. 131–45.

Sadrin, Anny. "Why D.I.J.O.N.? Crossing Forbidden Boundaries in *Dombey and Son*." *Dickens, Europe and the New Worlds*. 14–21.

Sage, Victor. "Negative Homogeneity: *Our Mutual Friend*, Richard Owen, and the 'New Worlds' of Victorian Biology." *Dickens, Europe and the New Worlds*. 212–26.

Sanders, Andrew. *Dickens and the Spirit of the Age*. Oxford: Clarendon P.

Schlicke, Paul. "Editing the *Oxford Companion to Dickens*." *The Dickensian* 95 (Winter 1999): 206–11.

———. "The 'Other World' of 'A Lazy Tour of Two Idle Apprentices.' " *Dickens, Europe and the New Worlds*. 194–99.

Schor, Hilary M.. *Dickens and the Daughter of the House*. Cambridge: Cambridge UP. Cambridge Studies in Nineteenth Century Literature and Culture 25.

Sell, Roger D. "Modernist Readings Mediated: Dickens and the New Worlds of Later Generations." *Dickens, Europe and the New Worlds*. 294–99.

Steward, Douglas. "Anti-Oedipalizing *Great Expectations*: Masochism, Subjectivity, Capitalism." *Literature & Psychology*. 45(3): 29–50.

Thomas, Ronald R. "Spectacle and Speculation: The Victorian Economy of Vision in *Little Dorritt*." *Dickens, Europe and the New Worlds*. 34–46.

Thornton, Sara. "Foreign Bodies: Acceptance and Rejection of the Alien in the Dickensian Text." *Dickens, Europe and the New Worlds*. 169–80.

Vlock, Deborah. *Dickens, Novel Reading, and the Victorian Popular Theatre*. Cambridge: Cambridge UP.

West, Gilian. "Little Dorrit: 'Thirty Years ago . . . .' " *The Dickensian* 95 (Winter 1999): 212–28.

———. "Huffam and Son." *The Dickensian* 95 (Spring 1999): 5–18.

INDEX

373